REMEMBERING
THE
COVENANT
A COMMENTARY ON
THE BOOK OF MORMON

VOLUME 2

Denver C. Snuffer, Jr.

Published in the United States by Mill Creek Press.
Mill Creek Press is a registered trademark of Mill Creek Press, LLC.
www.millcreekpress.com

ISBN-10: 0-9891503-1-3
ISBN-13: 978-0-9891503-1-6

Printed in the United States of America on acid-free paper.

First Edition

Cover design by Mill Creek Press.

Contents

VOLUME 2

ALMA 13

It may as well be a dream. It involves our collective slumber. We get pictures in our head when we are taught some truth and presume that the picture is accurate. Then after we have repeated the "truth" often enough, we go on to believe the picture must be all-inclusive.

Once we've arrived at that point, the truth no longer matters. Our minds are made up. We've decided the answers, and no further evidence will be considered.

This certainty is reinforced when more people reach the same conclusion because they share the same picture in their head. You get together with others and testify that you are all in possession of the truth; not only **the** truth, but **ALL** of the truth. Before long every one of the group can pass a lie-detector test about the truth as they explain it.

As a result, this herd is incapable of ever seeing the picture differently. They cannot open their minds to the idea that their picture is skewed or off. It is most certainly incomplete. It is, in fact, so far short of the whole story that when any part of the remaining, missing information is shown to them they are certain it is a lie.

It is painful to part with our suppositions and the traditions we hold dear. It is painful to admit there may be much more of the picture we have not yet considered, much less seen. It causes anxiety and fear. So much fear in fact, that when it comes to "eternal truth," people literally put their lives in jeopardy if they denounce the falsehoods of the herd and proclaim the truth to those whose peace of mind and self-identity is tied to the incomplete and misleading picture they believe holds all truth.

Latter-day Saints are not immune from this process. We have wanted a complete, well defined statement of our faith since the time of Joseph Smith. We crave an "orthodox" faith so we, like the Historic Christians, can proclaim what is true and right and what is error and heresy. It gives us security. It is false security, purchased at the price of closed minds. It gives us hope. It is false hope, based on the foolishness of the deluded.

As we water down even further the true principles of what our faith contains by requiring Relief Society and High Priests to labor over a Gospel Essentials Manual as the sole fodder for our spiritual fare, we strain every particle of solid food out of the diet. The remaining gruel is so thin, lacking in substance, that we become universally malnourished. Yet in that emaciated state, as our bellies distend from the bloating of starvation, we all proclaim how well fed we are. Our bellies are swollen! We have enough of the word of God! We need no more of the word of God! All is well! Better than well, we prosper in the land of promise!

When you surrender your superstitions and arrogance and read the scriptures for the first time with an open mind, they will astonish you. They will condemn you. They will demand you repent, open your heart, and receive more. They will offer you the bread of life, a living fountain of revelation from which, if you draw, you will find not only sustenance, but also the capacity to recognize that there are those who are starving.

We still weep for Zion; for Zion has fled.

Try reading Alma Chapter 13 and take **LITERALLY** every word there. Don't bring any pictures in your head and read them into the text. Forget every popular and correlated notion ever spoken about the priesthood for a moment and just look at the words. You will be shocked. If you can bring yourself to do that, then read the Book of Mormon again. It was written for our day, testifying **against** us. A former group of inhabitants who failed and were destroyed wrote their best advice and sent it to us. We are the ones being warned. We are in a great deal of peril. Our church, if the Book of Mormon is true, is filled with corruption and priestcraft.

Or, on the other hand, just chant that "you know (*insert the subject of choice here*) is true" and throw about the "name of Jesus Christ" as you do. It is a tried and true mantra, which when repeated often enough, can dull the senses and reinstate the slumber we are so often wrapped. So relax. Hum to yourself a hymn and you will soon be back asleep.

A few days ago I directed you to Alma 13. I suggested that it be read without preconceptions and you let the words just acquire whatever meaning they appear to have in the chapter itself. Some of you have begun that process and have raised questions. I thought I might revisit the chapter to open up a few ideas for those who haven't begun the exercise. Here's the first verse:

Alma 13:1

"And again, my brethren, I would cite your minds forward to the time when the Lord God gave these commandments unto his children; and I would that ye should remember that the Lord God ordained priests, after his holy order, which was after the order of his Son, to teach these things unto the people."

Why "cite your minds forward?" Especially since it was talking in the past tense? Why is this idiom in the verse? How would Joseph

Smith know about this kind of word usage? (Perhaps this is an indication the text is translated from another language rather than being composed in English.)

Why "the Lord God ordained priests?" Were they ordained by God indeed? Was there another man involved in conferring that authority? Did it necessarily come from God alone? What priesthood is it that is referred to?

What is "after his holy order?" Is this Aaronic? Is this Melchizedek? Or is this something different? There are three orders of priesthood, the third being "Patriarchal" as explained in *Beloved Enos*. Which one is this verse referring to of the three?

What form of priesthood is "after his holy order, which was after the order of his Son?" Are all three? Or is there one that is distinguished by being uniquely after the order of His Son?

What "things" are these people to "teach . . . unto the people?" Is there something associated with what is contained in the chapter that alone is the province of those possessing the "holy order" to teach? If so, why is that?

What is going on here? Is this deeper doctrine than we normally encounter? If so, why has it eluded our attention? If our preconceptions have blinded us to this material, then why would we want to ever read scripture through the blinding lens of the notions we have inherited? Is this part of the wicked "traditions of our fathers" that the Book of Mormon warn us against?

Oh ye Gentiles . . .

Now I'm missing the weekly Book of Mormon class I taught for so many years. There I could go ahead and discuss all the answers. My home was too small for the crowds and I wasn't going to export it to a less sacred place where the Spirit would not permit me to teach. Well, the questions are better than merely giving answers, as I have said before. If you can learn to ask good questions, then you can go to the Lord and get the answers. Who knows where that dialogue will lead you.

Alma 13:2

"And those priests were ordained after the order of his Son, in a manner that thereby the people might know in what manner to look forward to his Son for redemption."

Now this is important stuff here. We are really being told something quite amazing. Look at these words!

To be "ordained after the order of his Son" it must be done "in a manner that thereby the people might know in what manner to look forward to his Son for redemption." Did you get that?

Think about these words carefully.

The "manner" must be in a way which will let people know or understand how to "look forward to His Son for redemption."

So, let's clear away the institutional garbage that surrounds our thinking.

- Christ WAS NOT ordained by being sustained by a congregation.
- Christ WAS NOT ordained by having hands laid upon Him by another man.
- Christ DID NOT carry a credential with Him or a certificate of priestly authority.
- Christ WAS NOT part of the established priestly hierarchy.

We have no record of His ordination at all. We only have established, priestly class officials asking Christ about where He got His authority from. And we have Christ simply refusing to answer their question.

Christ showed that He in fact held priestly authority by His demonstration of power. More importantly, He taught profound truths with such passing simplicity and convincing prose that His message necessarily came from a higher source. In word and deed He put on display His power and authority.

But what is the verse in Alma speaking about? How does one become "ordained" in such a manner that people learning of it will then know how to look forward (or back) to the Savior and understand His redeeming power?

Do they put on display, by the words and precepts they speak, the profound simplicity and convincing prose of the angels themselves? Are they able to show their ordination by speaking words of eternal life, as He did?

How does this "ordination" acquire or show redeeming power?

How can obtaining authority by ordination to this priesthood be something which will let people know their Lord better?

What is really going on for those who hold actual priestly authority, being ordained in the required manner? Do they acquire more than administrative authority from an institution? Do they receive power from on high? Can you get it anywhere other than from on high? Is this why the power of the priesthood is inseparably connected with the powers of heaven? What have we Saints been doing? Practicing? Holding ourselves forth to possess?

Where can we get this ordination after the order of the Son of God?

Forget what you've been taught. Read the Book of Mormon and remove the condemnation under which this people labor. Really study its words. They are alien to your prejudices and presumptions. But they ARE in fact the words of life. You really can get closer to God by abiding its precepts than through any other book! Amazingly, this is one of the very precepts which necessarily forces you to draw closer to God!

What a marvelous work and a wonder! Will the wonder never cease? (Only if you reject it.) It is a font of living water which con-

stantly renews and floods forth more and new information endlessly, until at last we are also caught up in the visions of eternity and know our Lord. Then we needn't ask another to know the Lord, for all shall know Him.

I labor to help you know Him; to bring you to Him. The primary means to accomplish that remains the Book of Mormon. But only if you actually let it speak to you and reveal its many hidden secrets.

Alma 13:3

"And this is the manner after which they were ordained—being called and prepared from the foundation of the world according to the foreknowledge of God, on account of their exceeding faith and good works; in the first place being left to choose good or evil; therefore they having chosen good, and exercising exceedingly great faith, are called with a holy calling, yea, with that holy calling which was prepared with, and according to, a preparatory redemption for such."

It is too much! Too great of words for men to possess! Consider what they refer us to.

Called and prepared FIRST! From the foundation of the world!

So here priesthood has its beginning before this world even was organized. There is a necessary link between those hallowed days and power here. No person has authority here unless it was first obtained there.

How was it obtained first—before the foundation of the world?

It was because of the foreknowledge of God. And what was God's foreknowledge based upon? Their "exceeding faith and good works!"

How can a person have "faith" when they stand in the presence of God? Do they now have knowledge? This was before the mortal estate, right? If so, then how can there be faith? What good works were involved?

Then, too, the "faith" and the "good works" were done as a result of the person having been "left to choose between good and evil." Now this is surprising! You mean that before Adam partook of the fruit of the tree of knowledge of good and evil (i.e., before the foundation of the world) that some people had already obtained a knowledge of good and evil, been tempted, exhibited good works and acquired faith? How so? When and where did they do that? What does that tell us about them? Is this why Joseph said there were "sons of God who exalted themselves to be gods before the world was made?" (*Teachings of the Prophet Joseph Smith (TPJS)*, 375.) When and where and how did they do this? And was this required for any person to be able to claim they now have priestly authority here? Or is it only those who have the "holy order after the Son of God?" Is there something about these men's "holy calling" that distinguishes them from others here? If so, what is it? Who are these men? Are they always going to be from unlikely sources and places, so that people can know how to recognize the Lord?

Then, too, we have them in a class of people who had been through a "preparatory redemption" already. What does that mean? What does it imply? How did they qualify? How long have these souls been working on the process of redemption and thereby qualify through their faith and good works to hold authority in this estate? Who are they?

Oh, now my head is spinning. Can this doctrine really be true? Why do we know so little about it? Why did Joseph talk about it, but we have simply nothing to add? Indeed, we deny it exists . . . why is that?

This is certainly an interesting chapter. Fearsome and interesting. What a threatening, terrible, majestic, holy and challenging book this Book of Mormon turns out to be after all.

Alma 13:4

"And thus they have been called to this holy calling on account of their faith, while others would reject the Spirit of God on account of the hardness of their hearts and blindness of their minds, while, if it had not been for this they might have had as great privilege as their brethren."

The result of what went on before is the reason for the ordination or calling. That is, "thus they have been called." Meaning that all of what went into the earlier experiences, i.e., being left to choose between good and evil, and having chosen good, having "faith" and good works, is the reason for their ordination. These souls are not novices. They are not getting authority here for the first time. They come with power from beyond this earth, bringing it with them to this earth. They qualified before and elsewhere.

All of this is "on account of their faith." All things are obtained through faith. That is explained in the Sixth Lecture, quoted here. Faith is a principle of power. It is capable of making things happen. There must be a connection between faith and power; between faith and priesthood.

Others reject the Spirit of God and, therefore, do not have this power. These others may claim to have authority, but they do not really receive power from the Spirit of God. They are animated by a different source.

What, then, causes someone who has a little authority "as they suppose" (they don't really have it, you see), to attempt to use that pretense to control and dominate others? The answer is contained in revelations already in print. It is their pride, their insecurities, the need to control, to be praised and celebrated, the need to gratify their

vain ambition. These are character flaws. They cover up these flaws by claiming to have priestly authority from God.[362]

They are the world's Pharaohs, not the world's Abrahams. Their hearts are hard, their minds blind.

They do not hear the Spirit of God, and therefore none of the powers of heaven are with them.

This was/is their choice. They could have had the same privilege. But, alas, they prefer instead their own aggrandizement. They prefer monuments built with their names engraven on them. There is no message of truth and hope coming from them. Their words (the only things which really endure), will fall to the ground unfulfilled. They will not be remembered. They will return without a saved soul.

What stunning doctrines we have stumbled upon here! I'm getting worried about things as I look about. This Book of Mormon is alarming . . .

---

[362] D&C 121:33–44 "Behold, there are many called, but few are chosen. And why are they not chosen? Because their hearts are set so much upon the things of this world, and aspire to the honors of men, that they do not learn this one lesson—That the rights of the priesthood are inseparably connected with the powers of heaven, and that the powers of heaven cannot be controlled nor handled only upon the principles of righteousness. That they may be conferred upon us, it is true; but when we undertake to cover our sins, or to gratify our pride, our vain ambition, or to exercise control or dominion or compulsion upon the souls of the children of men, in any degree of unrighteousness, behold, the heavens withdraw themselves; the Spirit of the Lord is grieved; and when it is withdrawn, Amen to the priesthood or the authority of that man. Behold, ere he is aware, he is left unto himself, to kick against the pricks, to persecute the saints, and to fight against God. We have learned by sad experience that it is the nature and disposition of almost all men, as soon as they get a little authority, as they suppose, they will immediately begin to exercise unrighteous dominion. Hence many are called, but few are chosen. No power or influence can or ought to be maintained by virtue of the priesthood, only by persuasion, by long-suffering, by gentleness and meekness, and by love unfeigned; By kindness, and pure knowledge, which shall greatly enlarge the soul without hypocrisy, and without guile—Reproving betimes with sharpness, when moved upon by the Holy Ghost; and then showing forth afterwards an increase of love toward him whom thou hast reproved, lest he esteem thee to be his enemy; That he may know that thy faithfulness is stronger than the cords of death."

Alma 13:5–6

> "Or in fine, in the first place they were on the same standing with their brethren; thus this holy calling being prepared from the foundation of the world for such as would not harden their hearts, being in and through the atonement of the Only Begotten Son, who was prepared— And thus being called by this holy calling, and ordained unto the high priesthood of the holy order of God, to teach his commandments unto the children of men, that they also might enter into his rest—"

So there wasn't some great advantage for these people who hold actual priestly authority. We learn that "in the first place they were on the same standing with their brethren." Where was that "first place?" Is it also "from the foundation of the world" referred to earlier?

What does it mean that they were "on the same standing with their brethren" while in that first place?

What was it about these who receive authority that qualified them to receive the "holy calling" from the foundation of the world? What does it mean that they "would not harden their hearts" in the first place? If they didn't do it then, will they do it now?

Is foreknowledge about these individual's qualifications based on prior performance? Can you determine that since they did not harden their hearts in the first place, they will not begin to harden their hearts now?

What about the "atonement of the Only Begotten Son, who was prepared" made them qualified? Did they accept Him there? Did they soften their hearts there toward Him? Are they capable of having redeeming faith in Him here because they first acquired it there?

Is all this necessary to have preceded ordination here? If it was not acquired there, can an ordination here have any effect?

What, then, do those who qualify do? What does it mean "to teach his commandments unto the children of men?"

Is there something different between teaching commandments on the one hand, and "that they [who are taught] also might enter into his rest" on the other hand? Are the two linked together? Is it necessary to both "teach his commandments unto the children of men, that they also might enter into his rest" to show such priestly authority? That is, can anyone, regardless of their true ordination to authority teach commandments? But does it take something more, some higher ordination in order to bring those taught "to enter into His rest?" If so, what is the difference? How can you recognize such teachings if they are ever put on display?

Did Joseph Smith exhibit such powerful teachings?

Did Enoch?

Did Melchizedek? Abraham? Elijah? Elisha? Nephi? The Brother of Jared? Enos? Others?

Do we see that today? If so, where? Does anyone have the audacity to presume they can bring another soul back to the Lord's rest? Maybe Joseph Smith's comment on this point is appropriate: ""The things of God are of deep import and time and experience and careful and ponderous and solemn thoughts can only find them out. Thy mind O man if thou wilt lead a soul into salvation must search into and contemplate the darkest abyss and the broad expanse of eternity, thou must commune with God." (*Documentary History of the Church* (*DHC*) 3:295.) I'd like to meet such a man. They seem to be rather infrequent residents of this fallen world . . .

Alma 13:7

"This high priesthood being after the order of his Son, which order was from the foundation of the world; or in other words, being without beginning of days or end of years, being prepared from eternity to all eternity, according to his foreknowledge of all things—"

Now we encounter comments that everyone seems to use about this priesthood. It is "without beginning of days or end of years." It is "from the foundation of the world."

It is "prepared from eternity to eternity."

When did eternity end and mortality begin?

When does mortality end and eternity begin again?

What does the phrase "from eternity to eternity" really refer to?

Do we pass "from eternity" then back "to eternity" as part of this mortal experience?

What went on before, back in the first "eternity?" We read elsewhere of this peaceful existence during "millennial" conditions, which end with rebellion, disputes and a war. Was Satan loosed in an earlier eternity after some season of peace to stir the hearts of men to anger one with another?[363] Was he cast out to hell, or the Telestial Kingdom, where we presently reside? What went on? How often would the Lord have gathered us as a hen gathers her chicks, but we would not be gathered? (I suppose His asking and the lack of an answer implies a great number.)

What is it about what went on before, in the earlier "eternity," that allows God to possess His perfect "foreknowledge of all things" now?

What is this strange doctrine and the implications which flow from them? Was Joseph Smith trying to tell us this in the later Nauvoo talks? (Maybe we should read them again . . .)

How is one to take it all in? How is the priesthood tied to this prior eternity? Why do we get side-tracked into the subject of "from

---

[363] Revelation 20:7–9 "And when the thousand years are expired, Satan shall be loosed out of his prison, And shall go out to deceive the nations which are in the four quarters of the earth, Gog and Magog, to gather them together to battle: the number of whom is as the sand of the sea. And they went up on the breadth of the earth, and compassed the camp of the saints about, and the beloved city: and fire came down from God out of heaven, and devoured them."

eternity to eternity" when we learn about this endless priesthood which is without beginning of days or end of years?

What is really going on? How can we learn of the truth? Is there no prophet who can declare it to us?

The suspense is killing me. I'm hoping to get answers. I'm hoping you want them too. I'm confident if you ask the Lord, He will answer you. He intends to pour out knowledge upon the heads of the Saints. If we will stop making others accountable for what we learn, and go to Him to receive what He offers, by the power of the Holy Ghost you may know the truth of all things. I read that somewhere . . . But the words are mine, now.

Alma 13:8

"Now they were ordained after this manner—being called with a holy calling, and ordained with a holy ordinance, and taking upon them the high priesthood of the holy order, which calling, and ordinance, and high priesthood, is without beginning or end—"

The manner of such person's ordination is described but—

What does it mean to be "called with a holy calling?" Is there something about the nature of this "calling" that is different from an interview and being "found worthy of advancement in the priesthood" as we commonly see? What is a "holy calling" anyway? Why does this kind of priestly calling get described exclusively as "holy" by its nature? Is there some contact with God required (who is the source of all holiness) as part of this "holy calling?"

Then we have the description of their ordination. What does it mean to be "ordained with a holy ordinance?" Does our practice of laying on hands, conferring the Aaronic Priesthood and ordaining to the office of Priest answer to this description? What is the "holy ordinance" that is done to confer this priesthood?

Can we automatically rule out the entirety of Aaronic and most of the Melchizedek priesthood offices when we see the words: "taking upon them the high priesthood of the holy order?" Is there some office we are aware of which is appropriately described as "taking upon them the high priesthood of the holy order?" Think about that for a moment.

If this is a "holy calling" and it results in the person receiving it "taking upon them the high priesthood of the holy order" isn't this something perhaps quite different from what we do to disseminate the priesthood? And if all the Aaronic Priesthood and most of the Melchizedek Priesthood offices are not what we would appropriately call "the high priesthood of the holy order" then are we talking about either of these two commonly held priesthoods anyway?

Then we have the interesting addition that the "calling, and ordinance, and high priesthood, is without beginning or end" for those involved. That is, without reference to mortality. It was held before coming here, it will endure after leaving here. It is "endless" in the sense it comes "from eternity to eternity" as set out in the preceding verse.

This is potentially quite different from the manner in which we practice priestly ordinations in the church today. I suppose that some will want to confine all this description to our practices. They are free to see it in that way if they choose. I'm just asking if it is more likely that the words have a different meaning than we have associated with them before. If that is possible, then perhaps we ought to be asking the Lord to inform us more about the matter, rather than presuming we already possess what is being described here.

It may just be that our hopes for some great, eternal reward hinge upon getting to the bottom of this matter. It may just be that God's control over and involvement with the "holy calling" and "holy ordinance" of having the "high priesthood after the Son of God" is immediate and direct. It may be that this "holy ordinance" will only come from that God who employs no servant at the gate, but is Himself the gatekeeper.[364] Wouldn't that be wonderful. Think about it—no flawed process. No fooled bishop or stake president letting someone obtain an office for which they are completely unsuited. It sort of makes sense.

Alma 13:9

> "Thus they become high priests forever, after the order of the Son, the Only Begotten of the Father, who is without beginning of days or end of years, who is full of grace, equity, and truth. And thus it is. Amen."

Several things about this formulation are interesting. Most interesting is the closing declaration, **"And thus it is. Amen."** It is iconic. It is as if the statement were an authorized, serious message, intended to be accompanied by the requisite formalities to let the reader know that this is serious stuff. This is "most holy." This is not just a passing description. It holds terrible, eternal significance. So the material that preceded it holds important keys to understanding. Important warnings and knowledge. Perhaps, as a result of the concluding punctuation, we should be very, very careful about the words that preceded it. [This is why I'm conducting this exercise.]

Now look at the beginning—

"Thus they become . . . " These individuals have become something. The "high priests" about whom this material has been written have been in the process of becoming something holy from before the foundation of the world. This is pre-earth or pre-mortal existence stuff. The history, or background leading up to finding a holy

---

[364] 2 Nephi 9:41 "O then, my beloved brethren, come unto the Lord, the Holy One. Remember that his paths are righteous. Behold, the way for man is narrow, but it lieth in a straight course before him, and the keeper of the gate is the Holy One of Israel; and he employeth no servant there; and there is none other way save it be by the gate; for he cannot be deceived, for the Lord God is his name."

high priest in mortality is eons in the making. It goes back to before this world had been reorganized.

" . . . high priests forever . . . " This priestly authority and holy order is not mortal. It is without beginning in this mortal phase of existence.

Now comes the formula of the authority: "after the order of the Son, the Only Begotten of the Father, who is without beginning of days or end of years, who is full of grace, equity, and truth." Look at it in pieces.

- After the order of the Son

- After the order of the Only Begotten of the Father

- After the order of Him who is without beginning of days or end of years

- After the order of Him who is full of grace

- After the order of Him who is full of equity

- After the order of Him who is full of truth.

What does it mean to be "begotten" of the Father?[365]

What does it mean to be a "son" of the Father?[366]

---

[365] Psalms 2:7 "I will declare the decree: the Lord hath said unto me, Thou art my Son; this day have I begotten thee."

[366] 1 John 3:1–3 "Behold, what manner of love the Father hath bestowed upon us, that we should be called the sons of God: therefore the world knoweth us not, because it knew him not. Beloved, now are we the sons of God, and it doth not yet appear what we shall be: but we know that, when he shall appear, we shall be like him; for we shall see him as he is. And every man that hath this hope in him purifieth himself, even as he is pure."

What does it mean to be full of "grace?"[367]

What does it mean to be full of "equity?"[368]

What does it mean to be full of "truth?"[369]

This is interesting. What are we to make of such "holy" men who are "high priests after the order of the Son of God?"

Do you think *we* make a man such a thing by sustaining him in Ward, Stake and General Conferences? Can *we* make one of them at all?

If we never realize who they are, does that mean they don't exist? Does it mean they weren't ordained before the foundation of the world?

If they come, minister in obscurity, never hold high office and never have a single building at BYU, BYU Hawaii or BYU Idaho named after them, are they any less?

Does our recognition of them make them any more?

Are they here to be recognized? Are they here just to teach so that others may be brought back to God by learning His commandments and enter into His rest?

---

[367] D&C 93:11–20 "And I, John, bear record that I beheld his glory, as the glory of the Only Begotten of the Father, full of grace and truth, even the Spirit of truth, which came and dwelt in the flesh, and dwelt among us. And I, John, saw that he received not of the fulness at the first, but received grace for grace; And he received not of the fulness at first, but continued from grace to grace, until he received a fulness; And thus he was called the Son of God, because he received not of the fulness at the first. And I, John, bear record, and lo, the heavens were opened, and the Holy Ghost descended upon him in the form of a dove, and sat upon him, and there came a voice out of heaven saying: This is my beloved Son. And I, John, bear record that he received a fulness of the glory of the Father; And he received all power, both in heaven and on earth, and the glory of the Father was with him, for he dwelt in him. And it shall come to pass, that if you are faithful you shall receive the fulness of the record of John. I give unto you these sayings that you may understand and know how to worship, and know what you worship, that you may come unto the Father in my name, and in due time receive of his fulness. For if you keep my commandments you shall receive of his fulness, and be glorified in me as I am in the Father; therefore, I say unto you, you shall receive grace for grace."

[368] Proverbs 2:9 "Then shalt thou understand righteousness, and judgment, and equity; yea, every good path."

[369] D&C 93:24 "And truth is knowledge of things as they are, and as they were, and as they are to come;"

This is quite different than what I've been told in Gospel Doctrine class. It is beginning to look and feel a lot like what Joseph Smith was saying right at the end in the Nauvoo period. I wonder why we neglect this today?

Alma 13:10

"Now, as I said concerning the holy order, or this high priesthood, there were many who were ordained and became high priests of God; and it was on account of their exceeding faith and repentance, and their righteousness before God, they choosing to repent and work righteousness rather than to perish;"

Immediately following the formula, the explanation continues that "many" were able to become ordained as such "high priests of God." But the way they did this was through several specific actions.

They had "exceeding faith." What do you suppose "exceeding faith" means? Why not "faith?" What is the difference between "faith" and "exceeding faith?"

They went through "repentance." So we know they made the same kinds of mortal mistakes as we do. They experience the bitter and then are able to prefer the sweet. They knew what it was like to feel the bitterness of hell, because they felt the sting of sin. So they repented. These great souls are NOT perfect, after all! They "repented" because they didn't do it right the first time. What a refreshing idea. They weren't fake. They didn't feign virtue. They had failing. They were filled with life, made errors, and needed to repent. They were not immune to the circumstances of this fallen world.

More importantly, do the terms "exceeding faith" and "repentance" go together? That is, do you necessarily have to possess "exceeding faith" in order to become one who fully "repents?" If so, why? How is it done? This may be an important clue to the process of "keeping the second estate" and "proving" that you are ready to move on. Perhaps it is in this manner that some will then have "glory added upon their heads forever," (Abraham 3:26) and in another cycle of existence and eternal progression then also join in the ranks of those belonging to the "holy order after the Son of God."

These called persons are, despite everything, "righteous before God." God measures differently than do we. Being "righteous before God" may not mean the same thing we think "righteous" means. We want outward signs, symbols, dress, grooming and conformity. God looks at the intent of the heart.

Interestingly, they "choose to repent and work righteousness rather than to perish." What do you suppose that means? First, they "repent," then they "work righteousness." Because of this, they do not "perish." So do these things all go together? Can a person "repent" but then not "work righteousness?" Does a person have to "repent" and "work righteousness" in order to not "perish?"

Alma 13:11

"Therefore they were called after this holy order, and were sanctified, and their garments were washed white through the blood of the Lamb."

If you understand these phrases, this verse clarifies the matter.

Being called into this holy order requires a person to be more than a church member, or a follower, or a believer. They need to be "sanctified."

"Their garments were washed white through the blood of the Lamb." No small feat!

To have white garments is to have the blood and sins of your generation removed from you. To be purified. To be sanctified by the Lamb—removing from you, and taking upon Himself the responsibility to answer for whatever failings you have.

This is not ritual purity. This is purity in fact.

The person described by this phrase is qualified to stand in the presence of God without sin. Clean of all blood and sin—righteous forever. He is Christ's, and Christ is the Father's, and all that each of them will be is the same; for we shall see Him as He is, because we will be like Him. To be like Him is to be sanctified.

I can use the words, but I am powerless beyond that. This is more than you think it is. Words are inadequate to explain it. Eye hath not seen, nor ear heard, nor has it entered **into the heart of man** what great things the Lord has in mind by inheriting these promises. Indeed, to receive an understanding is **to cease to be a man and become something else altogether**. A stranger and sojourner here, but a resident with God in another condition altogether. It is written by the Lord concerning them: "These are they who are come unto Mount Zion, and unto the city of the living God, the heavenly place, the holiest of all. These are they who have come to an innumerable company of angels, to the general assembly and church of Enoch, and of the Firstborn. These are they whose names are written in heaven, where God and Christ are the judge of all. These are they who are just men made perfect through Jesus the mediator of the new covenant, who wrought out this perfect atonement through the shedding of his own blood." (D&C 76:66–69)

Such persons are still in this world, but they are also associated with innumerable others who are not present here. Although mortals associate with each other, these individuals obtain a higher order. They connect with a higher plane, because a more sure word has been spoken to them. As a result they belong to an order of holy priesthood. That priesthood is an order without beginning of days or end of years, from eternity to eternity. This new, higher order, when it occurs can be the spark through which heaven itself can return to the earth.

To others looking in from outside, these are words without meaning, or definition. To those who hold this priestly position, these words are a perfect fit. The gulf between the two positions is so great that even a common vocabulary won't make meanings connect.

We proclaim we "have the truth" but we do not preach it. We claim to have authority, but we have no power to redeem and exalt. We pretend it is unlawful to preach mysteries, yet Alma is preaching the deepest doctrines to the non-converted. If we preach the truth, it will attract those whose lives are empty. Why would they join us if what we offer is as trite and superficial as the false religions they already believe?

Is there no need to cry repentance to this generation with power and authority? With the tongue of an angel? To cry out as the Book of Mormon declares the message to the non-believing and skeptical?

It does raise some troubling concerns as we claim to be the "true church" but do not act the part as shown in these scriptures. How are we justified in masking the fullness, hiding the mysteries, putting away deep doctrine that will save, and still proclaim that we are the "only true and living church upon the earth?" Does "living" require us to create sons and daughters of God who are "come to an innumerable company of angels, to the general assembly and church of Enoch, and of the Firstborn?" If so, why do we hear so little about it in our day?

I suppose our audacity springs from our history? If we have lost something vital that conflicts with our current understanding of the history that GUARANTEES us that we are perfect, and that we cannot be misled, then we wouldn't want to acknowledge that. Thank goodness for these guarantees. It does let us relax a bit, doesn't it? Broad and wide are the guarantees we have inherited. We don't need to worry about that narrow and strait fringe who rummage about in the mysteries.

Alma 13:12

> "Now they, after being sanctified by the Holy Ghost, having their garments made white, being pure and spotless before God, could not look upon sin save it were with abhorrence; and there were many, exceedingly great many, who were made pure and entered into the rest of the Lord their God."

If the earlier verse were not clear enough, the point is reiterated again here. These people are "sanctified by the Holy Ghost" as a result of "having their garments made white." They are "pure and spotless before God!"

This is the reason they can enter His presence. He has accepted them because just like Him, they are without sin. They were not perfected by their own acts. The earlier reference to their repentance makes that clear. They become pure and spotless before God because they have done what was asked of them to become clean. They have repented.

Now, measure the effects of their repentance. It has been so complete, so heartfelt, and deeply prized that they "could not look upon sin save it were with abhorrence." It is this notion that underlies the mistaken idea that once someone's calling and election has been made sure they are required to suffer for their own sins, because they have knowledge they are redeemed. This is a twisted view, designed by the adversary to discourage those who might otherwise seek and find.

It is not that the atonement ceases to operate for the redeemed. The atonement continues to cover the on-going sins of these redeemed souls which arise from their foolishness, mistakes, errors of comprehension, and the things they don't understand yet. Christ does not require them to do what they don't know is a requirement yet. As the gentle and kind Lord, He will forgive all they do that is wrong, while He reveals through greater light and knowledge a higher path. As He unfolds to their understanding more light, they can measure their conduct according to that greater light.

As they gain greater truth and light they see things how they really are. Right and wrong are seen differently. What once was "right" is now wrong as greater light and truth is received. What was once "wrong" is now seen clearly, without all the errors of understanding held before.

The spotlessness is because their heart is right. They WANT to please their Lord. They WANT to be like Him. Sin is not tempting because it is contrary to Him whom they love.

The abhorrence they feel at sin is not within them. It is not the temptations they struggle against. That is not the meaning at all. It is what they see all about them. The lost souls are the object of their compassion and care. They WANT to have others redeemed and saved from this lost and fallen world. The fruit they tasted is something they desire to share. They WANT many, an exceeding many, to share with them in the hope that can be won by repentance.

They would shout *"flee from Babylon"* if they thought it would do any good. But shouting does no good among a darkened and benighted people. They may speak the words of an angel to others, but it is up to others to decide whether they will listen. It will be a still, small, quiet pleading they make to others. Within their entreaties will be found the Master's words.

Many may claim to speak in His name, but only these few have the ability to speak with His approval. These are holy men, possessing words of eternal life. In them will be found truths that come from eternity and that will save to all eternity.

Only a few will listen. That won't detract from the power of the message delivered by those who are after the holy order of the Son of God, for their words can save any who will listen.

What an interesting chapter we have found here. And we are only a dozen verses into it! We should press on.

Alma 13:13

"And now, my brethren, I would that ye should humble yourselves before God, and bring forth fruit meet for repentance, that ye may also enter into that rest."

Think about what you're reading here. Alma is essentially declaring himself as one of those possessing this priesthood because he is inviting others to enter into the rest which these people enjoy. That is, "come, join in the rest of the Lord."

Alma has just revealed something profound about himself. It is subtle, but nonetheless true. In meekness he has proffered an invitation. He has not set himself up to be admired. He does not consider himself better. He has delivered the invitation to those to whom he is ministering, just as you would expect someone possessing this great, holy calling to do.

All the more remarkable is that he extends this invitation to an unredeemed, critical, reproachful audience of unconverted. He does not shield them from these great mysteries.

He does not flinch or hold back because it would be to "cast pearls before swine." He knows where the line is drawn, for in the preceding chapter they have explained to an audience that there are mysteries withheld from the public.[370] There are things kept from public knowledge and obtained only by heed and diligence. The line involves sacred ordinances, NOT higher knowledge. You give that and you make converts. You withhold it and you blend into the morass of churches who teach merely a form of godliness without any power to save.[371]

It was the same during Christ's ministry. The line is drawn as sacred events turn to ordinances. They are withheld. NOT the teaching of deep doctrine.

So when we refuse to discuss "mysteries" and limit our correlated curriculum to an approved list of 52 subjects, recycling them endlessly, we are not in conformity with the pattern shown in the Book of Mormon. The "most correct book" condemns us. But, then again, so does the word of the Lord precisely because we are not following the Book of Mormon.[372]

The highest form of acceptance and redemption is to have your calling and election made sure; to be washed and cleansed from sin

---

[370] Alma 12:9–11 "And now Alma began to expound these things unto him, saying: It is given unto many to know the mysteries of God; nevertheless they are laid under a strict command that they shall not impart only according to the portion of his word which he doth grant unto the children of men, according to the heed and diligence which they give unto him. And therefore, he that will harden his heart, the same receiveth the lesser portion of the word; and he that will not harden his heart, to him is given the greater portion of the word, until it is given unto him to know the mysteries of God until he know them in full. And they that will harden their hearts, to them is given the lesser portion of the word until they know nothing concerning his mysteries; and then they are taken captive by the devil, and led by his will down to destruction. Now this is what is meant by the chains of hell."

[371] JS–H 1:19 "I was answered that I must join none of them, for they were all wrong; and the Personage who addressed me said that all their creeds were an abomination in his sight; that those professors were all corrupt; that: 'they draw near to me with their lips, but their hearts are far from me, they teach for doctrines the commandments of men, having a form of godliness, but they deny the power thereof'."

[372] D&C 84:55–57 "Which vanity and unbelief have brought the whole church under condemnation. And this condemnation resteth upon the children of Zion, even all. And they shall remain under this condemnation until they repent and remember the new covenant, even the Book of Mormon and the former commandments which I have given them, not only to say, but to do according to that which I have written—"

every whit. Alma is preaching this to unconverted, investigating, potential converts. Today we won't even permit the subject to be raised
in adult Sunday School, Priesthood, or Relief Society meetings because it is considered to be "too sensitive" for the members to consider. Have we, the Gentiles, rejected "the fullness of the Gospel?"[373]
Not as long as any of us (like salt or leaven) keep these doctrines alive.

If you want to know about this fullness and how to obtain it,
then read the books I have written. That is what they are about.
Alma was right! His message was true!

Let all come and partake. Everyone is invited. No institutional
control should be used to prevent your search into this matter. It is
right in the Book of Mormon. Though the institution may be condemned for neglecting it, you don't need to be.

So, let's turn to the next verse and see what wonders continue to
unfold before our eyes . . .

Alma 13:14

"Yea, humble yourselves even as the people in the days of
Melchizedek, who was also a high priest after this same order
which I have spoken, who also took upon him the high
priesthood forever."

We have named a portion of the priesthood after Melchizedek.
(It is not, however, the form which Melchizedek held. That is another
topic I am not going to address here now. This area is complete mush
in the minds of Latter-day Saint writers and commentaries. I can't

---

[373] 3 Nephi 16:10 "And thus commandeth the Father that I should say unto you: At
that day when the Gentiles shall sin against my gospel, and shall reject the fulness of
my gospel, and shall be lifted up in the pride of their hearts above all nations, and
above all the people of the whole earth, and shall be filled with all manner of lyings,
and of deceits, and of mischiefs, and all manner of hypocrisy, and murders, and priestcrafts, and whoredoms, and of secret abominations; and if they shall do all those
things, and shall reject the fulness of my gospel, behold, saith the Father, I will bring
the fulness of my gospel from among them."

straighten that out on this blog. I might take it up in a book and go through it methodically there.)

What is important is that the great events of Melchizedek's time began when people humbled themselves and accepted the teachings of this "high priesthood" holder and were, thereby, saved. Not only saved but also led into a fellowship which eventually turned into a City of Peace, or City of Salem, or Jerusalem, which was taken into heaven.

This prototype was so influential in the thinking of all who followed, that the high priesthood was named after Melchizedek. Even though he held Patriarchal Priesthood with its associated sealing power, he was the one after whom Melchizedek Priesthood was named in the form it was later transmitted which lacked sealing authority. (Again, another topic.)

What is important in this verse is the connection between the existence of the one holding this authority (Melchizedek), and a humble people who would accept and follow those teachings. The result of the combination of the two was that God came and dwelt among them.

This is a pattern that followed the previous pattern with Enoch. This was the pattern Joseph wanted to return through his teaching and ministry. Joseph wasn't able to accomplish it. We now hope to see it someday occur in the unfolding history of The Church of Jesus Christ of Latter-day Saints. The most recent book on this subject, now on sale at Deseret Book (unfortunately a red-flag for me) urges the idea that the only Zion we should expect to see will come when the church president allows or directs it to happen.

This verse suggests what is needed is 1) humble people willing to accept teaching from a high priest after the ancient order and 2) a person having that authority who will teach.

What does this do to our current accepted model?

If Zion is to return, how will it return? Will it mirror what the Book of Mormon is teaching here?

Is the church president the one who will bring this gathering to pass?

Is the church president teaching doctrine about the fullness which will bring others into the rest of the Lord?

Has the church president brought a company into the Lord's presence? Attempted to do so? Taught or written about how that will happen? (If so, can someone point that out to me so I can read the talk, get the book or watch the video.)

How can I know I would actually have followed Melchizedek and become a part of his city by what I do today? (I'd like to be among them, you see.)

Alma 13:15

"And it was this same Melchizedek to whom Abraham paid tithes; yea, even our father Abraham paid tithes of one-tenth part of all he possessed."

Abraham, father of the righteous, paid tithe to this Melchizedek. Not the reverse.

I've already commented that I believe Melchizedek (whose name means "king and priest") was in fact Shem. I believe those who disagree (McConkie and Joseph Fielding Smith) base their conclusion on the words of D&C 84:14 which reads: "Which Abraham received the priesthood from Melchizedek, who received it through the lineage of his fathers, even till Noah;". I believe the lineage referred to there is from the fathers who preceded Noah. But Noah was Shem/Melchizedek's father.

Abraham received the priesthood which had been promised to him by God, from Melchizedek. He (Abraham) already had the records of the fathers.[374] He already had the promise of priestly authority.[375] So the question should be asked as to why Abraham would need to be ordained by Melchizedek when the Lord was speaking directly to him and could have taken care of that directly. It is an important question. It is necessary to understand why the question should be asked and also what the answer is.

First, why would Abraham, who was directly in contact with God, be sent to another to receive the priesthood? What sense does it make the Lord would make him wait and send him to another? Particularly when Abraham had understanding that stretched into heavens and also possessed the records of the fathers, back to Adam. Why do that?

You should struggle with this question yourself. I feel like I'm robbing you by answering. Nevertheless, Abraham needed to be endowed and Melchizedek was set up to provide to Abraham the endowment. Therefore to receive the ordinance (Abraham was raised by apostates who had not provided that for him), he was sent to Melchizedek from whom he received necessary ordinances. As long

---

[374] Abraham 1:31 "But the records of the fathers, even the patriarchs, concerning the right of Priesthood, the Lord my God preserved in mine own hands; therefore a knowledge of the beginning of the creation, and also of the planets, and of the stars, as they were made known unto the fathers, have I kept even unto this day, and I shall endeavor to write some of these things upon this record, for the benefit of my posterity that shall come after me."

[375] Abraham 2:6–9 "But I, Abraham, and Lot, my brother's son, prayed unto the Lord, and the Lord appeared unto me, and said unto me: Arise, and take Lot with thee; for I have purposed to take thee away out of Haran, and to make of thee a minister to bear my name in a strange land which I will give unto thy seed after thee for an everlasting possession, when they hearken to my voice. For I am the Lord thy God; I dwell in heaven; the earth is my footstool; I stretch my hand over the sea, and it obeys my voice; I cause the wind and the fire to be my chariot; I say to the mountains—Depart hence— and behold, they are taken away by a whirlwind, in an instant, suddenly. My name is Jehovah, and I know the end from the beginning; therefore my hand shall be over thee. And I will make of thee a great nation, and I will bless thee above measure, and make thy name great among all nations, and thou shalt be a blessing unto thy seed after thee, that in their hands they shall bear this ministry and Priesthood unto all nations;"

as the ordinances needed to be performed and there was an officiator there to accomplish it, the Lord sent Abraham to Melchizedek.

Abraham also received the accouterments of kingship that descended from Adam. Melchizedek was the reigning high priest on the earth, Abraham was to replace him at his passing, and Melchizedek had awaited the promised successor's arrival for years. When at last Abraham arrived, Melchizedek was able to provide ordinances, answer questions, minister as was needed, then turn over the accouterments of kingship and withdraw from this earth. No sooner had Abraham been prepared than Melchizedek and his city also withdraw to join Enoch's people.

Second, why were tithes paid to a great high priest who would shortly be translated? What need was there for tithing?

The form the tithing took was not a check or bank draft. It was animals, food and usable material. What was provided would be used in sacrifices, feasts, celebrations and decoration of the temple maintained by Melchizedek. In short, Abraham provided material through his tithing that could be incorporated into the celebrations to which he was invited and from which he derived his own blessing and endowment. He gave, in turn he received.

Now, if you do not understand the concept of meekness and its importance for one who should hold this holy priesthood, then you do not understand either Melchizedek or Abraham. Each was a minister who served others. Each was a faithful guide because neither sought to be greater than another. They were great servants, who could be trusted with great authority because they did not seek their own will. They were interested in following the Lord's will. Even at the price of great inconvenience and sacrifice to them. They were willing to sacrifice all things, and were therefore called to the work.

Alma 13:16

"Now these ordinances were given after this manner, that thereby the people might look forward on the Son of God, it being a type of his order, or it being his order, and this that they might look forward to him for a remission of their sins, that they might enter into the rest of the Lord."

Notice the shifting back to "ordinances" from the discussion of priesthood. What ordinances? What manner?

Why would what happened with Melchizedek and Abraham be something pointing to the Son of God?

Why would such an ordination and ordinance always be something that would prepare people to understand and accept the Son of God?

How was it a "type" of the Son of God's order?

What is this referring to in plain language? Is it that the ordinances will reveal a pattern that will unmistakably point back to the ministry of Christ? How?

What is there in conferring priesthood and endowing with understanding that points to Christ? Was Christ endowed with knowledge? Power? Authority? From on-high? When? What account do we have of it? Was it at His baptism when the voice of God declared, "thou art my Son, this day have I begotten thee" (which wording was deliberately changed during the Fourth Century Christological debates to read instead: "this is my beloved Son, in whom I am well pleased")? How does this identify both the holder of this holy order of priesthood and confirm Christ's ministry as the Son of God?

More importantly, why are these things not being taught to us today? This is such basic and important doctrine that Alma is teaching it as introductory material to a potential group of converts. But as faithful members of the Church we aren't even familiar with them. What have we been doing with the Gospel we received?

Why was the "manner" something which would let those who learned about it know and identify the Lord?

Do we expect to follow Christ? If so, why aren't we anxious to learn about this holy order? Can we follow Him unless we do what is necessary to take upon us that same holy order? If so, then how are we to find it today? Who teaches about it?

It is interesting to read this chapter of Alma. It reinforces that the Book of Mormon is still being neglected. We cycle through it every four years. Perhaps we are still neglecting it's true message? I think this chapter gets lumped in with three others and covered in a 50 minute class every four years. Maybe that is what is meant by "neglect."

Alma 13:17–18

"Now this Melchizedek was a king over the land of Salem; and his people had waxed strong in iniquity and abomination; yea, they had all gone astray; they were full of all manner of wickedness; But Melchizedek having exercised mighty faith, and received the office of the high priesthood according to the holy order of God, did preach repentance unto his people. And behold, they did repent; and Melchizedek did establish peace in the land in his days; therefore he was called the prince of peace, for he was the king of Salem; and he did reign under his father."

He was a king over people who had "waxed strong" in both "iniquity" and also "abomination." Keep in mind that "waxing strong" means to be increasingly determined or committed. "Iniquity" is generally evil practice, but "abomination" involves the *religious justification* of wrongdoing. That is, something becomes "abominable" when it is motivated out of a false form of religious observance or is justified because of religious error.

The people to whom Melchizedek would minister were not simply in error, they were motivated by a false set of religious beliefs and errors. The result was that "they had all gone astray." They were "full of all manner of wickedness." This was a challenging audience for this man to minister to and try to convert to the truth.

Melchizedek began by "exercising mighty faith" in order to understand the truth and discern the difference between truth and error. Remember how difficult it is to be taught truth. It is more difficult to learn truth than it is to perform miracles.[376] Despite this, Melchizedek was able to set aside all he beheld and through faith acquire an understanding of the truth for himself. Conferred upon him as part of this education was the priestly authority with which to minister to others.

He "did preach repentance unto his people." This required him to expose the errors, show them they were involved in iniquity and to expose how their religious errors had made them abominable. This preaching is always most difficult because it confronts the audience with a challenge to their mistaken beliefs, and false religion. There is a risk of violence when this happens. People who entertain abominable religious practices are more often moved to violence than to repentance. The Lord was greeted with violence. So was Lehi, Isaiah, Nephi, Samuel the Lamanite, Abinadi, Peter, Paul, Stephen, James, Zacharias and too many others to mention. To their credit, and to Melchizedek's, the preaching resulted in repentance.

---

[376] 3 Nephi 17:2–7 "I perceive that ye are weak, that ye cannot understand all my words which I am commanded of the Father to speak unto you at this time. Therefore, go ye unto your homes, and ponder upon the things which I have said, and ask of the Father, in my name, that ye may understand, and prepare your minds for the morrow, and I come unto you again. But now I go unto the Father, and also to show myself unto the lost tribes of Israel, for they are not lost unto the Father, for he knoweth whither he hath taken them. And it came to pass that when Jesus had thus spoken, he cast his eyes round about again on the multitude, and beheld they were in tears, and did look steadfastly upon him as if they would ask him to tarry a little longer with them. And he said unto them: Behold, my bowels are filled with compassion towards you. Have ye any that are sick among you? Bring them hither. Have ye any that are lame, or blind, or halt, or maimed, or leprous, or that are withered, or that are deaf, or that are afflicted in any manner? Bring them hither and I will heal them, for I have compassion upon you; my bowels are filled with mercy."

The serious errors, iniquity, and abominations of these people did not prevent Melchizedek from establishing a Zion. These people were able to acquire "peace in the land" because of their repentance. As used here, however, peace means more than the absence of violence, it means the presence of the Lord.

The statement that he established peace as the King of Salem (Shalom means peace) and "he did reign under his father" is a play on words. Which "father" is being identified in the statement. Was it Noah, or Gabriel? (A man who would also be translated and have a ministry as the Lord's herald before the birth of John the Baptist and Christ.) Or was the "father" Him would would declare that Melchizedek was "begotten" as a "son of God?" It likely meant both. But it is also likely written this way to let those who do not understand what is being said to read it in a way that conceals the dual meanings. The scriptures are filled with such dual meanings.

What is hopeful for us today, is that no matter how much "iniquity" and religious error we engage in that results in our "abominations" in our pride and foolishness, we still may be candidates to receive something similar to what befell the City of Salem. The first step is to acquire the presence of this priesthood through individual repentance.

We envy these ancients. But we do nothing to try and follow the pattern revealed to us in their course. The Book of Mormon is a course in ancient failure and ancient success. We just do not respect what we have in that volume.

Alma 13:19–20

"Now, there were many before him, and also there were many afterwards, but none were greater; therefore, of him they have more particularly made mention. Now I need not rehearse the matter; what I have said may suffice. Behold, the scriptures are before you; if ye will wrest them it shall be to your own destruction."

The "many before him, and also . . . many afterwards" in this sermon is not just a reference to believers, but to those who held this "holy order after the Son of God." It it a reference to those who were made clean and pure by their repentance. It is those who, having been called by the Lord, chosen to this holy order, having their calling and election secure, hold power as a result of this relationship with God.

But none of these, before or since, (at the time of the writing by Alma) who held authority were greater than Melchizedek. As a result, he merited particular mention to identify those who held the holy priesthood after the order of the Son of God. It was merited because his example and his ministry illustrated perfectly what the "holy order" was intended to accomplish. It is designed to save others.

It was not to exalt the man.

It was not to bring attention to the man. It was not to amass praise or a following.

It was not to make the man a ruler over others. It was not to gain control or domination.

It was not to subjugate or force compulsive obedience upon the souls of men.

It was to serve and exalt those to whom he ministered. His greatness was derived by the fruit of saved, exalted souls whom he saved. There is no record of a single sermon preached by Melchizedek. We have evidence of the following things he did with his authority and power:

- He received tithes from Abraham.[377]

- He ordained Abraham.[378]

- He saved an entire population from iniquity and abominations, and converted them to the truth.[379]

- He made those he converted qualified to behold the Lord's presence.[380]

- He performed a form of ceremony with Abraham involving breaking bread and wine.[381]

He served. He blessed. He produced exalted souls. He was not great by what he received, but by what he did with what he received to bless and exalt others.

We would see this if we understood the scriptures. We would not be following a false tradition wherein men are famous, celebrity-like, fawned over, held up to acclaim and given the authority to exercise control over men. This is a false model that the Gentiles follow, and

---

[377] Alma 13:15 "And it was this same Melchizedek to whom Abraham paid tithes; yea, even our father Abraham paid tithes of one-tenth part of all he possessed."

[378] D&C 84:14 "Which Abraham received the priesthood from Melchizedek, who received it through the lineage of his fathers, even till Noah;"

[379] Alma 13:18 "But Melchizedek having exercised mighty faith, and received the office of the high priesthood according to the holy order of God, did preach repentance unto his people. And behold, they did repent; and Melchizedek did establish peace in the land in his days; therefore he was called the prince of peace, for he was the king of Salem; and he did reign under his father."

[380] Alma 13:11 "But Melchizedek having exercised mighty faith, and received the office of the high priesthood according to the holy order of God, did preach repentance unto his people. And behold, they did repent; and Melchizedek did establish peace in the land in his days; therefore he was called the prince of peace, for he was the king of Salem; and he did reign under his father."

[381] Genesis 14:18–19 "And Melchizedek king of Salem brought forth bread and wine: and he was the priest of the most high God. And he blessed him, and said, Blessed be Abram of the most high God, possessor of heaven and earth:"

not the way in which true priesthood holders operate.[382] No one possessing power from heaven will do this.[383]

Now, if you make this mistake and follow in this false tradition, it will be to your own destruction. Alma has warned you.

What a marvelously relevant book this Book of Mormon is for our own day! It is almost as if they saw our time, knew what we would struggle with, and had teachings designed to let us see the error and repent. I truly believe that we can get closer to God by abiding the precepts of the Book of Mormon than we can from any other book! Joseph Smith was right.

Now we see this startling continuation in the next two verses.

Alma 13:21–22

"And now it came to pass that when Alma had said these words unto them, he stretched forth his hand unto them and cried with a mighty voice, saying: Now is the time to repent, for the day of salvation draweth nigh; Yea, and the voice of the Lord, by the mouth of angels, doth declare it unto all nations; yea, doth declare it, that they may have glad tidings of great joy; yea, and he doth sound these glad tidings among all his people, yea, even to them that are scattered abroad upon the face of the earth; wherefore they have come unto us."

---

[382] Matthew 20:25–28 "But Jesus called them unto him, and said, Ye know that the princes of the Gentiles exercise dominion over them, and they that are great exercise authority upon them. But it shall not be so among you: but whosoever will be great among you, let him be your minister; And whosoever will be chief among you, let him be your servant: Even as the Son of man came not to be ministered unto, but to minister, and to give his life a ransom for many."

[383] D&C 121:36–37 "That the rights of the priesthood are inseparably connected with the powers of heaven, and that the powers of heaven cannot be controlled nor handled only upon the principles of righteousness. That they may be conferred upon us, it is true; but when we undertake to cover our sins, or to gratify our pride, our vain ambition, or to exercise control or dominion or compulsion upon the souls of the children of men, in any degree of unrighteousness, behold, the heavens withdraw themselves; the Spirit of the Lord is grieved; and when it is withdrawn, Amen to the priesthood or the authority of that man."

Now we get to some things which the record does not fully disclose, but does allow those with eyes to see behold it. Be careful how you respond to this, because some correct answers are not going up if they cross a line. But think of the answers to these questions:

Why does he "stretch forth his hand?" What does that signify?

In what way would that become significant, even a sign that he is a true messenger?

Why does he now "cry with a mighty voice" to make the call?

What is a "mighty voice?" Is it distinguished by volume or is there something more and quite different about it? Importantly, it is not "loud" but instead "mighty." Is that significant? How? Why?

What does it mean that "*the Lord*, by the mouth of angels, doth declare it?" Who is really speaking? Who is He speaking through? What person is delivering the message? How is Alma identifying himself in this "mighty cry" he makes?

Who are these angels sent to all nations?

What is the difference in this statement by Alma and the others who can speak with tongue of angels?[384]

If one should possess such a right or commission, then whose words are they actually speaking?

---

[384] 2 Nephi 31:13–14 "Wherefore, my beloved brethren, I know that if ye shall follow the Son, with full purpose of heart, acting no hypocrisy and no deception before God, but with real intent, repenting of your sins, witnessing unto the Father that ye are willing to take upon you the name of Christ, by baptism—yea, by following your Lord and your Savior down into the water, according to his word, behold, then shall ye receive the Holy Ghost; yea, then cometh the baptism of fire and of the Holy Ghost; and then can ye speak with the tongue of angels, and shout praises unto the Holy One of Israel. But, behold, my beloved brethren, thus came the voice of the Son unto me, saying: After ye have repented of your sins, and witnessed unto the Father that ye are willing to keep my commandments, by the baptism of water, and have received the baptism of fire and of the Holy Ghost, and can speak with a new tongue, yea, even with the tongue of angels, and after this should deny me, it would have been better for you that ye had not known me."

2 Nephi 32:2 "Do ye not remember that I said unto you that after ye had received the Holy Ghost ye could speak with the tongue of angels? And now, how could ye speak with the tongue of angels save it were by the Holy Ghost?"

Why do His sheep hear HIS voice? Even when spoken by another man or empowered priestly minister?

What does Alma actually say about his own authority as he delivers this warning? What can Alma lead you to inherit if you will heed his counsel and warning? How can we know he is a true messenger sent by the Lord?

If the Lord sends these messages and messengers to all His people, have they been sent to us? If so, where would we be able to find them and hear their message? How are we to know they are true ministers? Should I just trust that some institutional office and office holder is a guaranteed place in which to locate such a true minister? If it is always that convenient, why hasn't the Lord implemented that system before, instead of letting people have their free agency and permitting them to make mistakes? Why did the Lord allow Eli, Caiphus and Annas become High Priests? Why didn't He come up with this neat system before? [Clearly our system makes it so much easier. It throws God's fairness into question, since He made is so much harder for earlier Israelites to figure out where the truth was being proclaimed. I think the Lord must owe them an apology.]

Well, more can be said, but I leave it to you to reach your own conclusions about this startling comment coming from a true messenger. It makes one wonder why we've been missing it, as it has been before us for so many years.

"Why reveal a sacred sign?" First, "reveal" may not be the case because 1) it was not in connection with covenant-making, 2) it was accompanied with warning of judgment, not ceremonial in a Temple setting, 3) the audience may already know the meaning, in which case nothing is being "revealed", though they may be reminded, and if not, then 4) if the audience did not know the meaning then nothing is "revealed" to the audience who, in ignorance, will not associate keys or meaning to it.

Further, even you do not know the sign used unless it has been shown to you by revelation. You can know that a sign was used, but which is not stated.

Alma 13:23

"And they are made known unto us in plain terms, that we may understand, that we cannot err; and this because of our being wanderers in a strange land; therefore, we are thus highly favored, for we have these glad tidings declared unto us in all parts of our vineyard."

This doctrine contained in the scriptures was understood by this audience. The same audience who was full of iniquity and abominations because of their false religious traditions. It was in "plain terms" in the scriptures, if one doesn't "wrest" them to their destruction.

To "wrest" means to apply such twisted reasoning that the philosophies of men are mingled with scriptures so that the result is error.

The object of the scriptures is to make matters "plain" and prevent people from "erring" in their effort to follow God.

What is the difference between someone who with their scriptures before them, finds their message sufficiently "plain" and "understood" that they "cannot err," and someone who has the same set of scriptures and engages in "iniquity" and "abominations" because of their false religious ideas? How can someone who is religious be certain they are not among those who err, but is instead among those who find holiness and develop faith to repent?

How do we know which side of this line we are on?

Both sides are religious. Both sides have their traditions and teachings. Both sides are sincere and following what they believe to be true. However, one is engaged in "abominations" because of their false beliefs, and the other has entertained angels and received such cleansing that their garments are white before God. One side does not understand their awful state. But the other is certain of their promise of exaltation and purity before God.

So, how certain are you? Do you know you are pure before God? Holy? Having entered into His holy order after the order of the Son of God? Or do you entertain some doubt about whether the traditions which you value are actually based on the truth? Is it possible that you "err" or "wrest" the scriptures as part of your religious tradition?

According to Alma, all of this care by the Lord is because they are "wanderers in a strange land." Meaning that they are in this spot at this time because they have been taken from Jerusalem, the land of their forefathers, and placed in a new, promised land. They have been persecuted and evicted from land by their aggressive cousins. All of this to stir them up to repentance. It is God's care for them, God's careful tutelage of them, that leads them to receive this profound understanding. They are on God's errand, and therefore entitled to God's guidance. God is providing the "glad tidings" which will permit repentance to occur.

So, applying Alma's teaching to us, we should ask ourselves if we have repented? If we have received a message from angels declaring glad tidings? If we have received what we would recognize as a message from the Lord by someone declaring repentance? Or do we have a weak tradition which assures us that we are right, while letting us entertain abominable (false, religious-based) errors in our beliefs?

These are troubling questions. Worth careful, solemn and ponderous thought. Perhaps even prayerful thought where we ask the Lord if these things are not true. And if we ask with real intent, He may make the truth known to us. At least that is what He has said through past messengers. I see no reason why it would not work for us. It's at least worth a try, isn't it?

Powerful teachings from Alma. But then again, one should expect nothing less from a true messenger bearing a holy order of power and authority after the order of the Son of God. A weak and vacillating voice telling us all is well and we're going to be fine just seems wrong by comparison. At least I would think so.

Alma 13:24

"For behold, angels are declaring it unto many at this time in our land; and this is for the purpose of preparing the hearts of the children of men to receive his word at the time of his coming in his glory."

If "angels are declaring it unto many" at the time of Alma's remarks, why are they not declaring it unto many now? Are we any less important than they were? If we are as important, then why are we not hearing of this now?

What is the definition of "angels" who are doing this "declaring" to "many?" Was Alma included? If so, what is it that turns a man from a mortal to ministering angel? Can a mortal become a ministering angel? How would that occur? What would it require? Can we thereby entertain angels unawares?[385]

If an angel comes to visit with a man, gives him a message, and the man then declares it, are they both made "angels" by this message? Are "angels" always either deceased or unborn? If they are, then why did Joseph teach that "there are no angels who minister to this earth but those who do belong or have belonged to it?"[386] If angels "do belong" to the earth are they still mortal?

---

[385] Hebrews 13:2 "Be not forgetful to entertain strangers: for thereby some have entertained angels unawares."

[386] D&C 130:5 "I answer, Yes. But there are no angels who minister to this earth but those who do belong or have belonged to it."

How would you recognize such a person? Would it be the same way the Lord was known before He showed Himself to the disciples on the Road to Emmaus?[387]

If it is the "hearts" which are to be prepared, then does this relate to the disciples "hearts burning within them" as the Lord spoke to them while in the way? Why do His sheep hear His voice? How do they hear his voice?

Why is preparing "the hearts" enough to prepare a people to "receive His word?" Is it more important to "receive His word" than to receive His person? Why would that be so?

Why are we unable to receive Him in His glory until after our hearts have first "received His word?"

It is more difficult to be taught than to have faith for miracles.[388] Even should you behold the Lord "in His glory" just as the Nephites, it would still be more difficult for you to have the faith to be taught by Him and accept what He has to teach than for Him to perform a miracle.

How alike all the generations of men are. How very relevant, therefore, these words remain for us!

---

[387] Luke 24:32 "And they said one to another, Did not our heart burn within us, while he talked with us by the way, and while he opened to us the scriptures?"

[388] 3 Nephi 17:2–8 "I perceive that ye are weak, that ye cannot understand all my words which I am commanded of the Father to speak unto you at this time. Therefore, go ye unto your homes, and ponder upon the things which I have said, and ask of the Father, in my name, that ye may understand, and prepare your minds for the morrow, and I come unto you again. But now I go unto the Father, and also to show myself unto the lost tribes of Israel, for they are not lost unto the Father, for he knoweth whither he hath taken them. And it came to pass that when Jesus had thus spoken, he cast his eyes round about again on the multitude, and beheld they were in tears, and did look steadfastly upon him as if they would ask him to tarry a little longer with them. And he said unto them: Behold, my bowels are filled with compassion towards you. Have ye any that are sick among you? Bring them hither. Have ye any that are lame, or blind, or halt, or maimed, or leprous, or that are withered, or that are deaf, or that are afflicted in any manner? Bring them hither and I will heal them, for I have compassion upon you; my bowels are filled with mercy. For I perceive that ye desire that I should show unto you what I have done unto your brethren at Jerusalem, for I see that your faith is sufficient that I should heal you."

Alma 13:25

"And now we only wait to hear the joyful news declared unto us by the mouth of angels, of his coming; for the time cometh, we know not how soon. Would to God that it might be in my day; but let it be sooner or later, in it I will rejoice."

This comment is made in expectation that the Nephites will be told by heaven as soon as Christ is born. " . . . we only wait to hear the joyful news declared unto us by the mouth of angels . . . "

Angels declared it to the shepherds near Bethlehem.[389] Alma expected a similar announcement.

"We only wait to hear the joyful news." He *expected* the news to be shared. He knew they would have the announcement. He *expected* the angels to declare the arrival. He knew heaven would not leave these people without a herald of the news.

Imagine that. A prophet confident that the Lord will do nothing without first making known to the people His secrets![390] It is one thing to teach this concept. It is another to live it. Alma is living it. Therefore angels did come and did make things known to him.

What does it take to have faith like this?

---

[389] Luke 2:8–15 "And there were in the same country shepherds abiding in the field, keeping watch over their flock by night. And, lo, the angel of the Lord came upon them, and the glory of the Lord shone round about them: and they were sore afraid. And the angel said unto them, Fear not: for, behold, I bring you good tidings of great joy, which shall be to all people. For unto you is born this day in the city of David a Saviour, which is Christ the Lord. And this shall be a sign unto you; Ye shall find the babe wrapped in swaddling clothes, lying in a manger. And suddenly there was with the angel a multitude of the heavenly host praising God, and saying, Glory to God in the highest, and on earth peace, good will toward men. And it came to pass, as the angels were gone away from them into heaven, the shepherds said one to another, Let us now go even unto Bethlehem, and see this thing which is come to pass, which the Lord hath made known unto us."

[390] Amos 3:7 "Surely the Lord God will do nothing, but he revealeth his secret unto his servants the prophets."

If you do not possess this kind of faith, can you be saved? Moroni taught that the absence of such faith condemns the people who no longer have such things happening among them.[391]

Do we expect the Lord to tell US about things by the mouth of angels before they happen? Or do we expect the Lord will tell someone inside the bowels of an organization, and we will get some announcement through the prescribed channels, thereby relieving us from obtaining the ministry of angels? Then why is the visitation of angels an Aaronic (lowest) priesthood key?[392] This is the right of young people beginning at age 12, mind you. Should we expect the angelic heralds to come to everyone, 12 year of age or older? Why or why not?

Alma knows it will happen. But he does not know when it will happen. He would like it to have been in his day. It was not. But whether it was to happen in his life or afterwards, he nonetheless had faith, knew angels, awaited the message, and rejoiced at the idea of His coming.

How meek! How faithful! No wonder such a man possessed and knew the details of this holy order from God. No wonder he could teach with authority about it. How great the lesson he has left for any who will take seriously the message he taught.

Faith of this sort should be the common heritage of the Lord's people. It was never intended that an elite, distant hierarchy would be put between God and His people. If you are His, then you should KNOW Him. If you do not know Him, then you are not His. Heed

---

[391] Moroni 7:36–37 "Or have angels ceased to appear unto the children of men? Or has he withheld the power of the Holy Ghost from them? Or will he, so long as time shall last, or the earth shall stand, or there shall be one man upon the face thereof to be saved? Behold I say unto you, Nay; for it is by faith that miracles are wrought; and it is by faith that angels appear and minister unto men; wherefore, if these things have ceased wo be unto the children of men, for it is because of unbelief, and all is vain."

[392] D&C 84:26 "And the lesser priesthood continued, which priesthood holdeth the key of the ministering of angels and the preparatory gospel;"

His voice when you hear it. No matter how surprising a place or person from which it may come. If it is His voice, then you have heard Him.

Alma 13:26

"And it shall be made known unto just and holy men, by the mouth of angels, at the time of his coming, that the words of our fathers may be fulfilled, according to that which they have spoken concerning him, which was according to the spirit of prophecy which was in them."

Here is a simple, but compound thought. Alma is saying this:

There were "fathers" who recorded words of prophecy.

The "fathers" had the "spirit of prophecy which was in them."

These words of the prophetic fathers promised that "the mouths of angels" will declare Christ's birth into the world.

The declaration of Christ's birth will come to "just and holy men" by these angels.

So, Alma is assured that the promises will be fulfilled. He knows this because the fathers who revealed the promises were trustworthy and had the spirit of prophecy.

Now comes the real question: What does it mean that "just and holy men" will be the ones to whom the angels will come and make the declaration?

Is this a description of those who hold the same priesthood as Melchizedek discussed by Alma? If so, then does access to that priestly order after the order of the Son of God put the possessors into contact with heavenly messengers? Can a person hold that authority and not receive messages from angels from time to time?

Who is it among us who begins an address by referring to the angel who visited the them the preceding night?[393]

I have to assume that this is the kind of information that would be generally known among faithful followers of Christ's Gospel. After all, Alma is speaking to apostates, non-believers and critics who hold a false and abominable religion. One would expect that such things are not really so sacred that they can't be preached. Why would it be "off limits" to us and be something freely declared as part of a missionary effort in the Book of Mormon? So assuming it ought to be known, *if it is occurring*, is this among us? Where? Who has received these angelic messengers? Where are these "just and holy" men who entertain angelic ministers?

Or is it that we don't expect angels, so we don't entertain them? Perhaps they come and we don't notice them? Perhaps we are blind that we cannot see, deaf because we will not hear, and our minds are darkened because we will not abide the teachings of the Book of Mormon? What is going on with us, when we compare and measure ourselves against this message from Alma?

Should I be concerned?

Is all well?

Will we endure sound doctrine?[394]

---

[393] 2 Nephi 10:3 "Wherefore, as I said unto you, it must needs be expedient that Christ—for in the last night the angel spake unto me that this should be his name—should come among the Jews, among those who are the more wicked part of the world; and they shall crucify him—for thus it behooveth our God, and there is none other nation on earth that would crucify their God."
3 Nephi 7:15 "And it came to pass that Nephi—having been visited by angels and also the voice of the Lord, therefore having seen angels, and being eye-witness, and having had power given unto him that he might know concerning the ministry of Christ, and also being eye-witness to their quick return from righteousness unto their wickedness and abominations;"

[394] 2 Timothy 4:3 "For the time will come when they will not endure sound doctrine; but after their own lusts shall they heap to themselves teachers, having itching ears;"

Alma 13:27

"And now, my brethren, I wish from the inmost part of my heart, yea, with great anxiety even unto pain, that ye would hearken unto my words, and cast off your sins, and not procrastinate the day of your repentance;"

This is the reality of those who hold this holy order. They feel absolute charity toward others. It causes them "great anxiety even unto pain" to consider how others might be lost. This was exactly the same charity that motivated the born-again sons of Mosiah to perform their missionary labors at great personal peril.[395]

When you hear such a man after this order speaking in plain, even blunt words, it is not because they are unkind. It is not because they are uncharitable or brash. It is because they are filled with care, concern, and longing to share eternal life with those who would otherwise be lost.

Look at his words. What does it mean that Alma's motivation now comes from "the inmost part of my heart?" How is it possible that Alma can have such concern that it causes him "great anxiety even unto pain?" Why does he long so for others to "hearken unto his words?"

Is this motivation for Alma the same as he described Melchizedek having? Is the plea to "cast off your sins" the same plea which Melchizedek made to his people?

If this is the plea of both Melchizedek and Alma, and it is a burden which causes pain for fear that the mission would fail, where do we find such souls today crying repentance? Are they among us? Do we have ministers using the words of angels, declaring a message

---

[395] Mosiah 28:3 "Now they were desirous that salvation should be declared to every creature, for they could not bear that any human soul should perish; yea, even the very thoughts that any soul should endure endless torment did cause them to quake and tremble."

from heaven, who suffer anxiety and pain at the thought we will not repent?

Are you one of them? If you are not, then why procrastinate? Why not also join in the process? All that is required is repentance to make yourself clean, followed by keeping the word of God until you entertain angels, receive your assignment, and having been commissioned to then proclaim repentance to others.

Alma is inviting people to join the order after the Son of God, becoming thereby sons of God themselves. This is the great message of the Book of Mormon. I've discussed in six books the mysteries of godliness, using primarily the Book of Mormon as the scriptural source to explain these doctrines. It is the most correct book we have to set out these doctrines and inform us of the process. It is interesting how little of that message we've uncovered as yet.

Alma 13:28

> "But that ye would humble yourselves before the Lord, and call on his holy name, and watch and pray continually, that ye may not be tempted above that which ye can bear, and thus be led by the Holy Spirit, becoming humble, meek, submissive, patient, full of love and all long-suffering;"

Alma's formula is quite direct and clear:

"Humble yourselves:" Without humility you are not teachable. Humility and the capacity to accept new truth are directly related. This is the character flaw that prevents the Lord from teaching the Nephites when He appeared to them. They THOUGHT they already knew things. Therefore nothing that contradicted their false notions would be accepted. Christ advised the Nephites who saw Him descend from heaven to go prepare themselves for His teaching. "Therefore, go ye unto your homes, and ponder upon the things which I have said, and ask of the Father, in my name, that ye may understand, and prepare your minds for the morrow, and I come unto you again." (3 Nephi 17:3.) This was the Lord telling these witnesses that they were not humble enough to be taught—even by Him! So the first requirement is no small matter. Are you really humble? Can you accept truth if it is taught to you? Even if it contradicts your traditions? Even if it alienates you from family, friends, comfortable social associations, your neighbors?[396] See, humbling yourself is not just some droop-faced, hang-dog expression to wear on your countenance. Rather it is opening your heart up to higher things.

"Call upon God:" Not just prayer. Call upon Him. To call is to invite Him to come. How do you call Him? By devoting yourself, in humility, to living every principle He has taught to you through His messengers and in His scriptures. It's not a laundry list of "to-do's." It is meekness and prayerful watching; humbling yourself and accepting what His spirit will advise you to do. When He testifies to you that you are hearing a true principle, accept it. No matter the effect it may have upon your life. Change your life, but never abandon His truths. Call, listen, and obey what you are told. Never close that line of communication. Don't trust a message which does not come from Him.

"Watch and pray:" Answers may come in many ways. Be watchful so you don't miss them when they are given to you. Pray that you might be seeking, preparing your mind to behold what He sends. Stay tuned, and stay attuned. Without such diligence you will miss His messages, that come sometimes frequently, but from unexpected sources.

"That ye may not be tempted above that which ye can bear:" Implicit in this is that you may be tempted beyond what you can bear.

---

[396] Matthew 19:29 "And every one that hath forsaken houses, or brethren, or sisters, or father, or mother, or wife, or children, or lands, for my name's sake, shall receive an hundredfold, and shall inherit everlasting life."

So how do you avoid falling? Does humility and calling upon God and watching and praying insure that you can avoid an excess of temptation? How would they all go together? In particular, how would being "humble" be a protection against this kind of temptation?

Alma connects all this together with the word: "thus." Meaning as a consequence of the foregoing. As a result of what he's just told you. As a product of this approach, you will then "be led by the Holy Spirit." You can't do what comes next without being so led. It isn't in you. Not without help from within through the Holy Spirit.

So, if you do all the above, and then acquire the Holy Spirit to be your guide, then it follows that you will "become humble, meek, submissive, patient, full of love and all long-suffering." You won't be imitating humility, but you will be humble with the Holy Spirit's assistance. You won't feign meekness, but you will acquire the power to be meek (in the sense it is explained in *Beloved Enos*). You won't pretend to submission, patience, love and long suffering, but you will be these things as a result of the Spirit within you. This will be your character. Not as the world understands such things, but through the power of the Spirit to lay hold upon such things.

Formulas like this one are inspired statements, providing a road map to the Lord's methods of changing lives. Alma is making such a declaration and invitation in this sermon. It is amazing, really. How succinctly he cuts to the core of the matter.

Alma 13:29

> "Having faith on the Lord; having a hope that ye shall receive eternal life; having the love of God always in your hearts, that ye may be lifted up at the last day and enter into his rest."

Here you have faith, hope and charity (or love). You only have a fraction of the understanding of what faith in the Lord means until you have done as Alma is explaining here. True "faith" which is a principle of power, is acquired by the method Alma is preaching.

Hope that one can receive eternal life is not the vague optimism that it might happen—it is a certitude. You have the promise. You know you will have eternal life. You haven't died and entered into the resurrected state yet. Between the time of the promise and the time you leave this sphere, you have hope. (The way it is used here is defined in *Eighteen Verses*.)

When God has promised you eternal life then you have "the love of God always in your heart." It is there through the indelible promise He has made. He has changed your status. He has declared through His own voice what great thing you have become. Therefore it is by knowledge alone that such love resides in the heart of man.

This life will end. But you will be raised up. You know when you are lifted up in the last day it will be the power of God that raises you. Such power as God employs to lift a man up confers upon such a person eternal life. The promise alone is a power, conferring the right to lay hold on eternal life when the moment comes. No power in earth or hell can rescind God's word.[397] It cannot be done. Therefore, you have knowledge that you will not only be raised from the dead, but "lifted up" as well. Powers, principalities, dominions, exaltations are all promised as yours.

This is how you attain to "rest." It is the "rest of the Lord" as soon as the promise is made by Him. It is His rest when you inherit it in the last day. The words of the promise are enough to guarantee the inheritance. Therefore once the promise is made it is true enough that you have entered into the rest of the Lord. However, until you

---

[397] D&C 1:38 "What I the Lord have spoken, I have spoken, and I excuse not myself; and though the heavens and the earth pass away, my word shall not pass away, but shall all be fulfilled, whether by mine own voice or by the voice of my servants, it is the same."

depart this life, you remain subject to the difficulties of mortality. Graduation is assured, but you must tarry for a little while here.

As one possessing this hope, being filled with faith, hope and charity, it becomes your responsibility to raise up others. Hence the ministry of Alma, and Alma's exposition on the ministry of Melchizedek. God does send true messengers. They can lead you in the way of life and salvation.

Alma 13:30

> "And may the Lord grant unto you repentance, that ye may not bring down his wrath upon you, that ye may not be bound down by the chains of hell, that ye may not suffer the second death."

Alma's closing remark here is a prayer. He is asking that the Lord "grant unto you repentance." This is an interesting cause-and-effect way to state the proposition. We cause it by our desire and willingness to become humble and repent. The Lord causes it because without His atoning sacrifice it could not be done.

We receive the effect because we are cleansed by our acts, humility and willingness to accept what is offered. The Lord receives the effect because He has allowed us to join Him in being pure and holy. He acquires a brother (or, more correctly a son). But He has no jealousy, allowing His brothers/sons to sit upon His own throne.[398] He wants to have "all things in common" with us.

Alma's petition goes further to ask that the wrath of God not be poured out upon these people to whom he is preaching. There are, of course, two levels of wrath. One is temporal—here and now. The wicked are often punished here by letting them pursue their own evil course until it destroys them. Repentance in that sense relieves them

---

[398] Revelation 3:21 "To him that overcometh will I grant to sit with me in my throne, even as I also overcame, and am set down with my Father in his throne."

of the physical, emotional, social, military, economic, and interpersonal disasters they bring upon themselves by their ruinous pursuit of destructive behavior.

The other is eternal—meaning coming after this life. That second "wrath" is a result of leaving this life with accountability for what happened here, and the lack of preparation for the moment when "judgment" is rendered. That "judgment" consists of you finally facing reality. When you are in His presence you can accurately measure the difference between what you are and what He wanted you to become—i.e., like Him. The gulf is so great that you would rather be in hell than in the presence of a just and holy being when you are stained with the blood and sins of your generation.[399]

I have been in the presence of President Ronald Reagan. I met with President Spencer W. Kimball at the law school at BYU when he would come to visit with his son, who was a criminal law professor there. I shook hands and spoke with Chief Justice Warren Burger for about a half hour in the law library at BYU. I have appeared at the US Supreme Court, the Utah Supreme Court, argued before Federal and State courts in Utah, Idaho, Arizona, Texas, California, Virginia, Washington DC, New York, Oregon, Nevada, Montana and New Mexico. I have seen Congress in session. Although a boy at the time, I was there when President Kennedy came to Berlin and spoke at Checkpoint Charlie, giving his *"Ich Bin Ein Berliner"* speech. I have seen many other men who have shaped history. But there simply is no comparison between these mere children, these insubstantial and powerless creatures, and the holiness, power, majesty and glory of the one True Man, clothed in light. You may see what the world reckons as a "great man" and think he was impressive. But you come from

---

[399] Mormon 9:4 "Behold, I say unto you that ye would be more miserable to dwell with a holy and just God, under a consciousness of your filthiness before him, than ye would to dwell with the damned souls in hell."

the presence of glory with only one conclusion: Surely man is nothing, which I had never before supposed.[400]

It is awful, fearful and dreadful to be in the presence of God. You realize the horror of your own darkness.[401] You cry out with the realization that you are unclean, living your life among the unclean, and you are not ready for His presence.[402] You are not prepared, and all your careful pretensions dissolve until you stand naked, revealed, hollow and unworthy to stand in His presence.

How, then, does a man stand in His presence? Through the merits and mercy and grace of this, our Lord.[403] If your mouth is un-

---

[400] Moses 1:10 "And it came to pass that it was for the space of many hours before Moses did again receive his natural strength like unto man; and he said unto himself: Now, for this cause I know that man is nothing, which thing I never had supposed."

[401] Genesis 15:7–18 "And he said unto him, I am the Lord that brought thee out of Ur of the Chaldees, to give thee this land to inherit it. And he said, Lord God, whereby shall I know that I shall inherit it? And he said unto him, Take me an heifer of three years old, and a she goat of three years old, and a ram of three years old, and a turtledove, and a young pigeon. And he took unto him all these, and divided them in the midst, and laid each piece one against another: but the birds divided he not. And when the fowls came down upon the carcases, Abram drove them away. And when the sun was going down, a deep sleep fell upon Abram; and, lo, an horror of great darkness fell upon him. And he said unto Abram, Know of a surety that thy seed shall be a stranger in a land that is not theirs, and shall serve them; and they shall afflict them four hundred years; And also that nation, whom they shall serve, will I judge: and afterward shall they come out with great substance. And thou shalt go to thy fathers in peace; thou shalt be buried in a good old age. But in the fourth generation they shall come hither again: for the iniquity of the Amorites is not yet full. And it came to pass, that, when the sun went down, and it was dark, behold a smoking furnace, and a burning lamp that passed between those pieces. In the same day the Lord made a covenant with Abram, saying, Unto thy seed have I given this land, from the river of Egypt unto the great river, the river Euphrates:"

[402] Isaiah 6:5 "Then said I, Woe is me! for I am undone; because I am a man of unclean lips, and I dwell in the midst of a people of unclean lips: for mine eyes have seen the King, the Lord of hosts."

[403] 2 Nephi 2:8 "Wherefore, how great the importance to make these things known unto the inhabitants of the earth, that they may know that there is no flesh that can dwell in the presence of God, save it be through the merits, and mercy, and grace of the Holy Messiah, who layeth down his life according to the flesh, and taketh it again by the power of the Spirit, that he may bring to pass the resurrection of the dead, being the first that should rise."

clean, He will use an ordinance to cleanse your lips.[404] If you are covered by the blood and sins of your generation, He will cleanse them.[405] If you cannot stand, He will raise you up with His own hand.[406] He is the God of mercy. Your discomfort is relieved by what He does, and this not of yourself, lest you should boast. There is nothing in you from which to boast other than the merit and mercy and love and sacrifice given to you by Him.

How can He love so? It defies explanation. Words fail. You can search your lifetime through every word you have ever seen or heard—nothing comes close to being able to describe it. It cannot be spoken . . . Too sacred for language to capture. Beyond our power. So, you are left saying only: "Come, see."

---

[404] Isaiah 6:6–7 "Then flew one of the seraphims unto me, having a live coal in his hand, which he had taken with the tongs from off the altar: And he laid it upon my mouth, and said, Lo, this hath touched thy lips; and thine iniquity is taken away, and thy sin purged."

[405] John 13:5–13 "After that he poureth water into a bason, and began to wash the disciples' feet, and to wipe them with the towel wherewith he was girded. Then cometh he to Simon Peter: and Peter saith unto him, Lord, dost thou wash my feet? Jesus answered and said unto him, What I do thou knowest not now; but thou shalt know hereafter. Peter saith unto him, Thou shalt never wash my feet. Jesus answered him, If I wash thee not, thou hast no part with me. Simon Peter saith unto him, Lord, not my feet only, but also my hands and my head. Jesus saith to him, He that is washed needeth not save to wash his feet, but is clean every whit: and ye are clean, but not all. For he knew who should betray him; therefore said he, Ye are not all clean. So after he had washed their feet, and had taken his garments, and was set down again, he said unto them, Know ye what I have done to you? Ye call me Master and Lord: and ye say well; for so I am."

[406] Daniel 10:5–10 "Then I lifted up mine eyes, and looked, and behold a certain man clothed in linen, whose loins were girded with fine gold of Uphaz: His body also was like the beryl, and his face as the appearance of lightning, and his eyes as lamps of fire, and his arms and his feet like in colour to polished brass, and the voice of his words like the voice of a multitude. And I Daniel alone saw the vision: for the men that were with me saw not the vision; but a great quaking fell upon them, so that they fled to hide themselves. Therefore I was left alone, and saw this great vision, and there remained no strength in me: for my comeliness was turned in me into corruption, and I retained no strength. Yet heard I the voice of his words: and when I heard the voice of his words, then was I in a deep sleep on my face, and my face toward the ground. 10 And, behold, an hand touched me, which set me upon my knees and upon the palms of my hands."

How, then, can a man come to the judgment and not feel the wrath which they might have overcome by His grace and mercy? Through the merits of Him bestowing upon a man the power to stand in His presence.

Alma's pain at the thought of these people perishing was real. He was powerless to bring them to Christ. That power consists only in the authorized and truthful declaration of an invitation to come to Him. But the choice remained in those who, having heard, must decide for themselves whether they will repent. They were free to choose iniquity and abominations. Alma was only able to invite.

The invitation, if rejected, will cause those who die to die yet again. The way is broad which leads to such eternal deaths.[407]

Alma 13:31

"And Alma spake many more words unto the people, which are not written in this book."

This is often the case. John's Gospel ended with this observation:

"And there are also many other things which Jesus did, the which, if they should be written every one, I suppose that even the world itself could not contain the books that should be written." (John 21:25.) Records are incomplete. We do not have the full account of Christ's acts and words. We don't have Alma's either.

Mormon was the editor of this portion of the Book of Mormon. He was the one who determined to omit portions what Alma said to these people on this occasion. From what Mormon left for us to read, his intent is clear. He wanted us to understand the bigger picture of God's dealings with man, man's possession of priestly power, and the importance of repentance and defeating religious error.

---

[407] D&C 132:25 "Broad is the gate, and wide the way that leadeth to the deaths; and many there are that go in thereat, because they receive me not, neither do they abide in my law."

Mormon had seen us, and included specific warnings addressed to us, the Gentiles. He cautioned us about the Book of Mormon as follows:

"And then, O ye Gentiles, how can ye stand before the power of God, except ye shall repent and turn from your evil ways? Know ye not that ye are in the hands of God? Know ye not that he hath all power, and at his great command the earth shall be rolled together as a scroll? Therefore, repent ye, and humble yourselves before him, lest he shall come out in justice against you—lest a remnant of the seed of Jacob shall go forth among you as a lion, and tear you in pieces, and there is none to deliver."[408]

Mormon knew the book would initially be in the hands of the Gentiles. So you can know we are identified as "Gentiles" in the Book of Mormon. Also, Joseph Smith declared in the dedicatory prayer for the Kirtland Temple that we are identified with the Gentiles.[409] Although Brigham Young and President Joseph Fielding Smith taught that Joseph was a "pure blooded Ephraimite." (*Doctrines of Salvation* 3:253–254)

The selected materials that Mormon gave to us were targeted to the purpose of the Book of Mormon. The title page (written by Moroni) tells us the purpose: "Written to the Lamanites, who are a remnant of the house of Israel; and also to Jew and Gentile—Written by way of commandment, and also by the spirit of prophecy and of

---

[408] Mormon 5:22–24 "And then, O ye Gentiles, how can ye stand before the power of God, except ye shall repent and turn from your evil ways? Know ye not that ye are in the hands of God? Know ye not that he hath all power, and at his great command the earth shall be rolled together as a scroll? Therefore, repent ye, and humble yourselves before him, lest he shall come out in justice against you—lest a remnant of the seed of Jacob shall go forth among you as a lion, and tear you in pieces, and there is none to deliver."

[409] D&C 109:59–60 "We ask thee to appoint unto Zion other stakes besides this one which thou hast appointed, that the gathering of thy people may roll on in great power and majesty, that thy work may be cut short in righteousness. Now these words, O Lord, we have spoken before thee, concerning the revelations and commandments which thou hast given unto us, who are identified with the Gentiles."

revelation—Written and sealed up, and hid up unto the Lord, that they might not be destroyed—To come forth by the gift and power of God unto the interpretation thereof—Sealed by the hand of Moroni, and hid up unto the Lord, to come forth in due time by way of the Gentile."

Gentiles would receive, translate and disseminate the Book of Mormon. But the Gentiles are prophesied to fail in their faith. They are to become full of their own abominations. When they reject the fullness of the Gospel, then it will be taken from them and given back to the remnant.[410]

Mormon is using the message from Alma to provide to the Gentiles (who will reject the invitation), an opportunity to understand the fullness which was offered to them. It was intended to remove from them the excuse that they were not given an opportunity and did not understand. Therefore, the Book of Mormon's primary purpose, to make the Gentiles aware and accountable for their failure, is accomplished by Mormon including this portion of Alma's teachings. The fact that other portions were left out mean that they would not have contributed to the task before Mormon.

A few of the Gentiles happily may be numbered with the remnant.[411] That is conditioned upon their repentance. The degree and completion of that repentance is shown by this portion of the sermon by Alma which Mormon preserved for us.

---

[410] 3 Nephi 16:10–11 "And thus commandeth the Father that I should say unto you: At that day when the Gentiles shall sin against my gospel, and shall reject the fulness of my gospel, and shall be lifted up in the pride of their hearts above all nations, and above all the people of the whole earth, and shall be filled with all manner of lyings, and of deceits, and of mischiefs, and all manner of hypocrisy, and murders, and priestcrafts, and whoredoms, and of secret abominations; and if they shall do all those things, and shall reject the fulness of my gospel, behold, saith the Father, I will bring the fulness of my gospel from among them. And then will I remember my covenant which I have made unto my people, O house of Israel, and I will bring my gospel unto them."

[411] 3 Nephi 16:13 "But if the Gentiles will repent and return unto me, saith the Father, behold they shall be numbered among my people, O house of Israel."

We are on notice. We are accountable for how we react to that notice. For the most part, the expectation is that we tell one another in reassuring words that "all is well." and that "Zion prospers," and to generally allow our souls to be cheated while we are led carefully down to hell.[412] Still, some few will follow Christ, despite the leaders' teachings that will cause them to err.[413]

The Book of Mormon is a record that will be used as evidence we have been warned. In plain language and with sufficient truth to hold us all accountable, this is the standard by which we are to find our way back to the Lord in this last dispensation before His return. We remain, of course, under condemnation because we are unwilling to do that.[414]

What a great and terrible book. What an alarming message. It is no wonder we neglect it so.

---

[412] 2 Nephi 28:21–25 "And others will he pacify, and lull them away into carnal security, that they will say: All is well in Zion; yea, Zion prospereth, all is well—and thus the devil cheateth their souls, and leadeth them away carefully down to hell. And behold, others he flattereth away, and telleth them there is no hell; and he saith unto them: I am no devil, for there is none—and thus he whispereth in their ears, until he grasps them with his awful chains, from whence there is no deliverance. Yea, they are grasped with death, and hell; and death, and hell, and the devil, and all that have been seized therewith must stand before the throne of God, and be judged according to their works, from whence they must go into the place prepared for them, even a lake of fire and brimstone, which is endless torment. Therefore, wo be unto him that is at ease in Zion! Wo be unto him that crieth: All is well!"

[413] 2 Nephi 28:14 "They wear stiff necks and high heads; yea, and because of pride, and wickedness, and abominations, and whoredoms, they have all gone astray save it be a few, who are the humble followers of Christ; nevertheless, they are led, that in many instances they do err because they are taught by the precepts of men."

[414] D&C 84:57 "And they shall remain under this condemnation until they repent and remember the new covenant, even the Book of Mormon and the former commandments which I have given them, not only to say, but to do according to that which I have written—"

3 NEPHI 16

3 Nephi 16:7

"Behold, because of their belief in me, saith the Father, and because of the unbelief of you, O house of Israel, in the latter day shall the truth come unto the Gentiles, that the fulness of these things shall be made known unto them."

This is a teaching from the first day of Christ's visit with the Nephites. It is a quote from Christ.

The time frame in which the Gentiles were to have "belief in [Christ,]" and merit a special blessing as a result, was the time immediately following the Judean ministry. The Gospel would be taken to the Gentiles and they would believe. The Jews were going to reject Him and oppose His faith, the Gentiles would welcome it and have belief.

Now the words Christ spoke and Nephi's record preserved were from "the Father." Christ's explanation of these prophecies originate with His Father.

Gentiles will believe. Moreover, the "house of Israel" will not believe in Him. The result of that acceptance and rejection is the juxtaposition of the roles of Gentiles and Israel.

Whereas, the Gospel came to the Jews first, and by the Jews it was transmitted to the Gentiles, later the opposite will occur. The pattern will reverse. It will go from the last back to the first. (It is an historic chiasm.)

Accordingly, the Gentiles will be the ones to whom the restoration of the "fullness" will come in the latter day. The reward for earlier faithfulness is later recognition and reward.

Now, it should take no amount of brilliant insight to realize that the restoration involved Joseph Smith. A man of English descent. May have some Israelite blood in him from the earlier Diaspora of the Lost Ten Tribes, but he is nevertheless the one through whom the restoration was brought. He is necessarily identified as a "Gentile" in this prophecy by Christ, given by the Father. If Joseph Smith is NOT a Gentile, then the whole promise of the Father and word of the Son is defeated. Therefore, you may know for a surety that the Gentiles are not those nasty non-members. It is US. WE are the Gentiles who receive the first offer in the last offering.

The "others" (nonLDS) are not necessarily a focus for the Book of Mormon prophecies. They inherit the blessing of being here, as Nephi foresaw. They are blessed to be on the land, but they are not given anything other than a conditional possession. They are those who get offered the restored Gospel when it returned, and if they accept it they become part of the prophetic subject. When, however, they reject the offered restoration, then they are background and will be swept away just as the Saints who reject the fullness of the Gospel will be swept away.

So it was that the Father determined and Christ taught that the Gentiles would be the ones to whom the Gospel message would first come in our day. Now we have it. (Or had it anyway.)

This movement from Israel to Gentile and from Gentile to Israel is evening the playing field. This is balancing out the record of history. It is not that one is more favored than another. Rather it is that each one will have a suitable turn and opportunity to receive what the Lord offers. In the end, no people will be able to say the opportunities were unfair, unequal, or more challenging for one than for another. [I leave it to you to determine why that is so when lives come and go across generations and one dispensation may include different people than another. It raises the question as to how certain we should be about some of our premises. That, however, is too far afield at the moment. And it may not matter anyway. Today is the day of salvation, not yesterday or tomorrow. So we should confine ourselves to solving the problem we face at the moment.]

The promise is that the "fullness of these things" will come to the Gentiles. What things? What does it mean that the "fullness" will be coming to the Gentiles? Have the Gentiles in fact received it?

If we received it, what have we done with it? Do we still have it? If not, how do I know that? What will happen if we have not retained that fullness?

Fortunately for us, Christ will answer all those questions as He moves along in the message He delivers here.

3 Nephi 16:8

"But wo, saith the Father, unto the unbelieving of the Gentiles—for notwithstanding they have come forth upon the face of this land, and have scattered my people who are of the house of Israel; and my people who are of the house of Israel have been cast out from among them, and have been trodden under feet by them;"

So now the time frame is the latter day when the Gentiles have been given this restoration of the fullness. This comment moves forward from the reasons of the restoration to the Gentiles (earlier faithfulness) to the time when the Gentiles have received the fullness.

To make the time frame abundantly clear to both the Nephites and to us, the Lord explains in passing that the Gentiles will come to "this land." The full description of them coming is set out in the earlier prophecy of Nephi as set out at length in 1 Nephi 13 & 14. But here Christ reminds the audience that when the Gentiles come, they will "scatter my people who are of the house of Israel."

Gentiles certainly did come. They did scatter the remnants who were on the American continent. Not only did they scatter them, but they also "cast out" and "trodden down" those populations who were here when the Gentiles arrived. Smallpox wiped out the Great Plains Indians. There were an estimated 20 million plus Plains Indians when Columbus arrived. Smallpox all but annihilated them. So few survived that by the time of the western push of the United States, it was believed the Great Plains had never been populated.

To say they were "trodden underfoot" is descriptive. The native populations were destroyed. They were conquered. They died. Their remains returned to the earth upon which the Gentiles trod.

You must keep this image in mind as you read about the future of the Gentiles being trodden underfoot. We will get to that later in this same prophecy by Christ.

"Wo" is pronounced upon those Gentiles who are 'unbelieving' toward the Gospel. This is confirmed again in Section 76, describing those who are Telestial. They are religious, and follow even true messengers. However, they follow, believe in, trust and hope for salvation from the messenger, but fail to have faith, believe in, trust and receive salvation through Christ. They even claim to follow Christ. But they fall short of having a saving testimony of Him. It warns: "And the glory of the telestial is one, even as the glory of the stars is one; for as one star differs from another star in glory, even so differs one from another in glory in the telestial world; For these are they who are of Paul, and of Apollos, and of Cephas. These are they who say they are some of one and some of another—some of Christ and some of John, and some of Moses, and some of Elias, and some of

Esaias, and some of Isaiah, and some of Enoch; But received not the gospel, neither the testimony of Jesus, neither the prophets, neither the everlasting covenant."[415]

There is a great gulf between those who claim they follow Christ and those who receive the "testimony of Jesus." There is a difference between claiming to follow a recognized authority such as Paul, Apollos, Cephas, Moses, Elias, Esaias, Isaiah, John or Enoch on the one hand and "receiving the prophets" on the other.

How easy it is to quote a dead prophet. How unlikely it always is to recognize a living one.

What is meant then by saying "they are of Christ" on the one hand, and saying, "receive not the Gospel, neither the testimony of Jesus?" on the other. How do you reconcile these two things? One damns to the Telestial Kingdom, the other exalts.

How perilous it is for the latter day Gentiles!

3 Nephi 16:9

"And because of the mercies of the Father unto the Gentiles, and also the judgments of the Father upon my people who are of the house of Israel, verily, verily, I say unto you, that after all this, and I have caused my people who are of the house of Israel to be smitten, and to be afflicted, and to be slain, and to be cast out from among them, and to become hated by them, and to become a hiss and a byword among them—"

---

[415] D&C 76:98–101 "And the glory of the telestial is one, even as the glory of the stars is one; for as one star differs from another star in glory, even so differs one from another in glory in the telestial world; For these are they who are of Paul, and of Apollos, and of Cephas. These are they who say they are some of one and some of another—some of Christ and some of John, and some of Moses, and some of Elias, and some of Esaias, and some of Isaiah, and some of Enoch; But received not the gospel, neither the testimony of Jesus, neither the prophets, neither the everlasting covenant."

Notice once again the Lord's motivation for speaking these words: The Father's "mercies" and the Father's "judgments" are what drives the coming events in history. The Father is in control and Christ does not question or gainsay the results. The Father's mercy is not questioned by Christ, nor is there any degree of shame shown for the terrible circumstances which follow from His "mercies." Nor does Christ hesitate to announce the Father's "judgments" despite the anxiety which some may feel at hearing the future.

Truth should be delivered in a forthright and plain manner, whether the result is fearful or vindicating; whether you take joy in the news or you cower at what is to come.

Notice, however, that when the Father's judgment has been given, then the Lord assumes personal responsibility for the punishment to be inflicted. He does not say it is the Father's punishment. It is His own. Christ will personally be the one who "caused my people who are of the house of Israel to be smitten." Christ will personally "afflict" and "slay" the people. The Father decides, Christ fulfills. He seeks no cover, looks to no-one else to be held to account, He does as His Father judges.

Why would Christ assume responsibility to "smite" to "afflict" and to "slay" when it is the Father's judgment?

What does this tell us about Christ's acceptance of the Father's decisions?

Is (or has) there been some good result from those whom Christ calls "my people" (i.e., His people) being smitten, afflicted, slain, and cast out by the Gentiles? If so, what good has come to the Lord's people? How can these things that have lasted now for over two hundred years have been beneficial to the Lord's people? What can we learn about the Lord calling afflicted, smitten and outcast people as "His people" despite their centuries of subordination?

What does the Gentile "hatred" of the Lord's people do to diminish the Lord's plans for them? What does casting them out and making them a "hiss and a byword" by the Gentiles do to remove the Lord's promised blessing and covenant to "His people?"

What foolish pride allows Gentiles to measure the Lord's people as stricken, smitten of God and afflicted?[416]

Why would the Gentiles be put in this position? Why would Israel? What does it do to the Gentiles' ability to see through the deception of their time into truth which is timeless?[417]

How should the Gentiles view their momentary triumph and unchallenged possession of the land promised to others?

Why are those smitten and afflicted called by the Lord "my people" and the Gentiles referred to as "Gentiles?"

Is the irony of this beginning to dawn on you? Maybe you should re-read the title page of the Book of Mormon.[418]

---

[416] Isaiah 53:4 "Surely he hath borne our griefs, and carried our sorrows: yet we did esteem him stricken, smitten of God, and afflicted."

[417] D&C 93:24 "And truth is knowledge of things as they are, and as they were, and as they are to come;"

[418] Title Page of the Book of Mormon: "Wherefore, it is an abridgment of the record of the people of Nephi, and also of the Lamanites—Written to the Lamanites, who are a remnant of the house of Israel; and also to Jew and Gentile—Written by way of commandment, and also by the spirit of prophecy and of revelation—Written and sealed up, and hid up unto the Lord, that they might not be destroyed—To come forth by the gift and power of God unto the interpretation thereof—Sealed by the hand of Moroni, and hid up unto the Lord, to come forth in due time by way of the Gentile—The interpretation thereof by the gift of God. An abridgment taken from the Book of Ether also, which is a record of the people of Jared, who were scattered at the time the Lord confounded the language of the people, when they were building a tower to get to heaven—Which is to show unto the remnant of the House of Israel what great things the Lord hath done for their fathers; and that they may know the covenants of the Lord, that they are not cast off forever—And also to the convincing of the Jew and Gentile that Jesus is the Christ, the Eternal God, manifesting himself unto all nations—And now, if there are faults they are the mistakes of men; wherefore, condemn not the things of God, that ye may be found spotless at the judgment-seat of Christ."

3 Nephi 16:10

"And thus commandeth the Father that I should say unto you:
At that day when the Gentiles shall sin against my gospel, and
shall reject the fulness of my gospel, and shall be lifted up in
the pride of their hearts above all nations, and above all the
people of the whole earth, and shall be filled with all manner
of lyings, and of deceits, and of mischiefs, and all manner of
hypocrisy, and murders, and priestcrafts, and whoredoms, and
of secret abominations; and if they shall do all those things,
and shall reject the fulness of my gospel, behold, saith the
Father, I will bring the fulness of my gospel from among
them."

These words come from the Father.

The Father has commanded Christ to speak them.

This material is important to understand.

"At the day when the Gentiles shall sin against the Gospel . . . " Not IF.
Not SHOULD THEY HAPPEN TO DO SO. It is in the day
WHEN the Gentiles SHALL sin against the Gospel.

The Father has already seen this happen.[419] He has told Christ to
speak about it. But it is before the Father and therefore He can speak
with knowledge of the coming rejection by the Gentiles.

What do the Gentiles do as they reject the Gospel? They *"shall be
lifted up in the pride of their hearts above all nations . . . above all the people of
the whole earth."* Read again the prior post. The Gentiles take their inheritance of the promised land as their birthright. They presume
God's favor. They mistake their probation and testing as proof of
having God's favor. They are on trial, and presume they aren't being
tested.

---

[419] D&C 130:7 "But they reside in the presence of God, on a globe like a sea of glass
and fire, where all things for their glory are manifest, past, present, and future, and are
continually before the Lord."

What, then, do the Gentiles do with their highly favored status? The list is sobering:

- Lyings
- Deceits
- Mischiefs
- All manner of hypocrisy
- Murders
- Priestcrafts
- Whoredoms
- Secret combinations

Read the list and contemplate how much of this is among us. If we do not murder, do we delight in bloodshed? Are we warlike? Are there people whom we kill daily somewhere in the world to project our national will and great power?

Notice that hypocrisy leads to murder. Murder leads to priestcrafts. Priestcrafts lead to whoredoms. Are we seeing a progression here? By the time we have whoredoms, have we already passed through murders and priestcrafts?

What are priestcrafts?[420] What does it mean to seek the welfare of Zion? Is "Zion" the same thing as the institutional church? What is the difference? Can a person seek the welfare of Zion without seeking to succeed inside the institutional church? What is the difference between seeking to be a "light unto the world," on the one hand, and seeking the welfare of Zion, on the other? Can one seek to be a light pointing to Zion, and never be a "light unto the world?" What is the world? What is Zion? How are they different? Can one who seeks the welfare of Zion ever get praise from the world? Can a person curry favor with the world while also seeking to benefit Zion?

---

[420] 2 Nephi 26:29 "He commandeth that there shall be no priestcrafts; for, behold, priestcrafts are that men preach and set themselves up for a light unto the world, that they may get gain and praise of the world; but they seek not the welfare of Zion."

REMEMBERING THE COVENANT

If not hiring a whore, do we nonetheless watch with delight the portrayal of sexual license to entertain us, fill our thoughts, satisfy our lusts? Do you need to hire a prostitute to be practicing "whoredoms?" Utah is one of the largest consumers of pornography in the US. Hence, the continual return to this subject in General Conference.

When they do this, in turn the Gentiles will "reject the fullness of my Gospel." To reject the fullness is not to reject the Gospel itself. As we have seen, some fragment of the Gospel remains even when it has turned into "iniquity" and "abomination." Without some fractured segment of the Gospel to salve the conscious and let the people feel good about their sins, there couldn't be "abominations."

It is not the "Gospel" which is lost. Rather it is the "fullness of my Gospel" which is rejected and then taken away. It is first rejected, then it is forfeited. The Gentiles lose their entitlement to possess what they have rejected.

The Father has decreed it will happen. The Gentiles will change the ordinance and break the everlasting covenant.[421] What ordinance? What change? Has it happened? If not, what will be required to make a change and lose the "everlasting covenant" by the Gentiles? I hope to avoid that.

3 Nephi 16:11

"And then will I remember my covenant which I have made unto my people, O house of Israel, and I will bring my gospel unto them."

When the Gentiles have rejected the fullness of the Gospel, the Lord's memory will be stirred. He will "remember His covenant" again.

---

[421] Isaiah 24:5 "The earth also is defiled under the inhabitants thereof; because they have transgressed the laws, changed the ordinance, broken the everlasting covenant."

Notice the covenant He will remember is for "His people," whose interests and inheritance will now be vindicated. His words will be fulfilled. The Father's promises will all be realized. But "His people" are not the Gentiles. His people are the remnant to whom the Gospel will come as a matter of covenant and inheritance to reclaim a fallen people. This is the re-grafting of the natural branches referred to in Jacob 5.[422] It is important to note that the Lord of the vineyard was directly involved with the few servants assigned to accomplish this final work of gathering together.[423]

---

[422] Jacob 5:67–75 "And the branches of the natural tree will I graft in again into the natural tree; And the branches of the natural tree will I graft into the natural branches of the tree; and thus will I bring them together again, that they shall bring forth the natural fruit, and they shall be one. And the bad shall be cast away, yea, even out of all the land of my vineyard; for behold, only this once will I prune my vineyard. And it came to pass that the Lord of the vineyard sent his servant; and the servant went and did as the Lord had commanded him, and brought other servants; and they were few. And the Lord of the vineyard said unto them: Go to, and labor in the vineyard, with your might. For behold, this is the last time that I shall nourish my vineyard; for the end is nigh at hand, and the season speedily cometh; and if ye labor with your might with me ye shall have joy in the fruit which I shall lay up unto myself against the time which will soon come. And it came to pass that the servants did go and labor with their mights; and the Lord of the vineyard labored also with them; and they did obey the commandments of the Lord of the vineyard in all things. And there began to be the natural fruit again in the vineyard; and the natural branches began to grow and thrive exceedingly; and the wild branches began to be plucked off and to be cast away; and they did keep the root and the top thereof equal, according to the strength thereof. And thus they labored, with all diligence, according to the commandments of the Lord of the vineyard, even until the bad had been cast away out of the vineyard, and the Lord had preserved unto himself that the trees had become again the natural fruit; and they became like unto one body; and the fruits were equal; and the Lord of the vineyard had preserved unto himself the natural fruit, which was most precious unto him from the beginning. And it came to pass that when the Lord of the vineyard saw that his fruit was good, and that his vineyard was no more corrupt, he called up his servants, and said unto them: Behold, for this last time have we nourished my vineyard; and thou beholdest that I have done according to my will; and I have preserved the natural fruit, that it is good, even like as it was in the beginning. And blessed art thou; for because ye have been diligent in laboring with me in my vineyard, and have kept my commandments, and have brought unto me again the natural fruit, that my vineyard is no more corrupted, and the bad is cast away, behold ye shall have joy with me because of the fruit of my vineyard."

[423] Jacob 5:72 "And it came to pass that the servants did go and labor with their mights; and the Lord of the vineyard labored also with them; and they did obey the commandments of the Lord of the vineyard in all things."

This is to be done after the Gentiles (who are the European Latter-day Saints who descend from the bloodlines that overran and dispossessed the native people in North America), have rejected the fullness of the Gospel. Therefore, you should not expect that the institutional church, controlled as it is by those very same bloodlines, will be the means through which this final effort will be accomplished.

When the time comes, the Lord will "bring [His] gospel to them." How will He do this? What "laborers" should we expect to be sent? How, if the Gentiles have rejected the fullness of His Gospel, will the Gentiles be involved?

Can Gentiles who are lifted up in the pride of their hearts above all nations of the earth assist? If not, then what Gentiles can assist?

Isn't Ephraim to be involved? After all, they have the birthright. Are they not involved?

If they are, who will it be from among Ephraim?

How can the remnant to whom these blessings are promised, have still among them a few descendants of Ephraim? Why will Manassah, through the remnant, build the New Jerusalem, yet it will be Ephraim through whom the blessings are conferred upon the returning Lost Tribes?[424]

How can the New Jerusalem be the property of the remnant, but there be a group of Ephraimite who bestow crowns? What must these Ephraimite possess to be able to accomplish this task? How

---

[424] D&C 133:26–34 "And they who are in the north countries shall come in remembrance before the Lord; and their prophets shall hear his voice, and shall no longer stay themselves; and they shall smite the rocks, and the ice shall flow down at their presence. And an highway shall be cast up in the midst of the great deep. Their enemies shall become a prey unto them, And in the barren deserts there shall come forth pools of living water; and the parched ground shall no longer be a thirsty land. And they shall bring forth their rich treasures unto the children of Ephraim, my servants. And the boundaries of the everlasting hills shall tremble at their presence. And there shall they fall down and be crowned with glory, even in Zion, by the hands of the servants of the Lord, even the children of Ephraim. And they shall be filled with songs of everlasting joy. Behold, this is the blessing of the everlasting God upon the tribes of Israel, and the richer blessing upon the head of Ephraim and his fellows."

can they possess it and not be lifted up in pride above all other people of the whole earth? How can such power be put upon some group and they remain willing to ever bend the knee and confess before Him whose right it is to rule?

How can the Gentiles both reject the fullness of the Gospel, yet there be some who are of Ephraim who are able to bestow crowns?

What an interesting picture begins to emerge. Gentile rejection, but a tiny group of Ephraimite servants whose lives are lived so as to bestow blessings upon others.

The main body in the New Jerusalem coming from the remnant, who are to build the City of the New Jerusalem, yet within that City a functioning group of Ephraimites who will crown others with glory. All this preparatory to the Lord's return to a City set upon a hill which cannot be hid. To a location in the tops of the everlasting mountains, where all will gather from every nation.

Well, let's keep going to see how much we can figure out from the scriptures to correct our foolish traditions about these future roles and perhaps gain an even better idea of locations.

The relative size is referred to by the Lord in a number of places where He contrasts the "few there be who find it" with the "many who go in thereat." He also uses the parable of wise and foolish virgins. I take the meaning of "virgin" who are attired in wedding garments and have both oil and lamps to mean those who have: 1) been endowed; 2) been sealed; 3) come into possession of both oil and a lamp—meaning the Spirit has visited with them and they have shown its fruits at some point in their lives. From this group half will be unprepared at His coming and kept from the wedding feast.

There are others, and perhaps a post would be better than a comment. But the point is not to discourage anyone. It is to make us take a sober inventory of our lives and what we do with the Gospel we've been given. Are we taking it seriously enough? Do we do what we can to follow Him? Are we safely aboard, or yet in peril? If aboard, are we crying repentance and warning our neighbor? Do we really love Him? Do we love His children?

Whether the Church's leadership is or is not going to lead us there remains an open question. As with all things, they and we are free to choose. But their choice should not affect yours, or mine.

3 Nephi 16:12

"And I will show unto thee, O house of Israel, that the Gentiles shall not have power over you; but I will remember my covenant unto you, O house of Israel, and ye shall come unto the knowledge of the fulness of my gospel."

Gentiles shall NOT have power over Israel. Gentiles, filled with pride, claiming to hold the power of God, sitting in the Temple of God and acting as if they were God, will lose their grip.[425] They will be cast down like Lucifer, after claiming they would sit in the congregations of the north, like the Gods.[426]

---

[425] 2 Thessalonians 2:2–4 "That ye be not soon shaken in mind, or be troubled, neither by spirit, nor by word, nor by letter as from us, as that the day of Christ is at hand. Let no man deceive you by any means: for that day shall not come, except there come a falling away first, and that man of sin be revealed, the son of perdition; Who opposeth and exalteth himself above all that is called God, or that is worshipped; so that he as God sitteth in the temple of God, shewing himself that he is God."

[426] Isaiah 14:13–15 "For thou hast said in thine heart, I will ascend into heaven, I will exalt my throne above the stars of God: I will sit also upon the mount of the congregation, in the sides of the north: I will ascend above the heights of the clouds; I will be like the most High. Yet thou shalt be brought down to hell, to the sides of the pit."

These Gentiles will not have "power" over the house of Israel, though they may claim to possess great authority.[427] What, then, is the difference between Gentiles lacking "power" but holding authority?

How will the Lord remember the covenant?

What does it mean to come to "the knowledge" of something, rather than to start believing in something?

What does it mean to have the "fulness of [His] Gospel?"

What does "knowledge . . . of the fulness" imply about the degree to which it will be revealed as part of remembering the covenant?

Why is the Gentile rejection of the fullness tied to the house of Israel receiving the fullness?

Are the basic Gospel Principles the same as the fullness? If not, what is the difference? What do the Gentiles risk when they reject the fullness and focus instead upon the basic principles?

How perilous is it for the Gentiles to suppress the mysteries of godliness and retain only the most basic of doctrines as their focus?

Unto whom is the Lord to teach doctrine? Who is prepared to hear? Are they necessarily to be first weaned from milk and prepared to understand meat?[428] If that is so, then what do we need to do to wean ourselves off the milk and be prepared to receive weightier matters?

---

[427] D&C 121:36–37 "That the rights of the priesthood are inseparably connected with the powers of heaven, and that the powers of heaven cannot be controlled nor handled only upon the principles of righteousness. That they may be conferred upon us, it is true; but when we undertake to cover our sins, or to gratify our pride, our vain ambition, or to exercise control or dominion or compulsion upon the souls of the children of men, in any degree of unrighteousness, behold, the heavens withdraw themselves; the Spirit of the Lord is grieved; and when it is withdrawn, Amen to the priesthood or the authority of that man."

[428] Isaiah 28:9–10 "Whom shall he teach knowledge? and whom shall he make to understand doctrine? them that are weaned from the milk, and drawn from the breasts. For precept must be upon precept, precept upon precept; line upon line, line upon line; here a little, and there a little"

When will these things be? How will you know when the spirit begins to withdraw from the Gentiles and blessings begin to be poured out on others of the house of Israel?

3 Nephi 16:13–14

> "But if the Gentiles will repent and return unto me, saith the Father, behold they shall be numbered among my people, O house of Israel. And I will not suffer my people, who are of the house of Israel, to go through among them, and tread them down, saith the Father."

Here Gentiles are given hope. Although as a group, they will fall away and reject the fullness, if there are any among them who "repent and return" they may still be numbered among those who are the Lord's people. Those whom He calls "my people." Those dear to Him by covenant and promise.

The few who do will be required to "repent and return." Why do they need to "repent?" Why do they need to "return?" What have they been doing that will require this "repentance" and "return?"

Does it mean they will not remain in the way, but will have been led out of it? Will they necessarily have to abandon the abominations, or false beliefs, which have become part of their religious traditions?

Where did these false religious ideas arise? If the Gentiles inherit the fullness of the Gospel, then reject the fullness, what did they first receive? What did they do with what they received?

How can some few still persist and be numbered among the house of Israel? What must those who "repent and return" accomplish? How will they be able to accomplish this?

Nephi had described these "few" earlier in a prophecy about our day in 2 Nephi 28:14: "They wear stiff necks and high heads; yea, and because of pride, and wickedness, and abominations, and whoredoms, they have all gone astray save it be a few, who are the humble followers of Christ; nevertheless, they are led, that in many instances they do err because they are taught by the precepts of men."

What does it mean to have "all gone astray?" Does "all" truly mean "all?" How can a "few, who are the humble followers of Christ" exist? Do these "few" "nevertheless err?"

What causes the "few" to err? What does it mean that they are "led, that in many instances they do err?" What does it mean to be "taught by the precepts of men?" Wasn't that the very problem that provoked the Restoration in the first place? Weren't men teaching for doctrines the commandments of men? Did that produce only a form of godliness, which had no power?[429]

Those who "repent and return" will be spared from being trodden down and torn up. Others of the Gentiles, who do not "repent and return" are destined, like the original inhabitants of this land, to be trodden down and torn up. Their inheritance here is probationary. If they fail the probation, they will be swept away. The Gentiles will be gone, just as the earlier civilizations are gone. It will be the Father's doing.

3 Nephi 16:15

> "But if they will not turn unto me, and hearken unto my voice, I will suffer them, yea, I will suffer my people, O house of Israel, that they shall go through among them, and shall tread them down, and they shall be as salt that hath lost its savor, which is thenceforth good for nothing but to be cast out, and to be trodden under foot of my people, O house of Israel."

---

[429] JS–H 1:19 "I was answered that I must join none of them, for they were all wrong; and the Personage who addressed me said that all their creeds were an abomination in his sight; that those professors were all corrupt; that: 'they draw near to me with their lips, but their hearts are far from me, they teach for doctrines the commandments of men, having a form of godliness, but they deny the power thereof.'"

The Gentiles, to whom the restoration of the Gospel came, will fail to repent and return to the Lord, and will doom themselves to destruction.

The land reverts back to those to whom it was originally promised. They, the rightful heirs, will "go through among them, and shall tread them down." What does it mean to be "tread down?"

When salt has lost its savor, it becomes useless. The preservative has become a contaminant. The corruption, the abominable religion, is worse than what they were before inheriting the fullness of the Gospel. They have sinned against a greater light. And in the process they have rejected the Greatest Light of all.

What did the Gentiles do to become salt without savor? Why are they good for nothing but to be cast out? Why is it appropriate that the Gentiles who previously cast out and trod down previous inheritors should now be trodden down? What did the earlier heirs do to merit destruction at the hands of the Gentiles? How does the cycle seem to repeat itself in the actions of both of these peoples?

Why do the trodden down peoples, who were the first heirs, remain the "Lord's people" even when they have been dispossessed of the land and destroyed by the Gentiles? Why are the first to become the last, and the last to become the first? Why do such cycles of history repeat themselves? Why is the Book of Mormon unable to help the Gentiles avoid this cycle of destruction? Was the Book of Mormon intended to help the Gentiles avoid their fate? What did the Gentiles do with the Book of Mormon instead of using it as a guide to avoid destruction?

These prophecies are spoken by Christ, but ordained by the Father. What does it tell us about the Father's involvement with this unfolding history? How does the "foot of my people" reflect symbolically upon the process of destruction? If the Gentiles have rejected the fullness of the Lord's Gospel, but the feet of those who cry peace are beautiful upon the mountains, why do the one people get trodden and the others tread upon them? Why are clean feet preserved and the filthy cast out and trodden down?

How serious a matter is this Gospel? How should we conduct ourselves toward the Gospel? What is the Gospel's fullness?

This becomes more than interesting; it is gripping.

3 Nephi 16:16

"Verily, verily, I say unto you, thus hath the Father commanded me—that I should give unto this people this land for their inheritance."

As a result of the their behavior, the Gentiles forfeit the land. The ones who inherit the land will be "this people" or the ones to whom Christ was speaking. The land will belong to the remnant—those who were standing before Christ at the time of this address.

Now, the actual inheritors will not be those people, but those who claim the right as descendants through their fathers. It will not, and cannot be the Gentiles. There were no European migrants in the audience when Christ spoke on this occasion.

We need to know who "this people" is to know who will inherit the land.

We also need to know what "this land" was to be able to know if the Gentiles who inherited the "land of liberty"[430] which would "never fall into captivity except for wickedness" was North

---

[430] 2 Nephi 10:11 "And this land shall be a land of liberty unto the Gentiles, and there shall be no kings upon the land, who shall raise up unto the Gentiles."

America.[431] Hence the relevance of knowing the location of the
Book of Mormon lands.

That is such a side-track that I hesitate to even revisit the subject.
I will only add that there are arguments for both North American
and Central America. I think the better argument is for North
America.

The various possessors of the land all have the same condition:
They either follow Christ as they occupy the ground or they are
swept away and others who will follow Christ will supplant them.

This was established by covenant with Lehi generations before
Christ visited with and taught Lehi's descendants. Lehi recorded the
covenant:

> "Wherefore, I, Lehi, have obtained a promise, that inasmuch
> as those whom the Lord God shall bring out of the land of
> Jerusalem shall keep his commandments, they shall prosper

---

[431] 2 Nephi 1:6–11 "Wherefore, I, Lehi, prophesy according to the workings of the
Spirit which is in me, that there shall none come into this land save they shall be
brought by the hand of the Lord. Wherefore, this land is consecrated unto him whom
he shall bring. And if it so be that they shall serve him according to the commandments which he hath given, it shall be a land of liberty unto them; wherefore, they shall
never be brought down into captivity; if so, it shall be because of iniquity; for if iniquity shall abound cursed shall be the land for their sakes, but unto the righteous it shall
be blessed forever. And behold, it is wisdom that this land should be kept as yet from
the knowledge of other nations; for behold, many nations would overrun the land, that
there would be no place for an inheritance. Wherefore, I, Lehi, have obtained a promise, that inasmuch as those whom the Lord God shall bring out of the land of Jerusalem shall keep his commandments, they shall prosper upon the face of this land; and
they shall be kept from all other nations, that they may possess this land unto themselves. And if it so be that they shall keep his commandments they shall be blessed
upon the face of this land, and there shall be none to molest them, nor to take away
the land of their inheritance; and they shall dwell safely forever. But behold, when the
time cometh that they shall dwindle in unbelief, after they have received so great blessings from the hand of the Lord—having a knowledge of the creation of the earth, and
all men, knowing the great and marvelous works of the Lord from the creation of the
world; having power given them to do all things by faith; having all the commandments
from the beginning, and having been brought by his infinite goodness into this precious land of promise—behold, I say, if the day shall come that they will reject the
Holy One of Israel, the true Messiah, their Redeemer and their God, behold, the
judgments of him that is just shall rest upon them. Yea, he will bring other nations
unto them, and he will give unto them power, and he will take away from them the
lands of their possessions, and he will cause them to be scattered and smitten."

upon the face of this land; and they shall be kept from all other nations, that they may possess this land unto themselves. And if it so be that they shall keep his commandments they shall be blessed upon the face of this land, and there shall be none to molest them, nor to take away the land of their inheritance; and they shall dwell safely forever. But behold, when the time cometh that they shall dwindle in unbelief, after they have received so great blessings from the hand of the Lord—having a knowledge of the creation of the earth, and all men, knowing the great and marvelous works of the Lord from the creation of the world; having power given them to do all things by faith; having all the commandments from the beginning, and having been brought by his infinite goodness into this precious land of promise—behold, I say, if the day shall come that they will reject the Holy One of Israel, the true Messiah, their Redeemer and their God, behold, the judgments of him that is just shall rest upon them. Yea, he will bring other nations unto them, and he will give unto them power, and he will take away from them the lands of their possessions, and he will cause them to be scattered and smitten." (2 Nephi 1:9–11.)

Christ's words dovetail with the covenant made with Lehi. The same Lord announcing them both. That condition and lease of this land remains conditional. Keep the conditions and you may be preserved to inherit the land and be numbered with the house of Israel. Violate them and be swept away.

So we see that the times of the Gentiles, as they end, become quite perilous for the Gentiles upon the land. They will forfeit their hold, however improbable it may seem to them at the present. Christ's Father has declared it so. Who, then, can disannul?

The many confident assurances of God's favor we have do give us comfort, don't they? They are either true and right, and we have little to fear. Or they are among the abominations that allow foolish, vain and false notions lull us to sleep. The difference between those

two propositions is quite alarming. I hate it when we have to make
hard choices.

3 Nephi 16:17–20

> "And then the words of the prophet Isaiah shall be fulfilled,
> which say: Thy watchmen shall lift up the voice; with the voice
> together shall they sing, for they shall see eye to eye when the
> Lord shall bring again Zion. Break forth into joy, sing to-
> gether, ye waste places of Jerusalem; for the Lord hath com-
> forted his people, he hath redeemed Jerusalem. The Lord hath
> made bare his holy arm in the eyes of all the nations; and all
> the ends of the earth shall see the salvation of God."

Given the scholarly arguments over the meaning and application
of Isaiah, here we encounter a profound insight from Christ. He
attributes this quote from Isaiah to the coming events in the Americas. In this declaration by Christ we learn Isaiah was NOT speaking
of the return to the Middle East for these events to unfold. Instead
the "waste places of Jerusalem" are nowhere near Jerusalem. It is
another place, far away, where the residue of Jerusalem's scattered
people are wasted, then restored again. It is also plural. One is here,
in the Americas, on an "isle of the sea."[432] Now we can know from
Christ's own interpretation that Jerusalem's "waste places" are scattered throughout the world. This land is one of them.

Then we see something odd. After the removal of the Gentiles,
there is joy, rejoicing, singing together, seeing eye to eye, and a return
to Zion. The emotional setting seems at odds with what we antici-
pate. Destroying Gentiles and having the trauma of those days would

---

[432] 2 Nephi 10:20 "And now, my beloved brethren, seeing that our merciful God has
given us so great knowledge concerning these things, let us remember him, and lay
aside our sins, and not hang down our heads, for we are not cast off; nevertheless, we
have been driven out of the land of our inheritance; but we have been led to a better
land, for the Lord has made the sea our path, and we are upon an isle of the sea."

seem to produce mourning and lamentation. It does not. Instead it produces singing in joy.

To redeem Jerusalem is to re-establish the promised heirs upon their own land, and bring again Zion. Whatever bottle-neck of destruction needed to bring that triumph to pass will be worth it. So great will be the peace that follows that it will wipe away all tears. Truth, saving doctrine and being fed by Christ's own message will end all laments.[433]

How is the Lord's "holy arm" made bare? How will "the eyes of all nations" see it? What will the ends of the earth behold, as the salvation of God takes place? Why is it "all the ends of the earth" which will behold it?

What does it mean to "see eye to eye" when Zion is brought again?

Why is Zion to be "brought again" rather than re-built?

If the Lord is to comfort His people, what will that "comfort" include? Why has He consistently used the word "comfort" to describe His visit with people?

Why, when the waste places are redeemed, does it say "Jerusalem" will be redeemed? Is redeeming the "waste places" the same as redeeming "Jerusalem" itself? How does that affect the meaning of other scriptures?

Why are "singing together" and "seeing eye to eye" connected in the same thought?

What does it mean to "become one" as a people? Can we ever accomplish that by acquiring enough "sameness" or "uniformity" in conduct, thought and speech? Is it worth any effort at all to mimic one another? If we are to "become one" how should each of us

---

[433] Revelation 7:17 "For the Lamb which is in the midst of the throne shall feed them, and shall lead them unto living fountains of waters: and God shall wipe away all tears from their eyes."

proceed to accomplish that? How does Christ expect us to become "one?"[434]

Only the Lord can "bring it again." That is why He is said to "bring" it rather than for others to build it. All the labor may come from men, but it will the the Lord's command, Lord's direction, Lord's word which will cause it. Until He speaks it, it simply cannot come again. Hence the need for us to be able to speak with Him. He cannot bring it until a people exist who will listen to Him (or those who speak His words, no matter how unlikely the source they may seem to be). Oddly, until such spokesmen or spokeswomen should be listening to Him, and then He tells them to begin, and in turn a group should be here who would listen and hear Him in that call, there is simply no need to worry about Zion.

There are some great comments on the previous posts. I've not wanted to interrupt what I was doing to address them. Before moving on to another set of scriptures relating to those questions and comments, here are a few responses:

To whom has the Book of Mormon been written?

What possible good would it be for a message to be written for an audience who would never read the Book of Mormon?

If the term "Gentiles" is sometimes quite broad (and it is in some contexts), does the message get addressed to all of them? Is the message tailored to those who would read the book?

If the warnings are read to apply only to non-LDS occupants of the land, then what do the warnings accomplish? Do they make us proud? Do they make us feel better than "them," since only "they"

---

[434] 1 John 3:2 "Beloved, now are we the sons of God, and it doth not yet appear what we shall be: but we know that, when he shall appear, we shall be like him; for we shall see him as he is."

are condemned and not us? What kind of a warning is it if the only ones being warned are those who will never read the book?

Does The Church of Jesus Christ of Latter-day Saints at least retain the power and authority to preach the Gospel and administer the rites of baptism, and laying on of hands for the gift of the Holy Ghost? When I prayed, as the missionaries were instructing me, I got an answer that led me to baptism. I believe that baptism to be authoritative and approved by the Lord. Does anyone think the church lacks the authority to baptize for the remission of sins? I do not. If, therefore, the church has that authority, does it not continue to occupy an important, even central role in the Lord's work?

If you teach someone, and they want to "convert" and be baptized, would you not baptize them into The Church of Jesus Christ of Latter-day Saints?

What is the mission field for The Church of Jesus Christ of Latter-day Saints? Who is not included?

If all the world is the mission field for the church, what, then, becomes the mission field for the Church of the Firstborn? [I do not hold that the Church of the Firstborn is a formal organization, existing here as a formal order. I believe its members associate with others who are not of this world, and consequently the Church of the Firstborn is never in competition with The Church of Jesus Christ of Latter-day Saints.]

Would members of the Church of the Firstborn not pay tithes to The Church of Jesus Christ of Latter-day Saints? Would they not attend its meetings? Would they not support its programs? Would they not use The Church of Jesus Christ of Latter-day Saints to assist them in raising their children? Would they not have their families baptized into The Church of Jesus Christ of Latter-day Saints? Even if they held authority given them directly from the Lord, would they not continue to be faithful members of The Church of Jesus Christ of Latter-day Saints? To uphold and respect the authorities who are given the duty to preside?

Until the Lord brings again Zion, where should we all join in fellowship?

Would members of the Church of the Firstborn ever envy those presiding in The Church of Jesus Christ of Latter-day Saints? Ever challenge their right to preside? Did Christ ever try and displace Caiaphus? Did He not admonish us to follow His example?

Does The Church of Jesus Christ of Latter-day Saints limit the amount of light you can acquire by your own heed and diligence?[435] Can any man prevent God from pouring out knowledge upon you if you will receive it in the proper way?[436] Can any soul approach the Lord, see His face, and know that He is?[437]

Of what relevance is it if other Saints give no heed or are not willing to receive knowledge from the Lord? Should we belittle them? If not, what then is our responsibility toward them?[438]

What does it mean to let a "light shine?"

Why, upon seeing that light, would someone "glorify **your** Father who is in heaven" rather than heap praise and attention upon you?

---

[435] D&C 130:18–19 "Whatever principle of intelligence we attain unto in this life, it will rise with us in the resurrection. And if a person gains more knowledge and intelligence in this life through his diligence and obedience than another, he will have so much the advantage in the world to come."

[436] D&C 121:32–33 "According to that which was ordained in the midst of the Council of the Eternal God of all other gods before this world was, that should be reserved unto the finishing and the end thereof, when every man shall enter into his eternal presence and into his immortal rest. How long can rolling waters remain impure? What power shall stay the heavens? As well might man stretch forth his puny arm to stop the Missouri river in its decreed course, or to turn it up stream, as to hinder the Almighty from pouring down knowledge from heaven upon the heads of the Latter-day Saints."

[437] D&C 93:1 "VERILY, thus saith the Lord: It shall come to pass that every soul who forsaketh his sins and cometh unto me, and calleth on my name, and obeyeth my voice, and keepeth my commandments, shall see my face and know that I am;"

[438] 3 Nephi 12:16 "Therefore let your light so shine before this people, that they may see your good works and glorify your Father who is in heaven."

What is it about the nature of the light which you are to shine that produces notice of the Father rather than notice of you?

David Christensen's definition of "whoredoms" was interesting. Whether you take the meaning in 1830, or you take our modern sexual meaning, would it change the result of any analysis? One fellow who worked at the Church Office Building told me that approximately 60% of active adult male members of the church regularly view pornography.

Kisi also raised a question regarding Ishmael's Ephraimite lineage. Orson Pratt, Franklin D. Richards, and Erastus Snow all said Joseph Smith mentioned in passing that the lost 116 pages included a reference to Ishmael's lineage and he was from Ephraim. Does this change anything? If so, how? What other outcome might then be possible? Would this potentially even further limit the Gentile involvement?

On the subject of Joseph's statements contained in the Nauvoo era transcripts: These were the very materials from which Joseph's talks were reproduced. *The Documentary History of the Church*, by Joseph Smith, Jr., was compiled from these original materials. When *The Teachings of the Prophet Joseph Smith* was prepared, it was done using these materials. The paper I wrote included the original source materials, not the derivative compilations.

As to the importance and reliability of these materials, first, those involved were the leading church fathers at the time. Thomas Bullock was the official scribe for Joseph Smith during the Nauvoo talks. His versions were kept at Joseph's request and were official accounts. Second, the Joseph Smith Papers project now underway through the Church Historian's Office is attempting to make more of these original source materials available to the Saints. If they are not important, then the Church would not be investing millions of man-hours and dollars to bring the sources into the hands of the Saints.

It is not wise to dismiss as "mud" the very kinds of materials that give the best source for Joseph's teachings. Indeed, D&C 130 is an amalgam of comments Joseph made in a talk given April 2, 1843, recorded by some of the very same scribes used in the paper I wrote. I'm just using original materials, rather than derivative, second hand interpretations made years later by others who were not present (or living) when the statements were made by Joseph.

1 NEPHI 13

The role of gentiles in the history of this land, promised to Lehi's descendants, is not just covered in the Lord's words. It is set out in some detail by Nephi. Therefore, we will look at some of Nephi's prophecy from 1 Nephi 13.

1 Nephi 13:30

> "Nevertheless, thou beholdest that the Gentiles who have gone forth out of captivity, and have been lifted up by the power of God above all other nations, upon the face of the land which is choice above all other lands, which is the land that the Lord God hath covenanted with thy father that his seed should have for the land of their inheritance; wherefore, thou seest that the Lord God will not suffer that the Gentiles will utterly destroy the mixture of thy seed, which are among thy brethren."

This comes after an explanation of how the gentiles will flee oppression in another land (Europe), come here, and overtake this land. Nephi has been shown the establishment of a great church that alters the teachings to be given by Christ to the Jews. Then the prophecy continues with the above statement.

Flight from captivity has brought the Gentiles here. They came here (originally) for religious freedom. They wanted to follow their conscious when it came to matters of God and belief. This land was a land of religious freedom for these gentiles.

They then were "lifted up by the power of God above all other nations." This "lifting up" is not only to enjoy religious freedom to worship God. It also included the power to retain that freedom against any foreign threat to remove it. Therefore, ancillary to the religious freedom, the gentiles were necessarily given economic and military might with which to retain that freedom against "all other nations." But the "power of God" which "lifted [them] up" is conditioned upon them always serving the God of this land, who is Jesus Christ.[439] The power of God cannot be used to protect a wicked people.

The land is "choice above all other lands." Why is that so? What is it about the American continent which makes it more "choice" than any other location on earth?

Notice that here again Nephi is told that the land has been given to Lehi's descendants as "the land for their inheritance." Whatever dispossession the gentiles cause, these people have God's covenant to return the land to them. What does it mean to have this land promised by God through covenant to Lehi's descendants? Does that promise contain any condition? Will these people forfeit their right if they are wicked? If they will not forfeit the right, then what will happen to them if they cease to serve the God of this land?

Because of the covenant, the Lord will "not suffer that the Gentiles will utterly destroy" the covenant people? Note the "mixture of thy seed" mentioned to Nephi. Why is Nephi promised a "mixture of thy seed" will be preserved? Does gentile oppression remove the

---

[439] Ether 2:12 "Behold, this is a choice land, and whatsoever nation shall possess it shall be free from bondage, and from captivity, and from all other nations under heaven, if they will but serve the God of the land, who is Jesus Christ, who hath been manifested by the things which we have written."

promises to Lehi and Nephi? If not, what then do the promises assure them?

Why does God make a covenant to a worthy prophet-patriarch and bind Himself to fulfill the promise even with a posterity which may not be similarly faithful? Has the Lord done this before with Abraham? With Isaac? With Jacob? With Noah? Even though we knew nothing of these covenants when the gentiles overran the land, are they nonetheless God's promise and something which He will fulfill? How certain should we be that the Lord will deliver this land back to those who descend from Lehi and Nephi?

Why can a righteous prophet-patriarch obtain such promises from the Lord? What reason is there for such covenants to be made? Can they still be made? How? What did Lehi and Nephi do to qualify to receive such a covenant? Was there any intermediary? Will the Lord employ a servant when making such a covenant?

Well, this is interesting stuff. Worth continuing to consider, I think.

1 Nephi 13:31–32

"Neither will he suffer that the Gentiles shall destroy the seed of thy brethren. Neither will the Lord God suffer that the Gentiles shall forever remain in that awful state of blindness, which thou beholdest they are in, because of the plain and most precious parts of the gospel of the Lamb which have been kept back by that abominable church, whose formation thou hast seen."

The gentiles are limited in how far they may go. Although the covenant people will be smitten and afflicted, they will not be utterly destroyed. Diminished, broken to the dust, but not altogether lost. And, no matter what afflictions they may be called to endure, the Lord intends to give them this, their promised land.

A hopeful note sounds for the gentiles: The Lord will not let them "forever remain in that awful state of blindness" they are in when they arrive here. The Lord has commended the gentiles for coming to this land. They did so in response to the Spirit of God which "wrought" upon them.[440] The gentiles came out of captivity and humbled themselves before God.[441] The gentiles were given the "power of the Lord" because of their humility.[442] In the preceding verse, the power of God was how they were delivered from their captivity.[443] Despite all this, these gentiles are "in that awful state of blindness."

How can the gentiles be both blessed to inherit all the Lord's assistance and yet in an awful state of blindness?

What caused them to be blind?

If something is "plain" in the scriptures what must it include?

If something is "precious" in the scriptures what must it include?

If something both "plain" and "precious" has been removed, what has happened to the scriptures?

What does it mean to be blind? What does it mean to "stumble?"

What does it mean to cause plain and precious things "to be held back?"

Does any organization or group which "holds back" plain and precious things become part of that "abominable church?" Since

---

[440] 1 Nephi 13:13 "And it came to pass that I beheld the Spirit of God, that it wrought upon other Gentiles; and they went forth out of captivity, upon the many waters."

[441] 1 Nephi 13:16 "And it came to pass that I, Nephi, beheld that the Gentiles who had gone forth out of captivity did humble themselves before the Lord; and the power of the Lord was with them."

[442] Ibid.

[443] 1 Nephi 13:30 "Nevertheless, thou beholdest that the Gentiles who have gone forth out of captivity, and have been lifted up by the power of God above all other nations, upon the face of the land which is choice above all other lands, which is the land that the Lord God hath covenanted with thy father that his seed should have for the land of their inheritance; wherefore, thou seest that the Lord God will not suffer that the Gentiles will utterly destroy the mixture of thy seed, which are among thy brethren."

"abominable" requires the use of religion to suppress truth or impose a false form of truth, can the definition of "abominable church" be limited to Historic Christianity? What about a modern church, even a restorationist church like the Community of Christ (formerly RLDS) which suppresses or abandons truth? If they "hold back" truth, do they join in the collective assembly of false religions called the "abominable church?" Even it they came through Joseph Smith and accept the Book of Mormon?

What are the "plain and most precious" parts of the Gospel, anyway? Would it have anything to do with knowing Christ? Since this is life eternal, to "know" Him, would it be a simple and plain, but most precious teaching to urge people to part the veil of unbelief and behold their Lord?[444]

Where do we hear that message preached today? I think when I find such a message taught, I will give heed to it.

Nephi's vision of these events does inform us, does it not?

1 Nephi 13:33–34

"Wherefore saith the Lamb of God: I will be merciful unto the Gentiles, unto the visiting of the remnant of the house of Israel in great judgment. And it came to pass that the angel of the Lord spake unto me, saying: Behold, saith the Lamb of God, after I have visited the remnant of the house of Israel—and this remnant of whom I speak is the seed of thy father—wherefore, after I have visited them in judgment, and smitten them by the hand of the Gentiles, and after the Gentiles do stumble exceedingly, because of the most plain and precious parts of the gospel of the Lamb which have been kept back by that abominable church, which is the mother of harlots, saith the Lamb—I will be merciful unto the Gentiles in that day, insomuch that I will bring forth unto them, in

---

[444] John 17:3 "And this is life eternal, that they might know thee the only true God, and Jesus Christ, whom thou hast sent."

mine own power, much of my gospel, which shall be plain and precious, saith the Lamb."

Here is meat indeed! What amazing truths unfold in this announcement!

Notice the definition of the "remnant" to whom the prophecies apply has now been given. The distinction between the "gentiles" and the "remnant" are apparent here. Notice that although the gentiles will receive "much of my gospel" they will still remain identified as "Gentiles." We may refer to the restored church as "latter-day Israel" or similar terms, but the Book of Mormon vocabulary applies the term "Gentiles" to us. This is akin to the "Samaritans" many of whose blood was as Jewish as those who were exiled to Babylon and returned. Even Christ didn't acknowledge they were Jewish.

Why is it that the gentiles receive "much of my gospel" rather than the "fullness of my Gospel?" As you consider that, remember Joseph used to lament about the Saints' unwillingness to be taught new truths. Here are two of his comments:

> "There has been a great difficulty in getting anything into the heads of this generation. It has been like splitting hemlock knots with a corn-dodger for a wedge, and a pumpkin for a beetle. Even the Saints are slow to understand." (*DHC* 6:184).

> "Paul ascended into the third heavens and he could understand the three principle rounds of Jacob's ladder—the telestial, the terrestrial, and the celestial glories or kingdoms, when Paul saw and heard things which were not lawful to utter. I could explain a hundredfold more than I ever have of the glories of the kingdoms manifested to me in the vision were I permitted and were the people ready to receive them." (*DHC* 5:402.)

Joseph administered a form of endowment ceremony in Nauvoo, but told Brigham Young that he would have to finish it. Joseph initiated a few in the manner he received, but was not content with the form of the endowment. Brigham Young reported that Joseph told him, *"Brother Brigham, this is not arranged right. But we have done the best we could under the circumstances in which we are placed, and I wish you to take this matter in hand and organize and systematize all these ceremonies."* (See *Journal of L. John Nuttal,* 1:18–19, quoted in Truman G. Madsen, *Joseph Smith the Prophet,* Salt Lake City: Bookcraft, 1999, 97.)

Joseph also initiated a practice of sealing others to him, as the Patriarchal head of a dispensation. The nature of Patriarchal authority Joseph administered is different from what we currently understand or teach. Today we "seal" families together in genealogical lines based upon birth or legal adoption. Our families are tied together in what we understand was the intended purpose of Elijah's prophecy about "turning hearts of the fathers to the children, and the children to the fathers" so that the earth would not be smitten with a curse at the Lord's return. But Joseph's practice was somewhat different.

Joseph, who received the revelations on this matter, attempted to set out the manner in which the "family" will be constituted in eternity. He used Christ's comment in Matthew 19:29 to support the idea that those who are worthy will be placed in a family organization that would be completely restructured in the resurrection.[445] Orson Hyde later constructed a diagram of this teaching and published it in the *Millennial Star* Vol. 9 [15 January 1847], 23–24. If you search for that online you can find it. You need both the diagram and the explanation to understand the teaching. It is also in *The Words of Joseph Smith,*

---

[445] Matthew 19:29 "And every one that hath forsaken houses, or brethren, or sisters, or father, or mother, or wife, or children, or lands, for my name's sake, shall receive an hundredfold, and shall inherit everlasting life."

297. Please find and read it. You need to understand that teaching, which came to Orson Hyde from Joseph Smith.

As a result of this teaching, beginning with Joseph Smith and continuing until Wilford Woodruff discontinued it, sealing for eternity was not done in family lines. It was done instead to bind those who had received the Gospel to Joseph Smith, as the Patriarchal head of this dispensation. Joseph's teaching was followed by Brigham Young, who sealed himself to Joseph as his (Joseph's) son. John D. Lee, who was executed for the Mountain Meadows Massacre, was another sealed to Brigham Young as his son. Heber Grant's mother was sealed to Joseph Smith, although his father was Jedediah Grant. As a result he (President Grant) considered himself Joseph's son. That's a side issue.

Returning to the gentile inheritance of "much of my gospel" referred to above, does it suggest that the gentiles are not/never were given generally or as a group possession of "the fullness?" Is "much of my gospel" something worth considering? Can you be certain Joseph delivered all he could or would, were the Saints willing to receive it? If it was "much" rather than "the fullness" then how does that change things?

Assuming "much of my gospel" includes (as it tells us) those things which "shall be plain and precious" then do the gentiles have enough to allow them to receive an audience with Christ as the promised Second Comforter from John's Gospel?[446] If so, then will not Christ, along with the Holy Ghost, teach you all things needed, even if the gentiles are not in possession of the "fullness" of it all?[447]

---

[446] John 14:18, 23 "I will not leave you comfortless: I will come to you. . . . Jesus answered and said unto him, If a man love me, he will keep my words: and my Father will love him, and we will come unto him, and make our abode with him."

[447] John 14:26 "But the Comforter, which is the Holy Ghost, whom the Father will send in my name, he shall teach you all things, and bring all things to your remembrance, whatsoever I have said unto you."

This is important to understand. Nephi makes it clear how the gentiles can become adopted into the promised line and inherit a place among the chosen people who will be preserved, inherit this land, and be numbered among the house of Israel. While that jumps us ahead a bit, it is directly connected here. The first two verses of the next chapter state the following:

> "And it shall come to pass, that if the Gentiles shall hearken unto the Lamb of God in that day that he shall manifest himself unto them in word, and also in power, *in very deed*, unto the taking away of their stumbling blocks—And harden not their hearts against the Lamb of God, they shall be numbered among the seed of thy father; yea, they shall be numbered among the house of Israel; and they shall be a blessed people upon the promised land forever; they shall be no more brought down into captivity; and the house of Israel shall no more be confounded." (1 Nephi 14:1–2)

If the gentiles will hearken to the Lamb, He will manifest Himself to them. What does that mean?

What does it mean to manifest Himself to us "in word?" What does it mean to manifest Himself to us "in power?" What does it mean to manifest Himself to us "in very deed?"

How would Christ manifesting Himself to you in word, in power, and in deed "take away your stumbling block?"

These are the means promised by the Book of Mormon to deliver gentiles so that they may become "a blessed people upon the promised land forever" so as to never be brought down into captivity. But to know this would require you to come into possession of the fullness. Gentile possession of the fullness does not come from group-think, or group possession of some institutional magic. It comes by the same means as salvation has come to mankind from the beginning. The Catholics don't have it and can't give it to you. No institutional church has the means to deliver the gentiles. It will come, if it comes at all, from Christ and on the same conditions as saved Joseph Smith, Paul, Alma, Moroni, Peter, Moses, Enoch, Abraham and others.

Now there is a great deal to understand about how to move from having "much of the Gospel" to having a fullness of it. But it was always planned for that final step to be taken by you with the Lord. After all, He is the gatekeeper who employs no servant between you and Him.[448] This is why true servants will always point you to Him. False ones will claim they can save you, they have power to bring you to Him, they have been entrusted to open the door for you. The "gatekeeper" however does not need a doorman. Nor can He be fooled by men making pretensions to have authority while lacking any of His power. You must confront Him; or, to use His description, you must be comforted by Him.

If Joseph taught the organization of the Celestial Kingdom would involve reconstructed "family units" based upon the capacity of the individuals' involved, did he understand doctrine differently than we now do? Why were the original sealings performed to bind people to Joseph as the Patriarch? Why was that continued through Wilford Woodruff? Why was it discontinued? Although it was replaced with a method that provides us with sentimental associations, is there something about our understanding that is less complete, less accurate and less of how Christ intends to organize the eternal family?

It is clear from these verses in 1 Nephi 13 that the Lord intends to make redemption available to the gentiles, if they will receive it. But the primary means was never intended to be an institution. It was intended to be the Book of Mormon. The Book of Mormon

---

[448] 2 Nephi 9:41 "O then, my beloved brethren, come unto the Lord, the Holy One. Remember that his paths are righteous. Behold, the way for man is narrow, but it lieth in a straight course before him, and the keeper of the gate is the Holy One of Israel; and he employeth no servant there; and there is none other way save it be by the gate; for he cannot be deceived, for the Lord God is his name."

speaks right over the heads of those who are trying to distract you from returning to Christ. You must either seek and find Him while here, or remain in this Telestial state worlds without end. His invitation is extended. He will open the gate.

Where will we find true doctrine taught? From what source does it come? Will He not, as He has promised, send true messengers to warn before He cuts off and divides asunder? If you do not understand this it is because you will not ask Him.

So, let us press on. I find this is more interesting a Gospel than I had at first imagined. Truly, such things do not enter into the heart of man. They must be revealed, or they stand unknown. Fortunately for us, the Lord has provided the Book of Mormon and sent Joseph Smith to establish a foundation from which we gentiles may derive hope.

1 Nephi 13:35

> "For, behold, saith the Lamb: I will manifest myself unto thy seed, that they shall write many things which I shall minister unto them, which shall be plain and precious; and after thy seed shall be destroyed, and dwindle in unbelief, and also the seed of thy brethren, behold, these things shall be hid up, to come forth unto the Gentiles, by the gift and power of the Lamb."

It is the Lamb who makes this promise. He declares He will "manifest" Himself to Nephi's seed. Christ promises the same thing (to "manifest" Himself) to the gentiles in our day.[449] This original promise would be repeated by later Book of Mormon prophets.

The descendants of Nephi to whom the Lord would manifest Himself "shall write many things" which the Lord would minister.

---

[449] 1 Nephi 14:1 "And it shall come to pass, that if the Gentiles shall hearken unto the Lamb of God in that day that he shall manifest himself unto them in word, and also in power, in very deed, unto the taking away of their stumbling blocks—"

What does the qualification "many things" imply? Is "many" the same as "all things?"

The things to be written are what Christ "shall minister unto them." Is this limited to His ministry after His resurrection? Would it include all things which He "ministered" to them, even through prophetic ministers sent by Him?

Here again the words "plain and precious" are repeated. Why is this phrase used? What does it mean? Why was this what was removed by the "great and abominable church," but replaced through the things to be written by the Nephites? Is the fact Christ "ministered" to the Nephites, over a thousand-year dispensation, through many different ministers, in many different settings, alone evidence of something "plain and precious" to us? When Nephi would later write:

> "Wo be unto him that shall say: We have received the word of God, and we need no more of the word of God, for we have enough! For behold, thus saith the Lord God: I will give unto the children of men line upon line, precept upon precept, here a little and there a little; and blessed are those who hearken unto my precepts, and lend an ear unto my counsel, for they shall learn wisdom; for unto him that receiveth I will give more; and from them that shall say, We have enough, from them shall be taken away even that which they have. Cursed is he that putteth his trust in man, or maketh flesh his arm, or shall hearken unto the precepts of men, save their precepts shall be given by the power of the Holy Ghost Wo be unto the Gentiles, saith the Lord God of Hosts! For notwithstanding I shall lengthen out mine arm unto them from day to day, they will deny me; nevertheless, I will be merciful unto them, saith the Lord God, if they will repent and come unto me; for mine arm is lengthened out all the day long, saith the Lord God of Hosts." (2 Nephi 28:29–32)

Is not speaking to the Lord, and more importantly hearing from Him the most plain, the most precious of things? Would the Lord have ever promised to come, take up His abode[450] and sup with you[451] if He did not mean it? Does the Book of Mormon reiterate the promises given in the New Testament? Have they been restored to us by the Book of Mormon?

Here again we find the word "destroyed" used. "Destroyed" does not mean complete eradication. It means the loss of order, political independence and social coherence. Many will die, but they will not cease to exist.

What does "dwindle in unbelief" mean? Will anything be kept, although they should "dwindle?" Can a people "dwindle" and yet retain some truths?

It is not just the Nephite descendants who will "dwindle in unbelief," but "also the seed of thy brethren," the Lamanites. Whatever truths remain will not permit them to have on-going access to the Lord's presence. However, that does not mean they will not have Divine favor, does it? After all, the Lord gives to everyone precisely what will be best for them to know according to His wisdom.[452] Does dwindling mean that people are altogether lost to some portion of God's teachings and favor? How is it possible to determine if any people from any society are not being brought wisely along by the Lord?

---

[450] John 14:23 "Jesus answered and said unto him, If a man love me, he will keep my words: and my Father will love him, and we will come unto him, and make our abode with him."

[451] Revelation 3:20–21 "Behold, I stand at the door, and knock: if any man hear my voice, and open the door, I will come in to him, and will sup with him, and he with me. To him that overcometh will I grant to sit with me in my throne, even as I also overcame, and am set down with my Father in his throne."

[452] Alma 29:8 "For behold, the Lord doth grant unto all nations, of their own nation and tongue, to teach his word, yea, in wisdom, all that he seeth fit that they should have; therefore we see that the Lord doth counsel in wisdom, according to that which is just and true."

The teachings that Christ will "minister" to the Nephites will be written, and then "these things shall be hid up, to come forth unto the Gentiles" at the appointed time. Why write them? Why preserve them? Why are the records of His acts important for others to learn about? Why would a record of His dealings need to eventually be brought to light? Will all His dealings eventually be brought to light?[453] If He, therefore, imparts His word to you, what becomes your responsibility?

What does the coming forth of the Nephite record "by the gift and power of the Lamb" mean? Will this same pattern repeat?[454] Will the "gift and power of the Lamb" be on display again? Will this "make bare His arm?" Will people finally consider things which they have previously ignored?[455] Can you and I consider them now?

1 Nephi 13:36

"And in them shall be written my gospel, saith the Lamb, and my rock and my salvation."

Christ's Gospel is in the Book of Mormon. I've written books explaining just how much of His Gospel is contained in the Book of Mormon. When writing *The Second Comforter* I found the Book of Mormon was the best source to explain the process. In the Preface to *Eighteen Verses* I wrote (and meant) the following: "I am convinced

---

[453] 2 Nephi 29:13 "And it shall come to pass that the Jews shall have the words of the Nephites, and the Nephites shall have the words of the Jews; and the Nephites and the Jews shall have the words of the lost tribes of Israel; and the lost tribes of Israel shall have the words of the Nephites and the Jews."
D&C 133:30 "And they shall bring forth their rich treasures unto the children of Ephraim, my servants."

[454] D&C 133:26 "And they who are in the north countries shall come in remembrance before the Lord; and their prophets shall hear his voice, and shall no longer stay themselves; and they shall smite the rocks, and the ice shall flow down at their presence."

[455] Isaiah 52:15 "So shall he sprinkle many nations; the kings shall shut their mouths at him: for that which had not been told them shall they see; and that which they had not heard shall they consider."

the Book of Mormon is the preeminent sacred text for our times. All other volumes of scriptures are not just inferior to it, but vastly so." (*Ibid*, iii.)

The Book of Mormon contains Christ's Gospel. It also contains His "rock" and His "salvation." What is the "rock" contained within it?

John Hall thought the better translation of Christ's colloquy with Peter would have included the Lord identifying Peter not as a "rock" but as a "seer stone." And upon the stone or seership would the Lord build His church.

I've thought the Book of Mormon was more a Urim and Thummim than a book. It is a tremendous source of subject matter upon which to ponder, oftentimes drawing a veil at critical moments while inviting the reader to ponder, pray and ask to see more. Used in that fashion, the Book of Mormon can open the heavens and make any person a seer indeed.

The words of a prophet are best understood by a prophet. If you can come to understand the Book of Mormon's words, you can become a prophet. Or, more correctly, a seer before whom scenes of God's dealings with mankind, past, present and future, will be put on display.

> "But a seer can know of things which are past, and also of things which are to come, and by them shall all things be revealed, or, rather, shall secret things be made manifest, and hidden things shall come to light, and things which are not known shall be made known by them, and also things shall be made known by them which otherwise could not be known." (Mosiah 8:17)

Another way to interpret the "rock" is found in *Eighteen Verses* where I discussed the meaning of 1 Nephi 1:6.[456] The meaning of

---

[456] 1 Nephi 1:6 "And it came to pass as he prayed unto the Lord, there came a pillar of fire and dwelt upon a rock before him; and he saw and heard much; and because of the things which he saw and heard he did quake and tremble exceedingly."

the "rock" before Lehi (who wrote in Egyptian and would therefore understand meanings) would mean Ma'-at. Facsimile 2 figure 4, for example, shows the image of the Horus Hawk atop a rock and on the heavenly boat.

Still another meaning is found in the Book of Moses where Christ uses the term as a proper noun, or name for Himself.[457] He is "the Rock of Heaven." In this instance the meaning of the above verse is that you can find the Lord within the Book of Mormon. (Remember that E.B. Grandin's print shop provided all punctuation and capitalizations to the first edition. It was actually John H. Gilbert who did the work, which he described in a written recollection of the events dated 8 September 1892. (John Gilbert's September 8, 1892 recollections). If this was a proper noun and Gilbert did not capitalize it, we still don't. But that would not mean the word "rock" ought not to be rendered instead "Rock" as a proper name for Christ.)

The "salvation" to be found in the Book of Mormon is the same as salvation to be found in all the Gospel. That is, by finding Christ. For life eternal consists in coming to know Christ, and in turn Christ introducing you to the Father.[458] It is this *appearing* which Joseph Smith referred to as literal, not figurative.[459]

The prophetic message of the Book of Mormon is deeper and more profound the closer you examine it. It begins to become quite unlikely Joseph Smith could have produced such wisdom unless it

---

[457] Moses 7:53 "And the Lord said: Blessed is he through whose seed Messiah shall come; for he saith—I am Messiah, the King of Zion, the Rock of Heaven, which is broad as eternity; whoso cometh in at the gate and climbeth up by me shall never fall; wherefore, blessed are they of whom I have spoken, for they shall come forth with songs of everlasting joy."

[458] John 17:2–3 "As thou hast given him power over all flesh, that he should give eternal life to as many as thou hast given him. And this is life eternal, that they might know thee the only true God, and Jesus Christ, whom thou hast sent."

[459] D&C 130:3 "John 14:23—The appearing of the Father and the Son, in that verse, is a personal appearance; and the idea that the Father and the Son dwell in a man's heart is an old sectarian notion, and is false."

truly is an ancient document. Of course the critics labor to make it seem so, but they haven't seriously examined its contents to see what it says.

1 Nephi 13:37

"And blessed are they who shall seek to bring forth my Zion at that day, for they shall have the gift and the power of the Holy Ghost; and if they endure unto the end they shall be lifted up at the last day, and shall be saved in the everlasting kingdom of the Lamb; and whoso shall publish peace, yea, tidings of great joy, how beautiful upon the mountains shall they be."

Now we encounter words that require us to know meanings first. For the Lord's "Zion" to be brought forth, we need to know what "Zion" means. What is it? When the Lord calls it "my Zion" does it belong to Him. Will the Lord be the one who "brings again Zion" as stated earlier in the 3 Nephi materials of Christ's prophecy?[460] What are the role of people in "seeking to bring forth His Zion?"

Will they actually "bring again Zion" or is that the Lord's doing? Unless the Lord determines to "bring again Zion" will men be able to accomplish it? Even if they are quite sincere and determined? What, then, must precede Zion's return?

Even if they are not given the commission or command to participate in Zion's return, will they nevertheless be blessed if they seek to bring it again? Is the promised "gift and power of the Holy Ghost" promised to those who would seek to bring forth Zion? What does that mean? How could anyone accomplish that?

What does it mean to "publish peace?"

What does it mean to "publish tidings of great joy?"

---

[460] 3 Nephi 16:18 (quoting Isaiah 52:8): "Thy watchmen shall lift up the voice; with the voice together shall they sing, for they shall see eye to eye when the Lord shall bring again Zion."

How does the "publishing of peace" and "tidings of great joy" relate to having your feet become beautiful upon the mountains?

Why feet "upon the mountains?" What "mountains?" Are these literal, or figurative, or both? If the "mountains" are a symbol, what do they symbolize?

The feet of those who walk upon the mountains crying peace are beautiful[461] because they are clean from the blood and sins of their generation.

In the ancient ceremonies involving animal sacrifice, blood was shed upon the ground and the feet of those involved in the rites became bloody. The blood of the sacrifice upon the feet became a symbol of the sins for which the sacrifice was offered.

The feet of those who walk upon the mountains crying peace are cleansed from that blood. Christ's washing of His Apostles' feet was to symbolize this cleansing which He alone could provide. He employs no servant to provide such a cleansing.[462] These feet, washed by Him are, therefore, beautiful because they connote the sanctity of the one crying peace.

"Crying peace" because the only thing which stills the mind of man, and brings rest from the trouble of this world, is the atonement of Christ. That is why it is called "the rest of the Lord." When cleansed, it becomes the consuming desire of those who are clean to bring others to partake. Just like Lehi's dream, when those who had eaten of the fruit of the tree of life ate, they immediately invited others to come and join them.

---

[461] Isaiah 52:7 "How beautiful upon the mountains are the feet of him that bringeth good tidings, that publisheth peace; that bringeth good tidings of good, that publisheth salvation; that saith unto Zion, Thy God reigneth!"

[462] 2 Nephi 9:41 "O then, my beloved brethren, come unto the Lord, the Holy One. Remember that his paths are righteous. Behold, the way for man is narrow, but it lieth in a straight course before him, and the keeper of the gate is the Holy One of Israel; and he employeth no servant there; and there is none other way save it be by the gate; for he cannot be deceived, for the Lord God is his name."

"Upon the mountains" because the mountain is nature's symbol of the ascent to God. The climb represents repentance and purification of the soul. When a person stands upon the top of the mountain, she appears to be part of heaven itself and no longer earthbound. Her profile is with the sky, symbolizing the completion of the ascent back to God.

It is beautiful. All of it is beautiful. All of it is a reflection of the purity and intelligence of God, whose ways are higher than man's ways as the heavens are higher than the earth.[463]

Tuesday I went to the Salt Lake Temple early with a missionary who reported to the MTC on Wednesday. I teach him in priest quorum. I wanted to make sure before his departure that the "endowment" he received would include some details of what the Mountain of the Lord's House was intended to confer. Young men are still teachable. I'd really like to move to the Primary, however. Primary kids, despite their energy, have open hearts and they are willing to receive. By the time we get to teach LDS adults, there is just too much idolatry to deal with . . .

1 Nephi 13:38

> "And it came to pass that I beheld the remnant of the seed of my brethren, and also the book of the Lamb of God, which had proceeded forth from the mouth of the Jew, that it came forth from the Gentiles unto the remnant of the seed of my brethren."

Roles and definitions continue to be established here. Nephi's seed has been "destroyed" and only a "mixture" of his blood remains at the time of these events. Nephi has taken to calling them

---

[463] Isaiah 55:8–9 "For my thoughts are not your thoughts, neither are your ways my ways, saith the Lord. For as the heavens are higher than the earth, so are my ways higher than your ways, and my thoughts than your thoughts."

"the seed of my brethren" rather than a "mixture" of his (Nephi's) seed.

The "book of the Lamb of God" is later identified as the record we know as the New Testament. Altered, limited, with plain and precious materials removed, nevertheless called the "book of the Lamb of God." Acceptance of this New Testament book, notwithstanding its limitations and omissions, is akin to Christ referring to the Temple of Herod as His "Father's house" despite the fact that it had been profaned.

Although Christ called Herod's Temple His Father's house, He did not commune with His Father there. Christ visited with angelic ministers on the Mount of Transfiguration[464], in the Garden of Gethsemane[465], in the wilderness[466], and alone while apart from others. But there is no record of Him entertaining angels while in Herod's Temple. Though the Temple had been profaned and was unworthy to receive such visitors, Christ still honored the site and referred to it in sacred terms. This is a great key to understanding Christ's language here.

The "book of the Lamb of God" is revered and held in extraordinary esteem, as is evidenced by the terminology used in this revelation to Nephi. Nevertheless the book is corrupted, changed, with many plain and precious things removed.

Can the book that has come to the "seed of Nephi's brethren" be said to be less than a fullness? Can the book be called "the book of

---

[464] Matthew 17:1–3 "And after six days Jesus taketh Peter, James, and John his brother, and bringeth them up into an high mountain apart, And was transfigured before them: and his face did shine as the sun, and his raiment was white as the light. And, behold, there appeared unto them Moses and Elias talking with him."

[465] Luke 22:43 "And there appeared an angel unto him from heaven, strengthening him."

[466] Matthew 4:11 "Then the devil leaveth him, and, behold, angels came and ministered unto him."

the Lamb of God?" If it can be called "the book of the Lamb of God" can it also be said to contain a fullness?

[Here's a modern detour in question-asking: Do you focus on the book's value and worth by calling it the "book of the Lamb of God" or do you focus on the book's failings by saying many plain and precious things have been removed? If you do the one are you "positive" and "hopeful" and "Christ-like?" And if you focus on the other are you "negative" and "judgmental" and "un-Christ-like?" Is Nephi being fair and accurate by including the book's limitations? Or is he just another crank, tearing down the good works and valuable intent of others? Should he repent of his negativity? Ought we be offended? These kinds of questions are more a reflection of our own insecurities and foolishness than they are helpful to understanding Christ's "strange act" unfolding before our disbelieving eyes.[467]]

This "book of the Lamb of God" will originate from the Jews, be brought by gentiles, and provided to the "remnant" who are identified with the "seed of Nephi's brethren." Since we can recall the history of these events, and know it is talking of the New Testament, we can see the various identities. New Testament converts from Judaism to Christianity, including the Apostles, Seventy, and Paul, are called "Jews." The descendants of the Puritans, English Colonies, American States and United States who dispossessed the native peoples are all referred to as "gentiles" in the prophecy. (I'm ignoring Central and South American for the moment.) The natives will include among them some faction which is the "seed of my brethren" that is the "remnant" about whom these promises are being made.

---

[467] D&C 101:93–93 "What I have said unto you must needs be, that all men may be left without excuse; That wise men and rulers may hear and know that which they have never considered; That I may proceed to bring to pass my act, my strange act, and perform my work, my strange work, that men may discern between the righteous and the wicked, saith your God."

The question remains as to the identity of the "remnant" about whom these prophecies are speaking.

I know side-issues are arising throughout this discussion. But I've been focusing only on the "remnant" for weeks now. I won't depart from that single subject, despite the temptations that arise from questions flooding in on tangents. Bear with me. We'll eventually get to other issues.

I've debated whether it is even possible to cover this subject on a blog. This is an experiment. I'm trying to cover a topic that should rightly be put into a book. Whether it will work or not is still an open question. I think it is helpful even if the ultimate objective can't be met. We'll press forward and see how it turns out.

1 Nephi 13:39

> "And after it had come forth unto them I beheld other books, which came forth by the power of the Lamb, from the Gentiles unto them, unto the convincing of the Gentiles and the remnant of the seed of my brethren, and also the Jews who were scattered upon all the face of the earth, that the records of the prophets and of the twelve apostles of the Lamb are true."

We know the New Testament will come forth first and get into the hands of the "remnant" of the promised people. It will get into their hands BEFORE some other materials will also come forth.

When did that happen? Was it something that occurred before the publication of the Book of Mormon in 1830? Which native tribes received copies of the New Testament before the "other books" came forward? What are these "other books" referred to here? They "came forth by the power of the Lamb" but came "after" the New Testament was given to the "remnant." What books have come forth "by the power of the Lamb" to your knowledge? Apart from the Book of Mormon, Doctrine and Covenants, Book of Moses, Book of Abraham and Joseph Smith History and Matthew, what other books would qualify? Did all these come after the "remnant" had first received the New Testament "book of the Lamb of God?"

The effect of the "other books" will be to "convince" the gentiles as well as "the remnant of the seed of my brethren" of the truth of the New Testament and "records of the prophets." Have the gentiles become convinced? Have the "remnant" become convinced? Have the Jews who were scattered upon all the face of the earth become convinced? Are they convinced of the truth of "the records of the prophets" even if they are not yet convinced of the truth of the "twelve apostles of the Lamb?"

Is this a serial progression? That is, does it come and convince the gentiles first? Then, having convinced them, does it next convince the "remnant?" Then, after having convinced both the gentiles and the "remnant," does it in turn convince the scattered Jews? If serial, what stage of the unfolding of these events is happening now? What is needed before the phase would be completed and the next one begin?

What does it mean that "other books" will come forth? What kinds of "books" would they be? Who would have written them? Why would they come "by the power of the Lamb" only to meet the criteria? Is a good commentary written by CES among the promised "books" coming forward? What about the *Ensign*?

How would you be able to recognize a book coming "by the power of the Lamb" in fulfillment of this promise? Will these "books" be recognized as scripture? Do they include discoveries at Qumran and Nag Hammadi? Was Hugh Nibley working on such projects, and if so, was he among those in whom the "power of the Lamb" was working?

This verse has potential for broad application. It raises questions worth contemplating and may surprise you at some of the issues it requires us to confront. Such are the Lord's dealings with mankind in every generation. We are made prayerful because He gives us great subjects with which to grapple.

1 Nephi 13:40–41

> "And the angel spake unto me, saying: These last records, which thou hast seen among the Gentiles, shall establish the truth of the first, which are of the twelve apostles of the Lamb, and shall make known the plain and precious things which have been taken away from them; and shall make known to all kindreds, tongues, and people, that the Lamb of God is the Son of the Eternal Father, and the Savior of the world; and that all men must come unto him, or they cannot be saved. And they must come according to the words which shall be established by the mouth of the Lamb; and the words of the Lamb shall be made known in the records of thy seed, as well as in the records of the twelve apostles of the Lamb; wherefore they both shall be established in one; for there is one God and one Shepherd over all the earth."

The "books" that the prior verse referred to are now called "records" by the angel. The "records" will be among and originate from the gentiles. The purpose of the "records" is to establish the truth of the original records of "the twelve apostles of the Lamb." The purpose of the whole is to confirm the reality of Christ in His mortal ministry. Christ, who came to earth, lived and died as a mortal, was the Savior of mankind. The New Testament record confirming His ministry, sacrifice and resurrection is true! Their testimonies of Christ are reliable. He is our Savior and our God!

The "plain and precious" things that got removed will be returned to us. I've spoken of that before and won't repeat it again here. But the "plain and precious" things will become known to "all kindreds, tongues and people" again.

I was thinking about what was required for Joseph Smith to be able to get a message out in his day. He needed a printing press, which he could not afford. He needed Martin Harris to give a $3,000 note backed by a mortgage on his home to motivate the printer to make the first printings of the Book of Mormon. He needed an army of disciples to distribute the material on foot or horseback. He needed an infrastructure that went well beyond his individual means. Today Joseph would need a keyboard and an internet connection. He could speak to more people in a few minutes, across a wider swath of the globe, as a single individual acting alone, than he was able to speak to through an army of followers who uprooted their lives to follow his teachings.

We continue to make great sacrifices in purse and time to send missionaries throughout the world even today. In truth, if Joseph Smith had access to the internet he could have restored more things to more people in less time than has been done from 1830 to the present. It makes you wonder—if the truth were not packaged, marketed, focus-grouped through approved language, and accompanied by supporting photos and digital graphics—if the truth were simply spoken plainly, would it have any effect? Does it need an infrastructure of trained professional marketing to accompany it? Does it need a slick website to attract His sheep? Is His voice enough?

What if someone were to declare "that all men must come unto the Lamb of God, who is the Son of the Eternal Father, and the Savior of the world, or they cannot be saved." What if they were to declare in sober words that the Lamb of God lives still! That He had appeared to and spoken with the one making the declaration. Would there yet be those who would hear and repent?

Would that message be drowned out by the chorus of foolish and vain things being spoken in the name of Jesus Christ by those who, despite having real intent and sincere desire, have not been given power to declare His words? Would such a message only be another bit of entertainment for the bored and curious to give but passing notice? Could the world be given such a message and warned, but fail to see what it is they are being offered for one last time before the harvest is to begin? If so, would we notice?

The verse raises interesting options for the Lord to fulfill His promises in ways which have only come into existence in the last few years. He certainly does have the ability to "hasten His work" when He chooses.[468]

---

[468] D&C 88:73 "Behold, I will hasten my work in its time."

Should someone choose to come, the verse reports: "they must come according to the words which shall be established by the mouth of the Lamb; and the words of the Lamb shall be made known in the records of thy seed, as well as in the records of the twelve apostles of the Lamb." What does that include? Authoritative baptism? Authoritative bestowal of the gift of the Holy Ghost? Prophecy? Revelation? The "rock" of seership we discussed a few days ago? How must they come? The Book of Mormon suggests it must be through the gate of revelation.[469] Without revelation you cannot obtain the testimony of Jesus; which is the spirit of prophecy.[470] Or, in other words, unless you find prophets who can bear testimony of Him, you have not yet found the means for salvation. This becomes quite interesting and important. Very frank about the conditions for salvation.

Then the promise is that all these witnesses, all these records, and all these disciples are to become "one." "[T]hey both (records) shall be established in one; for there is one God and one Shepherd over all the earth" who in turn makes people to be "one" as well. A great assembly, a general congregation and Church of the Firstborn.

How great a promise has been offered to those who will receive! What good, however, is it to offer a gift if the one to whom it is offered refuses to accept?[471]

---

[469] Moroni 10:4–5 "And when ye shall receive these things, I would exhort you that ye would ask God, the Eternal Father, in the name of Christ, if these things are not true; and if ye shall ask with a sincere heart, with real intent, having faith in Christ, he will manifest the truth of it unto you, by the power of the Holy Ghost. And by the power of the Holy Ghost ye may know the truth of all things"

[470] Revelation 19:10 "And I fell at his feet to worship him. And he said unto me, See thou do it not: I am thy fellowservant, and of thy brethren that have the testimony of Jesus: worship God: for the testimony of Jesus is the spirit of prophecy."

[471] D&C 88:33 "For what doth it profit a man if a gift is bestowed upon him, and he receive not the gift? Behold, he rejoices not in that which is given unto him, neither rejoices in him who is the giver of the gift."

1 Nephi 13:42

"And the time cometh that he shall manifest himself unto all nations, both unto the Jews and also unto the Gentiles; and after he has manifested himself unto the Jews and also unto the Gentiles, then he shall manifest himself unto the Gentiles and also unto the Jews, and the last shall be first, and the first shall be last."

Christ showed Himself to the Jews during His mortal ministry. He showed Himself to the Nephites after His resurrection.

He visited others, who have also kept records of His appearances to them. The full extent of the records that have been kept has not become apparent to us yet. Nephi would report in the final summation of his lifelong ministry the following about the many records to come forth:

"Wherefore, because that ye have a Bible ye need not suppose that it contains all my words; neither need ye suppose that I have not caused more to be written. For I command all men, both in the east and in the west, and in the north, and in the south, and in the islands of the sea, that they shall write the words which I speak unto them; for out of the books which shall be written I will judge the world, every man according to their works, according to that which is written. For behold, I shall speak unto the Jews and they shall write it; and I shall also speak unto the Nephites and they shall write it; and I shall also speak unto the other tribes of the house of Israel, which I have led away, and they shall write it; and I shall also speak unto all nations of the earth and they shall write it. And it shall come to pass that the Jews shall have the words of the Nephites, and the Nephites shall have the words of the Jews; and the Nephites and the Jews shall have the words of the lost tribes of Israel; and the lost tribes of Israel shall have the words of the Nephites and the Jews. And it shall come to pass that my people, which are of the house of Israel, shall be gathered home unto the lands of their possessions; and my word also shall be gathered in one. And I will show unto them that fight against my word and against my people, who are of the house of Israel, that I am God, and that I covenanted with Abraham that I would remember his seed forever." (2 Nephi 29:10–14)

The "lost tribes of Israel" are plural. However many the number may be, each kept records and they are to come into our possession at some point in fulfillment of this prophetic promise.

All of this was foreseen by Zenos even before Isaiah. Zenos tells us the lost tribes of Israel will be spread all about, into the "nethermost" parts of the earth:

"And these will I place in the nethermost part of my vineyard, whithersoever I will, it mattereth not unto thee; and I do it that I may preserve unto myself the natural branches of the tree; and also, that I may lay up fruit thereof against the season, unto myself; for it grieveth me that I should lose this tree and the fruit thereof. And it came to pass that the Lord of the vineyard went his way, and hid the natural branches of the tame olive-tree in the nethermost parts of the vineyard, some in one and some in another, according to his will and pleasure." (Jacob 5:13–14)

Where is "nethermost?" How many were there?

When Christ informed the Nephites of His post-resurrection ministry, He informed them He would be visiting the various Israelite people: "But now I go unto the Father, and also to show myself unto the lost tribes of Israel, for they are not lost unto the Father, for he knoweth whither he hath taken them." (3 Nephi 17:4.) He visited the Nephites. They were an organized body, led by prophets, expecting His birth and death. There were other organized believers who also looked for His coming. What their prophets told them, and how they understood His ministry will be in their records. What He taught them when He visited with them after His resurrection will also be in their records. It is likely to mirror the Nephite experience and record. However, it is undoubtedly true that we will again learn how involved a Redeemer He has been. Should we already realize that from what we've been given? We ought to welcome His direct ministry among us. Somehow we find His intimate involvement hard to comprehend. We think, if someone should acknowledge they have seen Him, that such a person is somehow special, different, or unique. It ought to be commonplace.

In the unfolding ministry of the Lord, the Jews were the first, but will be the last, to receive again His ministry. The gentiles have been given the Gospel. The remnant will be receiving it from them—soon.

1 NEPHI 14

1 Nephi 14:1–2

"And it shall come to pass, that if the Gentiles shall hearken unto the Lamb of God in that day that he shall manifest himself unto them in word, and also in power, in very deed, unto the taking away of their stumbling blocks—And harden not their hearts against the Lamb of God, they shall be numbered among the seed of thy father; yea, they shall be numbered among the house of Israel; and they shall be a blessed people upon the promised land forever; they shall be no more brought down into captivity; and the house of Israel shall no more be confounded."

I've referred to these verses before. When Elder Mark E. Peterson claimed the Lord would not visit with "gentiles" but only with the house of Israel, relying upon 3 Nephi 15:23[472], it was my view that the 3 Nephi statement of Christ was as to His immediate post-resurrection appearances to the various scattered lost tribes. He had no commission from the Father to appear to the gentiles in that time frame. These verses are about a different, much later time. These are speaking of the time when the Book of Mormon (record of the

---

[472] 3 Nephi 15:23 "And they understood me not that I said they shall hear my voice; and they understood me not that the Gentiles should not at any time hear my voice—that I should not manifest myself unto them save it were by the Holy Ghost."

Nephites) would come into the possession of the gentiles. The gentiles will, if they hearken to the "Lamb of God IN THAT DAY," have the Lamb manifest Himself to them. Today is THAT DAY. It is now when the gentiles are promised He will manifest Himself to us, in "word" and in "power" and "in very deed."

His assignment immediately post-resurrection was to visit with each of the still organized, prophet-led, but scattered children of Israel. They had been put into the "nethermost" parts of the earth. He went to and visited with each of them serially. He did not visit with gentiles during that ministry.

But in the time following the publication of the Book of Mormon, and as part of removing the stumbling blocks of the gentiles, He is to visit the gentiles "in word" and "in power" and "in deed" so that it will "take away their stumbling blocks."

What does it mean to stumble? What is a "stumbling block?" What kinds of things would impede you from walking back to the presence of God? How will Christ's ministry in "word, power and deed" to gentiles remove these things?

It is AFTER the ministry of "word, power and deed" when the stumbling blocks are removed, that the gentiles are then "numbered among the seed of thy father." Note that they are not numbered among other branches of Israel. Note that they are not sealed to their fathers and made Ephraimites descended from other branches. They are to be "numbered among the seed of thy father" or counted as part of Lehi's seed. They are, in short, to be sealed to Lehi as their Patriarch and father. It is necessary to understand the doctrine discussed in this post.

This was always a part of the Gospel. Joseph Smith understood it and practiced it. Today we think it was an oddity that got corrected at the time of Wilford Woodruff. However, if you read the Book of Abraham you realize that the adoption of people into an inheritance was always the manner the Celestial Kingdom was to be organized here. Look at the Lord's discussion/explanation to Abraham:

> "My name is Jehovah, and I know the end from the beginning; therefore my hand shall be over thee. And I will make of thee a great nation, and I will bless thee above measure, and make thy name great among all nations, and **thou shalt be a blessing unto thy seed after thee,** that in their hands they shall bear this ministry and Priesthood unto all nations; And I will bless them through thy name; for **as many as receive this Gospel shall be called after thy name, and shall be accounted thy seed,** and shall rise up and bless thee, as their father; And I will bless them that bless thee, and curse them that curse thee; and in **thee (that is, in thy Priesthood) and in thy seed (that is, thy Priesthood),** for I give unto thee a promise that this right shall continue in thee, and in thy seed after thee (that is to say, the literal seed, or the seed of the body) shall all the families of the earth be blessed, even with the blessings of the Gospel, which are the blessings of salvation, even of life eternal." (Abraham 2:8–11)

Those who receive the same priesthood (Patriarchal) from the time of Abraham forward become his (Abraham's) seed. Therefore they become his (Abraham's) inheritance and posterity, sealed to him as a part of his family.

This was the priesthood that was bestowed upon Joseph Smith, as a result of which he received the promises of Abraham. While looking for references to Abraham throughout D&C 132 is interesting, I'll just take an excerpt. [PLEASE forget about plural wives while you read this. Think only about Patriarchal Priesthood and the authority which was with Abraham and renewed in Joseph. It is that issue that I want to focus, and not to become side-tracked on plural marriage. At some point I'll spend a few weeks on that side issue, *not now*.]

"I am the Lord thy God, and will give unto thee the law of **my Holy Priesthood**, as was ordained by me and my Father before the world was. **Abraham received all things, whatsoever he received, by revelation and commandment, by my word, saith the Lord**, and hath entered into his exaltation and sitteth upon his throne. **Abraham received promises concerning his seed**, and of the fruit of his loins—from whose loins ye are, namely, my servant Joseph—which were to continue so long as they were in the world; and as touching Abraham and his seed, out of the world they should continue; both in the world and out of the world should they continue as innumerable as the stars; or, if ye were to count the sand upon the seashore ye could not number them. This promise is yours also, because ye are of Abraham, and **the promise was made unto Abraham; and by this law is the continuation of the works of my Father, wherein he glorifieth himself.** Go ye, therefore, and do the works of Abraham; enter ye into my law and ye shall be saved." (D&C 132:28–32)

Exaltation came through this priesthood, which linked together the fathers and the children of promise. The priestly sealing together of Patriarchs into a family that will endure as the government in heaven was the object of the Gospel in every generation. We are returning, at the end, to what it was at the beginning. However, the way in which it was to occur was "by my word" and "by revelation and commandment" so that the person knows he is to have a part in the Father's kingdom. It was not to be merely a distant expectation, uncertain in origin and doubtful in authority. It was to be certain, not doubtful: "The more sure word of prophecy means a man's knowing that he is sealed up unto eternal life, by revelation and the spirit of prophecy, through the power of the Holy Priesthood."[473] It is di-

---

[473] D&C 131:5 "(May 17th, 1843.) The more sure word of prophecy means a man's knowing that he is sealed up unto eternal life, by revelation and the spirit of prophecy, through the power of the Holy Priesthood."

rectly connected with this Patriarchal Priesthood, the same authority which belonged to Abraham, the possession of which by any man makes him the seed of Abraham.

Returning to the subject of "remnant" and "gentiles," the Book of Mormon prophecies still do not refer to the latter-day gentiles as anything other than "gentiles" even when they are "numbered among the seed of Lehi." Gentiles retain in prophecy their identification with "gentiles" although they are adopted as Lehi's seed. Hence Joseph Smith's reference in the Kirtland Temple dedicatory prayer to the Latter-day Saints as "gentiles" by identity.[474] Whenever a gentile manages to acquire this adoption, they do not become identified as the "remnant" as a result. Instead, they become heirs to share in the promised blessings, but as "gentiles." They will get to assist the "remnant" but as "gentiles" not as the "remnant." Still, those who are adopted as Lehi's seed inherit with the "remnant" the Lord's promises. But they are nevertheless called in prophecy "gentiles" throughout.

The priesthood held by Melchizedek was Patriarchal. The "City" was a family, sealed to him. They came into the order through the authority given to him to seal on earth and in heaven.

We have two divisions of priesthood in the Church, one which we call Melchizedek and one which we call Aaronic. These are not the same as what Melchizedek held, because in the Melchizedek order sealing authority is not generally granted.

Moses had authority from Jethro, but also visited with the Lord face to face, at which time the Lord gave him a work to do. The work was greater than the authority given by Jethro, and of necessity included all keys to accomplish it (as I have explained earlier in a post about keys accompanying assignments).

---

[474] D&C 109:60 "Now these words, O Lord, we have spoken before thee, concerning the revelations and commandments which thou hast given unto us, who are identified with the Gentiles."

Lehi was a descendant of Abraham, Isaac, Jacob and Joseph; as was Joseph Smith. There is no conflict with Joseph as Dispensation head being the Patriarch of all who came after him, and Lehi being the father of all gentiles who convert in this dispensation.

Go back and review the chart from Orson Hyde I referred to earlier and you will see that genealogical order does not control, but worthiness and capacity control. How the eternal family will be structured will be the result of what the Lord knows to be the right, joyful, best and holiest of family orders.

1 Nephi 14:3–4

"And that great pit, which hath been digged for them by that great and abominable church, which was founded by the devil and his children, that he might lead away the souls of men down to hell—yea, that great pit which hath been digged for the destruction of men shall be filled by those who digged it, unto their utter destruction, saith the Lamb of God; not the destruction of the soul, save it be the casting of it into that hell which hath no end. For behold, this is according to the captivity of the devil, and also according to the justice of God, upon all those who will work wickedness and abomination before him."

Now I wish Nephi would only prophecy smooth things to us.[475] But once again here we find him being negative. He needs to repent or he's going to lose readers.

The "great pit" is an interesting symbol. Remember when the brothers sought to kill Joseph? Before they sold him into slavery, they put him into a pit in which there was no water.[476] They stripped

---

[475] Isaiah 30:10 "Which say to the seers, See not; and to the prophets, Prophesy not unto us right things, speak unto us smooth things, prophesy deceits:"

[476] Genesis 37:23–24 "And it came to pass, when Joseph was come unto his brethren, that they stript Joseph out of his coat, his coat of many colours that was on him; And they took him, and cast him into a pit: and the pit was empty, there was no water in it."

him of his sacred garment—not of "many colors" but of "sacred markings." Having stripped him of the garment that belonged to the heir, and assured him of his exaltation, they cast him into a pit without water. He descended, as the damned, into the waterless pit. This pit symbolizes the damned souls in spirit prison who, without deliverance from the waters of baptism, are left to suffer.[477] Joseph's pit without water is a reminder of how the ordinances that pass us through the water are the means of deliverance. (Hence the Red Sea and rebirth of Israel as they emerged from Egypt.) Christ also alluded to this in His parable of Lazarus, when the torment could only be cooled by covenantal water.[478]

Well the abominable church offers ordinances, but they leave people in a pit, without redemption and in need of authoritative washing to cleanse from sin. The devil and his children are the founders of this great and abominable order. They seek to cheat mankind of salvation. If they can cause even a little error that robs power from the ordinances performed, they can keep mankind captive. For death and hell will claim all those who have not been redeemed from the awful pit.

How unkind would it be to fail to warn people of this risk they face? How unkind would it be to allow them to proceed into the afterlife unprepared, uncleansed, and unredeemed? Which would be better, to stay silent while the idolatry of the Latter-day Saints robs them of redemption, or to speak up and warn? Men and institutions will never redeem a man. Idolizing an institution will damn every participant. Idolizing men will damn those false religionists. In the Latter-day Saint community we have two groups: Those who are

---

[477] Zechariah 9:12 "Turn you to the strong hold, ye prisoners of hope: even to day do I declare that I will render double unto thee;"

[478] Luke 16:24 "And he cried and said, Father Abraham, have mercy on me, and send Lazarus, that he may dip the tip of his finger in water, and cool my tongue; for I am tormented in this flame."

humble and follow Christ, but who are taught by the precepts of men and err.[479] And the rest are those who follow men and worship the institution and proclaim "All is well" with their faith. For the first group there is hope, so long as they are able to find the truth.[480] For the rest, they will become heirs of this prophecy of Nephi's, all the while assuring one another that the odds are they are going to be exalted.

The goal in every generation is to become Zion. To do that you must have a return of a Patriarchal head, as in Enoch's day or in Melchizedek's day, wherein they organized again after the pattern of heaven. A family. One. Where all things are in common because there is a loving environment where all are of equal worth. No one aspires to be a leader, but all become sons and daughters, brothers and sisters, husbands and wives where the care of all is as natural as family affection for one another.

The devil and his children seek to fragment, to divide, and to keep mankind from organizing into a family where the hearts of fathers are with the children and the hearts of children are toward their fathers. When you divide up into separate clans or divided families, while still paying tribute to the honored position of "family life" among the divided clans and families, you still have only a form of godliness without any power. This is the goal of the devil. It will prevent Zion from ever being brought again. It will leave people unorganized and unprepared to assume a place in the government of

---

[479] 2 Nephi 28:14 "They wear stiff necks and high heads; yea, and because of pride, and wickedness, and abominations, and whoredoms, they have all gone astray save it be a few, who are the humble followers of Christ; nevertheless, they are led, that in many instances they do err because they are taught by the precepts of men."

[480] D&C 123:12 "For there are many yet on the earth among all sects, parties, and denominations, who are blinded by the subtle craftiness of men, whereby they lie in wait to deceive, and who are only kept from the truth because they know not where to find it—"

God, which is His eternal and singular extended family, where all are one.

The references to the "hell that hath no end" is that same play on words that is defined in D&C 19:5–12.[481] It is a place of torment, where people suffer as in the Telestial Kingdom, or the world in which you presently reside (to paraphrase the Endowment). How long will people endure such an experience? Until they repent.[482] What if they do not repent? They will suffer, worlds without end.[483]

All of this according to "the justice of God."

Notice that people arrive here because of the "abominable church" that will always be ready to preach to you false, vain and foolish doctrines. They will offer anything to distract you and keep you from seeing the Lord "bring again Zion." They will use the words of Zion to preach a false faith. They are "abominable" because their false teachings are clothed in the vocabulary of truth.

---

[481] D&C 19:5–12 "Wherefore, I revoke not the judgments which I shall pass, but woes shall go forth, weeping, wailing and gnashing of teeth, yea, to those who are found on my left hand. Nevertheless, it is not written that there shall be no end to this torment, but it is written endless torment. Again, it is written eternal damnation; wherefore it is more express than other scriptures, that it might work upon the hearts of the children of men, altogether for my name's glory. Wherefore, I will explain unto you this mystery, for it is meet unto you to know even as mine apostles. I speak unto you that are chosen in this thing, even as one, that you may enter into my rest. For, behold, the mystery of godliness, how great is it! For, behold, I am endless, and the punishment which is given from my hand is endless punishment, for Endless is my name. Wherefore—Eternal punishment is God's punishment. Endless punishment is God's punishment."

[482] D&C 76:99–101 "For these are they who are of Paul, and of Apollos, and of Cephas. These are they who say they are some of one and some of another—some of Christ and some of John, and some of Moses, and some of Elias, and some of Esaias, and some of Isaiah, and some of Enoch; But received not the gospel, neither the testimony of Jesus, neither the prophets, neither the everlasting covenant."

[483] D&C 76:109–112 "But behold, and lo, we saw the glory and the inhabitants of the telestial world, that they were as innumerable as the stars in the firmament of heaven, or as the sand upon the seashore; And heard the voice of the Lord saying: These all shall bow the knee, and every tongue shall confess to him who sits upon the throne forever and ever; For they shall be judged according to their works, and every man shall receive according to his own works, his own dominion, in the mansions which are prepared; And they shall be servants of the Most High; but where God and Christ dwell they cannot come, worlds without end."

At that day even the very elect will be the targets of deception. Those claiming falsely to be "prophets" will arise and lead away many. They will show great wonders, spacious and glorious buildings, feats of charity and good will. But the elect will not be deceived, though they may be troubled.[484] They will not be deceived because they treasure up His words. They know His voice, recognize when it speaks, and will use it to keep them from deception. They will have entertained angels, who will have gathered them, and will be waiting for His return.[485]

Now, indeed, is the great day of Satan's power; who rules from the rivers to the ends of the earth and there are none to molest him or make him afraid. We look for the day when, again, a voice will cry out in the wilderness saying to walk in the strait path of the Lord. It would be interesting if that should happen to see who would recognize it, and who would want to know instead "by what authority" such a voice cries out.

Well, there's more to the verse than this. Ask yourself:

- Why is it a "great pit which hath been digged for the destruction of men?"
- Who is it that "shall fill" it?
- What does "utter destruction" mean?
- What does the phrase "not the destruction of the soul, save it be the casting of it into that hell which hath no end" refer to?

---

[484] JS–Matthew 1:22–25 "For in those days there shall also arise false Christs, and false prophets, and shall show great signs and wonders, insomuch, that, if possible, they shall deceive the very elect, who are the elect according to the covenant. Behold, I speak these things unto you for the elect's sake; and you also shall hear of wars, and rumors of wars; see that ye be not troubled, for all I have told you must come to pass; but the end is not yet. Behold, I have told you before; Wherefore, if they shall say unto you: Behold, he is in the desert; go not forth: Behold, he is in the secret chambers; believe it not;"

[485] JS–Matthew 1:37 "And whoso treasureth up my word, shall not be deceived, for the Son of Man shall come, and he shall send his angels before him with the great sound of a trumpet, and they shall gather together the remainder of his elect from the four winds, from one end of heaven to the other."

- Why is this "according to the captivity of the devil?"

- Why is this "also according to the justice of God, upon all those who will work wickedness and abomination before him?"

It is an interesting insight into the patience of God, the eternal purposes of God, and the endless, even "worlds without end" which will be provided for all those who will not repent. What a vast, eternal work God has set about to accomplish! Imagine bringing to pass the immortality and eternal life of man! What an endless process such a work may entail! Why would anyone procrastinate the day of their repentance?

1 Nephi 14:5

> "And it came to pass that the angel spake unto me, Nephi, saying: Thou hast beheld that if the Gentiles repent it shall be well with them; and thou also knowest concerning the covenants of the Lord unto the house of Israel; and thou also hast heard that whoso repenteth not must perish."

Again a reminder that Nephi's teachings come from an angel. He's not on his own errand in making these things known. I doubt a person of good faith and common sense would ever dare to make declarations as Nephi does unless he had received the message from such a source. Joseph put it this way: "None but fools will trifle with the souls of men. How vain and trifling have been our spirits, our conferences, our councils, our meetings, our private as well as public conversations—too low, too mean, too vulgar, too condescending for the dignified characters of the called and chosen of God, according to the purposes of His will, from before the foundation of the world!" (*DHC* 3:295–96.) Nephi was no fool. He wanted us to understand these teachings came from a higher source, and not man's wisdom. Indeed, what man can open up the mysteries that have remained hidden? Either God makes them known or they remain a mystery!

I believe the wisest course would have been for all our teachers, from Joseph till today, to either declare what the Lord and His angels have made known to them or to remain silent. Had that been the practice our libraries would undoubtedly be sparse. But what few books that remained would be the "best books" worthy of study.[486] I understand that not all have faith. But teachers do a profound disservice whenever they pontificate about something they do not understand. No-one is an "authority" who has not received intelligence from the Lord or His angels. They are simply trying to be helpful, or seeking to magnify a calling, but they are not on His errand. Alas, the full extent of this problem cannot be known. All those who have spoken in His name, but without His instruction and direction, have indeed taken His name in vain. This will be a great burden for those who have chosen to use His name in violation of a fundamental commandment to the contrary.[487]

The happy news is that "if the Gentiles repent" is always a condition for moving forward. We can't get through carrying on our backs the false, vain and foolish traditions men have handed to us. We must lay them down. Unless we do so we wind up exactly at the point when this Dispensation began: suffering under doctrine which con-

---

[486] D&C 88:118 "And as all have not faith, seek ye diligently and teach one another words of wisdom; yea, seek ye out of the best books words of wisdom; seek learning, even by study and also by faith."

[487] Exodus 20:7 "Thou shalt not take the name of the Lord thy God in vain; for the Lord will not hold him guiltless that taketh his name in vain."

sists merely of the commandments of men, having a form of godliness without power.[488]

What must gentiles do to "repent?" All gentiles, including those who have accepted the Restoration and who claim to believe the Book of Mormon . . . What must they do? To answer that look again carefully at the Lord's condemnation of us:

> "And your minds in times past have been darkened because of unbelief, and because you have treated lightly the things you have received— Which vanity and unbelief have brought the whole church under condemnation. And this condemnation resteth upon the children of Zion, even all. And they shall remain under this condemnation until they repent and **remember the new covenant, even the Book of Mormon and the former commandments which I have given them, not only to say, but to do according to that which I have written**—That they may bring forth fruit meet for their Father's kingdom; otherwise there remaineth a scourge and judgment to be poured out upon the children of Zion." (D&C 84:54–58.)

Then Nephi's angel-minister reminds Nephi of two different thoughts: 1) There are covenants with the house of Israel. So they will be remembered. 2) Whoever repents will find things will be well. Nephi was told: "thou also knowest concerning the covenants of the Lord unto the house of Israel; and thou also hast heard that whoso repenteth not must perish." The result is that even though the gentiles are not given a covenant status, they are nonetheless included within the promise that it is well with whoever should repent. Ac-

---

[488] JS–H 1:19 "I was answered that I must join none of them, for they were all wrong; and the Personage who addressed me said that all their creeds were an abomination in his sight; that those professors were all corrupt; that: 'they draw near to me with their lips, but their hearts are far from me, they teach for doctrines the commandments of men, having a form of godliness, but they deny the power thereof'."

cordingly, if they will repent, the gentiles will not perish but will have eternal life.

How beautiful upon the mountains are the feet of those who declare that God reigneth and will deliver His people. How merciful it is that the Lord God will accept all those as His people who will repent and come unto Him.

1 Nephi 14:6

"Therefore, wo be unto the Gentiles if it so be that they harden their hearts against the Lamb of God."

Interestingly, rather than shouting out in rejoicing that all who repent will escape punishment, the angel instead pronounces a "wo" upon the gentiles. It is almost as if the future of the gentile conduct inspires nothing but pessimism for the angel. It inspires another warning and condemnation for the gentiles who, having received the Book of Mormon and other sacred writings, are then fully responsible to repent.

Notice that the relationship is between the "Lamb of God" and the gentiles. It is not between the gentiles and "leaders" or "prophets" or "administrators" or "general authorities" or even messengers. It is between the gentiles and "the Lamb of God."

Why that specific a relationship? Why is it exclusively between the individual and Christ?

Read again the description of the Telestial folk who return "worlds without end" to their condemnation: "And the glory of the telestial is one, even as the glory of the stars is one; for as one star differs from another star in glory, even so differs one from another in glory in the telestial world; For these are they who are of Paul, and of Apollos, and of Cephas. These are they who say they are some of one and some of another—some of Christ and some of John, and some of Moses, and some of Elias, and some of Esaias, and some of Isaiah, and some of Enoch; But received not the gospel, neither the testimony of Jesus, neither the prophets, neither the everlasting covenant." (D&C 76:98–101.)

From what you've now learned can you see how one might follow even a true messenger but fail to gain "the testimony of Jesus?"

Can you now understand why, although you have followed messengers, you may have not in fact received the "everlasting covenant?"

The Temple is a type and shadow. It is a symbol of the real thing, but it is not the real thing. The "everlasting covenant" is taught there. But to gain it you must receive it through "the testimony of Jesus." Is this "testimony of Jesus" yours? Or is it rather Jesus testifying to you? If it is He testifying to you, then what must His testimony be?

In light of that what does it mean then to "harden your hearts against the Lamb of God?" As you answer that, keep in mind His formula in D&C 93:1: "Verily, thus saith the Lord: It shall come to pass that every soul who forsaketh his sins and cometh unto me, and calleth on my name, and obeyeth my voice, and keepeth my commandments, shall see my face and know that I am." Here Christ is but reiterating the message of the Book of Mormon.

Then how do you repent? I was asked about idolatry among the Saints. Anything that separates you from the Lamb of God is an idol. Cast it aside and come to Him. Why we have idols between us and the Lord is as different as one person is from another. Almost without exception, it comes as a result of a false tradition handed down. Your false traditions are based on your life's experiences while another's false traditions are based on theirs. No matter what they are or how they were acquired, whatever separates Christ from you must be set aside.

Come to HIM. Not to me or any other. Only He can save you.

No wonder that after making great promises to the gentiles, *if they will but repent*, the angel cries out "wo be unto the Gentiles!" They won't receive: 1) the Gospel, neither 2) the testimony of Jesus, neither 3) the prophets sent to warn them and the message given to them, neither 4) the everlasting covenant offered to them.

Will you?

It's amazing the power (or influence) of one word: repent. There is quite a linguistic history of this one word. It comes from French *penitire* (to regret), from the Latin *poenitire* (make sorry), and *poene* (pain, punishment, penalty). Some say that it was used when translating to keep "the masses" in constant subjection to the (Catholic) Church. Back in the day, you could pull out your purse and "pay" for sins, or you could do penitence (self punishment) by whipping yourself or whatever. It's interesting how these "negative" Gentile definitions have worked their way into how view repentance today.

Contrast that with the word used in the Greek translation of the Bible: Metanoia (meta meaning change or turn, as in metamorphosis; and noia meaning mind or heart, as in paranoia). The Greek term for repentance, metanoia, denotes a change of mind, a reorientation, a fundamental transformation of outlook, of an individual's vision of the world and of her/himself, and a new way of loving others and the Universe. It involves, not mere regret of past evil but a recognition by a person of a darkened vision of her/his own condition, in which sin, by separating her/him from Deity, has reduced her/him to a divided, autonomous existence, depriving her/him of both her/his natural glory and freedom.

There is also an Aramaic version of repentance: *tubu*. It means return or come home.

1 Nephi 14:7

> "For the time cometh, saith the Lamb of God, that I will
> work a great and a marvelous work among the children of
> men; a work which shall be everlasting, either on the one hand
> or on the other—either to the convincing of them unto peace
> and life eternal, or unto the deliverance of them to the hard-
> ness of their hearts and the blindness of their minds unto
> their being brought down into captivity, and also into destruc-
> tion, both temporally and spiritually, according to the captivity
> of the devil, of which I have spoken."

There will be a time when the accounts will all be settled. Everything will become everlasting and people will either inherit eternal
lives and move forward, or they will return to be destroyed both
temporally and spiritually again. Joseph Smith commented in the
King Follett Discourse about the process of gaining exaltation. He
said, "you must begin with the first, and go on until you learn all the
principles of exaltation. But it will be a great while after you have
passed through the veil before you will have learned them. It is not
all to be comprehended in this world; it will be a great work to learn
our salvation and exaltation even beyond the grave."

Death and hell are the devil's domain. He's the god of that world,
and since we have death and suffering here, he calls himself the god
of this world. Those who come here are subject to his buffeting, and
his will. They are tormented, tempted, troubled, and then they die.
While captive here, they endure the insults of the flesh, and the difficulties of trying to find their way back to God.

Those who find Him, however, are able to receive "peace and life
eternal" through a higher way. The devil is bound for them, and they
are able to be "added upon" by the experiences and difficulties here.

All of this is called a "great and marvelous work" to occur
"among the children of men." Note it isn't the "remnant" or the
"gentiles" but "the children of men." Why so? Is everyone invited?

Why, if everyone is invited, will it largely only affect the "remnant," and the "gentiles," and the "scattered Israel," and "Jews?" What about the "heathen," since they are also "the children of men?" Don't they also have part in the first resurrection?[489] Will even some of them be included among the "children of men" who behold this "great and marvelous work?"

Why is it **"everlasting"** whether it is for "peace and eternal life" or "captivity and destruction?" Isn't *"Everlasting"* another of God's names just like *"Eternal"* and *"Endless?"*[490] If so, then what does the "everlasting peace and eternal life," and "everlasting captivity and destruction" really involve? [You really need to read that paper I've been emailing out if you haven't read it already.]

Why does God want us to respond to His message and get out of this Telestial Kingdom into another, higher kingdom? Why does He want us to become like Him? How is this experience able to make us more like Him?

If one is involved in the "continuation of the lives"[491] is that distant and second-hand? Or does God (or the Gods) get involved directly with His/Their children?[492]

---

[489] D&C 45:54 "And then shall the heathen nations be redeemed, and they that knew no law shall have part in the first resurrection; and it shall be tolerable for them."

[490] D&C 19:10–12 "For, behold, the mystery of godliness, how great is it! For, behold, I am endless, and the punishment which is given from my hand is endless punishment, for Endless is my name. Wherefore—Eternal punishment is God's punishment. Endless punishment is God's punishment."

[491] D&C 132:22 "For strait is the gate, and narrow the way that leadeth unto the exaltation and continuation of the lives, and few there be that find it, because ye receive me not in the world neither do ye know me."

[492] Abraham 3:24–25 "And there stood one among them that was like unto God, and he said unto those who were with him: We will go down, for there is space there, and we will take of these materials, and we will make an earth whereon these may dwell; And we will prove them herewith, to see if they will do all things whatsoever the Lord their God shall command them;"

What causes "hardness of their hearts?" What causes "blindness of their eyes?" Why are those whose hearts are hard unable to receive Christ? Why are those who are blind unwilling to see Him?

This cycle of inviting people to come to the Lamb of God has been going on for some time now. When mankind generally rejected Him after the time of Noah, there was a chosen people who were given a sacred tradition. Ultimately they got proud, failed to recognize Him when He came, rejected His message, and killed Him. Gentiles converted and became the inheritors of His teachings. Then the gentiles began to persecute the previously chosen people for generations. In this verse the gentiles are remembered, sacred materials are entrusted to them with an obligation to spread that sacred material back to the earlier chosen people. However, for the gentiles to be able to accomplish this they need to hold onto the sacred materials and teachings. You simply can't spread abroad what you've failed to retain.

If the gentiles let the sacred materials and teachings fall into disuse, forfeit their priesthood by draining it of any power, and have nothing to offer the previously chosen people, then the gentiles will be cast off, trodden under foot and destroyed, as we have earlier seen.

This verse reminds us what is at stake: Eternity. Or at least God's judgment. It'll be embarrassing to return to Him unimproved and un-added upon. Particularly when His hand was stretched out to us all the day long. Gentiles who do as they are asked are given all the blessings of the chosen people. Those who do not are rejected and destroyed.

As a friend and I discussed last week, Hindu's advise us to get off the wheel and return to God. They may be onto something with that thought. One eternal round, indeed . . .

1 Nephi 14:8–9

"And it came to pass that when the angel had spoken these words, he said unto me: Rememberest thou the covenants of the Father unto the house of Israel? I said unto him, Yea. And it came to pass that he said unto me: Look, and behold that great and abominable church, which is the mother of abominations, whose founder is the devil."

The dialogue between Nephi and the angel is interrupted. Nephi is brought into the dialogue as the angel interrupts and asks Nephi a question. You should ask yourself why an angel behaves in this manner? Why interrupt the teaching by asking Nephi questions?

And what a question it is: " Rememberest thou the covenants of the Father unto the house of Israel?" Once again, it is the "covenants of the Father" that is important and controls what is being taught and all history involved. It remains not only "in the beginning" but throughout "is the Word of God." Consider how broadly the "Word" of God may be applied:

- Christ is the "Word of God" because He lived and did all in conformity with the will of the Father.[493]

- All of creation came into being because of the Father's Word, or power.[494]

- Christ's spoken Word had such power as to astonish onlookers.[495]

---

[493] 3 Nephi 11:11 "And behold, I am the light and the life of the world; and I have drunk out of that bitter cup which the Father hath given me, and have glorified the Father in taking upon me the sins of the world, in which I have suffered the will of the Father in all things from the beginning."

[494] Mormon 9:17 "Who shall say that it was not a miracle that by his word the heaven and the earth should be; and by the power of his word man was created of the dust of the earth; and by the power of his word have miracles been wrought?"

[495] Luke 4:32, 36 "And they were astonished at his doctrine: for his word was with power. . . . And they were all amazed, and spake among themselves, saying, What a word is this! for with authority and power he commandeth the unclean spirits, and they come out."

- Nothing of power hereafter will exist unless obtained by the Father's Word.[496]

- Moses made water come forth from the rock by the Father's Word.[497]

- Joseph Smith was able to bring the Book of Mormon forth because of the Father's word.[498]

- His Word is "quick" and "powerful" and can cut like a two-edged sword.[499]

- It was by this Word of God that Enoch had power to hold at defiance the armies of nations.[500]

Without the "covenants of the Father" the best laid plans, the most noble aspirations, the desire to have Zion return, will all fail. It will return by a covenant or not at all. It will return in strict conformity with His covenant, His Word, and not according to the vain desires of men.

---

[496] D&C 132:13 "And everything that is in the world, whether it be ordained of men, by thrones, or principalities, or powers, or things of name, whatsoever they may be, that are not by me or by my word, saith the Lord, shall be thrown down, and shall not remain after men are dead, neither in nor after the resurrection, saith the Lord your God."

[497] 1 Nephi 17:29 "Yea, and ye also know that Moses, by his word according to the power of God which was in him, smote the rock, and there came forth water, that the children of Israel might quench their thirst."

[498] Mormon 8:16 "And blessed be he that shall bring this thing to light; for it shall be brought out of darkness unto light, according to the word of God; yea, it shall be brought out of the earth, and it shall shine forth out of darkness, and come unto the knowledge of the people; and it shall be done by the power of God."

[499] D&C 11:2 "Behold, I am God; give heed to my word, which is quick and powerful, sharper than a two-edged sword, to the dividing asunder of both joints and marrow; therefore give heed unto my word."

[500] Moses 7:13 "And so great was the faith of Enoch that he led the people of God, and their enemies came to battle against them; and he spake the word of the Lord, and the earth trembled, and the mountains fled, even according to his command; and the rivers of water were turned out of their course; and the roar of the lions was heard out of the wilderness; and all nations feared greatly, so powerful was the word of Enoch, and so great was the power of the language which God had given him."

The angel is setting up a contrast for Nephi. First he asks if Nephi remembers the Father's covenants, to which Nephi responds that he does remember them. Now, often in the Book of Mormon the word "remember" is used to mean "keep." If that is the way it is used here, then Nephi is being asked if he keeps the covenants of the Father, so far as they apply to him. Using that meaning, the angel is inquiring about Nephi's worthiness to receive more. Or, in other words: "Do you follow the Father's commandments?" "Yes." "Then I will show you more." Reminding Nephi that the only reason he is beholding these things is because of his obedience and sacrifice. Or, to put it more plainly, reminding US that this kind of information and learning from angelic ministers comes as a consequence of following everything taught to you before. You receive more because you follow what you already have.

Now, after the inquiry and answer, the contrast is shown—On the one hand: The Covenants of the Father. On the other hand: the Great and Abominable Church.

God's covenants are strict and apply in a very precise manner. The great whore uses religion to promise to all people everywhere their desires for being comforted in their sins. The great and abominable church does not want you to forsake your sins, but to retain them and expect God will forgive and overlook them. The great and abominable church wants you to believe that the way is broad and many will enter into exaltation. This whore teaches that no matter your conduct, the odds are you are going to be exalted. So eat, drink and be merry. If God is going to be upset He will merely beat you with a few stripes and promote you into the kingdom of God anyway.[501]

This contrast is drawn for Nephi because these are two extremes. Both of them are religious. One is founded on a true religion, the other is a false religion. One follows the Father's covenants and will result in God's promised results. The other follows the commandments of men who have mingled their own philosophies with scripture so that their doctrines are all corrupt. They share a vocabulary, but nothing else. For one, to "repent" is to return to God's presence, for the other "repent" is to satisfy institutional demands and surrender to control by others. The angel uses the contrast because this is where mankind finds themselves. We live between these two choices. Our eternal consequences hinge on how we choose. Among all sects there are good people who are blinded by the craftiness of deceitful men.[502] Even though they may be honorable, by surrendering to deceit they forfeit the crown.[503]

This contrast is shown to Nephi, and shared by him with us, because we are always facing the dilemma of choosing between those who will promise you everything and give you nothing, and those who warn you to repent, as a result of which you may receive everything. Oddly, mankind seems to prefer the former.

---

[501] 2 Nephi 28:8 "And there shall also be many which shall say: Eat, drink, and be merry; nevertheless, fear God—he will justify in committing a little sin; yea, lie a little, take the advantage of one because of his words, dig a pit for thy neighbor; there is no harm in this; and do all these things, for tomorrow we die; and if it so be that we are guilty, God will beat us with a few stripes, and at last we shall be saved in the kingdom of God."

[502] D&C 123:12 "For there are many yet on the earth among all sects, parties, and denominations, who are blinded by the subtle craftiness of men, whereby they lie in wait to deceive, and who are only kept from the truth because they know not where to find it—"

[503] D&C 76:74–76 "Who received not the testimony of Jesus in the flesh, but afterwards received it. These are they who are honorable men of the earth, who were blinded by the craftiness of men. These are they who receive of his glory, but not of his fulness."

1 Nephi 14:10

"And he said unto me: Behold there are save two churches only; the one is the church of the Lamb of God, and the other is the church of the devil; wherefore, whoso belongeth not to the church of the Lamb of God belongeth to that great church, which is the mother of abominations; and she is the whore of all the earth."

There are and always have been two churches only. One is true. Its members belong to the Lamb of God. The Lamb, and their Father.

Either you belong to the elect family of Christ, the Church of the Firstborn, or you don't. All other religions and philosophies are false. Read again the description of those who are saved. (See *What's in a name?*) There are only "two," and one of them is not the Catholic Church, nor the Presbyterian Church, nor the Lutheran Church, nor The Church of Jesus Christ of Latter-day Saints. However, the ordinances received through The Church of Jesus Christ of Latter-day Saints are expected for those who belong to "the church of the Lamb of God," but there is not a complete overlap of the "church of the Lamb of God" and The Church of Jesus Christ of Latter-day Saints.

Therefore, based on what Nephi says above, unless we are part of that body of believers whose Father is Christ, and who posses a covenant from Him that they will be His, we belong to the whore of all the earth, a church of abominations. Those who are believers are they who He has declared to His Father " . . . having been true and faithful in all things."

The other and all-inclusive great church is comprised of all philosophies, all belief systems, all unbelief systems, all rationalizations, all theories and vanities that distract people from repenting and following Christ. These vary from very good things that are uplifting, and possess even great portions of truth, to the degrading and perverse. This all-inclusive church is a "whore" because she is completely indiscriminate and open for all to have her acceptance and affection. She welcomes you. The only requirement being that you have false beliefs.

She will make you rich, or she will make you covet riches. If she gives them to you it is to corrupt you. If she withholds them from you, it is so you will lust and envy what you do not have.

Look at her list of trade goods, given in the description of her fall by John the Revelator:

> "And the merchants of the earth shall weep and mourn over her; for no man buyeth their merchandise any more: The merchandise of gold, and silver, and precious stones, and of pearls, and fine linen, and purple, and silk, and scarlet, and all thyine wood, and all manner vessels of ivory, and all manner vessels of most precious wood, and of brass, and iron, and marble, And cinnamon, and odours, and ointments, and frankincense, and wine, and oil, and fine flour, and wheat, and beasts, and sheep, and horses, and chariots, and slaves, and souls of men." (Revelation 18:11–13.)

The final two on the list are the reason for the other items. The earlier ones lead inevitably to slavery and loss of the souls of men. The devil, who founded her, is not interested in anything other than slavery and the loss of your soul.

The great illusion of a whore is to imagine she likes you. To imagine she cares for you. To imagine she desires what you desire and is cooperating with you because she finds you attractive, appealing, and that you fulfill her longing. It is a lie, an illusion and a fraud. Her bodily diseases are less virulent than her contamination of the soul. Empty, false, vain and foolish thoughts occupy the imagination of those who have intercourse with the great whore. She prefers the lie, relies on it. You would not be her customer if not for the lies.

What an amazing congruence of sexual images and religious failing have been given to us by Nephi and John the Revelator. How apt!

How perfect! Imagining something that is degrading and debilitating to be sacred. It is a work of a god or a devil. And of course it is for us to decide between them.

The whore does have her allures, doesn't she? How many of us are in her embrace, speaking of love and Jesus and the joy of the Saints, while remaining wretched, poor, foolish and lost? She offers you vanity as a religion. "Vanity" because it is vain, or without any effect to save, i.e., without power. Only a form of godliness, nothing real.

Such powerful deception as is implied in these verses demands our attention. It ought to force us forward to seek and obtain a more sure word of prophecy, so we **know our God and covenant directly with Him**. It should make us refuse all the imitations, all the deceptions, all those who pretend to speak truth, and instead demand that true messengers be sent from whom we can be taught further light and knowledge.

There's the rub, isn't it? How to tell the one from the other? A concealed and veiled resurrected Christ laid aside all glory and walked with two of His disciples for approximately seven miles on the day of His resurrection. After His departure, the one asked the other: **"And they said one to another, Did not our heart burn within us, while he talked with us by the way, and while he opened to us the scriptures?"** (Luke 24:32.) Undoubtedly the reason they already knew it was Him was because truth has power that vanity does not. Therefore, it appears that before our eyes are opened, we must determine truth first. I've written about this in the Appendix to *Eighteen Verses*.

Interesting cause and effect. Interesting the Lord would open the scriptures to touch their hearts. What a powerful pattern the Lord has given for those who follow Him.

1 Nephi 14:11–12

"And it came to pass that I looked and beheld the whore of all the earth, and she sat upon many waters; and she had dominion over all the earth, among all nations, kindreds, tongues, and people. And it came to pass that I beheld the church of the Lamb of God, and its numbers were few, because of the wickedness and abominations of the whore who sat upon many waters; nevertheless, I beheld that the church of the Lamb, who were the saints of God, were also upon all the face of the earth; and their dominions upon the face of the earth were small, because of the wickedness of the great whore whom I saw."

The whore has "dominion" over all. All nations. All kindreds. All tongues. All people. She has dominion over them all. What does "dominion" mean?

Notice the "church of the Lamb of God" are referred to as "the Saints of God."

The Saints on the other hand, were "few" in number by comparison with the great dominion of the whore.

The Saints numbers are few because of "the wickedness and abominations of the whore." How would the whore's wickedness and abominations cause the Saints to be "few" in number? What trouble must the Saints overcome because of the whore's widespread wickedness? What challenges must the Saints overcome because of the whore's universal abominations? How do they "overcome" these challenges?[504]

What does it mean the whore "sits upon many waters?"[505] Why are they likened to water?[506]

---

[504] D&C 76:53 "And who overcome by faith, and are sealed by the Holy Spirit of promise, which the Father sheds forth upon all those who are just and true."

[505] Revelation 17:15 "And he saith unto me, The waters which thou sawest, where the whore sitteth, are peoples, and multitudes, and nations, and tongues."

[506] Genesis 49:4 "Unstable as water, thou shalt not excel; because thou wentest up to thy father's bed; then defiledst thou it: he went up to my couch."

Note the Saints are also "upon all the face of the earth" but are not said to be "sitting upon many waters." They do have, however, "dominions" (in the plural). Why is the whore's dominion singular, while the Saint's plural? The whore's control is one, but the Saints are divided into sub-grouPsalms Why? Will they be led by various prophets from various locations?[507]

This fragmentation of the Saints is set in a time frame of this prophecy and it will not last. However it will exist before the wrath poured out upon the whore begins.

Why is the whore much more successful than the church of the Lamb of God? Or, more importantly, is the number of those involved in these two different cultures any indication of their relative standing before the Lord? If not, then what matter? Is it the quantity of those who are following a particular creed or organization, or the quality of the knowledge some few possess of the Lord?

Will getting more people to join the Church change the outcome of this prophecy from Nephi?

What is important, then, for those who want to be on the right side of this divide? How do they become one of the "few" who are Saints belonging to the Lamb of God?

How should "success" be defined? By numbers, buildings, activity and wealth or possession of knowledge of Christ? If success has nothing to do with numbers, buildings, activity and wealth, why do we concern ourselves with them? If it has something to do with knowledge of Christ, why are so few able to declare they know Him? Who can state they have seen Him? Who can testify as a witness of Him? How successful have we been in distributing the knowledge of the Son of God?

---

[507] D&C 133:26 "And they who are in the north countries shall come in remembrance before the Lord; and their prophets shall hear his voice, and shall no longer stay themselves; and they shall smite the rocks, and the ice shall flow down at their presence."

Where should our efforts be focused? Is the Book of Mormon important in accomplishing what the Lord expects from His Saints?

What interesting information Nephi has given us in this verse. But it gets more interesting as it proceeds further . . .

1 Nephi 14:13

"And it came to pass that I beheld that the great mother of abominations did gather together multitudes upon the face of all the earth, among all the nations of the Gentiles, to fight against the Lamb of God."

Did you notice that? The whore is also a "mother?" Why is that? What do we learn from that bit of information? Just how loyal will the deceived be to the institution they regard as their great mother? It's no wonder they react with such hostility at the threat posed by the Lamb of God.

Now did you notice also that the fight is against "the Lamb of God" and not the "Saints?" They are opposed to Christ and are going to fight against Him.

This is akin to David's response to Goliath:

"Thou comest to me with a sword, and with a spear, and with a shield: but **I come to thee in the name of the Lord of hosts, the God of the armies of Israel, whom thou hast defied. This day will the Lord deliver thee into mine hand**; and I will smite thee, and take thine head from thee; and I will give the carcasses of the host of the Philistines this day unto the fowls of the air, and to the wild beasts of the earth; that all the earth may know that there is a God in Israel. And all this assembly shall know that **the Lord saveth not with sword and spear: for the battle is the Lord's, and he will give you into our hands**." (1 Samuel 17:45–47)

David knew the fight was between the Lord and Goliath, not between him and Goliath. Therefore the advantage was all the Lord's.

The coming fight will be between those who regard the worldly order as their mother, and the Lamb of God.

Did you notice also that the great mother whore includes "all the nations of the Gentiles?" Meaning that included among this great false order will be the United States, the greatest of the Gentile nations. We've been told in modern revelation that along with all other nations, the United States will be destroyed.[508] We disbelieve this and hope to save the nation. We want to follow the counsel of the Lord to make friends of the mammon of unrighteousness, that when we fail we may be received into everlasting habitations.[509] Your affiliations here will serve you here, but you will not be trusted with true riches.[510] The result is that we have no choice but to flee.

Well, the great whore wants to defeat the Lamb, but she cannot get access to Him. She must settle for destroying His teachings, His doctrines, His ordinances. She will target these truths because they link the Lord to some few who are here. She will at every turn deceive, mislead, corrupt and discourage. She understands that the fight is with the Lord, but to destroy Him she must destroy all that testifies truthfully of Him.

All that is corrupt and corrupted is welcomed by her. All that fails to redeem the souls of men and return them to the Lord's presence is welcomed here in her dominion. She will confer tax benefits, hon-

---

[508] D&C 87:6 "And thus, with the sword and by bloodshed the inhabitants of the earth shall mourn; and with famine, and plague, and earthquake, and the thunder of heaven, and the fierce and vivid lightning also, shall the inhabitants of the earth be made to feel the wrath, and indignation, and chastening hand of an Almighty God, until the consumption decreed hath made a full end of all nations;"

[509] Luke 16:9 "And I say unto you, Make to yourselves friends of the mammon of unrighteousness; that, when ye fail, they may receive you into everlasting habitations."

[510] Luke 16:11 "If therefore ye have not been faithful in the unrighteous mammon, who will commit to your trust the true riches?"

ors, protection and awards upon those who cannot teach the doctrines that save. Wealth will amass, privileges will be given, and the great whore's dominion will expand to include "all churches" in these last days.[511] Persecution is the heritage of the righteous because this world has no part in Christ.[512] When the righteous are no longer persecuted, and the honors and awards of men begin to be bestowed upon any religion, you may know they have made friends of the children of mammon.

She cannot destroy Him, so she will turn her anger upon those who preserve His doctrine, His teachings, His truths and destroy them that He may be cast out of this world. This is her plan.

But this battle is between principalities and dominions involving spiritual wickedness in high places, and not just flesh and blood.[513] Therefore we should fear not, because the battle is, always was, and always will be the Lord's.[514]

1 Nephi 14:14

"And it came to pass that I, Nephi, beheld the power of the Lamb of God, that it descended upon the saints of the

---

[511] 2 Nephi 28:12–14 "Because of pride, and because of false teachers, and false doctrine, their churches have become corrupted, and their churches are lifted up; because of pride they are puffed up. They rob the poor because of their fine sanctuaries; they rob the poor because of their fine clothing; and they persecute the meek and the poor in heart, because in their pride they are puffed up. They wear stiff necks and high heads; yea, and because of pride, and wickedness, and abominations, and whoredoms, they have all gone astray save it be a few, who are the humble followers of Christ; nevertheless, they are led, that in many instances they do err because they are taught by the precepts of men."

[512] John 14:30 "Hereafter I will not talk much with you: for the prince of this world cometh, and hath nothing in me."

[513] Ephesians 6:12 "For we wrestle not against flesh and blood, but against principalities, against powers, against the rulers of the darkness of this world, against spiritual wickedness in high places."

[514] D&C 105:14 "For behold, I do not require at their hands to fight the battles of Zion; for, as I said in a former commandment, even so will I fulfil—I will fight your battles."

church of the Lamb, and upon the covenant people of the
Lord, who were scattered upon all the face of the earth; and
they were armed with righteousness and with the power of
God in great glory."

Once the whore sets about to destroy the Lamb of God, He does
not remain in His pavilion away. He takes up the fight for His Saints.

What is the "power of the Lamb of God?"

Why does this "power" "descend" upon the Saints?

Why are there two groups identified, "the Saints of the Lamb of
God," and also, "upon the covenant people of the Lord?" Are these
the same or two different groups? If two, what is to happen in this
descending of "power" upon these two?

Why are the "Saints" and the "covenant people" both "scattered
upon all the face of the earth?" Why are they not gathered together
in one place?

What does it mean to be "armed with righteousness?"

Why are "righteousness" and "the power of God" two different things?

Do the "covenant people" have to have "righteousness" to re-
ceive the "power of God?" Are they blessed for the covenant's sake?
What about the others? Who are "righteous" and their protection?
Are they protected for righteousness sake?

Assuming the "power of God" is given to protect these groups,
do they need munitions? Do they need intercontinental firepower?
Do they need to form an army for their own defense?

What is the "power of God in great glory?" Will the children of
the great whore be able to behold this "power of God in great
glory," or will it be hidden from them? If hidden, will they sense
something? Will fear fall upon them that they flee from the presence

of this glory? Wasn't that the case with Daniel's friends?[515] Wasn't that the case with the companions of Saul?[516] Will Zion not be protected by this "power of God?"[517] If it is to be like the days of Noah,[518] then won't there be someone who can speak the word of God and mountains flee, armies held at defiance, and rivers turned out of their course?[519]

Will the same things happen that happened at the time of the great flood? If so, how much relevance does the history from Enoch through Noah have to our day? Should we be familiar with that pattern to know how the pattern may repeat itself?

What can you do to be numbered with those who will be spared? Does the known history of the antediluvians tell you anything about how you need to prepare? Since Enoch had 365 years to develop a people who were worthy to be spared, how much greater a work will it be to prepare now that life spans are generally less than 90 years? How great a work lies before you?

---

[515] Daniel 10:7 "And I Daniel alone saw the vision: for the men that were with me saw not the vision; but a great quaking fell upon them, so that they fled to hide themselves."

[516] JST–Acts 9:7 "And *they who were journeying* with him *saw indeed the light, and were afraid; but they heard not the voice of him who spake to him.*"

[517] D&C 45:70 "And it shall be said among the wicked: Let us not go up to battle against Zion, for the inhabitants of Zion are terrible; wherefore we cannot stand."

[518] Luke 17:26–27 "And as it was in the days of Noe, so shall it be also in the days of the Son of man. They did eat, they drank, they married wives, they were given in marriage, until the day that Noe entered into the ark, and the flood came, and destroyed them all."

[519] Moses 7:13 "And so great was the faith of Enoch that he led the people of God, and their enemies came to battle against them; and he spake the word of the Lord, and the earth trembled, and the mountains fled, even according to his command; and the rivers of water were turned out of their course; and the roar of the lions was heard out of the wilderness; and all nations feared greatly, so powerful was the word of Enoch, and so great was the power of the language which God had given him."

1 Nephi 14:15–16

"And it came to pass that I beheld that the wrath of God was poured out upon that great and abominable church, insomuch that there were wars and rumors of wars among all the nations and kindreds of the earth. And as there began to be wars and rumors of wars among all the nations which belonged to the mother of abominations, the angel spake unto me, saying: Behold, the wrath of God is upon the mother of harlots; and behold, thou seest all these things—"

God's wrath is "poured out" and takes a specific form: "wars and rumors of wars among all the nations and kindreds." People go to war. The "wicked kill the wicked."[520]

The wicked get to destroy one another, but they do not get to destroy the righteous.[521]

The destruction of God's judgment will be "among all the nations which belonged to the mother of abominations." But that was all nations, was it not? Therefore, what nation will not be at war in this coming day?

The angel makes a point of stating what Nephi is beholding: "Behold, the wrath of God is upon the mother of harlots." How is this God's wrath? The answer is that when God is angry, He with-

---

[520] D&C 63:33 "I have sworn in my wrath, and decreed wars upon the face of the earth, and the wicked shall slay the wicked, and fear shall come upon every man;"
Proverbs 11:5 "The righteousness of the perfect shall direct his way: but the wicked shall fall by his own wickedness."
Mormon 4:5 "But, behold, the judgments of God will overtake the wicked; and it is by the wicked that the wicked are punished; for it is the wicked that stir up the hearts of the children of men unto bloodshed."

[521] 1 Nephi 22:16 "For the time soon cometh that the fulness of the wrath of God shall be poured out upon all the children of men; for he will not suffer that the wicked shall destroy the righteous."

draws His spirit.[522] And when He withdraws His spirit from one, He generally pours it out on another.[523] When His spirit withdraws, men are left to their natural, carnal state, filled with envy, jealousy, covetousness, ambition and greed. When the heavens become silent, the judgments of God follow.[524]

This is the means by which the tares ripen in iniquity, and the wheat ripens in righteousness. However, to preserve the spirit among those to be saved in the last days, it will be necessary for the same priesthood, the same calling, to be in possession of those to be pre-

---

[522] Helaman 6:35 "And thus we see that the Spirit of the Lord began to withdraw from the Nephites, because of the wickedness and the hardness of their hearts."
Helaman 13:8 "Therefore, thus saith the Lord: Because of the hardness of the hearts of the people of the Nephites, except they repent I will take away my word from them, and I will withdraw my Spirit from them, and I will suffer them no longer, and I will turn the hearts of their brethren against them."

[523] Helaman 6:34–36 "And thus we see that the Nephites did begin to dwindle in unbelief, and grow in wickedness and abominations, while the Lamanites began to grow exceedingly in the knowledge of their God; yea, they did begin to keep his statutes and commandments, and to walk in truth and uprightness before him. And thus we see that the Spirit of the Lord began to withdraw from the Nephites, because of the wickedness and the hardness of their hearts. And thus we see that the Lord began to pour out his Spirit upon the Lamanites, because of their easiness and willingness to believe in his words."

[524] Revelation 8:1 "And when he had opened the seventh seal, there was silence in heaven about the space of half an hour."
D&C 88:95 "And there shall be silence in heaven for the space of half an hour; and immediately after shall the curtain of heaven be unfolded, as a scroll is unfolded after it is rolled up, and the face of the Lord shall be unveiled;"

served. Otherwise they can't ripen into wheat.[525] For the wheat are destined for Celestial Glory and eternal life.[526] This cannot be realized without a covenant[527] and the testimony of Jesus to them.[528]

How should we each proceed?

---

[525] D&C 86:1–11 "Verily, thus saith the Lord unto you my servants, concerning the parable of the wheat and of the tares: Behold, verily I say, the field was the world, and the apostles were the sowers of the seed; And after they have fallen asleep the great persecutor of the church, the apostate, the whore, even Babylon, that maketh all nations to drink of her cup, in whose hearts the enemy, even Satan, sitteth to reign—behold he soweth the tares; wherefore, the tares choke the wheat and drive the church into the wilderness. But behold, in the last days, even now while the Lord is beginning to bring forth the word, and the blade is springing up and is yet tender—Behold, verily I say unto you, the angels are crying unto the Lord day and night, who are ready and waiting to be sent forth to reap down the fields; But the Lord saith unto them, pluck not up the tares while the blade is yet tender (for verily your faith is weak), lest you destroy the wheat also. Therefore, let the wheat and the tares grow together until the harvest is fully ripe; then ye shall first gather out the wheat from among the tares, and after the gathering of the wheat, behold and lo, the tares are bound in bundles, and the field remaineth to be burned. Therefore, thus saith the Lord unto you, with whom the priesthood hath continued through the lineage of your fathers—For ye are lawful heirs, according to the flesh, and have been hid from the world with Christ in God—Therefore your life and the priesthood have remained, and must needs remain through you and your lineage until the restoration of all things spoken by the mouths of all the holy prophets since the world began. Therefore, blessed are ye if ye continue in my goodness, a light unto the Gentiles, and through this priesthood, a savior unto my people Israel. The Lord hath said it. Amen."

[526] D&C 101:65 "Therefore, I must gather together my people, according to the parable of the wheat and the tares, that the wheat may be secured in the garners to possess eternal life, and be crowned with celestial glory, when I shall come in the kingdom of my Father to reward every man according as his work shall be;"

[527] D&C 132:20 "Then shall they be gods, because they have no end; therefore shall they be from everlasting to everlasting, because they continue; then shall they be above all, because all things are subject unto them. Then shall they be gods, because they have all power, and the angels are subject unto them."

[528] D&C 76:51–57 "They are they who received the testimony of Jesus, and believed on his name and were baptized after the manner of his burial, being buried in the water in his name, and this according to the commandment which he has given—That by keeping the commandments they might be washed and cleansed from all their sins, and receive the Holy Spirit by the laying on of the hands of him who is ordained and sealed unto this power; And who overcome by faith, and are sealed by the Holy Spirit of promise, which the Father sheds forth upon all those who are just and true. They are they who are the church of the Firstborn. They are they into whose hands the Father has given all things—They are they who are priests and kings, who have received of his fulness, and of his glory; And are priests of the Most High, after the order of Melchizedek, which was after the order of Enoch, which was after the order of the Only Begotten Son."

Can anyone make you "wheat" if you do not the things the Lord commands you to do?[529]

Can anyone give you "oil" for your lamp?

What is your responsibility to obtain these things?

When the time comes that all nations of the earth are at war with one another as the means for the Lord's wrath to be poured out upon the wicked, what is the role of the righteous? Will they join in the battle? Will they be spared?[530]

Why does the Lord not require the righteous to shed the blood of the wicked? Why would He use the wicked to destroy the wicked?

If His spirit withdraws from the world, but remains with His Saints, what peril is there if the Saints don't also withdraw from the world?

Will citizenship in both Babylon and Zion be possible? Will Zion need a bank?

1 Nephi 14:17

"And when the day cometh that the wrath of God is poured out upon the mother of harlots, which is the great and abominable church of all the earth, whose founder is the devil, then, at that day, the work of the Father shall commence, in preparing the way for the fulfilling of his covenants, which he hath made to his people who are of the house of Israel."

Now we get some indication of timing. A great deal has been described, but the timing of the events has been left out until now.

---

[529] Luke 6:46 "And why call ye me, Lord, Lord, and do not the things which I say?"

[530] D&C 45:68–71 "And it shall come to pass among the wicked, that every man that will not take his sword against his neighbor must needs flee unto Zion for safety. And there shall be gathered unto it out of every nation under heaven; and it shall be the only people that shall not be at war one with another. And it shall be said among the wicked: Let us not go up to battle against Zion, for the inhabitants of Zion are terrible; wherefore we cannot stand. And it shall come to pass that the righteous shall be gathered out from among all nations, and shall come to Zion, singing with songs of everlasting joy."

The "day cometh that the wrath of God is poured out upon the mother of harlots"—that is, when the great and abominable church is caught up in worldwide violence, every nation at war with its neighbor or within itself. It is when those events are underway "the work of the Father shall commence" to fulfill all the prior commitments and covenants.

First, the great whore will reel and stagger as a drunkard, drunk with her own blood.

Then the "work of the Father" will "commence." What does it mean to "commence?" Why choose such a desperate hour to begin?

Are there signs of this international and internal violence already afoot? Is the work of the Father now commenced?

The "commencement" of the work is "for the fulfilling of His covenants." What does it mean to "fulfill?" Will every whit of His covenants be all completed, all finished, all kept?[531]

Interestingly, the "fulfilling of His covenants which He hath made to His people who are of the house of Israel" is not divided into "remnant" and "gentile." At the time when His final work begins, all of "the house of Israel" will be remembered, in whatever scattered place they may be found. Why the change? Why no longer focus upon the "remnant" and "Jew" and "gentile" and "scattered house of Israel?" Why does He now call them all "his people?"

Do the fractures heal? Do the divided groups come together at last? Will the scattered, lost and forgotten remains of Israel be found throughout the world?[532] Will the results be a restoration of all Israel,

---

[531] D&C 1:38 "What I the Lord have spoken, I have spoken, and I excuse not myself; and though the heavens and the earth pass away, my word shall not pass away, but shall all be fulfilled, whether by mine own voice or by the voice of my servants, it is the same."

[532] Jacob 5:67–68 "And the branches of the natural tree will I graft in again into the natural tree; And the branches of the natural tree will I graft into the natural branches of the tree; and thus will I bring them together again, that they shall bring forth the natural fruit, and they shall be one."

no matter what group they may have been identified with previously?[533] Will these divided, but remembered people become one at last?[534]

How much purging will be needed to bring this to pass?[535]

If the work has begun, are there "servants" already here beginning to move the now wild branches back to their natural roots?[536] How does one respond and return to their natural roots? Who is

---

[533] Jacob 5:72–73 "And it came to pass that the servants did go and labor with their mights; and the Lord of the vineyard labored also with them; and they did obey the commandments of the Lord of the vineyard in all things. And there began to be the natural fruit again in the vineyard; and the natural branches began to grow and thrive exceedingly; and the wild branches began to be plucked off and to be cast away; and they did keep the root and the top thereof equal, according to the strength thereof."

[534] Jacob 5:74 "And thus they labored, with all diligence, according to the commandments of the Lord of the vineyard, even until the bad had been cast away out of the vineyard, and the Lord had preserved unto himself that the trees had become again the natural fruit; and they became like unto one body; and the fruits were equal; and the Lord of the vineyard had preserved unto himself the natural fruit, which was most precious unto him from the beginning."

[535] Jacob 5:71 "And the Lord of the vineyard said unto them: Go to, and labor in the vineyard, with your might. For behold, this is the last time that I shall nourish my vineyard; for the end is nigh at hand, and the season speedily cometh; and if ye labor with your might with me ye shall have joy in the fruit which I shall lay up unto myself against the time which will soon come."
D&C 45:68–71 "And it shall come to pass among the wicked, that every man that will not take his sword against his neighbor must needs flee unto Zion for safety. And there shall be gathered unto it out of every nation under heaven; and it shall be the only people that shall not be at war one with another. And it shall be said among the wicked: Let us not go up to battle against Zion, for the inhabitants of Zion are terrible; wherefore we cannot stand. And it shall come to pass that the righteous shall be gathered out from among all nations, and shall come to Zion, singing with songs of everlasting joy."
D&C 133:9–12 "And behold, and lo, this shall be their cry, and the voice of the Lord unto all people: Go ye forth unto the land of Zion, that the borders of my people may be enlarged, and that her stakes may be strengthened, and that Zion may go forth unto the regions round about. Yea, let the cry go forth among all people: Awake and arise and go forth to meet the Bridegroom; behold and lo, the Bridegroom cometh; go ye out to meet him. Prepare yourselves for the great day of the Lord. Watch, therefore, for ye know neither the day nor the hour. Let them, therefore, who are among the Gentiles flee unto Zion."

[536] Jacob 5:70 "And it came to pass that the Lord of the vineyard sent his servant; and the servant went and did as the Lord had commanded him, and brought other servants; and they were few."

the "tree of life?" How do we reattach ourselves to Him?[537] What of those who would have you attach yourselves to them, to become their disciples, to follow what they claim as their right to lead and control you?[538] How must they lead, if not by exercising control and dominion?[539]

[As long as we are in Section 121, there is an important but still unrecognized truth in that revelation. The caution in Section 121 about abuse is directed in whole at The Church of Jesus Christ of Latter-day Saints. Among other things, it is warning the LDS Church not to persecute the Lord's Saints, and thereby fight against God.[540] It has been traditionally interpreted by the LDS Church to the complete contrary. The LDS teaching turns the warning on its ear, and reads it to mean that you shouldn't fight against the LDS Church! The warning, however, is addressed to the Church and warning it to exercise caution, least they find themselves fighting against the Lord's

---

[537] John 15:1–6 "I am the true vine, and my Father is the husbandman. Every branch in me that beareth not fruit he taketh away: and every branch that beareth fruit, he purgeth it, that it may bring forth more fruit. Now ye are clean through the word which I have spoken unto you. Abide in me, and I in you. As the branch cannot bear fruit of itself, except it abide in the vine; no more can ye, except ye abide in me. I am the vine, ye are the branches: He that abideth in me, and I in him, the same bringeth forth much fruit: for without me ye can do nothing. If a man abide not in me, he is cast forth as a branch, and is withered; and men gather them, and cast them into the fire, and they are burned."

[538] D&C 121:36–37 "That the rights of the priesthood are inseparably connected with the powers of heaven, and that the powers of heaven cannot be controlled nor handled only upon the principles of righteousness. That they may be conferred upon us, it is true; but when we undertake to cover our sins, or to gratify our pride, our vain ambition, or to exercise control or dominion or compulsion upon the souls of the children of men, in any degree of unrighteousness, behold, the heavens withdraw themselves; the Spirit of the Lord is grieved; and when it is withdrawn, Amen to the priesthood or the authority of that man."

[539] D&C 121:41–42 "No power or influence can or ought to be maintained by virtue of the priesthood, only by persuasion, by long-suffering, by gentleness and meekness, and by love unfeigned; By kindness, and pure knowledge, which shall greatly enlarge the soul without hypocrisy, and without guile—"

[540] D&C 121:38 "Behold, ere he is aware, he is left unto himself, to kick against the pricks, to persecute the saints, and to fight against God."

Saints, and thereby in turn fighting against the Lord. Read it carefully. It is not a caution to you or me, but a caution to the LDS Church itself. It means that there may be Saints of God who are at times at odds with, or critical of the LDS Church. When that happens, the LDS Church is warned to refrain from persecuting them, or else they may find themselves fighting against God. It is an unnoticed warning because the traditional interpretation is used to give the LDS Church protection against criticism.]

Now we jump to late in His ministry where Christ is teaching the Nephites.

3 Nephi 21

3 Nephi 21:1

"And verily I say unto you, I give unto you a sign, that ye may know the time when these things shall be about to take place—that I shall gather in, from their long dispersion, my people, O house of Israel, and shall establish again among them my Zion;"

Christ is telling the Nephites (and us) about timing. He will provide a "sign" to those who watch for such things. Contrary to what you've heard all your life about "signs," they are and always have been part of the true Gospel. They invariably follow faith, but do not and never have produced faith.[541] There are examples of signs throughout God's dealings with those who follow Him. (See, e.g., Helaman 14:4; Ezekiel 24:24; Exodus 10:2; Acts 2:22, among many others.) *We* are supposed to see signs, that we may know God is dealing with *us*.[542]

---

[541] D&C 63:9–10 "But, behold, faith cometh not by signs, but signs follow those that believe. Yea, signs come by faith, not by the will of men, nor as they please, but by the will of God."

[542] D&C 68:10–11 "And he that believeth shall be blest with signs following, even as it is written. And unto you it shall be given to know the signs of the times, and the signs of the coming of the Son of Man;"

Christ is giving a sign to us so we may understand when His Father's promises are being fulfilled.

The time when His Father's covenants are to be fulfilled will be the moment when Christ will "gather in, from their long dispersion, my people." Note it is "I" meaning Christ, who will do the gathering. Christ is the great husbandman of this, the Lord's vineyard. It is Christ who will personally do the gathering. How do you suppose Christ will "gather in" those whom He calls "His people?"

Notice how the gathered are referred to by Christ as "my people" and "house of Israel" and "my Zion." When the gathering is complete, the various groups are no longer separately identified. On the other side of this gathering they will be "one" people and a restored "house of Israel."

But note the sequence:

- First, gathering in from a long dispersion.
- Second, they convert into "my people" or the "house of Israel."
- Then they are "established" as "Zion."

Why does the Lord refer to it as "my Zion?" Can you have Zion without the Lord's presence? Can there be Zion without the Lord dwelling among them?[543] Notice in Enoch's City that it was the Lord who came and dwelt there, then later the Lord is the one who names or calls the people "Zion."

When the Lord calls it "my Zion" how literal is this? How directly will the Lord be involved?

---

[543] Moses 7:16–18 "And from that time forth there were wars and bloodshed among them; but the Lord came and dwelt with his people, and they dwelt in righteousness. The fear of the Lord was upon all nations, so great was the glory of the Lord, which was upon his people. And the Lord blessed the land, and they were blessed upon the mountains, and upon the high places, and did flourish. And the Lord called his people Zion, because they were of one heart and one mind, and dwelt in righteousness; and there was no poor among them."

If you want to have a place there, do your connections in a church, organization, fraternity, fellowship, quorum or brotherhood matter? If not, what association alone will allow you to participate? How important is the "testimony of Jesus?"

Read again the description of the group of Saints who are included with those who will comprise Zion. As you read, keep in mind all we have discussed up to this point as you recognize familiar words used below:

> "They are they who received the testimony of Jesus, and believed on his name and were baptized after the manner of his burial, being buried in the water in his name, and this according to the commandment which he has given— That by keeping the commandments they might be washed and cleansed from all their sins, and receive the Holy Spirit by the laying on of the hands of him who is ordained and sealed unto this power; And who overcame by faith, and are sealed by the Holy Spirit of promise, which the Father sheds forth upon all those who are just and true. They are they who are the church of the Firstborn. They are they into whose hands the Father has given all things— They are they who are priests and kings, who have received of his fulness, and of his glory; And are priests of the Most High, after the order of Melchizedek, which was after the order of Enoch, which was after the order of the Only Begotten Son. Wherefore, as it is written, they are gods, even the sons of God— Wherefore, all things are theirs, whether life or death, or things present, or things to come, all are theirs and they are Christ's, and Christ is God's. And they shall overcome all things. Wherefore, let no man glory in man, but rather let him glory in God, who shall subdue all enemies under his feet. These shall dwell in the presence of God and his Christ forever and ever." (D&C 76:51–62)

These, then are Zion. These are those who become "one" and are called by the Lord after they are gathered in the "house of Israel" and "my Zion."

3 Nephi 21:2–3

"And behold, this is the thing which I will give unto you for a sign—for verily I say unto you that when these things which I declare unto you, and which I shall declare unto you hereafter of myself, and by the power of the Holy Ghost which shall be given unto you of the Father, shall be made known unto the Gentiles that they may know concerning this people who are a remnant of the house of Jacob, and concerning this my people who shall be scattered by them; Verily, verily, I say unto you, when these things shall be made known unto them of the Father, and shall come forth of the Father, from them unto you;"

The sign Christ is giving requires a specific knowledge of a sequence of events. These verses begin to detail how you will recognize the sign as the proper chronology unfolds.

First, Christ's words which were "declared unto you" (meaning the Nephites) will be "made known unto the gentiles." So, the Nephites must receive both what Christ *has* declared and *will* declare to them before His ministry was completed. Then these Nephites must record or preserve the words Christ declared. These words, recorded by the Nephites must in turn, become "known unto the gentiles." This initial part of Christ's sign is directly tied to the Book of Mormon. However, what does it mean that the words of Christ must be "made known unto the gentiles?" We have them, but do we know them in the sense that is being used here?

Second, the gentiles must come to a knowledge of "this people (Nephite audience) who are a remnant of the house of Jacob." The gentiles must understand or "know" that the promises made to the "remnant" exist. Has that happened? If not, why not? Is it happening at the moment as you become aware of this information that has been in the Book of Mormon since its publication in 1830? (No wonder the Lord's condemnation of the Latter-day Saints.)

Note the Lord calls the audience, and in turn their posterity, "this people who are a remnant of the house of Jacob . . . this my people." It is important to know that the Lord describes them with this identity as "my people" throughout His sermon and prophecy. This careful limitation of the reference to the Lord's "people" should not be applied broadly. It does not include gentiles. We should not change His meaning. He is speaking about a single identified group as "my people" and it is those before Him and their descendants.

Now, although it is a parenthetical thought, He adds a third event in the chronology. The third event is the scattering of the "Lord's people" who are the "remnant" by the gentiles. It will happen before the second listed event, but it's the third tier of the sign Christ is giving.

[By the way, this scrambled chronology is one of the things that evidences it is authentic and not a product of Joseph Smith's imagination. The time-line is always scrambled somewhat when the Lord or His true prophets speak. Information is not presented to their minds in a chronological manner, and therefore it is grouped by subject, not by time.[544] Isaiah, for example, was always grouping information according to subject, not chronology. Indeed, when looking back on a sweeping revelation, it is not possible to reconstruct a time line of events shown to a prophet in vision without some considerable effort. But this is merely an aside.]

The fourth portion of the sign is when the gentiles, who have the words, and appreciate or "know" them, bring them to the attention of the remnant. When those standing before Christ, through their descendants, come to receive these words of Christ from gentiles who know them to be true, then the fourth portion of the sign will have occurred.

---

[544] D&C 130:7–8 "But they reside in the presence of God, on a globe like a sea of glass and fire, where all things for their glory are manifest, past, present, and future, and are continually before the Lord. The place where God resides is a great Urim and Thummim."

Notice how Christ attributes the coming forth of the Book of Mormon to the gentiles as the work of "the Father." Christ was and is directly involved, He is the husbandman and the true vine. But He does not take credit as the Son. He says this coming forth will be "of the Father." All things are done by Christ according to the will of the Father, to whom He always gives the credit. There is a profound lesson in that for each of us. We are only accomplishing something good, enduring and valuable as we conform to the will of the Father and His Son. Whenever we are on our own errand, it is foolishness and vanity.

The "sign" given to us will continue in the Lord's statement which follows. So let's turn to more . . .

3 Nephi 21:4

"For it is wisdom in the Father that they should be established in this land, and be set up as a free people by the power of the Father, that these things might come forth from them unto a remnant of your seed, that the covenant of the Father may be fulfilled which he hath covenanted with his people, O house of Israel;"

Christ attributes the wisdom of this plan to "the Father."

The gentiles will be set up "in this land." What land has become a land for free people "by the power of the Father?" The most common answer is the United States. That is the conclusion of Porter and Meldrum in their book *Prophecies and Promises—The Book of Mormon and the United State of America.*

The "wisdom of the Father" decrees that the gentiles will receive the record and the land where Christ visited the Nephites. Why is it wise for this to be the case?

From the gentiles, who inherit the record, the record will "come forth from them unto a remnant of your seed." The gentiles receive it first, then it will come from them to the "remnant." Who are the gentiles? Do the Latter-day Saints have the record? Even though they are in possession of the record, they are nonetheless called "gentiles"

Note that the "covenant of the Father" is the reason for these events to unfold. Why is the unfolding history of the remnant, gentiles and house of Israel to fulfill "the covenant of the Father?" What was/is Christ's role in the process? If Christ is directly involved, why is it nevertheless the "covenant of the Father?"

Christ refers to the objects of the covenant as "his people"—the Father's people. This is an important transition in the description. These people belong to the Father! Immortality and eternal life is a family affair. Christ's harvest of souls is for the glory of the Father. If there were any doubt of Christ's motivation and selfless service, His comments here remove that doubt.

From what source does the gentile freedom come?

If gentile freedom is based on the Father's power, how vulnerable is their hold on freedom if they rebel and reject the Father? How much credit can the gentiles take for establishing their land of freedom? To whom should gratitude flow for the gentile freedom?

The backdrop Christ gives to our history is wholly based on the Father's will, covenants and design for mankind. We tend to question how involved the Father and His Son are in the daily events of life. From Christ's statement here, how involved are they?

3 Nephi 21:5–6

"Therefore, when these works and the works which shall be wrought among you hereafter shall come forth from the Gentiles, unto your seed which shall dwindle in unbelief because of iniquity; For thus it behooveth the Father that it should come forth from the Gentiles, that he may show forth his power unto the Gentiles, for this cause that the Gentiles, if they will not harden their hearts, that they may repent and come unto me and be baptized in my name and know of the true points of my doctrine, that they may be numbered among my people, O house of Israel;"

Now keep in mind this is all within a "sign" Christ is telling to the Nephites. It is a "sign" of when the great latter-day work will begin to unfold.

What are "these works" referred to by Christ? Was it necessary for the "works which shall be wrought among you hereafter" to be included in the "works" the gentiles were to receive? Why? Why would the gentiles need to know of the great success and ultimate failure of Nephite faith? The greatest time in the Nephite history would be after Christ's visit, when they lived a united order. But the harrowing end described by Mormon and Moroni shows a depth of shocking evil. The violence, killing, cannibalism are disgusting to read and consider. Why did Christ want the "works which shall be wrought among you hereafter" to be included for the gentiles to have before them? What lessons would we not learn without these subsequent portions of the Nephite record?

Why do (from Christ's vantage point)/did (from our vantage point) the records need to come "from the gentiles?" And how did that "show forth [the Father's] power unto the gentiles?" What about the restoration was a visible display of the Father's power? Latter-day Saints have a "testimony" of the restoration, but gentiles seem unimpressed. The missionary effort among Americans today is nearly at a standstill. There are about as many people slipping into inactivity, or asking for their names to be removed as there are people volunteering to join at the present. So how is the restoration a display of "the Father's power" to the gentiles?

Does the Father use "small means" to display His power?[545] Is it possible for the Father to show forth His power and for people to miss it entirely? What kind of "power" is missed by those who reject it?

If they do not reject it, notice what the "Father's power" may lead the gentiles to receive:

- repentance
- baptism
- knowledge of the true points of Christ's doctrine
- being numbered among Christ's people, even Israel.

But if not, then they will be swept away by their own wickedness and violence.

Now it may not be appreciably "powerful" when the gentiles receive the Book of Mormon. But if they repent, and are baptized, and come to know the true points of His doctrine, how great a change will take place? How great a show of power is it when the only ones at peace are those who dwell in Zion?[546]

It is clear the Lord will only gather to Zion in the great day of calamity those who had previously seen in His "small means" the path to safety and redemption.

---

[545] 1 Nephi 16:29 "And there was also written upon them a new writing, which was plain to be read, which did give us understanding concerning the ways of the Lord; and it was written and changed from time to time, according to the faith and diligence which we gave unto it. And thus we see that by small means the Lord can bring about great things."
Alma 37:6 "Now ye may suppose that this is foolishness in me; but behold I say unto you, that by small and simple things are great things brought to pass; and small means in many instances doth confound the wise."

[546] D&C 45:68–71 "And it shall come to pass among the wicked, that every man that will not take his sword against his neighbor must needs flee unto Zion for safety. And there shall be gathered unto it out of every nation under heaven; and it shall be the only people that shall not be at war one with another. And it shall be said among the wicked: Let us not go up to battle against Zion, for the inhabitants of Zion are terrible; wherefore we cannot stand. And it shall come to pass that the righteous shall be gathered out from among all nations, and shall come to Zion, singing with songs of everlasting joy."

For the most part, the gentiles will be unimpressed with the Lord's stretched out arm. Gentiles will remain slow to respond, skeptical of the means, and dispute whether the Lord is really involved. Even those who claim to believe in His restored Book of Mormon and covenant will take lightly what He offers them. Only a few will be willing to undertake a form of repentance. But to receive "knowledge of the true points of my doctrine" it will require something more than half-hearted conversion.

How do you suppose "knowledge of Christ's true points of doctrine" would change you?

Why do you think it will be necessary to "repent" before you receive "knowledge of the true points of His doctrine?"[547]

Why are both of these ("repentance" and "knowledge of true points of doctrine") required before you can be "numbered among Christ's people?"

Why do some of the gentiles need to become so numbered? How will we know when that sign has occurred? Has it already? If not, then the sign isn't before us yet—But if so, then the sign has begun. Are you among those who have repented, been baptized, know the true points of His doctrine, and become numbered with His people?

3 Nephi 21:7

"And when these things come to pass that thy seed shall begin to know these things—it shall be a sign unto them, that they may know that the work of the Father hath already commenced unto the fulfilling of the covenant which he hath made unto the people who are of the house of Israel."

---

[547] John 7:17 "If any man will do his will, he shall know of the doctrine, whether it be of God, or whether I speak of myself."

Now the completion of the sign:

When all that has been described has happened, and the remnant will "begin to know these things," that beginning is the sign. Has it happened? Is it happening? Then who is the "remnant" that has or will "begin to know" about the Book of Mormon to fulfill the sign?

We've lost the history of Joseph Smith's efforts to locate the "remnant" of the Nephites. The first mission to locate them was called by revelation in the first 5 months after the church was organized.[548] Oliver was called and later that same month Peter Whitmer was also called.[549] This began an effort to locate the "remnant" that continued after the death of Joseph Smith. That will take some time to set out and cannot be dealt with in this post. We'll get to it.

When the remnant is at last identified, and have been given the Book of Mormon, and start to know about their history and the Lord's covenants with them, that will be the moment at which the "sign" given by Christ will have occurred.

It is when this happens that all of us will "know that the work of the Father hath already commenced." Or, in other words, the Father's hand is in motion to finish up what He promised to accomplish. What is it He intends to accomplish? What does it mean "fulfilling of the covenant?" What does the reference to "the people who are of the house of Israel" mean? How broadly will this final

---

[548] D&C 28:8–9 "And now, behold, I say unto you that you shall go unto the Lamanites and preach my gospel unto them; and inasmuch as they receive thy teachings thou shalt cause my church to be established among them; and thou shalt have revelations, but write them not by way of commandment. And now, behold, I say unto you that it is not revealed, and no man knoweth where the city Zion shall be built, but it shall be given hereafter. Behold, I say unto you that it shall be on the borders by the Lamanites."

[549] D&C 30:5–6 "Behold, I say unto you, Peter, that you shall take your journey with your brother Oliver; for the time has come that it is expedient in me that you shall open your mouth to declare my gospel; therefore, fear not, but give heed unto the words and advice of your brother, which he shall give you. And be you afflicted in all his afflictions, ever lifting up your heart unto me in prayer and faith, for his and your deliverance; for I have given unto him power to build up my church among the Lamanites;"

work of the Father spread? How many of those who are included in
the covenant to Israel will become affected by the Father's work fulfilling the covenant?

Assuming the work "commences" at that time, how long will it
take for the work to be completed? Will it be a single generation?[550]
How long is a "generation?"

Why is the fulfillment to result in "the house of Israel" being
given their covenant again?

How can we participate?

Why would the "sign" be given? If it was given to inform us, how
can we watch to behold the sign when it happens? Is there any indication that the sign is now unfolding?

If the organized church does not pay any attention to these
things, and does not search for the remnant as Joseph did, will that
change these promises? Will the covenant of the Father be forgotten
by Him if the Saints themselves forget about it? What effect does
our neglect have on the Father's covenants?

3 Nephi 21:8–9

"And when that day shall come, it shall come to pass that
kings shall shut their mouths; for that which had not been
told them shall they see; and that which they had not heard
shall they consider. For in that day, for my sake shall the Father work a work, which shall be a great and a marvelous

---

[550] JS–Matthew 1:34–37 "Verily, I say unto you, this generation, in which these things
shall be shown forth, shall not pass away until all I have told you shall be fulfilled. Although, the days will come, that heaven and earth shall pass away; yet my words shall
not pass away, but all shall be fulfilled. And, as I said before, after the tribulation of
those days, and the powers of the heavens shall be shaken, then shall appear the sign of
the Son of Man in heaven, and then shall all the tribes of the earth mourn; and they
shall see the Son of Man coming in the clouds of heaven, with power and great glory;
And whoso treasureth up my word, shall not be deceived, for the Son of Man shall
come, and he shall send his angels before him with the great sound of a trumpet, and
they shall gather together the remainder of his elect from the four winds, from one end
of heaven to the other."

work among them; and there shall be among them those who will not believe it, although a man shall declare it unto them."

Christ is quoting from Isaiah and applying the words to a specific time frame. It is post-gentile receipt of the Book of Mormon, post-delivery of that book to the remnant, and post-opportunity for gentiles to repent and know of the true points of His doctrine. When that happens, the Lord will be freed up to fulfill the covenants of the Father.

When the Father's covenants are in being fulfilled, "kings shall shut their mouths." That is, the noble of this world will not know what to say. They will be at a loss of words because of the Father's acts.

Things that haven't been "told them" will take place, and they will not understand.

Things that they never had taught to them will unfold, and they cannot comprehend, cannot get their hands around it all. It will dumbfound them.

Even when people who understand that the events are according to the Father's plan, and the Lord's covenant, they will not be able to believe it.

Too much! Too distressing! Too unexpected! Too great to take in! It will be confusion and distress, and the idea that God is behind it all will be unbelievable to them.[551]

Their plans for managing the world will be dashed and end. Their great investments will be lost. The control they imagined they had as "kings" will fade to dust.[552]

---

[551] Isaiah 52:15 "So shall he sprinkle many nations; the kings shall shut their mouths at him: for that which had not been told them shall they see; and that which they had not heard shall they consider."

[552] Haggai 2:22 "And I will overthrow the throne of kingdoms, and I will destroy the strength of the kingdoms of the heathen; and I will overthrow the chariots, and those that ride in them; and the horses and their riders shall come down, every one by the sword of his brother."

How can such splendor, such great and masterful arrangements, such glory in mankind become nothing? How can it all fall to the dust?[553]

It will be "great and marvelous" because it shows the Father's power and might. But it will be inconvenient and distressing, unbelievable and terrible.[554]

What is coming will leave proud men speechless and believing people vindicated. Everything will change.

Once again we see the tremendous relevance of Isaiah's words. You can search for language to capture our times and find no-one who has given phrases that capture this moment better than Isaiah. Even the Lord finds his words appropriate to quote as His own. Words of inspiration, given Isaiah by the Lord, become Isaiah's, then are taken by the Lord and used again as His. The symmetry of this chiasm is a reminder of how closely the Lord works with those He inspires. It is "His voice" even when the message comes from His servants. Who has ears to hear?

3 Nephi 21:10–11

"But behold, the life of my servant shall be in my hand; therefore they shall not hurt him, although he shall be marred because of them. Yet I will heal him, for I will show unto them that my wisdom is greater than the cunning of the devil. Therefore it shall come to pass that whosoever will not believe in my words, who am Jesus Christ, which the Father shall cause him to bring forth unto the Gentiles, and shall give unto

---

[553] Revelation 14:7–8 "Saying with a loud voice, Fear God, and give glory to him; for the hour of his judgment is come: and worship him that made heaven, and earth, and the sea, and the fountains of waters. And there followed another angel, saying, Babylon is fallen, is fallen, that great city, because she made all nations drink of the wine of the wrath of her fornication."

[554] Malachi 4:1 "For, behold, the day cometh, that shall burn as an oven; and all the proud, yea, and all that do wickedly, shall be stubble: and the day that cometh shall burn them up, saith the Lord of hosts, that it shall leave them neither root nor branch."

him power that he shall bring them forth unto the Gentiles, (it shall be done even as Moses said) they shall be cut off from among my people who are of the covenant."

This statement has caused endless conjecture. Who is the "servant?" Was this Joseph Smith? Wasn't it Joseph who was "given power to bring forth the words to the gentiles?" If Joseph was this "servant," then what does it mean he will be "marred," but the Lord will "heal him?" Is he coming back? Will Joseph be resurrected? Will he be born again?

Although Christ is speaking, this raises a matter worth addressing in connection with the statement. Therefore we'll take a bit of a detour and address it. First, the purpose of prophecy is not always to make a matter clear before it happens. Prophecy may not have a clear meaning before an event happens, but once it has happened it becomes apparent that the event was foretold. This keeps the prophecy from controlling the event, but allows those who have faith to see the Lord's hand in operation. Therefore, having some difficulty in attaching specific meaning to the prophecy is exactly in keeping with prophecy's traditional way of communicating an event.

Second, the words of prophecy are not always established in the same way. In fact, there are a variety of ways in which the language is fixed. Below are descriptions of the various ways the language of a prophecy comes about:

The Lord may give, announce or dictate the language and the prophet takes it down word for word. If this is the case, then the one who receives the language may not understand their meaning, even though they received the message. (In this case it is Christ who is speaking. We assume He would know fully the word's meaning. However, Christ has explained that His Father knows things that have been withheld from Him.[555] So, you cannot rule out that even in this case the language was given and the meaning withheld.)

Sometimes it is not the language or the words that are given to the prophet, but a vision is shown or opened and then the prophet is left to craft a description. In such cases the words are the prophet's, but the underlying meaning is the Lord's.

Sometimes a vision may be shown or opened, but when the prophet takes to write the description, the language is prescribed, or limited by inspiration. In this instance, the prophet's understanding may be greater than the words used, and the language will be designed to accomplish the Lord's purposes rather than to make what the prophet understands clear to the recipient.

With respect to when one or another form of language is in scripture, we may not always be able to tell. Section 76 is one example we know how the language came to us. There was a vision, opened to both Joseph Smith and Sydney Rigdon, and as the vision proceeded Joseph would dictate the words given to him by the Lord to describe what he and Sydney beheld. The words were the Lord's. The vision was greater or included more understanding for Joseph and Sydney than the words of the revelation. Hence Joseph's comment: "I could explain a hundred fold more than I ever have of the glories of the kingdoms manifested to me in the vision, were I permitted, and were the people prepared to receive them." (*TPJS*, 304.)

It is not important to fully understand the statement of Christ in this prophecy until AFTER it is fulfilled. Before it is fulfilled the following questions are interesting to contemplate as you think about its meaning:

---

[555] Mark 13:32 "But of that day and that hour knoweth no man, no, not the angels which are in heaven, neither the Son, but the Father."

Is the "servant" who will be "marred" and then "healed" a single individual, or a people with whom the Lord is working? If a people rather than an individual, then who is this servant?

If the ones who will cause the servant to be "marred" are plural, who are they? Are they a group, or groups? If groups, which are they? What is their affiliation with the "great and abominable church?"

What does it mean that the "servant" will not be "hurt" but will be "marred?" How can one be "marred" without being "hurt?"

Is the "servant" in verse 10 the same as the "him" in verse 11? Have the subjects changed? That is, can verse 10 be speaking about a people, but verse 11 be addressing a person whose work it was (or is) to bring forth Christ's words? If an individual, is Joseph Smith the only one who can qualify? Can others also bring forth words of Christ to the gentiles, and the gentiles given an opportunity to accept or reject the words at their peril?

If they risk being cut off by rejecting the words, then can more than Joseph Smith be qualified to be "(even as Moses said) they shall be cut off from among my people who are of the covenant." That is, when the latter-day prophets are sounding alarms and warning, is the message from Christ—no matter who speaks it—something, if rejected, will cause people to be cut off from the covenant?

How does one cut themselves off from the covenant? If you will not listen to Christ's words, do you thereby cut yourself off by not listening? Would that be true if Joseph Smith is a prophet and you reject him? Would that be true if Brigham Young were a prophet and you rejected him? What about an angel sent to you? What about someone like Abinadi, or John the Baptist, or some other unexpected messenger? Would the same be true anytime someone decided to reject a message authorized or sent from the Lord?

Now go back and re-read verses 10 and 11 with these questions in mind and see if you get a different meaning from them.

3 Nephi 21:12–14

"And my people who are a remnant of Jacob shall be among the Gentiles, yea, in the midst of them as a lion among the beasts of the forest, as a young lion among the flocks of sheep, who, if he go through both treadeth down and teareth in pieces, and none can deliver. Their hand shall be lifted up upon their adversaries, and all their enemies shall be cut off. Yea, wo be unto the Gentiles except they repent; for it shall come to pass in that day, saith the Father, that I will cut off thy horses out of the midst of thee, and I will destroy thy chariots;"

Notice again the distinction between the gentiles and the remnant.

The "remnant" will behave in a way which will "tread down and tear in pieces" the gentiles. As they do this, "none can deliver" the gentiles.

Unlike the previous slaughter of the remnant by the gentiles, this time it is the gentiles who are slaughtered at the hands of the remnant. Those who are "enemies" to the remnant will all be "cut off." What does "cut off" mean?

The woes of that coming time can all be avoided by the gentiles—predicated upon their willingness to "repent." So we return again to the recurring question of what it means to "repent?" How can "repentance" be the only means by which the gentiles survive the slaughter? What is it about gentile repentance that spares them from the wrath that is to be otherwise poured out upon them?

What symbol comes to mind when you think of "horses?" What does cutting out the horses symbolize?

Does the symbol of the "horses" and the symbol of the "chariots" go together? That is, does cutting out the horses and destroying the chariots express a single thought? If it does, what do the horses and chariots symbolize? How vulnerable is the American military might to destruction? What effect would symbolically destroying the horses and chariots of the American population have?

If the United States is to be engulfed in domestic violence, will it continue to have foreign military influence? Economic influence? Social and cultural influence?

Assuming the gentile population is swept away, trodden under foot and torn in pieces, what culture and social influence will remain?

What symbol does the lion among the beasts of the forest suggest? The young lion among the sheep? What is the difference between the beasts of the forest and the sheep? If both beasts and sheep are gentiles, then are the beasts different than the sheep? What sort of person called a gentile "beast" will be swept away? What kind of person called a gentile "sheep" will be torn in pieces? Why would both gentile beasts and gentile sheep need to "repent?" Does repentance of a "beast" and repentance of "sheep" take the same form? Why would both need repentance when they are so remarkably different in symbol? Is it enough alone to be a gentile sheep?

What message is being sent by this warning?

3 Nephi 21:15–18

"And I will cut off the cities of thy land, and throw down all thy strongholds; And I will cut off witchcrafts out of thy land, and thou shalt have no more soothsayers; Thy graven images I will also cut off, and thy standing images out of the midst of thee, and thou shalt no more worship the works of thy hands; And I will pluck up thy groves out of the midst of thee; so will I destroy thy cities."

Cleaning up things so that the course of wickedness comes to an end involves some highly specific purging. However, the description is not given to us so we can know what will be coming as much as it is given to us to guide our own conduct and beliefs.

"Cities will be cut off" means what? "Strongholds thrown down" refers to what? Interesting things to contemplate to be sure. But much more relevant are the warnings in what follows:

"Cut off witchcrafts" is a warning to those who engage in certain practices. What should you do to avoid being cut off as a result of being involved in "witchcraft?" What does that mean? Are only wiccans being warned by this?

Who are the "soothsayers" who are to be terminated? What constitutes "soothsaying?" Look that word up. It appears in interesting contexts. The typical example involves predictions made using means other than true prophecy. But you should look at it and ask yourself how it would apply in modern applications: in business, government, economics, weather—especially long-term weather, politics, etc.

What are "graven images?" What are "standing images?" Why are the "standing images" said to be "in the midst of thee?"

What does it mean to "worship the works of thy hands?" How can a person worship their own works?

What are the "groves" that are to be plucked up? Why are the groves also "in the midst of thee?" The ancient usage of groves involved fertility rites, sacred sexual practices, or the worship of intercourse. What modern versions of this ancient form of fertility worship would be similar to the ancient behavior as to merit being called the same thing?

What does it mean to have our "cities destroyed?" Does this have anything to do with the other prophecy that the final victory of Israel will inhabit the desolate cities of the gentiles?[556]

---

[556] Isaiah 54:3 "For thou shalt break forth on the right hand and on the left; and thy seed shall inherit the Gentiles, and make the desolate cities to be inhabited."

Remember this is Christ speaking. This is the Redeemer, the merciful author of our salvation. Therefore, you must conclude that these direful predictions are actually based on the overall long-term best interest of those involved. They are better off, improved and advanced by these judgments. Imagine that. The wrath of God is best visited upon those who are destroyed, rather than leaving them to continue the course they are headed in. It is an interesting thing to contemplate.

3 Nephi 21:19–20

"And it shall come to pass that all lyings, and deceivings, and envyings, and strifes, and priestcrafts, and whoredoms, shall be done away. For it shall come to pass, saith the Father, that at that day whosoever will not repent and come unto my Beloved Son, them will I cut off from among my people, O house of Israel;"

Notice that the first four defects that are to end, include "lyings, and deceivings, and envyings, and strifes." These are somewhat different than the next two. These first four are character flaws that lead to the next two.

The character flaws should not be thought of as defects in our ability to do business or conduct commerce. These are flaws leading to the failures of our redemption. Therefore, think of them as flaws in our beliefs, leading us to have what the Book of Mormon terms unbelief.

What lying goes on among us leads to priestcraft? How is our lying keeping us from knowing the Lord? What is it about our peculiar form of false belief that leads us to believe in, and spread about lying as part of the fallen, false faith we entertain?

What deceivings are part of our culture of unbelief? How is it we can celebrate the great priesthood "authority" we possess while acknowledging that it lacks any "power?" Are we deceiving ourselves? Are we alienated from God while thinking ourselves His peculiar people?

What envy is there among us? Has envy become a tool for church governance? If so, how does it become a tool for church governance? Have we built it right into our system at present?

Are we filled with strife? Is strife among us suppressing healthy exchange of ideas by labeling such discussion as "contention?" Is strife different from contention? Is uniformity of ideas and suppression of dissent something that will remove strife? If not, then why not?

These character flaws in turn lead to "priestcrafts" where people seek approval of the world but not the best interest of Zion.[557] Do we want popularity from the "world?" What is the "world?" Why would someone practicing priestcraft seek in particular to have approval and lead the world? Why is the distinction made between the interests of Zion and the interests of the world? Is public relations always focused on approval from the world? If so, why are we seeking such approval? Does the world's opinion of us matter? Why? When have the followers of Jesus been popular? What have they suffered for His name?[558]

Then we see "whoredoms" which we have discussed earlier. David Christensen's comment on the meaning of false religion is worth returning to read again in this post.

---

[557] 2 Nephi 26:29 "He commandeth that there shall be no priestcrafts; for, behold, priestcrafts are that men preach and set themselves up for a light unto the world, that they may get gain and praise of the world; but they seek not the welfare of Zion."

[558] Hebrews 11:36–40 "And others had trial of cruel mockings and scourgings, yea, moreover of bonds and imprisonment: They were stoned, they were sawn asunder, were tempted, were slain with the sword: they wandered about in sheepskins and goatskins; being destitute, afflicted, tormented; (Of whom the world was not worthy:) they wandered in deserts, and in mountains, and in dens and caves of the earth. And these all, having obtained a good report through faith, received not the promise: God having provided some better thing for us, that they without us should not be made perfect."

Then Christ sounds the alarm, attributing it to the Father. Repent. Come unto Christ. Otherwise you will be cut off. What does it mean to come to Christ? Read the short statement in D&C 93:1.[559] There is a succinct description of the process. You haven't come to Him until you have "seen His face and know that He is," or, in other words, until you hear from His own voice that He has atoned for your sins and He promises you a place in His kingdom.

All of these warnings are being given to orient you to what is important. The important thing is to come to Him. As Christ put it to Martha, "but one thing is needful."[560] Until we have come to Him, all our concerns about other matters must remain secondary. Of what good is it to know all mysteries, if we have not come to Him? This is why, in the middle of this warning of calamities to come, the Lord places this invitation to come to Him. He can help. He can restore and protect. But only if you are His.

3 Nephi 21:21–22

"And I will execute vengeance and fury upon them, even as upon the heathen, such as they have not heard. But if they will repent and hearken unto my words, and harden not their hearts, I will establish my church among them, and they shall come in unto the covenant and be numbered among this the remnant of Jacob, unto whom I have given this land for their inheritance;"

---

[559] D&C 93:1 "Verily, thus saith the Lord: It shall come to pass that every soul who forsaketh his sins and cometh unto me, and calleth on my name, and obeyeth my voice, and keepeth my commandments, shall see my face and know that I am;"

[560] Luke 10:38–42 "Now it came to pass, as they went, that he entered into a certain village: and a certain woman named Martha received him into her house. And she had a sister called Mary, which also sat at Jesus' feet, and heard his word. But Martha was cumbered about much serving, and came to him, and said, Lord, dost thou not care that my sister hath left me to serve alone? bid her therefore that she help me. And Jesus answered and said unto her, Martha, Martha, thou art careful and troubled about many things: But one thing is needful: and Mary hath chosen that good part, which shall not be taken away from her."

Again the warning and the promise. Vengeance and fury are terrible words. It will be the responsibility of Christ to inflict it, and Christ says it will be His. "I will execute vengeance and fury" not "the Father." This is Christ's assignment—His cup.

His fury will be executed upon disbelieving gentiles, as well as the offending and violent heathen. When the spirit withdraws and they are left to themselves, it is only the limits of their cruel imagination that will compass the torture and evil they will visit upon one another. He will allow it by withdrawing the light of Christ, or His spirit. Without conscience, without remorse, without affection, filled with anger and hatred, it will be vengeance and fury.

This is juxtaposed with the reminder that "if they will repent and hearken unto my words, and harden not their hearts" He will be with them. If they will follow His path, His light and spirit will not forsake them. They will not descend into the same violent vengeance and fury. They will remain at peace. They will have hope in Him.

For those who will "repent," and "hearken unto His words," He will establish "my church" among them. Does this mean The Church of Jesus Christ of Latter-day Saints, or the church of the Firstborn?

When His church is joined it is through "the covenant." What "covenant" is that? Merely baptism, or something more?

When the "covenant" is given them, they become "numbered among this remnant of Jacob." Who is that remnant? When they become "numbered" among them, what significance does that hold? Does it imply a covenantal link which, like being sealed to someone, makes you part of that eternal family line (as discussed earlier)?

Why is it necessary to become first in the covenant and numbered with the remnant before they receive the blessings of being "given this land for their inheritance?" What does the promise of land have to do with entering into a covenant? Can it ever be the same as the covenant made with Abraham if it does not involve an inheritance of land? If, therefore, the covenant of land is part of that new and everlasting covenant which was begun through Joseph, is this a promise of reuniting the recipients with the "fullness of the Gospel" as opposed to receiving "much of the Gospel" discussed in earlier posts?

What is the Lord setting out in this declaration and prophecy? How do we become part of those promises? Is this something which an institution can do for you? Must you repent and come to Christ in order to become a part of it? If so, why not repent?

3 Nephi 21:23–24

"And they shall assist my people, the remnant of Jacob, and also as many of the house of Israel as shall come, that they may build a city, which shall be called the New Jerusalem. And then shall they assist my people that they may be gathered in, who are scattered upon all the face of the land, in unto the New Jerusalem."

Who are those referred to as "my people?" "My people" are "the remnant of Jacob."

Who are those referred to as "they?" The "they" are gentiles who have repented, come to Christ, entered into a covenant with Him, received the fullness of His Gospel, become heirs, and received the promise of land, and a connection with the promises to the remnant.

So it will be these few, chosen, covenantal gentiles who will "ASSIST" the remnant.

- They won't lead them,
- preside over them,
- control them,
- subjugate them,
- nor dominate them.

They will "assist" them. What does "assist" mean? Who is taking the lead if the gentiles are only to "assist" in the process?

What will the remnant do? What city is to be built? Why is it called the New Jerusalem?

Forget everything you think you know about where the New Jerusalem is to be built. Most of the myth and traditions about it are based on incomplete and inaccurate recreations of the events.

Joseph sent the first missionaries to the Lamanites to find the place. The entire block of Native Americans east of the Mississippi, from the Delaware to the Cherokee, had been relocated at the time of the 1834 revelations regarding the New Jerusalem. At that brief moment in time, all of them were located just over the boundary of western Missouri. The closest you could get to them was Independence, Missouri. Since it was the remnant who would build the New Jerusalem, the obligation was to find them, preach to them, and assist them in building. But the missionaries couldn't do that. When they tried, they were sent out of the Indian Territory on the threat of being imprisoned. So Independence was as close as they could get.

The Native Americans have relocated and relocated again. Now they are nowhere near Independence. When Joseph fled Nauvoo in late June, days before his death, he was leaving for the Rocky Mountains where he intended to locate the remnant. He returned, was killed, and never made it out here.

Brigham Young tried to locate the remnant. In fact, the St. George Temple was built as the next fully functioning Temple at the chosen location precisely because it was intended to be near the remnant. In the very first endowment session, the Hopi Chief and his wife went through, received their endowment, and were sealed the next day. They were invited to try and connect with the remnant and this tribe was suspected as the one the Saints were to locate.

We've lost that fervor. We've assumed Independence is the site. We think we're going to build it. We have no clue we are only to "assist" and not control.

All of this is worth some study. But you're going to have to search back into history and ignore all the recent re-done and re-worked histories that ignore this early material. It's too much to get into in this post, but maybe I'll take it up at some point.

3 Nephi 21:25

"And then shall the power of heaven come down among them; and I also will be in the midst."

What does the "power of heaven" include? (We've already looked at 1 Nephi 14:14 which is speaking about this same event, you should read again that post.)

What is the difference between the "power of heaven" and the Lord's presence?

Why would the power of heaven come first, then the Lord?[561]

What would it require for you to be able to endure the presence of the Lord?[562]

---

[561] Moses 1:11 "But now mine own eyes have beheld God; but not my natural, but my spiritual eyes, for my natural eyes could not have beheld; for I should have withered and died in his presence; but his glory was upon me; and I beheld his face, for I was transfigured before him."

[562] Moses 1:2 "And he saw God face to face, and he talked with him, and the glory of God was upon Moses; therefore Moses could endure his presence."

If you are not prepared for His presence, what will your reaction be?[563]

Those who are directly in a covenant with Him, who have been promised forgiveness of their sins by Him, and who have sought and obtained His face, will be able to dwell in His presence. They will be prepared for His glory, have part in it, and thereby be protected when they are with Him.

If people have the "power of heaven" with them, do they need some other means to protect them as well? Why not?

Haven't we already been promised this as early as 1833?[564] What happened that we did not obtain these things? Have our Temples been kept undefiled? If not, why? Have we permitted the unclean to enter? If so, why? Is the glory of the Lord in our Temples? Can we behold His presence there? If not, why not?

If the promise was made to us in 1833 and we haven't realized it from then till now, then are we to be numbered among those who will have the Lord "in their midst" as set out in this verse? What should we do to change that?

---

[563] Mormon 9:3–5 "Then will ye longer deny the Christ, or can ye behold the Lamb of God? Do ye suppose that ye shall dwell with him under a consciousness of your guilt? Do ye suppose that ye could be happy to dwell with that holy Being, when your souls are racked with a consciousness of guilt that ye have ever abused his laws? Behold, I say unto you that ye would be more miserable to dwell with a holy and just God, under a consciousness of your filthiness before him, than ye would to dwell with the damned souls in hell. For behold, when ye shall be brought to see your nakedness before God, and also the glory of God, and the holiness of Jesus Christ, it will kindle a flame of unquenchable fire upon you."

[564] D&C 97:15–19 "And inasmuch as my people build a house unto me in the name of the Lord, and do not suffer any unclean thing to come into it, that it be not defiled, my glory shall rest upon it; Yea, and my presence shall be there, for I will come into it, and all the pure in heart that shall come into it shall see God. But if it be defiled I will not come into it, and my glory shall not be there; for I will not come into unholy temples. And, now, behold, if Zion do these things she shall prosper, and spread herself and become very glorious, very great, and very terrible. And the nations of the earth shall honor her, and shall say: Surely Zion is the city of our God, and surely Zion cannot fall, neither be moved out of her place, for God is there, and the hand of the Lord is there;"

By and large, the church has failed to honor the Book of Mormon, keep its terms and become heirs of its promises. Our collective failure does not prevent individual success. Individuals may still realize the blessings offered. But each of us must meet the exact same conditions. Having met them, however, nothing can prevent you from obtaining the blessings.

The Lord has been willing to bring individuals back into His presence on the same conditions throughout all time. Read again *The Second Comforter* if you do not remember what those conditions are. He is as willing to make you a citizen of Zion, member of the Church of the Firstborn, and part of the general assembly today[565], as in the future established Zion spoken of in the verses we have been reviewing. Many have done it in times past. Some have done it in our day. All are offered the same opportunity, but always on the same conditions.

The unchanging Gospel of Jesus Christ is always the same, and its blessings are always available.

3 Nephi 21:26

"And then shall the work of the Father commence at that day, even when this gospel shall be preached among the remnant of this people. Verily I say unto you, at that day shall the work of the Father commence among all the dispersed of my people, yea, even the tribes which have been lost, which the Father hath led away out of Jerusalem."

---

[565] D&C 76:66–69 "These are they who are come unto Mount Zion, and unto the city of the living God, the heavenly place, the holiest of all. These are they who have come to an innumerable company of angels, to the general assembly and church of Enoch, and of the Firstborn. These are they whose names are written in heaven, where God and Christ are the judge of all. These are they who are just men made perfect through Jesus the mediator of the new covenant, who wrought out this perfect atonement through the shedding of his own blood."

Christ reiterates again the work of the Father is only at its "commencement" when the fullness of the gentiles is completed. The gentile day ends, the message goes to the remnant, and then will the work "commence at that day."

We think the work was underway when Joseph initiated it. In one respect it was. But Joseph never lived to locate the remnant, nor to deliver the Book of Mormon to them, nor to see them return to believe in and obtain a renewal of their covenant with Jesus Christ. It was one of his great priorities. But Joseph was killed before the work advanced to the point which is called the "commencement" by the Lord in this prophecy.

The work of the Father consists in fulfilling covenants. His great latter-day work of bringing the return of the Gospel to the remnant, who had the promise, used Joseph Smith and the gentiles to lay a foundation. The work of the covenant, however, will commence when the gentiles hand off the restored truths, the record of the fathers, and the reminder of what great things are promised, to the remnant.

The work of the Father, once it commences, is not limited to restoring the remnant to their former status. It reaches to all those who had been "led away out of Jerusalem." Therefore, all of those tribes who are "lost" to us, but are not lost to the Father, will be brought back and restored to the Lord.

This restoration of the lost tribes and return of the covenant is a subject Isaiah wrote and rejoiced about. I do not intend to take that detour in this post, but if you read Isaiah (particularly those portions quoted by Nephi), you will see how great a focus this final restoration has been.

We call our time the Dispensation of the Fullness of Time, because our time is leading to that return to fullness. However, in one sense Joseph Smith was much like the Protestant fathers who laid a groundwork for a greater, further return of light. They did not see the full return. We might.

From the time of Joseph Smith until now, however, we have neglected or forgotten a great deal of what Joseph was given. There are doctrines we circulate today that are incomplete or misleading. We have not been diligent, and as a result our conferences, meetings, associations and discussions continue to be too low, too vulgar, too condescending from what we were called to receive.

How few or many of us will be permitted to participate in the on going process of the Restoration remains to be seen. However, when the fullness returns, those who become the heirs will look back on the era of the Latter-day Saints with much the same reaction as we look back on the Jewish era in which Christ lived. They will be astonished at the great principles of truth we discarded, neglected or ignored. They will wonder in astonishment at our groveling to gain acceptance from a doomed and ignorant religious tradition calling itself "Christianity." They will find it utterly incomprehensible that we argued we should be regarded as one of them, rather than proclaiming their doctrines are the commandments of men, having a form of godliness but lacking any power. They will wonder why we would trade the power of God for acceptance and popularity; particularly when we were told that pandering for popularity is at the heart of priestcraft. Why, they will ask, did the Latter-day Saints invest tithing in opinion polling and focus group testing to insure the language and opinions of doomed Babylon were employed in declaring what little we kept of the restored Gospel? Our failure will be clear to them, although we find it quite opaque. We still think we're approved by the Lord, even though our condemnation is set out in scripture.

The work of the Father will commence in the future. What is underway at present cannot be what was intended to bring the return of the Lord's Zion because we have neglected the ordinances, forgotten the teachings, and drifted into a "feel good" sentimentality which suggests that all of us are likely to be exalted. Using a gambling term to capture the grave risks we take, Deseret Book proclaims: "Odds Are, You're Going To Be Exalted"—while they risk damning all those who are willing to gamble with them on such foolish, vain and untrue notions. Nephi condemned that foolish idea long ago in a book which, if we kept its principles, would have spared us from our current plight.[566]

3 Nephi 21:27–28

> "Yea, the work shall commence among all the dispersed of my people, with the Father to prepare the way whereby they may come unto me, that they may call on the Father in my name. Yea, and then shall the work commence, with the Father among all nations in preparing the way whereby his people may be gathered home to the land of their inheritance."

When it begins in earnest and for the last time, it will be universal. There won't be an effort among one part of the vineyard which isn't mirrored by similar efforts in other parts of the vineyard. All the natural branches will be returned and reunited with the natural roots, as all are gathered again into one.

The Father will determine the timing. The Son will implement the plan. The process will require everyone, in every scattered part of the vineyard, to "come unto Christ." Unless they "come unto Christ," they will not be gathered and cannot be saved.

When they are brought again into their original state and begin to bear fruit, "they may call on the Father in [Christ's] name" with

---

[566] 2 Nephi 28:8 "And there shall also be many which shall say: Eat, drink, and be merry; nevertheless, fear God—he will justify in committing a little sin; yea, lie a little, take the advantage of one because of his words, dig a pit for thy neighbor; there is no harm in this; and do all these things, for tomorrow we die; and if it so be that we are guilty, God will beat us with a few stripes, and at last we shall be saved in the kingdom of God."

His approval and blessing. Without that, the "gathering home" cannot become a reality.

The Father's work will be "among all nations" because it will involve the judgment and destruction of all nations.[567]

This will "prepare the way." Why does the work need to happen "among all nations" for the way to be prepared?

What does it mean to now call all those who are to be included in this final gathering "his people" meaning the Father's people? Why would they end their long sojourn by becoming the "Father's people?" Christ has spoken of them being "His people" (meaning Christ's) but now the culmination will result in them becoming the "Father's people" as well.[568]

Notice that part of the final covenant being fulfilled involves re-gathering into the lands promised as their inheritance. This does not mean a single step. It means that the great work of the Father in destroying the nations, eliminating the wicked, and returning knowledge and a connection to Him through His Son, will prepare the way for the final step of gathering the chosen people into the lands of their inheritance.

There will be gatherings, and a great gathering, and at last a distribution of the survivors into their respective promised lands. Between the time of the great upheavals, and the time of the final distribution, there will be a season in which there will a great gathering in the

---

[567] D&C 87:6 "And thus, with the sword and by bloodshed the inhabitants of the earth shall mourn; and with famine, and plague, and earthquake, and the thunder of heaven, and the fierce and vivid lightning also, shall the inhabitants of the earth be made to feel the wrath, and indignation, and chastening hand of an Almighty God, until the consumption decreed hath made a full end of all nations;"

[568] D&C 76:92–95 "And thus we saw the glory of the celestial, which excels in all things—where God, even the Father, reigns upon his throne forever and ever; Before whose throne all things bow in humble reverence, and give him glory forever and ever. They who dwell in his presence are the church of the Firstborn; and they see as they are seen, and know as they are known, having received of his fulness and of his grace; And he makes them equal in power, and in might, and in dominion."

"Mountains"[569] where it will be a fearsome, even terrible thing for the wicked to contemplate.[570] This will be in "the tops of the mountains."[571] This will be where the New Jerusalem will exist. This will be before the final distribution into the various places of inheritance of the Lord's people.

Before the return to the lands of inheritance, however, there will be terrible days, the likes of which have only been seen in the final pages of the Nephite record.[572]

The choice is between the Lord, His offered redemption and protection, and destruction. The gentiles are now offered a choice while

---

[569] 2 Nephi 12:2 "And it shall come to pass in the last days, when the mountain of the Lord's house shall be established in the top of the mountains, and shall be exalted above the hills, and all nations shall flow unto it."

[570] D&C 45:68–70 "And it shall come to pass among the wicked, that every man that will not take his sword against his neighbor must needs flee unto Zion for safety. And there shall be gathered unto it out of every nation under heaven; and it shall be the only people that shall not be at war one with another. And it shall be said among the wicked: Let us not go up to battle against Zion, for the inhabitants of Zion are terrible; wherefore we cannot stand."

[571] Micah 4:1 "But in the last days it shall come to pass, that the mountain of the house of the Lord shall be established in the top of the mountains, and it shall be exalted above the hills; and people shall flow unto it."
2 Nephi 12:2 ""And it shall come to pass in the last days, when the mountain of the Lord's house shall be established in the top of the mountains, and shall be exalted above the hills, and all nations shall flow unto it."
Isaiah 2:2 "And it shall come to pass in the last days, that the mountain of the Lord's house shall be established in the top of the mountains, and shall be exalted above the hills; and all nations shall flow unto it."

[572] Mormon 6:6–22 "And it came to pass that when we had gathered in all our people in one to the land of Cumorah, behold I, Mormon, began to be old; and knowing it to be the last struggle of my people, and having been commanded of the Lord that I should not suffer the records which had been handed down by our fathers, which were sacred, to fall into the hands of the Lamanites, (for the Lamanites would destroy them) therefore I made this record out of the plates of Nephi, and hid up in the hill Cumorah all the records which had been entrusted to me by the hand of the Lord, save it were these few plates which I gave unto my son Moroni. And it came to pass that my people, with their wives and their children, did now behold the armies of the Lamanites marching towards them; and with that awful fear of death which fills the breasts of all the wicked, did they await to receive them. And it came to pass that they came to battle against us, and every soul was filled with terror because of the greatness of their numbers. And it came to pass that they did fall upon my people with the sword, and with the bow, and with the arrow, and with the ax, and with all manner of

reenacting the same poor judgment that led to their own loss of opportunity. That needn't be true of individuals. It seems apparent that the prophetic message of the Book of Mormon foretells gentile arrogance and pride, collectively claiming they are on the road to Zion, while they are instead doomed to repeating the errors of prior civilizations of this continent. We will get to that in the coming days, but for now we remain interested in the definition and destiny of the "remnant" of the prior occupants.

(What an interesting text this Book of Mormon proves to be. It makes one wonder why it would ever suffer from neglect.)

---

weapons of war. And it came to pass that my men were hewn down, yea, even my ten thousand who were with me, and I fell wounded in the midst; and they passed by me that they did not put an end to my life. And when they had gone through and hewn down all my people save it were twenty and four of us, (among whom was my son Moroni) and we having survived the dead of our people, did behold on the morrow, when the Lamanites had returned unto their camps, from the top of the hill Cumorah, the ten thousand of my people who were hewn down, being led in the front by me. And we also beheld the ten thousand of my people who were led by my son Moroni. And behold, the ten thousand of Gidgiddonah had fallen, and he also in the midst. And Lamah had fallen with his ten thousand; and Gilgal had fallen with his ten thousand; and Limhah had fallen with his ten thousand; and Jeneum had fallen with his ten thousand; and Cumenihah, and Moronihah, and Antionum, and Shiblom, and Shem, and Josh, had fallen with their ten thousand each. And it came to pass that there were ten more who did fall by the sword, with their ten thousand each; yea, even all my people, save it were those twenty and four who were with me, and also a few who had escaped into the south countries, and a few who had deserted over unto the Lamanites, had fallen; and their flesh, and bones, and blood lay upon the face of the earth, being left by the hands of those who slew them to molder upon the land, and to crumble and to return to their mother earth. And my soul was rent with anguish, because of the slain of my people, and I cried: O ye fair ones, how could ye have departed from the ways of the Lord! O ye fair ones, how could ye have rejected that Jesus, who stood with open arms to receive you! Behold, if ye had not done this, ye would not have fallen. But behold, ye are fallen, and I mourn your loss. O ye fair sons and daughters, ye fathers and mothers, ye husbands and wives, ye fair ones, how is it that ye could have fallen! But behold, ye are gone, and my sorrows cannot bring your return. And the day soon cometh that your mortal must put on immortality, and these bodies which are now moldering in corruption must soon become incorruptible bodies; and then ye must stand before the judgment-seat of Christ, to be judged according to your works; and if it so be that ye are righteous, then are ye blessed with your fathers who have gone before you. O that ye had repented before this great destruction had come upon you. But behold, ye are gone, and the Father, yea, the Eternal Father of heaven, knoweth your state; and he doeth with you according to his justice and mercy."

3 Nephi 21:29

> "And they shall go out from all nations; and they shall not go
> out in haste, nor go by flight, for I will go before them, saith
> the Father, and I will be their rearward."

When the time comes to redistribute the survivors to their respective promised lands of inheritance, they will not flee, nor will the
process be hurried. No one will pursue them. They will at last be free
to go to their homes without being molested along the way.

The Father will go before them. The Father will be on their rear
guard. His glory and His presence will be their shield and protection.

How will the earth respond to such a passage? Psalms 48:1–4
gives some idea of this great and joyful procession.[573] Psalms 67 is
another great anthem of this event.

Though the days before were terrible, in their wake all be comforted, for to know the Great Comforter is to know at last peace.
Isaiah could not refrain from adding to the anthems of praise of this
future event:

> "Thus saith the Lord, In an acceptable time have I heard thee,
> and in a day of salvation have I helped thee: and I will pre-
> serve thee, and give thee for a covenant of the people, to es-
> tablish the earth, to cause to inherit the desolate heritages;
> That thou mayest say to the prisoners, Go forth; to them that
> are in darkness, Shew yourselves. They shall feed in the ways,
> and their pastures shall be in all high places. They shall not
> hunger nor thirst; neither shall the heat nor sun smite them:
> for he that hath mercy on them shall lead them, even by the
> springs of water shall he guide them. And I will make all my
> mountains a way, and my highways shall be exalted. Behold,
> these shall come from far: and, lo, these from the north and

---

[573] Psalms 48:1–4 "Great is the Lord, and greatly to be praised in the city of our God,
in the mountain of his holiness. Beautiful for situation, the joy of the whole earth, is
mount Zion, on the sides of the north, the city of the great King. God is known in her
palaces for a refuge. For, lo, the kings were assembled, they passed by together."

from the west; and these from the land of Sinim. Sing, O heavens; and be joyful, O earth; and break forth into singing, O mountains: for the Lord hath comforted his people, and will have mercy upon his afflicted." (Isaiah 49:8–13)

This ultimate triumph was always intended to be the outcome. The end will be joyful. Though His covenant people may pass through the trials and rigors of mortality, the fruit offered to them is delicious even in times of tragedy and distress.[574] To make it through what is coming and endure to the final comfort, it will be necessary to come and plant that seed inside you now. Unless you do so, you will not have the strength to lay hold on the promises of the Lord.

The end will be worth all the shame and bitterness endured while the world still lies in sin and error.[575] The final triumph will be won by those who can endure the presence of the Father. This requires more than enduring the presence of the Son. Those who can rise to this glory must be sealed by the Holy Spirit of Promise, and become kings and priests, holding that same priesthood and bearing that same right which was in the beginning and is named after the Son of God. They will be everlasting, for they came from everlasting and have reconnected with that while here in mortality.

The Book of Mormon is a message of hope and triumph. But to win that triumph and possess that hope requires the reader to follow

---

[574] Alma 32:28 "Now, we will compare the word unto a seed. Now, if ye give place, that a seed may be planted in your heart, behold, if it be a true seed, or a good seed, if ye do not cast it out by your unbelief, that ye will resist the Spirit of the Lord, behold, it will begin to swell within your breasts; and when you feel these swelling motions, ye will begin to say within yourselves—It must needs be that this is a good seed, or that the word is good, for it beginneth to enlarge my soul; yea, it beginneth to enlighten my understanding, yea, it beginneth to be delicious to me."

[575] 2 Nephi 9:18 "But, behold, the righteous, the saints of the Holy One of Israel, they who have believed in the Holy One of Israel, they who have endured the crosses of the world, and despised the shame of it, they shall inherit the kingdom of God, which was prepared for them from the foundation of the world, and their joy shall be full forever."

the same path and take the same steps as all others who went before. There simply is not a way to avoid the rigors of the journey. It must change YOU. The work of the Father is to develop YOU. To do so it will require you to cooperate with Him. It is His work and His glory, but you must choose to let Him bring you along. Read Nephi's remarkable summary:

> "Behold, the Lord hath created the earth that it should be inhabited; and he hath created his children that they should possess it. And he raiseth up a righteous nation, and destroyeth the nations of the wicked. And he leadeth away the righteous into precious lands, and the wicked he destroyeth, and curseth the land unto them for their sakes. He ruleth high in the heavens, for it is his throne, and this earth is his footstool. And **he loveth those who will have him to be their God**. Behold, he loved our fathers, and he covenanted with them, yea, even Abraham, Isaac, and Jacob; and he remembered the covenants which he had made;" (1 Nephi 17:36–40)

Can you not see the pleading, the meekness and the humility in this description of our God?

Great is His wisdom and endless His mercy and the extent of His doings no man can find out! He makes Himself known to those who seek after Him, and those who cry out they do not know Him is only because they have chosen to ignore His plea!

We will return then to Nephi's writings and continue this effort to understand what great covenants the Book of Mormon lay before us if we choose to receive them.

A home or Temple is called "sacred space" because the Lord may come and dwell there. It is a place of refuge and peace. It would be good to have such a house right now. But, if not, "know ye not that ye are the Temple of God?" God can come and dwell with you, even if others will not permit Him. Since you are the Temple, you may become the sacred space to which He comes. The blood on the posts and lentil saved the occupants, for the sake of the righteous. For the want of a few Sodom was destroyed. Be the few. Be the leaven. Be the salt. If you are the Temple, you preserve more than yourself.

What makes any of you think you can become redeemed without bringing others with you? Why would you think that those given to associate with you are not a gift from God, deliberately in your life to permit you the high honor and great responsibility of showing by a godly walk what redemption can bring? Why shrug off others, thinking they will fail when you will succeed? You will only succeed if you minister to them in patience, all the while seeking their redemption even before your own. Christ came not to be ministered to, but to minister. Why would it be different for His servants?

We're still in a discussion to try and make sense of the present and future of Zion.

We have seen how priestly authority is more complex than a list of names on a page showing some connection to the Prophet Joseph Smith. We have examined how necessary it is to reconnect with heaven itself to have not just authority, but also power in the priesthood. That connection of power in the priesthood comes from the hand of God, not from another man. The powers of the priesthood are inseparably connected with the powers of heaven and the hand of God.[576]

Men do not make priests, God does. For those who have eyes to see, God's hand in priestly authority has been seen by endowed Latter-day Saints from Nauvoo onward. Men do not make prophets.

---

[576] D&C 121:36 "That the rights of the priesthood are inseparably connected with the powers of heaven, and that the powers of heaven cannot be controlled nor handled only upon the principles of righteousness."

God has reserved that right for Himself.[577]   God will call them whether or not men accept or recognize them.

We think we have a hope in membership in the church, but the scriptures offer us no reason for that hope. Hope lies in Christ.

We have seen how carefully the Book of Mormon distinguishes between the "remnant" to inherit great promises, and "gentiles" who must align themselves with Christ to become inheritors of those promises. We have seen how members of The Church of Jesus Christ of Latter-day Saints are always identified with the gentiles,[578] and not the remnant.

We have seen how the gentiles will be given authority over the remnant, and will be permitted to abuse and tread upon them for a season. We have seen that the promises once given the remnant will be given conditionally and for a season to the gentiles, who will receive the book written by the remnant's forebearers. The gentiles will become a great nation, and will be protected and powerful. They will be greater than any other nation on the earth. We have read how that will result in pride and foolishness.

We have seen that the gentiles will be swept away, just as the remnant was swept away. But those gentiles who will repent and receive Christ will receive a covenant entitling them to also belong to and possess this land as a place of inheritance.

Those gentiles who enter into this covenant, repent, come to Christ and receive Christ's presence will be preserved as the remainder of the gentiles' probation ends. When the time of the gentile dominance ends, they will be swept away.

---

[577] Numbers 12:6 "And he said, Hear now my words: If there be a prophet among you, I the Lord will make myself known unto him in a vision, and will speak unto him in a dream."

[578] D&C 109:60 "Now these words, O Lord, we have spoken before thee, concerning the revelations and commandments which thou hast given unto us, who are identified with the Gentiles."

We have seen that the gentiles who do not possess the covenant will become trodden under foot just as the remnant. The world will descend into darkness, as the Spirit and the Light of Christ withdraws from all but those who are chosen heirs. The wicked will destroy the wicked. The gathered faithful will have the Lord's Spirit as a protection and shield. The wicked will fear and not go near them, for they will be "terrible" to the wicked.

The covenant people will be gathered in the "tops of the mountains" where there will be a refuge and the Lord will be among them. When the destruction ends and the wicked have been swept away, the Father will return these gathered covenant people to their lands of promise. When He does, His hand will be over them, and will be their rear guard. Nothing and no-one will hurt or make them afraid.

This orients us to begin to consider more carefully what the gentiles have done and will do with their opportunity. So we return to Nephi's writings to look more carefully at ourselves and the perils we face.

All of this is an experiment to see if it is possible to have this kind of discussion take place on a blog. I used to teach a weekly Book of Mormon class where we examined the text carefully. In those ten years we were able to go from 1 Nephi 1:1 to Jarom 1:4. I know the material could be taught in that setting because the people were in front of me and I could take in what they were receiving as I taught. This is an alien way to teach, where disembodied words are put into a blog to be read by those who may or may not be attentive, diligent, prayerful and prepared. I cannot gage the effectiveness of this as well except from how the Lord assists me at my end. At the reader's end I am divided by circuitry, time and space and cannot measure as I could if you were in front of me.

I will continue the experiment, but remain doubtful that this will work as well as a book or a meeting would. In the end, the reader (or listener) must have the Spirit to be able to take in any light taught. So you will determine for yourself if you will receive what is offered. So, we will see . . .

2 NEPHI 28

2 Nephi 28:1–2

"And now, behold, my brethren, I have spoken unto you, according as the Spirit hath constrained me; wherefore, I know that they must surely come to pass. And the things which shall be written out of the book shall be of great worth unto the children of men, and especially unto our seed, which is a remnant of the house of Israel."

Nephi, as any prophetic writer, says what "the Spirit hath constrained" him to say. This is the very definition of using the Lord's name with permission and not using His name in vain.[579]

Nephi held power from God in the words he used. Therefore he could "know that they must surely come to pass" because he sealed them as he wrote them.[580] For any person holding the sealing authority (which is an indispensable part of the Patriarchal Priesthood discussed earlier), the authority requires an alignment between the prophet, the Lord and the Lord's will. See D&C 132:45–49, in par-

---

[579] Exodus 20:7: "Thou shalt not take the name of the Lord thy God in vain; for the Lord will not hold him guiltless that taketh his name in vain."

[580] D&C 1:38: "What I the Lord have spoken, I have spoken, and I excuse not myself; and though the heavens and the earth pass away, my word shall not pass away, but shall all be fulfilled, whether by mine own voice or by the voice of my servants, it is the same."

ticular verse 48 which mentions "by my word and according to my law"—which required Joseph to align himself with the Lord before using that power.[581] Those who have this authority will not do anything contrary to the will of the Lord.[582] It is because of this trust between the Lord and His messenger that the power is given to the man. Nephi was such a man. His book contained a seal upon it bearing the power of God.

Nephi knew.

Knowledge came from Christ.

Nephi knew Christ.[583]

Notice how Nephi refers to the "remnant" who are "our seed." Nephi refers to the remnant variously as:

---

[581] D&C 132:45–49 "For I have conferred upon you the keys and power of the priesthood, wherein I restore all things, and make known unto you all things in due time. And verily, verily, I say unto you, that whatsoever you seal on earth shall be sealed in heaven; and whatsoever you bind on earth, in my name and by my word, saith the Lord, it shall be eternally bound in the heavens; and whosesoever sins you remit on earth shall be remitted eternally in the heavens; and whosesoever sins you retain on earth shall be retained in heaven. And again, verily I say, whomsoever you bless I will bless, and whomsoever you curse I will curse, saith the Lord; for I, the Lord, am thy God. And again, verily I say unto you, my servant Joseph, that whatsoever you give on earth, and to whomsoever you give any one on earth, by my word and according to my law, it shall be visited with blessings and not cursings, and with my power, saith the Lord, and shall be without condemnation on earth and in heaven. For I am the Lord thy God, and will be with thee even unto the end of the world, and through all eternity; for verily I seal upon you your exaltation, and prepare a throne for you in the kingdom of my Father, with Abraham your father."

[582] Helaman 10:5 "And now, because thou hast done this with such unwearyingness, behold, I will bless thee forever; and I will make thee mighty in word and in deed, in faith and in works; yea, even that all things shall be done unto thee according to thy word, for thou shalt not ask that which is contrary to my will."

[583] 2 Nephi 11:3 "And my brother, Jacob, also has seen him as I have seen him; wherefore, I will send their words forth unto my children to prove unto them that my words are true. Wherefore, by the words of three, God hath said, I will establish my word. Nevertheless, God sendeth more witnesses, and he proveth all his words."

- descendants of his father Lehi[584]
- descendants of his brethren[585]
- his family's descendants or "our seed"[586]
- a mixture of Nephi's descendants who are among his brother's descendant's[587]

Nephi's primary line of descendants would be destroyed, but that destruction would not include all. There would remain a mixture of

---

[584] 1 Nephi 13:34 "And it came to pass that the angel of the Lord spake unto me, saying: Behold, saith the Lamb of God, after I have visited the remnant of the house of Israel—and this remnant of whom I speak is the seed of thy father—wherefore, after I have visited them in judgment, and smitten them by the hand of the Gentiles, and after the Gentiles do stumble exceedingly, because of the most plain and precious parts of the gospel of the Lamb which have been kept back by that abominable church, which is the mother of harlots, saith the Lamb—I will be merciful unto the Gentiles in that day, insomuch that I will bring forth unto them, in mine own power, much of my gospel, which shall be plain and precious, saith the Lamb."

[585] 1 Nephi 13:38–39 "And it came to pass that I beheld the remnant of the seed of my brethren, and also the book of the Lamb of God, which had proceeded forth from the mouth of the Jew, that it came forth from the Gentiles unto the remnant of the seed of my brethren. And after it had come forth unto them I beheld other books, which came forth by the power of the Lamb, from the Gentiles unto them, unto the convincing of the Gentiles and the remnant of the seed of my brethren, and also the Jews who were scattered upon all the face of the earth, that the records of the prophets and of the twelve apostles of the Lamb are true."

[586] 1 Nephi 15:13–14 "And now, the thing which our father meaneth concerning the grafting in of the natural branches through the fulness of the Gentiles, is, that in the latter days, when our seed shall have dwindled in unbelief, yea, for the space of many years, and many generations after the Messiah shall be manifested in body unto the children of men, then shall the fulness of the gospel of the Messiah come unto the Gentiles, and from the Gentiles unto the remnant of our seed—And at that day shall the remnant of our seed know that they are of the house of Israel, and that they are the covenant people of the Lord; and then shall they know and come to the knowledge of their forefathers, and also to the knowledge of the gospel of their Redeemer, which was ministered unto their fathers by him; wherefore, they shall come to the knowledge of their Redeemer and the very points of his doctrine, that they may know how to come unto him and be saved."

[587] 1 Nephi 13:30 "Nevertheless, thou beholdest that the Gentiles who have gone forth out of captivity, and have been lifted up by the power of God above all other nations, upon the face of the land which is choice above all other lands, which is the land that the Lord God hath covenanted with thy father that his seed should have for the land of their inheritance; wherefore, thou seest that the Lord God will not suffer that the Gentiles will utterly destroy the mixture of thy seed, which are among thy brethren."

blood that would include partial descent from Nephi.[588] The various bloodlines remained identified as Nephites, Jacobites, Josephites, Zoramites, Lamanites, Lemuelites and Ishmaelites.[589] Although it would be impossible, without revelation, for us to determine which of these lines a person might belong to today, the Lord nevertheless revealed in 1828 that these various divisions remain identified to Him.[590] No doubt, in time, He will restore to the remnant descendants this knowledge of their sacred paternity and eternal identity.

Their blood may be mixed, but the remnant remains. Nephi may have referred to them more often as descendants of his "brethren," but they have within them some of his blood as well. In the day of redemption and restoration, the promises will all be fulfilled. The whole of the family of Lehi will be represented in the remnant.

Notice Nephi's prophecy is that "words which shall be written out of the book" rather than the book itself. This is, of course, exactly what we have. The actual book has been withheld. Only words

---

[588] 1 Nephi 13:30–31 "Nevertheless, thou beholdest that the Gentiles who have gone forth out of captivity, and have been lifted up by the power of God above all other nations, upon the face of the land which is choice above all other lands, which is the land that the Lord God hath covenanted with thy father that his seed should have for the land of their inheritance; wherefore, thou seest that the Lord God will not suffer that the Gentiles will utterly destroy the mixture of thy seed, which are among thy brethren. Neither will he suffer that the Gentiles shall destroy the seed of thy brethren."

[589] Mormon 1:8 "And it came to pass in this year there began to be a war between the Nephites, who consisted of the Nephites and the Jacobites and the Josephites and the Zoramites; and this war was between the Nephites, and the Lamanites and the Lemuelites and the Ishmaelites."

[590] D&C 3:16–19 "Nevertheless, my work shall go forth, for inasmuch as the knowledge of a Savior has come unto the world, through the testimony of the Jews, even so shall the knowledge of a Savior come unto my people—And to the Nephites, and the Jacobites, and the Josephites, and the Zoramites, through the testimony of their fathers—And this testimony shall come to the knowledge of the Lamanites, and the Lemuelites, and the Ishmaelites, who dwindled in unbelief because of the iniquity of their fathers, whom the Lord has suffered to destroy their brethren the Nephites, because of their iniquities and their abominations. And for this very purpose are these plates preserved, which contain these records—that the promises of the Lord might be fulfilled, which he made to his people;"

from the book have been given us. But those words are intended to be of great worth to mankind, and in particular to the remnant.

This process is sacred, the promises are from the Lord. These words are given to us by Him, through a servant possessing authority to seal them up. We cannot prevent them from happening. We can, however, align ourselves with them and in turn be saved as well.

2 Nephi 28:3

"For it shall come to pass in that day that the churches which are built up, and not unto the Lord, when the one shall say unto the other: Behold, I, I am the Lord's; and the others shall say: I, I am the Lord's; and thus shall every one say that hath built up churches, and not unto the Lord—"

The Book of Mormon will become available to the remnant in a day when there will be "churches which are built up, and not unto the Lord." Generally this is interpreted by Latter-day Saints to mean OTHER churches, but not ours. However, the context requires all, including our own church, to be considered at risk as well. Here are the questions bearing on whether we (LDS) are among those being warned:

- Is the prophecy limited to the time before the Book of Mormon comes forth? (No; it will reach until the time when other records of the Lost Tribes are to come forth—a future event.[591])

---

[591] 2 Nephi 29:13–14 "And it shall come to pass that the Jews shall have the words of the Nephites, and the Nephites shall have the words of the Jews; and the Nephites and the Jews shall have the words of the lost tribes of Israel; and the lost tribes of Israel shall have the words of the Nephites and the Jews. And it shall come to pass that my people, which are of the house of Israel, shall be gathered home unto the lands of their possessions; and my word also shall be gathered in one. And I will show unto them that fight against my word and against my people, who are of the house of Israel, that I am God, and that I covenanted with Abraham that I would remember his seed forever."

- Is the prophecy about only those churches created by man, and not one intended to become Zion? (No.[592])

- Can a church established by the Lord become one which is not built up to Him? (Of course.[593])

- Does the promise that the Lord will never abandon His latter-day work[594] mean that the church He established will not drift into condemnation?

Should we therefore consider these warnings to be equally applicable to us Latter-day Saints as to the larger community of churches?

Nephi warns that each church will claim it is the Lord's. Do we do that? Each will claim divine authority and approval. Do we do that? Each will assert it belongs to the Lord. Do we do that? But the question Nephi focuses upon is whether it is "unto the Lord."

What does it mean for a church to be "unto the Lord?" What would the opposite be?

How certain are we that what we do as a church is building up to the Lord? Do the procurement practices of the church "build up unto the Lord?" Does the auditor's report in General Conference

---

[592] 2 Nephi 28:21–24 "And others will he pacify, and lull them away into carnal security, that they will say: All is well in Zion; yea, Zion prospereth, all is well—and thus the devil cheateth their souls, and leadeth them away carefully down to hell. And behold, others he flattereth away, and telleth them there is no hell; and he saith unto them: I am no devil, for there is none—and thus he whispereth in their ears, until he grasps them with his awful chains, from whence there is no deliverance. Yea, they are grasped with death, and hell; and death, and hell, and the devil, and all that have been seized therewith must stand before the throne of God, and be judged according to their works, from whence they must go into the place prepared for them, even a lake of fire and brimstone, which is endless torment. Therefore, wo be unto him that is at ease in Zion!"

[593] Ezekiel 44:10 "And the Levites that are gone away far from me, when Israel went astray, which went astray away from me after their idols; they shall even bear their iniquity."
Isaiah 53:6 "All we like sheep have gone astray; we have turned every one to his own way; and the Lord hath laid on him the iniquity of us all."
John 5:39 "Search the scriptures; for in them ye think ye have eternal life: and they are they which testify of me."

[594] D&C 138:44 "Daniel, who foresaw and foretold the establishment of the kingdom of God in the latter days, never again to be destroyed nor given to other people;"

even begin to allow you to make that determination? If some of the large and well-connected Latter-day Saint families own the businesses which contract with the church and have become wealthy by reason of trading with the church, is there some question which ought to be considered about "building up unto the Lord" in how business is conducted?

I explained how the church distinguishes between tithing money and "investment income" in a post on April 1, 2010. Does this seem consistent with the Lord's parable about the talents?[595] If in the parable, all returns realized on the money were the Lord's, why does the return on the Lord's tithing now become investment money to be used for commercial projects developing condominiums, shopping malls, banks, and other income-producing ventures? Who is benefiting? What careers and fortunes are being made? What families are being benefited? Are they the Lord?

Assuming the purpose of a church were to "build up unto the Lord" what single purpose would be most important? In the Book of Mormon, as I've explained earlier, the writers seek to have you trade unbelief for belief; then to trade belief for faith; then to come beyond faith and receive knowledge. The knowledge it would have you obtain is of Christ.[596]

---

[595] Luke 19:20–23 "And another came, saying, Lord, behold, here is thy pound, which I have kept laid up in a napkin: For I feared thee, because thou art an austere man: thou takest up that thou layedst not down, and reapest that thou didst not sow. And he saith unto him, Out of thine own mouth will I judge thee, thou wicked servant. Thou knewest that I was an austere man, taking up that I laid not down, and reaping that I did not sow: Wherefore then gavest not thou my money into the bank, that at my coming I might have required mine own with usury?"

[596] Ether 3:19 "And because of the knowledge of this man he could not be kept from beholding within the veil; and he saw the finger of Jesus, which, when he saw, he fell with fear; for he knew that it was the finger of the Lord; and he had faith no longer, for he knew, nothing doubting."

The lack of knowledge condemns a people who claim to be the Lord's. Nephi quoted Isaiah in 2 Nephi 15.[597]

"Therefore, my people are gone into captivity, because they have no knowledge; and their honorable men are famished, and their multitude dried up with thirst." (2 Nephi 15:13)

Captivity comes from a lack of knowledge. Joseph Smith warned that "a man is saved no faster than he gains knowledge." (*DHC* 5:588.) The ones who are considered "honorable" are "famished" because they lack knowledge. The "multitude" who follow the "honorable men" are in turn "dried up with thirst" because they are not taught enough to become saved.[598]

If the Lord promises to never abandon His latter-day work[599], does that mean men cannot abandon Him? Although men may abandon Him, can He work with you individually and "remember" His promises? Even if others are without knowledge, can you still obtain knowledge from Him? Though others may be "dried up with thirst" can you still obtain "living waters" from Him?

Can you rely upon the assertions from any church today that it is "built up unto the Lord?" How can you be "built up unto the Lord" even if you do not have any institution you can trust to bring to you

---

[597] You will not understand Nephi's purpose in quoting Isaiah if you are unacquainted with *Nephi's Isaiah*.

[598] 2 Nephi 28:14 "They wear stiff necks and high heads; yea, and because of pride, and wickedness, and abominations, and whoredoms, they have all gone astray save it be a few, who are the humble followers of Christ; nevertheless, they are led, that in many instances they do err because they are taught by the precepts of men."

[599] D&C 138:44 "Daniel, who foresaw and foretold the establishment of the kingdom of God in the latter days, never again to be destroyed nor given to other people;"

that knowledge? Was the Lord always intended to be directly involved in your life?[600]

If "captivity" comes from a lack of knowledge, and Joseph Smith tied knowledge to salvation, then why is the correlated curriculum of the church focusing less and less on doctrine? Why was the Relief Society and Priesthood Manual on *Teachings of the Presidents* volume on Joseph Smith carefully edited by the Correlation Department so as to support meanings somewhat different than Joseph's? If you think meanings were not changed, then go to the sources quoted in the *History of The Church* and read each of the whole statements made by Joseph from which the excerpts were taken. I leave it to you to decide if the edited versions in the church manual were or were not both incomplete and misleading. [Personally, I was dismayed. But I have a sensitivity to words that is quite acute, and therefore something left out that is important to me may not be significant to you. You must decide that question for yourself. You will find it an interesting exercise even if you disagree with my conclusion.]

If a church claims to be built up to the Lord, but does not attempt to confer knowledge of the Lord upon people, then how are you to seek after this knowledge? [We are going to be discussing Nephi's instruction to us about this very subject for the coming weeks. So keep the question in mind as we go forward.]

---

[600] Matthew 11:27–30 "All things are delivered unto me of my Father: and no man knoweth the Son, but the Father; neither knoweth any man the Father, save the Son, and he to whomsoever the Son will reveal him. Come unto me, all ye that labour and are heavy laden, and I will give you rest. Take my yoke upon you, and learn of me; for I am meek and lowly in heart: and ye shall find rest unto your souls. For my yoke is easy, and my burden is light."

Remember this is the promised day when all are intended to grow into knowledge of the Lord, from the least to the greatest.[601] "Those who remain" will remain because they have "knowledge" that will save them. Hence Joseph's teaching about the link between "knowledge" and "salvation." Also, the captivity spoken of by Nephi because people lack knowledge.

Go back to the post on Lecture 6 of the *Lectures on Faith*. If your church encourages you to become part of a broad mainstream without asking for the sacrifice of all things, then it is not requiring you to take the steps necessary to develop faith to save you. Rest assured, however, the Lord still has the same requirements, and He will work directly with you to develop you into a person who has the required knowledge. It was always intended to be individual. It is your quest. Others may encourage you along, but you must confront the process for yourself.

[Now, as a complete aside, I want to address the misapplication and overreaching misinterpretation of the idea one is "evil speaking" when a person explains something that concerns them. First, we are dealing with the souls of men. We are addressing salvation itself. If there is an error in doctrine or practice, everyone has an obligation to

---

[601] JS–H 1:41 "He also quoted the second chapter of Joel, from the twenty-eighth verse to the last. He also said that this was not yet fulfilled, but was soon to be. And he further stated that the fulness of the Gentiles was soon to come in. He quoted many other passages of scripture, and offered many explanations which cannot be mentioned here."
Joel 2:28–29 "And it shall come to pass afterward, that I will pour out my spirit upon all flesh; and your sons and your daughters shall prophesy, your old men shall dream dreams, your young men shall see visions: And also upon the servants and upon the handmaids in those days will I pour out my spirit."
D&C 84:96–97 "For I, the Almighty, have laid my hands upon the nations, to scourge them for their wickedness. And plagues shall go forth, and they shall not be taken from the earth until I have completed my work, which shall be cut short in righteousness—"

speak up, from the least to the greatest.[602] Second, the "truth" cannot ever be "evil." Though the truth may cut with a two edged sword, truth is not and cannot be "evil." Therefore, if someone should say something that is untrue or in error, then correct their doctrine, show the error, but do not claim what is good to be evil, nor support what is evil by calling it good.[603] Using a broad generalization to stifle a discussion of the truth is a trick of the devil, who is an enemy to your soul. It is not the way of our Lord. He was always open to questions, always willing to answer questions, ever willing to speak the truth even when it caused those with authority over Him to be pained by His words. We must follow Him, and not men, in that example. Even if we would personally prefer to not endure insults but remain silent. So, rather than condemn something as "evil speaking" that you believe to be wrong, explain the error and bring us all into greater understanding. But if something is true, then even if it disturbs your peace of mind, it cannot be evil.]

2 Nephi 28:4

"And they shall contend one with another; and their priests shall contend one with another, and they shall teach with their learning, and deny the Holy Ghost, which giveth utterance."

Nephi foresees that churches in our day will argue over the claim to have truth. When it comes to the Latter-day Saints, the relentless

---

[602] D&C 20:42, 46–47, 50–51, 59 (among other places): "And to teach, expound, exhort, baptize, and watch over the church; The priest's duty is to preach, teach, expound, exhort, and baptize, and administer the sacrament, And visit the house of each member, and exhort them to pray vocally and in secret and attend to all family duties. But when there is an elder present, he is only to preach, teach, expound, exhort, and baptize, And visit the house of each member, exhorting them to pray vocally and in secret and attend to all family duties. They are, however, to warn, expound, exhort, and teach, and invite all to come unto Christ."

[603] 2 Nephi 15:20 "Wo unto them that call evil good, and good evil, that put darkness for light, and light for darkness, that put bitter for sweet, and sweet for bitter!"

accusation made against us is that we aren't "Christian." This accusation is made by those who claim the right to define the word "Christian" to necessarily include acceptance of the creeds of Historic Christianity. These creeds are an amalgam of Neo-Platonic philosophy mingled with scripture.

We just ought to concede the point. We should proudly acknowledge we are NOT part of Historic Christianity. We disagree with Historic Christianity, and at a fundamental level we denounce it as false. We are a restoration of Primitive Christianity. We do not share in accepting the creeds which Christ Himself denounced as "an abomination in His sight."[604]

Oddly, from our end, we try and avoid the argument, fit in, claim we are "good Christians too," and part of the larger community of churches. There isn't as much fight left in us as there was once. Or, perhaps more correctly, our arguments are focused instead, toward those who attempt to preserve practices from the early part of the Restoration. In other words, we try to make ourselves seem more like Historic Christianity, and avoid or discard what once set us apart. We have inverted the picture from where we began. (Nephi will address that, as well.)

Although there are numerous examples of how we have altered our views to become more like other faiths, we can take just one to illustrate the point. We have abandoned plural marriage. But it is hard for us to claim the doctrine is false because it remains in Section 132 of the Doctrine and Covenants. While we do not practice it, and believe those who do have failed to stay on track, we cannot gainsay that the doctrine is true. Yet no other church is so vehement in de-

---

[604] JS–H 1:19 "I was answered that I must join none of them, for they were all wrong; and the Personage who addressed me said that all their creeds were an abomination in his sight; that those professors were all corrupt; that: 'they draw near to me with their lips, but their hearts are far from me, they teach for doctrines the commandments of men, having a form of godliness, but they deny the power thereof'."

nouncing and persecuting those who practice plural marriage. It is as if we want to lead the argument against the practice in order to distract people from the fact that the practice is approved in our scriptures.

Let me be clear that I do not advocate the practice nor recommend it. Nor do I think those who continue the practice do so either with approval or authority. I've explained the defects in their arguments to authority in *Beloved Enos,* and I am confident in the explanation given there. They do not possess the keys to continue that practice. Their own position is self-defeating.

Nor do I think these people will be given the hand of fellowship until Zion returns. But when it does, I do not expect those who follow the practice if plural marriage in a humble and devout way, having real intent, and proceeding prayerfully will be excluded from the gathering. It also seems self-evident that if John D. Lee, who was executed for the Mountain Meadows Massacre, has been reinstated to the privileges of the church, that those practicing plural marriage after the 1905 letter from President Joseph F. Smith will some day not also be reinstated to church membership.

Well, that was an aside merely to illustrate a point. We fail to contend about errors of other faiths, fail to defend our unique status, and in turn attack doctrines that we know to be true.

What Nephi will focus on in his prophecy is not the contention, but the absence of guidance from the Holy Ghost. This criticism will become the theme of the coming chapters. This collection of chapters at the end of 2 Nephi are his final warnings in which he tells us the great themes of prophecy that rest so heavily upon his soul. He is most alarmed that, in our day, men will " teach with their learning, and deny the Holy Ghost, which giveth utterance." What do you suppose it means to "teach with their learning?"

We know that other churches employ trained theological experts to professionally teach them as a paid clergy. We have always been critical of that approach because once a minister has been to college and been trained for the ministry, they mingle the philosophies of men with scripture. We have always been taught that even a child with the Spirit can edify a congregation in Sacrament by speaking with the influence of the Holy Ghost. We intend our meetings to be directed in word and thought by the Holy Ghost. But how much of what we are taught in our meetings and conferences are the result of man's learning? Of focus group opinion gathering? Of opinion polling? Of careful study of trends and development of data bases from social sciences? (See the post titled "Slippery".)

How much of what we are taught is from the "Spirit which giveth utterance?" How often are we fed as the Lord directed in D&C 84:85 through entirely spontaneous utterance?[605] If Joseph was commanded to speak spontaneously so the Spirit could direct him[606] then why is a Correlation Department allowed to control talks today and prevent any spontaneous speaking in our conferences?

I know the purpose behind correlation was to insure false doctrine was not taught. They seem to have instead insured that no doctrine is taught.

In my view, correlation has failed in its purpose. It has stifled the Spirit and stripped us of doctrine which should be prized and taught. Furthermore, it has not insured the doctrine it permits to be taught is true or consistent with scripture or earlier teachings.

---

[605] D&C 84:85 "Neither take ye thought beforehand what ye shall say; but treasure up in your minds continually the words of life, and it shall be given you in the very hour that portion that shall be meted unto every man."

[606] D&C 100:5–6 "Therefore, verily I say unto you, lift up your voices unto this people; speak the thoughts that I shall put into your hearts, and you shall not be confounded before men; For it shall be given you in the very hour, yea, in the very moment, what ye shall say."

D&C 24:5–6 "And thou shalt continue in calling upon God in my name, and writing the things which shall be given thee by the Comforter, and expounding all scriptures unto the church. And it shall be given thee in the very moment what thou shalt speak and write, and they shall hear it, or I will send unto them a cursing instead of a blessing."

Even though correlation has not prevented us from having errors of doctrine I do not believe an error of doctrine makes a person a bad man. Joseph Smith said:

"I did not like the old man being called up for erring in doctrine. It looks too much like the Methodist, and not like the Latter-day Saints. Methodists have creeds which a man must believe or be asked out of their church. I want the liberty of thinking and believing as I please. It feels so good not to be trammeled. It does not prove that a man is not a good man because he errs in doctrine." (*DHC* 5:340)

I do not believe anyone should ever be subject to church discipline for believing false doctrine. The false teaching should be overcome by teaching the truth, not by stifling discussion. The quickest way for truth to triumph is to allow free discussion. When we are open, the truth will always win out.

I agree with Joseph Smith that teaching false doctrine does not prove "that a man is not a good man." Take the *Proclamation on the Family*, for example. It states:

"All human beings —male and female—are created in the image of God. Each is a beloved spirit son or daughter of heavenly parents, and, as such, each has a divine nature and destiny. Gender is an essential characteristic of individual premortal, mortal, and eternal identity and purpose."

This statement conflicts with what President Joseph Fielding Smith taught in the arrangement prepared by Bruce R. McConkie (and therefore undoubtedly approved by Elder McConkie as well):

"Some of the functions in the celestial body will not appear in the terrestrial body, neither in the telestial body, and the power of procreation will be removed. I take it that men and women will, in these kingdoms, be just what the so-called Christian world expects us all to be: **neither man nor woman,** merely immortal beings having received the resurrection. (*Doctrines of Salvation* 2:287–288; emphasis added.)

In another place President Smith taught,

"Is not the sectarian world justified in their doctrine generally proclaimed, that **after the resurrection there will be neither male nor female sex?** It is a logical conclusion for them to reach and apparently is in full harmony with what the Lord has revealed regarding the kingdoms into which evidently the vast majority of mankind is likely to go." *(Answers to Gospel Questions* 4:66—a set that was also edited by Elder Bruce R. McConkie.)

If it is a grave offense to now err in doctrine, either President Smith and his son-in-law Elder McConkie should be condemned, or those who signed the *Proclamation on the Family* in September 1995 (the entire First Presidency and Quorum of the Twelve) should be condemned. They contradict one another. The Apostle Paul would seem to agree with President Smith and Elder McConkie.[607] The "Christian" world, of course, denounces marriage in eternity precisely because they disbelieve sexual identity ends with mortality. They base this upon Luke 20:34–35, Matthew 22:30, and Mark 12:25 as well as Paul's statement in Galatians.

It appears to me that someone errs in doctrine. Despite that, I absolutely DO NOT BELIEVE that either the First Presidency and Quorum of the Twelve in 1995, nor President Joseph Fielding Smith and Bruce R. McConkie are bad men. Nor do I think that the contradiction should be managed by the Correlation Department. I think it should stand and become something on which each of us consider, ponder, pray and reach some conclusion for ourselves. It isn't neces-

---

[607] Galatians 3:28 "There is neither Jew nor Greek, there is neither bond nor free, there is neither male nor female: for ye are all one in Christ Jesus."

sary for us to always have controversies taken away from us, particularly at the expense of losing our doctrine.

The approach now is to prevent spontaneous talks from being delivered under the influence of the Holy Spirit because of fear that we would excite criticism by contradicting one another. I think this is wrong. If we want to be cautious about doctrine, then we ought to call men who understand and teach doctrine to preside. I see trustworthy men and women on KBYU discussing doctrine all the time. Elder Packer was a Seminary Instructor before his call to be a General Authority, and he has always been reliable on doctrine. I would love to hear him speak spontaneously every time he speaks. Elder Scott, also, seems to me to be a man who, if allowed to speak without a prepared text would have a great deal to share. It would be delightful to hear him speak extemporaneously. There is something valuable enough when an inspired man does this that the D&C admonished Joseph Smith to only address the Saints in this manner. If that was the Lord's desire for Joseph, and it remains in the D&C, then it is little wonder we pay a price as a result of the correlation process.

This is what the verse we are considering here it telling us SHOULD be the case. We cannot help but "deny the Holy Ghost, which giveth utterance" when we do not permit the Holy Ghost the opportunity to inspire by giving spontaneous utterance.

President Brigham Young said,

> "What a pity it would be if we were led by one man to utter destruction! Are you afraid of this? I am more afraid that this people have so much confidence in their leaders that they will not inquire of themselves of God whether they are led by Him. I am fearful they will settle down in a state of blind self-security, trusting their eternal security in the hands of their leaders with a reckless confidence that in itself would thwart the purposes of God in their salvation, and weaken that influence they could give to their leaders, did they know for them-

selves, by the revelations of Jesus Christ, that they are led in the right way." (*JD* 9:149–50.)

Joseph Smith cautioned about trusting to much in the prophet and neglecting the duties devolving upon the Saints individually. And George Q. Cannon also taught the principle that you cannot trust leadership to save you.

> "It makes no difference what is written or what anyone has said, if what has been said is in conflict with what the Lord has revealed, we can set it aside. My words, and the teachings of any other member of the Church, high or low, if they do not square with the revelations, we need not accept them. Let us have that matter clear." (*Doctrines of Salvation* 3:203, emphasis in original.)

2 Nephi 28:5

> "And they deny the power of God, the Holy One of Israel; and they say unto the people: Hearken unto us, and hear ye our precept; for behold there is no God today, for the Lord and the Redeemer hath done his work, and he hath given his power unto men;"

The defect Nephi terms "deny the power of God" is an interesting matter to ponder. What do you suppose denying that power involves? How would it manifest itself in the way religious people go about their lives? Is praying without seeking an answer "denying" God's power? Is presuming you have an answer when your own desires are all you are considering perhaps also "denying" God's power?

I reflect on how many times I've learned something surprising, unanticipated, or which had never before entered into my mind. I think, too, about Joseph's comment before his First Vision that "it had never entered into [his] heart that all were wrong"[608], but the answer from God informed him otherwise. God's answers are quite often:

- unanticipated
- never something you would have considered
- inconvenient
- requiring of you something you would prefer not to give or do
- clear and unequivocal
- enough to make your frame shake as it penetrates your soul.

When prayer gets through to God and provokes an answer from Him, it is offered with a sincere heart, having real intent.[609] If a prayer is offered without a sincere heart, and while lacking real intent, is this "denying" the power of God?

If a minister lacks real intent, and does not go to God in mighty prayer, has never become acquainted with the "power of God," but proceeds to teach with their own learning anyway, do they deny the power of God?

In place of preaching what the Lord reveals, men will claim they teach correct "precepts." They have all the revelation they need, and they are now proceeding with the authority given them by God. But they don't hear from Him, don't have new revelation to deliver from Him, and do not expect God to be involved any longer.

---

[608] JS–H 1:18 "My object in going to inquire of the Lord was to know which of all the sects was right, that I might know which to join. No sooner, therefore, did I get possession of myself, so as to be able to speak, than I asked the Personages who stood above me in the light, which of all the sects was right (for at this time it had never entered into my heart that all were wrong)—and which I should join."

[609] Moroni 10:4 "And when ye shall receive these things, I would exhort you that ye would ask God, the Eternal Father, in the name of Christ, if these things are not true; and if ye shall ask with a sincere heart, with real intent, having faith in Christ, he will manifest the truth of it unto you, by the power of the Holy Ghost."
James 1:5 "If any of you lack wisdom, let him ask of God, that giveth to all men liberally, and upbraideth not; and it shall be given him."

In effect, God has become so distant that "there is no God to-day." He finished His work. He's given His authority to men.

Whether the claim is based on Protestant claims that authority is derived from the New Testament, and all men who believe have authority from God, or it is a Catholic claim to have a line of authority back to Jesus Christ, it is the same. Without some involvement from God in the church itself, the teachings end in the same conclusion: "God has given His power unto men." The institution has taken over. The claim is always that "the church is true" without regard to whether the Lord remains involved, revealing Himself to the church. This is what the Catholic Church has claimed for centuries God has finished His work and surrendered the "keys of authority" to the church. Now God has transmuted into a church, a Holy Roman Church, to which you may confess your sins, obtain absolution for your sins, and have entry into heaven provided to you.

With such a claim, why ask God for help? Why turn to a priesthood advancing such claims? Why make the difficult, inner changes that bring about real intent and faith in Christ? Why seek for and come into contact with "the power of God" if a church can be an adequate substitute?

How like the Catholics have we become?

Was Nephi only warning about Catholic error? Do his warnings apply equally to all?

2 Nephi 28:6

> "Behold, hearken ye unto my precept; if they shall say there is
> a miracle wrought by the hand of the Lord, believe it not; for
> this day he is not a God of miracles; he hath done his work."

This lack of faith in receiving answers to prayer from God leads to skepticism about any other manifestation by God. If the leader isn't having any experience with God, then they distrust claims by anyone else. Everyone is a fraud, if the leader can't receive an answer to prayer.

The root of this is jealousy and envy. But it is completely unfounded. Revelation received by another person has no limiting effect on what personal revelation you can receive. The Lord is willing to share with all. However, it is predicated on the same principle. If the leader were willing to humble himself and seek in the prescribed manner, he would receive the same result. Everyone is invited. No one is excluded.

Nicodemus came to Christ in the dark, and Christ taught him the same way He taught others. There are some sources which suggest Nicodemus was ultimately converted. If he was, there is little doubt that after his conversion, the spiritual life he had as one of the Lord's disciples was greater than that of a member of the Sanhedrin. The Lord was not unwilling to share with the Sanhedrin, but they were unwilling to receive Him. When one (Nicodemus) changed his heart, the Lord came to him.

This seething distrust and accusation of any who claim to experience the miraculous leads in turn to denouncing the gifts of God. When denounced, such gifts depart from us. We no longer hear about miracles, healings, visions, tongues, visitations, or other gifts experienced by those we read of in scripture. Therefore, when the presence of the gifts end, the record of scriptures ends. There is nothing to add, and so nothing is added.

Eventually the end of this spiritual journey into the dark is to denounce all things coming from the "hand of God." No "miracle wrought by the hand of God" will be acknowledged, but will be denounced instead. The position becomes unalterable: "God is not a God of miracles anymore." You must trust leaders and leadership. You will be deceived if you profess revelation or the miraculous. And so the approach into hell is carefully laid by argument, emotion and fear.

Nephi foresaw this. He is warning us against it. We should not be seduced into thinking God has finished His work. He hasn't. He is in the middle of fulfilling promises made generations ago to the "fathers." We inherit from the Lord the promises He made to them. Now is a great day of miracles, visits, visitations, dreams, and healings. The heavens are open, if you will ask with a sincere heart having real intent, He will manifest the truth unto you. God remains the same. His blessings remain predicated upon the same conditions.

Seek. Ask. Knock. It will all be unfolded to you. He is no respecter of persons.

2 Nephi 28:7–8

"Yea, and there shall be many which shall say: Eat, drink, and be merry, for tomorrow we die; and it shall be well with us. And there shall also be many which shall say: Eat, drink, and be merry; nevertheless, fear God—he will justify in committing a little sin; yea, lie a little, take the advantage of one because of his words, dig a pit for thy neighbor; there is no harm in this; and do all these things, for tomorrow we die; and if it so be that we are guilty, God will beat us with a few stripes, and at last we shall be saved in the kingdom of God."

This notion that religion should always encourage merriment and feasting has so taken hold that it becomes impossible to cry repentance. Anything that challenges a happy outlook is thought to be negative and of the devil. It creates the misunderstanding that the right to feel good about one's self is a higher obligation than the duty to teach repentance and forsaking sin.

If you are laden with sin,[610] it is of no consequence, for God intends that you be happy. It is of little matter that happiness cannot be found in sin[611], the gospel of positive attitude and flattery will triumph with the ungodly every time when it competes with a warning to repent and return to Christ.

The whole system has been worked out for us. The odds are you're going to be exalted. Deseret Book has taken a firm stand on that very subject. We have it from God, you see. Because Deseret Book is owned by the church, the church has been headed by a prophet, the prophet can't lead you astray, and therefore the odds are you're going to be exalted—Or so the reasoning goes.

If Nephi's warning is urged against the tide of permissiveness, supported by this false gospel of positive attitude and false hope, then the message must surely be meant by Nephi for someone other than us. We cannot possibly be among those who incorrectly believe the Lord will justify us in committing a little sin. We do not believe in the utility of a little lie, do we? We do not use words to take advantage of others do we?

What pits have we dug for our neighbors?

By what measure do we advocate to live life pleasantly and not fear death or judgment? How could we be taken with the notion that a little guilt will result in merely a "few stripes" from an irritated, but ultimately tolerant, and permissive God? What doctrine is it we advance that suggests all of us will, at last, be saved in the kingdom of God?

---

[610] Isaiah 1:4 "Ah sinful nation, a people laden with iniquity, a seed of evildoers, children that are corrupters: they have forsaken the Lord, they have provoked the Holy One of Israel unto anger, they are gone away backward."

[611] Alma 41:10 "Do not suppose, because it has been spoken concerning restoration, that ye shall be restored from sin to happiness. Behold, I say unto you, wickedness never was happiness."

Assuming this was meant to be a warning to *us, the readers of the Book of Mormon, and not to another audience who will never read the book because they aren't converted to it,* then how do we fit into this warning? Do we have a mistaken view of God's plan? What do we say, preach or believe that would provoke this warning from Nephi? Have you scrutinized the recent manuals from the Correlation Department to see if there is any basis for concern? Have you read the General Conference talks for hints of these teachings? Do you find them there?

How many articles do you find in the LDS *Church News, Ensign* and *New Era* which are positive, flattering and reassuring? How many articles confront you, call you to repent, warn you of the judgment and the duration of eternity?[612]

Why is the Book of Mormon constantly calling upon us to repent? Why are we not called relentlessly to repentance by our current leaders? Is there a disconnection between the message of the Book of Mormon and our modern messages? Has the Lord changed His mind? Was Nephi just a crank? Is the Book of Mormon a negative book not relevant to an enlightened people who are specially chosen by God for endless happiness and promised they will never be led astray? Why would the Book of Mormon be a message for us? Why do we have a book so negative in tone, pessimistic in its view of us, while we sit atop the promises of never again having to face an apostasy?

What accounts for this disparity?

---

[612] Enos 1:23 "And there was nothing save it was exceeding harshness, preaching and prophesying of wars, and contentions, and destructions, and continually reminding them of death, and the duration of eternity, and the judgments and the power of God, and all these things—stirring them up continually to keep them in the fear of the Lord. I say there was nothing short of these things, and exceedingly great plainness of speech, would keep them from going down speedily to destruction. And after this manner do I write concerning them."

An interlude by Bobby McFerrin: "Hmmmmmm, hmm, hmm, hmm, hmm, hmm, hmmmm, hmmmm, hm-hum-hm-hm . . . Don't worry. Be happy."

He's Mormon now, isn't he? I heard someone's friend's boyfriend baptized him when serving a mission in Southern California . . .

Poets and artists have been proclaiming the coming apocalypse in songs, art and movies for several decades. Nephi gives us the same message. But we spin happily out of control, loosed from the moorings and tossed by the approaching hurricane, all the while promising one another that it will all turn out right. We are special. We are chosen by God. Surely He will not judge us, nor hold us to account for what we believe. If we're mistaken, He owes it to us to give us a warning, and an opportunity to repent. Other than that sad account of the prior occupants of this land, He hasn't done that . . .

Oh. The Book of Mormon is important, isn't it?

The foolishness of the doctrines that Nephi is denouncing provokes such dismay that our own foolishness needs to be paraded out in all its stupidity. We just don't seem to get it. We're reading Nephi's warnings to us and pretending they were meant for everyone other than us. They aren't—they are aiming at us. Read the verse again and try to see our own teachings being laid bare. We are his target. We are his audience. We are being warned.

2 Nephi 28:9

"Yea, and there shall be many which shall teach after this manner, false and vain and foolish doctrines, and shall be puffed up in their hearts, and shall seek deep to hide their counsels from the Lord; and their works shall be in the dark."

The alarming use of the word "many" suggests this is to be a widespread problem in our time. These teachings are denounced as "false and vain and foolish." We should look at each one.

What does "false" mean? Does something have to be thoroughly and completely wrong to be false? Is it enough to be off by enough to rob the teaching of power? How many truths will a liar tell while trying to get you to believe an ultimate lie? How well does a deception work if there isn't some truth included in the message? So, then, how difficult will detecting the error be? May the very elect be deceived?[613] How will one be able to decide between a false and a true teaching?[614]

What does "vain" mean? Is the best meaning "futile" or "without power?" If a teaching robs you of power, deprives you of the Spirit, is that "vain?" What would you trade in exchange for having power in the Spirit? If a little flattery is enough, would you take the assurance that God loves you, and will never let you be deceived enough to get you to let go of the responsibility to ever have His Spirit to be with you?[615] If the current President of the Quorum of the Twelve has lamented our lack of power, is it really a lament about our vain beliefs? If so, what can you do about it? How can you avoid having your faith become vain?

What does "foolish" mean? Would something that is so poorly based, so weak and powerless to save, and utterly false be foolish? What about trusting a man to save you, rather than the Lord? What about the notion that there is a man who will be perfectly unable to

---

[613] Matthew 24:24 "For there shall arise false Christs, and false prophets, and shall shew great signs and wonders; insomuch that, if it were possible, they shall deceive the very elect."

JS–Matthew 1:22 "For in those days there shall also arise false Christs, and false prophets, and shall show great signs and wonders, insomuch, that, if possible, they shall deceive the very elect, who are the elect according to the covenant."

[614] Moroni 10:5 "And by the power of the Holy Ghost ye may know the truth of all things."

[615] Moroni 5:2 "O God, the Eternal Father, we ask thee, in the name of thy Son, Jesus Christ, to bless and sanctify this wine to the souls of all those who drink of it, that they may do it in remembrance of the blood of thy Son, which was shed for them; that they may witness unto thee, O God, the Eternal Father, that they do always remember him, that they may have his Spirit to be with them. Amen."

ever lead you astray? How foolish is it to trust your salvation to the inerrancy of a man?

What kind of a heart is "puffed up?" How would these false, vain and foolish doctrines result in a proud following? Why would they think themselves better than they are because of these doctrines?

What does it mean to "seek deep to hide their counsels from the Lord?" What does it mean to "seek deeply?" What foolish men would think they could ever "hide their counsel from the Lord?" Who would believe that God would be bound to follow what a man dictates—because they have keys to bind Him—rather than recognizing that the Lord alone holds all authority to judge and will alone determine all judgment?[616] How foolish is it to become a sycophant of priestly pretenders, hoping that they will save you in the day of judgment? Will appeasing an LDS authority be of any more value than kissing a Cardinal's ring when you are standing before the Lion of Israel to be judged? How well will the vain ceremonies and guarded conspiracies work in the day when everything is shouted from the rooftops?

What does it mean to have "works" which "shall be in the dark?" Does this just mean hidden? Does "darkness" also include the quality of the works? What kinds of work are "dark?" Can obliterating part of a sacred ceremony remove light and replace it with dark? Does curtailing the Saints' ability to discuss true principles, exercising control and dominion and compulsion to prevent knowledge from spreading all contribute to darkness in the minds of the Saints?

When is the last time you were encouraged in the Temple to understand and discuss the meaning of the Temple ceremonies? When was the last time you were told *not* to discuss the Temple meaning

---

[616] 3 Nephi 27:27 "And know ye that ye shall be judges of this people, according to the judgment which I shall give unto you, which shall be just. Therefore, what manner of men ought ye to be? Verily I say unto you, even as I am."

inside the Temple? If you can't discuss it inside the Temple, and you covenanted not to discuss it outside the Temple, then where can you discuss its meaning? How will you learn if you are unable to share ideas about the symbols and their meaning? Is it "dark" when the light of teaching is closed to view?

I don't know if any of you recall that Hugh Nibley was given access to the chapel in the Provo Temple to speak to waiting patrons about the meaning of the Temple for a number of years. While waiting for a session to begin, patrons could listen to and ask questions of Hugh Nibley in an atmosphere of sharing and getting answers. Today, in contrast, they discourage you from discussing anything about the Temple even inside the Temple. I refer to an incident in the Jordan River Temple in *The Second Comforter*. I was told to not discuss meanings while in the Celestial Room speaking with full time missionaries assigned to my stake. I presided over the missionary work of the stake and worked closely with these wonderful young men. But I was told to stop teaching them. This is common today. It ought to end. We will only understand sacred symbols if we are able to teach one another about what we have learned. When I think of the library of material I have had to get through to be able to understand, I am left to wonder at how difficult the process has been made for those who would sincerely and humbly like to seek after further light and knowledge by teaching one another.

We should welcome as much light and truth in our exchanges with one another as we have to offer; in the right setting and with the right Spirit. It is not casting pearls before swine when the audience is prepared, worthy and interested in obtaining knowledge for the right reason. Now even if you have the very best of audiences, in the most sacred setting, we are told to not discuss what may be of vital interest to a soul seeking to gain further light and knowledge by conversing with the Lord through the veil.

How little discarding of light must one cause before they are do-ing "works in the dark?" It is such a terrible question with such fear-ful results that I would hesitate to be the one who limits the Saints' ability to seek into truth.

Now, to balance things somewhat, I want to affirm several fun-damental truths:

- We are accountable for our own search into the truth.
- No one can limit you if you are searching with real intent having a contrite spirit and broken heart.
- There is no conflict between fulfilling your duties to the church on the one hand and your responsibilities to the Lord on the other.
- You cannot blame anyone else if you have not been diligent about your own search.
- In the end, whether there is active opposition or active assis-tance provided to you, it is necessary for you to make the internal changes and to follow the path.

No outside party will control what is yours alone to control. But the first step to be taken is to realize you really are personally respon-sible. You can't depend on others nor on an institution to do the work for you. But as you awaken to that recognition, you should not lose heart or become discouraged. Nothing has been lost collective-ly which you may not still lay claim upon for yourself.

I do think we could make a greater overall gentile success with a different, more benign attitude as a group. But even if you must work against a corrosive environment, you can still do it. You have the greatest tool in your hands. You truly can get closer to the Lord through the Book of Mormon than any other means. It is a guide-book written for us and for now.

2 Nephi 28:10–12

"And the blood of the saints shall cry from the ground against them. Yea, they have all gone out of the way; they have become corrupted. Because of pride, and because of false teachers, and false doctrine, their churches have become corrupted, and their churches are lifted up; because of pride they are puffed up."

Why does this mention the "blood of the saints?" What does it mean for their "blood to cry from the ground?" I've discussed this before, speaking of the earth's own spirit.

What does "all" include? Even us? If "they have all gone out of the way; they have become corrupted" includes us, what does that mean? How could we also be "out of the way?" Is Nephi right? What about Wilford Woodruff's claim that we would never be led astray? Can someone who promises to not lead you astray then lead you astray? How solid a guarantee does any man offer to you?

What does it mean to "have become corrupted?" Can a church be "true" and still be "corrupted?"[617]

What "pride" can religion impose upon people who believe false traditions? Does your faith make you "proud" to belong? Do you think it makes you better than others? Do you believe you're saved while others will be damned, because they don't share your faith? Does that make you lose sleep at night, and want to cry out to save them—or to relax and enjoy your security?

---

[617] D&C 84:53–58 "And by this you may know the righteous from the wicked, and that the whole world groaneth under sin and darkness even now. And your minds in times past have been darkened because of unbelief, and because you have treated lightly the things you have received—Which vanity and unbelief have brought the whole church under condemnation. And this condemnation resteth upon the children of Zion, even all. And they shall remain under this condemnation until they repent and remember the new covenant, even the Book of Mormon and the former commandments which I have given them, not only to say, but to do according to that which I have written—That they may bring forth fruit meet for their Father's kingdom; otherwise there remaineth a scourge and judgment to be poured out upon the children of Zion."

What does it mean that the faiths are "all out of the way?" Is there only one "way?" If so, how would you recognize the right "way" from the wrong one?

Who are "false teachers" that teach "false doctrine?" Does "false" include omission of important truths? If one teaches truths about Christ, but does not teach you how to return to His presence, is the teacher "false?" What would qualify someone to be "true" and teach the right "way?" How would you distinguish between true and false teachers? Between true and false doctrine?

How can "false teachers" corrupt a church? Can they corrupt any church? Even ours?

Why does becoming "puffed up" and "pride" follow false teachings? What is it about false religion that brings pride to its followers? How does false security caused by corrupt doctrine lead to "pride?"

What would the opposite religious attitude be for "pride?" Would humility, a broken heart and a contrite spirit be different than "pride?" What kind of teaching would cause a listener to become contrite, humble, meek and submissive? What kind of teaching would defeat pride and break a person's heart? Can you have both? Can you be "humble" and "broken hearted" and also be proud of your religion? If you cannot, then can you think deeply about your faith, your meetings, your conferences, your private as well as public conversations and ask yourself if the teachers to whom you listen lead you to pride? Lead you to humility? Lead you to contrition and repentance?

Who is Nephi describing? Is it possible it could apply to us along with all other organized faiths?

I have often heard my fellow-Saint speak of the sense of pride the Conference Center gives them. It is a great, spacious and technologically advanced center. I've thought the ceiling of that building looks somewhat like that very successful evangelist Joel Osteen's amazing church. I've wondered if the architectural firm took hints from other successful mega-churches when designing the Conference Center. Have you noticed how the dimmed lights and the magnified images, magnified voices and focus upon the great pulpit is designed to use all the modern audio-visual technology to create heroic images within the building for the audience? It is a technical marvel. Really state of the art. It is hard for me not to take some pride in it all. Anyone who wonders if our church is respectable, successful, powerful or advanced, who visits the facility will no doubt leave with the conclusion that, despite our humble origins, we certainly have made a success in the world for ourselves. It is a story of overcoming and prospering.

If those whose bloodstained footprints covered our westward migration could see what we've become, I wonder what delight (or disappointment) they would feel. Would they have any mixed emotions at seeing this monument in granite, glass, brass and walnut? The third-of-a-billion dollars we spent on it produced a landmark of splendor for the ages. Poor Joseph had only an open air bowery to use. Adam, too, used the open plains of Adam-Ondi-Ahman to meet. We are, of course, blessed with more resources to use as part of our "worship."

2 Nephi 28:13

"They rob the poor because of their fine sanctuaries; they rob the poor because of their fine clothing; and they persecute the meek and the poor in heart, because in their pride they are puffed up."

You must keep the prior verse in mind as you read this one. They are a continuation of thought.

It is an interesting thought to equate "fine sanctuaries" with "robbing the poor." Why do you suppose Nephi would make that equation? Does it give us any pause?

What "duty" would be owed to the poor that entitles them to come before a "fine sanctuary?"

Is there a duty to care for the poor that comes before the right of someone to wear "fine clothing?"

What does it mean to "persecute the meek?" Can you "persecute the meek" just by ignoring them? By neglecting them? Does any religion owe some duty to the meek? What obligation is owed to the meek by people of faith?

Who is "poor in heart?" What obligation do we all owe to the poor in heart?

Now look at the last phrase. It begins with "because." Isn't Nephi saying that our defects are all due to "our pride?" That is, "because of their pride they are puffed up" and this is the reason we "rob the poor." This is the reason we "persecute the meek." This is the reason we "persecute the poor in heart." Or, in other words, we are proud and puffed up and therefore we cannot help but cause these other offenses.

We necessarily ignore our obligations to the poor and meek because we are filled with pride. We don't give a second thought to what we're doing with resources entrusted to us to bless and benefit others, because we believe we are entitled to have "fine sanctuaries." We just presume we are justified in our "fine clothing" without regard to what we may owe others.

There is a moment in film that helps illustrate this verse. It is in the closing of the movie *Schindler's List*. The Allies had overrun the area and the Nazi rule had ended. As Schindler was receiving the gratitude of those who had been saved by his efforts, he was struck by what more he could have done. He was less interested in receiving gratitude than he was guilt ridden by how many more lives could have been saved had he parted with a ring. Had he parted with a car it would have secured other lives. The thought filled him with guilt. He had done some, it was undoubtedly true. But his conscious was filled with remorse because he could have done more. And in that setting, doing more was saving lives. He preferred a ring to another man's life. He preferred a car to a family's lives. It tormented him. If you can harrow up your mind to remember this scene, then think of what we might have done with the great resources we have been given in place of some of the monuments we have built.

Why do we need chapels at all? Why not meet in homes? What good could be done with the money we have invested in the chapels we have built? Joseph Smith built temples; he did not build chapels. General Conference was held in an outdoor bowery. Do we have anything to apologize for in how we use our resources? Were or are there poor toward whom the Lord would have preferred us to show mercy, and do more? There are families who have supplied church leadership from their large construction companies who have built projects for the church. I am told these relationships are natural. They call who they know and associate with, after all. I suppose that is true.

Nephi seems troubled by his view of us. We seem untroubled by his words. At least we don't seem to change our behavior much because of Nephi's counsel. We deflect it, and point to others as his real target.

Well, Nephi is nothing if not relevant to almost everything going on today.

2 Nephi 28:14

"They wear stiff necks and high heads; yea, and because of pride, and wickedness, and abominations, and whoredoms, they have all gone astray save it be a few, who are the humble followers of Christ; nevertheless, they are led, that in many instances they do err because they are taught by the precepts of men."

This is so sobering and relevant a verse that it is the first thing quoted in the dedication of the first book I wrote, *The Second Comforter: Conversing With the Lord Through the Veil.* This is our moment. Inside this foolish age there are nevertheless a "few, who are the humble followers of Christ." These are the salt which preserve the world. These are the leaven who keep us still from destruction.

"Stiff necks" do not bow in prayer and praise before a Lord to whom they regard themselves as unworthy. They are undaunted by their unworthiness. They think themselves justified, and therefore without any need to bow in reverence.

"High heads" do not tilt down to behold the less fortunate to whom they might have provided relief. They ignore the destitute and needy, preferring only to see those who are on their standing or above. Who can help elevate them? Who can give them an advantage? Who is a good contact to keep? The "high heads" will be careful about what social advantages come from associations, and will always pick carefully those whom they deign to notice.

But these stiff necks and high heads belong to those carrying a burden of sin. They are prideful, wicked, given to abominations and whoredoms. These are the ones who sit upon the labors of others, and fare sumptuously here. So long as your neck remains stiff and your head held high, you will never notice Lazarus lying at your gate.

But what of the "few, who are the humble followers of Christ?" What of them?

It is clear in this verse that they do NOT lead, but are instead being led. They are "led that in many instances they do err." That is, those who qualify to be called the "few, who are the humble followers of Christ" are not themselves leaders. They are being led by others.

The others who lead them "cause them to err." And why do they cause this? "Because they are taught by the precepts of men." Therefore, the humble true followers are misled into accepting false, foolish and vain (or powerless) beliefs because the ones who preside over them are only able to offer the "precepts of men." These "precepts of men" are unable to bring the "humble followers of Christ" to the knowledge of Him.

Keep in mind that the "precepts of men" are repeated by Nephi in this written sermon more than any other phrase. The learning used to lead is distracting, even damning, whenever it fails to lead to the Lord. Men's precepts cannot rescue us.

Why are not the "humble followers of Christ" doing the leading? Because they do not have the "stiff necks and high heads" to become noticed, to be added to the group of insiders. Their clothes are not costly, their home "sanctuaries" are insufficiently ornate. They are not the stuff of renown and recognition. They are, in a word, *the least*.

It is a troubling image which begins to emerge from Nephi's words. They are shocking for us to consider. If the alternatives are what Nephi seems to leave us, then how much better is it to be among the "few, who are the humble followers of Christ" than among those with the authority to lead them?

I do not believe any of us are in a position to fully understand our times. We live inside a cultural fog that makes our judgments inside the bubble distorted in ways Nephi did not experience from his vantage point. The Lord can give us a clearer perspective through revelation, as He did for Nephi. But we are not equipped to fully recognize our peril standing inside this age and culture.

The one thing that is abundantly clear is that Joseph Smith was right about the need to reconnect with God. His first and primary message remains the testimony of James 1:5.[618] If we lack wisdom, we should ask of God. God will give liberally to those who ask with a sincere heart, having real intent. Whether you believe Joseph's account or not, Joseph was pointing us to James and testifying James made a promise which God will fulfill. So test James. Ask with real intent. Perhaps you will begin to see how Nephi's words of warning are exactly what is needed to save us from our peril. At a minimum, the petition will make you closer to being one of the "few, who are the humble followers of Christ" because of your desire to know from Him the truth of your plight.

He always intends to save those who wait upon Him. Those who serve Him and do as He asks will never be forsaken. All that is required to qualify is to repent and come to Christ with sincere intent. No matter what else is going on, the Lord can take your life's circumstances and make them work to fulfill His work. And His work is your salvation and exaltation.

The first step is to recognize the peril you face. The second is to then do something about it. To take the first step without the second is worse than meaningless. It inspires fear and pessimism. That is wrong. Happiness is the goal of our existence. That comes from Christ. So do not just notice your plight, but make the necessary flight back to Him.

2 Nephi 28:15

"O the wise, and the learned, and the rich, that are puffed up in the pride of their hearts, and all those who preach false doctrines, and all those who commit whoredoms, and pervert the right way of the Lord, wo, wo, wo be unto them, saith the Lord God Almighty, for they shall be thrust down to hell!"

---

[618] James 1:5 "If any of you lack wisdom, let him ask of God, that giveth to all *men* liberally, and upbraideth not; and it shall be given him."

Now we reach a terrible point. Nephi records an inspired condemnation. For a person in Nephi's position, recording words of condemnation holds terrible significance. They are not written unless they are instructed to do so, because their words will be fulfilled. I've explained this in *Beloved Enos*.

Nephi pronounces three "*wo*'s." This is a three fold condemnation. It goes beyond this life. It will follow them into the hereafter.

Associated with the three "wo's" are three names used for God: "Lord God Almighty." It is a three fold assertion of divine authority. "Lord" refers to the Savior as Guide. "God" refers to Divine right and authority. "Almighty" refers to the irrevocable nature of the word used by God, and in turn the words given to Nephi. When you are confronted with all three, the "wo's" are pronounced by a power that cannot be altered.

This is more than a setback in the hopes of the "learned, and the rich" who are being condemned. This is a condemnation which reaches into hell itself. It is so significant a pronouncement that when you read it you should pause and think of the dreadful import for anyone who fits into the curse.

Those, who in their pride, use the precepts of men as the basis for their "preaching false doctrines," are not just wrong, they are damned for this perversion of the religion entrusted to them to preach in purity and truth.

In effect, they were given a precious and eternally significant treasure, and they have diverted it into something that makes them rich, puffed up, and powerful. It is tragic. It is pitiful—meaning it should inspire pity in each of us. These could be well meaning people who have fallen into this error. But they claim to preach the truth, using God's name in vain, while they spread a vain religion which cannot bring people to the knowledge of Christ.

Who would wish such a condemnation upon others? Who can read these words and not be moved with compassion and alarm for those who have fallen under this condemnation? Who would not remove it from those who are condemned if they could?

Nephi could not make a greater plea for the salvation of all those involved. The pronouncement is terrible and its implications eternal. Yet this verse seems to have escaped notice.

Who alone claims they are speaking for God Himself when they preach? Who could possibly qualify for this level of condemnation? This should make all of us think long and hard about any utterance we speak before we make our assertions "in the name of Jesus Christ." The thoughtlessness which accompanies that expression among the Saints is contrary to the seriousness of the condemnation we invite if we preach false doctrine while puffed up in pride; thereby perverting the right way of the Lord.

In an example which is chilling to read, the first anti-Christ we encounter in the Book of Mormon (Sherem) uses this phrase to justify his preaching. He accuses Jacob of "perverting the right way of God."[619] He brings himself under Nephi's curse. It was a small thing, therefore, for Jacob to reiterate the condemnation of Nephi against Sherem.[620] Jacob was merely repeating what Nephi had already pronounced. And since Nephi had sealed the condemnation, it would be Nephi, not Jacob, who was responsible for the cursing.

---

[619] Jacob 7:7 "And ye have led away much of this people that they pervert the right way of God, and keep not the law of Moses which is the right way; and convert the law of Moses into the worship of a being which ye say shall come many hundred years hence. And now behold, I, Sherem, declare unto you that this is blasphemy; for no man knoweth of such things; for he cannot tell of things to come. And after this manner did Sherem contend against me."

[620] Jacob 7:14 "And I said unto him: What am I that I should tempt God to show unto thee a sign in the thing which thou knowest to be true? Yet thou wilt deny it, because thou art of the devil. Nevertheless, not my will be done; but if God shall smite thee, let that be a sign unto thee that he has power, both in heaven and in earth; and also, that Christ shall come. And thy will, O Lord, be done, and not mine."

This threefold wo, and use of three titles for God, all suggest that teaching false doctrine and using man's learning, while being filled with pride is so grave an offense that great care should always be taken before teaching, preaching or expounding on the Gospel. Only a fool would undertake to do so without knowing their words are approved of God. You cannot take cover using a Correlation Department, or a commentary, or a scholar's words, or a selected bibliography. When you presume to preach the truth, you need to realize how serious a matter you are undertaking. Joseph Smith wrote from Liberty Jail:

> "The things of God are of deep import; and time, and experience, and careful and ponderous and solemn thoughts can only find them out. Thy mind, O man! if thou wilt lead a soul unto salvation, must stretch as high as the utmost heavens, and search into and contemplate the darkest abyss, and the broad expanse of eternity—thou must commune with God. How much more dignified and noble are the thoughts of God, than the vain imaginations of the human heart! None but fools will trifle with the souls of men.

> "How vain and trifling have been our spirits, our conferences, our councils, our meetings, our private as well as public conversations—too low, too mean, too vulgar, too condescending for the dignified characters of the called and chosen of God, according to the purposes of His will, from before the foundation of the world!" (DHC 3:295–296)

When we speak about Christ and His Gospel with others, we should do so with a sense of terrible awe and fear. If we have doubts about our message, we should remain silent rather than risk proclaiming what may be an error. It is a burden to be carefully undertaken.

As Nephi warns about our day, there will be many who will teach vain, foolish and false things coming from the precepts of men.

I believe these words from Nephi are primarily directed at the leaders, and only secondarily relevant to those who are following. The trends and direction are always set by leaders.

I know there are humble people reading this who want to condemn themselves and justify leaders. But taken in context, Nephi's condemnation must necessarily be primarily aimed at those who lead.

I wish it were otherwise. I cannot tell you how these words cause me grief. I take no delight in this.

It would be easier to stop than to go on. But this Book of Mormon is something we must study if we are going to remove our condemnation. And it seems as if no one is willing to face its words. So the burden remains upon us.

On "evil speaking" the following are relevant:

First, it is not "evil" to say what is true.

Second, it cannot be "evil speaking" when it comes from an accepted prophet (Nephi) and is found in the scriptures.

Third, if the Spirit underlays the concept or thought, it is not you speaking it is the Spirit. If the message which comes from the Lord, or the Spirit, then it is not even you speaking. You are voice, but it is another who speaks.

Fourth, a call to repent is not "evil" speaking; because if it were then we could never be urged to repentance. Because the issues involved in repentance are always going to be somewhat personal, cutting and difficult.

In the narrowest sense, "the Lord's anointed" would be those whom the Lord anoints. It would be those whom the Lord makes His, sealing them up to eternal life.

In the broadest sense, it would be anyone who has been through the Temple to receive their washings and anointings.

It is *not* the Lord. As to Him, there are other commandments which relate to using His name in vain, His status as our Savior, and other appropriate rules for respecting and worshiping Him. But it only takes a moment of reflection to see the Lord's anointed would be those whom He has anointed.

My guess is that the most natural reaction to the critique of Nephi of our modern-day church and its foibles tends to be defensive because have testimonies of the divine role the organization plays. Any criticism must be attempting to pry us away from membership in the organization. I don't think that's what's involved here at all.

Perhaps we fall slightly into the trap of first declaring that we need to stop assuming infallibility and perfection of leaders and organization and start getting our answers for ourselves from the Lord.

Unfortunately, next we then hold up the leaders and organization against the measure of infallibility and perfection are then tempted to examine the failings in detail and lament the error and failings we find.

Well, what did we expect, we just said that we don't assume perfection in leaders and earthly institutions. They haven't changed with this new revelation to us, but maybe we need to change our approach to them. We don't throw them out because of their failings, we turn to the Lord and put our faith *there*. He can tell us through his Spirit the truth of all things, including the truth of the the teachings of those who stand as his imperfect legal administrators on earth.

2 Nephi 28:16–17

"Wo unto them that turn aside the just for a thing of naught and revile against that which is good, and say that it is of no worth! For the day shall come that the Lord God will speedily visit the inhabitants of the earth; and in that day that they are fully ripe in iniquity they shall perish. But behold, if the inhabitants of the earth shall repent of their wickedness and abominations they shall not be destroyed, saith the Lord of Hosts."

Nephi warns against "turning aside the just for a thing of naught." A "thing of naught" means something without value. To "turn aside" is to leave or move away from. So he is telling you to be careful to not walk away from the truth being taught by a "just" or true source, and instead follow after something of no value.

This rejection of a true messenger and following after a false one inevitably results in "reviling that which is good." When you reject the truth you normally have to deal with a troubled conscious. The way to calm it is to "revile against" the thing you have rejected. Not only do people "revile against" the message, but they go on to "say that it is of no worth!"

Think about the general reception given to the Lord's messengers throughout scripture. They are always the object of criticism and reviling. Nephi is describing a syndrome here which always attaches to the true message and true messenger. They aren't valued, but thought "a thing of naught." The argument is always: "If what they had to say were important, it would come from someone more important." Content is ignored in favor of status.

Now the Lord allows this to go on and always has. But, as Nephi reminds us, there does come a time when the limit has been reached. When the limit has been reached, the end "will speedily visit the inhabitants of the earth." That is, when the time has come, the turn will be so swift that they cannot repent any longer. Judgment will overtake them too quickly.

The moment when they have reached the limit is described by Nephi as "fully ripe in iniquity." That means they will no longer even listen to the truth. They have completely closed minds. It would do no good to extend them further opportunity, because they will not take any advantage of it.

So they are scheduled for destruction.

But, Nephi reminds us, they can repent. If they will change their minds and come to Christ, He will forgive them and heal them. If they repent, they will be preserved from the destruction. However, as has already become clear, their destruction is due to the fact they are "fully ripe." So although repentance remains theoretically possible, and the Lord will accept even late return to Him, the offenders are committed to their offense. They are not likely to take advantage of the opportunity.

How humble it is for the Lord to be willing to accept the reluctant, tardy, and slow to repent. Nevertheless, He is willing to accept even them. He suffered for all, and will redeem as many as will come to Him. Initially, He won't destroy them with the wicked. Ultimately the outcome will depend upon how committed they are to the process of repentance. For to repent is to come to Him. They decide if His open arms will be where they finally embrace Him; or if they will stand afar off and think it too hard to surrender their sins and go further.

2 Nephi 28:18–19

"But behold, that great and abominable church, the whore of all the earth, must tumble to the earth, and great must be the fall thereof. For the kingdom of the devil must shake, and they which belong to it must needs be stirred up unto repentance, or the devil will grasp them with his everlasting chains, and they be stirred up to anger, and perish;"

Remember that this comes at the end of Nephi's ministry. He saw the vision of the great and abominable church at the beginning of his journey into the wilderness. There has been over forty years between the time of the earlier visions and the time of this summary of his great teachings.[621]

---

[621] 2 Nephi 5:34 "And it sufficeth me to say that *forty years had passed away, and we had already had wars and contentions with our brethren."

Between the time Nephi saw the visions (set out beginning in 1 Nephi 11) and the time of this final instruction, Nephi has had decades to ponder on the things he was shown in vision. He has, in fact, spent those years reflecting constantly upon the visions he received.[622] It is foolish to believe that Nephi, Joseph Smith, or any prophet understood what they saw the day they saw it. Only time, careful, solemn and ponderous thought can unravel what a person is shown in vision by the Lord. The understanding of a prophet is not static. It unfolds. Joseph's first impression of the first vision was personal. He thought it was a message to him about himself. By the time he had finished translating the Book of Mormon, organizing the church, and collecting a following, Joseph realized the first vision was not his, but it belonged at a minimum to a larger community of believers. Eventually he would come to see it belonged to the world. The version we have in the Pearl of Great Price reflects that changing understanding. In it he gives the first understanding in what he told his mother the day it happened: He learned that Presbyterianism was not true.[623]

So this statement goes back forty years earlier and Nephi's vision of the fall of the great whore. This universal false religion will fail. It will "fall." The "fall" will be "great." It will "tumble to the earth"—meaning that it will no longer stand on its own, but will altogether collapse.

---

[622] 2 Nephi 4:16 "Behold, my soul delighteth in the things of the Lord; and my heart pondereth continually upon the things which I have seen and heard."

[623] JS–H 1:20 "He again forbade me to join with any of them; and many other things did he say unto me, which I cannot write at this time. When I came to myself again, I found myself lying on my back, looking up into heaven. When the light had departed, I had no strength; but soon recovering in some degree, I went home. And as I leaned up to the fireplace, mother inquired what the matter was. I replied, "Never mind, all is well—I am well enough off." I then said to my mother, "I have learned for myself that Presbyterianism is not true." It seems as though the adversary was aware, at a very early period of my life, that I was destined to prove a disturber and an annoyer of his kingdom; else why should the powers of darkness combine against me? Why the opposition and persecution that arose against me, almost in my infancy?"

The purpose of this great calamity is to bring about repentance. The purposes of God, even in punishment, are to elevate and save others.

Notice the devil's tool that will be used in opposition to repentance: they will "be stirred up to anger, and perish." That is, to harden hearts and to blind eyes, anger will be the most effective tool. Rather than being humbled by the fall of the great whore, those who will continue to resist repentance will be angry for the losses. They will lament the loss of what they held so dearly.

This, then, is how the groups break down—For those who repent, the difficulties they encounter bring humility and contrition. For those who refuse to repent, they respond with anger at their trials.

This is the great watershed test. If your set backs in life humble you, then your heart is soft and you are a candidate for repentance. If you become angry, accuse God of causing evil, and refuse to be comforted, you are not a candidate for repentance. Your anger is a tool used to blind you. The one employing the tool is the enemy to your soul.

The trials and difficulties are gifts to stir you up to repentance. That is how you ought to respond. The only way to approach the Lord is through humility. Anything that aids you in becoming humble is good, merciful and just. You should view it as a gift. No matter the difficulty. Christ descended below it all; and none of us are greater than He.[624]

2 Nephi 28:20

"For behold, at that day shall he rage in the hearts of the children of men, and stir them up to anger against that which is good."

---

[624] D&C 122:8 "The Son of Man hath descended below them all. Art thou greater than he?"

One of the most effective ways to end thought or discussion is to get angry. Lawyers use anger as a tool to turn witnesses into thoughtless and emotional pawns. People make very bad decisions when they are angry. I've mentioned before my father's saying that he never spoke a word in anger than he did not later regret.

This is a time of great anger. Anger about religious ideas flows from insecurity and feeling threatened by the idea. It is not possible to have a discussion when people are insecure, angry and unwilling to be thoughtful about ideas.

This is the work of the devil. He succeeds when people close their minds and fill with anger at teachings which introduce ideas that challenge assumptions.

This is why the Jews wanted Christ killed. This is why they wanted to kill Lehi when he spoke of Christ. The teachings ran contrary to the presumptions, and as a result the response was emotional, angry and closed down thought and discussion.

Using fear to shut down people's ability to consider, ponder and pray is a technique used with amazing success. When you hear the argument that something will put you in peril, jeopardize your salvation, and to be afraid of the idea or discussion, you ought to ask yourself whether the notion that shutting down discussion seems right or not. Is it merely using fear to cause rage and anger? Can it be a tool to cause you to turn "against that which is good?"

All kinds of ideas need to be considered to bring you to the Lord. Closing down because of fear will hinder the process, as the devil knows.[625]

The tool of anger is the other side of fear.

---

[625] D&C 38:30 "I tell you these things because of your prayers; wherefore, treasure up wisdom in your bosoms, lest the wickedness of men reveal these things unto you by their wickedness, in a manner which shall speak in your ears with a voice louder than that which shall shake the earth; but if ye are prepared ye shall not fear."

The object of this is always to cheat your soul, close your mind, keep you from learning the truth.

Now is the great day of anger. Have you noticed how much of the discourse in public life is based upon fear and anger? Those larger social dynamics invade the community of Saints, as well. We are as vulnerable to this technique as the rest of society.

Be slow to anger, quick to forgive; open and prayerful. The great plan to cheat your soul will not succeed with you if you remain humble and open.

2 Nephi 28:21

> "And others will he pacify, and lull them away into carnal security, that they will say: All is well in Zion; yea, Zion prospereth, all is well—and thus the devil cheateth their souls, and leadeth them away carefully down to hell."

Now we have reached a point where the audience becomes unavoidably identified with the gentiles of the last days who claim to be assembling as "Zion." This term gets applied in the Book of Mormon in a highly selective way. It includes the following:

- Last days time frame;
- Post-restoration of the Book of Mormon;
- People who are either claiming or who have actually assembled together as Zion.

We are the only ones who fit this definition. Therefore the application of these verses to include us is required. We cannot point to others and say we are not among those being warned.

What does "pacify" mean?

What does "lull" mean?

What does "carnal security" mean?

If you have people who are pacified, lulled with carnal security, what kind of people are you speaking about?

Why would these people think they were "Zion?" What possible basis could people who are pacified, and lulled with carnal security have for thinking they are "Zion?"

What does it mean that "all is well in Zion?" What does it mean "Zion prospereth?" Does "all is well in Zion" mean the same thing as "Zion prospereth?" If not, what is the difference? Is one "spiritual" and the other "carnal?"

Can one be an attitude, while the other is a measurement or statistic? Can "all be well in Zion" mean that we have comfortable controls and guarantees in place which will protect us?

Can "Zion prospereth" mean new converts, new buildings, new numbers, more tithing receipts, growth and political influence? What else might it mean?

Do we satisfy the notion that "all is well in Zion?" That is, can you see a reason to say that Zion is well at present? Do our people say that?

Do we satisfy the notion that "Zion prospereth?" That is, can you see any reason to say that Zion is presently prospering? Do our people say that?

Why would it "cheat souls" to make them think "all is well in Zion" and that "Zion prospereth?"

Why would it lead people "carefully down to hell" for them to believe all is well and Zion prospers?

Can Zion ever relent? Can Zion tolerate a little sin? Does it cheat us if we are good, decent people, and we recognize we are good and decent? Even if we are good and honorable, can we be deceived?[626]

---

[626] D&C 76:75 "These are they who are honorable men of the earth, who were blinded by the craftiness of men."

How does prosperity blind us? Do John's words to the Laodiceans tell us how we can err?[627]

What quality does the devil employ to mislead us? Does being led away "carefully" mean it is harder to recognize the peril? Should it be hard to avoid deception? Why do those who take the Holy Spirit as their guide avoid this kind of deception?[628]

Can anyone qualify to receive guidance from the Holy Spirit?[629]

Can anyone qualify to receive Christ as their guide?[630]

What good does it do to follow even a true messenger, if you do not receive a testimony from Christ?[631]

To whom should you look for salvation?

Does part of the problem Nephi relates here grow out of the notion that being part of a group will matter? If you accept baptism and other saving ordinances from those with authority to minister them, but you do not come to Christ, will the ordinances alone save

---

[627] Revelation 3:17 "Because thou sayest, I am rich, and increased with goods, and have need of nothing; and knowest not that thou art wretched, and miserable, and poor, and blind, and naked:"

[628] D&C 45:57 "For they that are wise and have received the truth, and have taken the Holy Spirit for their guide, and have not been deceived—verily I say unto you, they shall not be hewn down and cast into the fire, but shall abide the day."

[629] Moroni 10:5 "And by the power of the Holy Ghost ye may know the truth of all things."

[630] D&C 93:1 "Verily, thus saith the Lord: It shall come to pass that every soul who forsaketh his sins and cometh unto me, and calleth on my name, and obeyeth my voice, and keepeth my commandments, shall see my face and know that I am;"

[631] D&C 76:98–101 "And the glory of the telestial is one, even as the glory of the stars is one; for as one star differs from another star in glory, even so differs one from another in glory in the telestial world; For these are they who are of Paul, and of Apollos, and of Cephas. These are they who say they are some of one and some of another—some of Christ and some of John, and some of Moses, and some of Elias, and some of Esaias, and some of Isaiah, and some of Enoch; But received not the gospel, neither the testimony of Jesus, neither the prophets, neither the everlasting covenant."

you? Since the ordinances do matter[632], what must you do after receiving them?[633] Is part of enduring to the end helping others within your own ward family? Can you just walk away from your obligations to the church after entering into the covenant of baptism?[634]

2 Nephi 28:22

"And behold, others he flattereth away, and telleth them there is no hell; and he saith unto them: I am no devil, for there is none—and thus he whispereth in their ears, until he grasps them with his awful chains, from whence there is no deliverance."

How can the devil "flatter" someone? Why would it be "flattery" to tell someone "there is no hell?" What does it mean that "there is no hell?" Have you ever heard this idea taught?

Historic Christians are fully persuaded of the existence of hell. We, on the other hand, have three degrees of *glory* in which the idea of hell is sometimes lost.

---

[632] Mark 16:16 "He that believeth and is baptized shall be saved; but he that believeth not shall be damned."
2 Nephi 9:23 "And he commandeth all men that they must repent, and be baptized in his name, having perfect faith in the Holy One of Israel, or they cannot be saved in the kingdom of God."

[633] D&C 20:25 "That as many as would believe and be baptized in his holy name, and endure in faith to the end, should be saved—"

[634] Mosiah 18:8–10 "And it came to pass that he said unto them: Behold, here are the waters of Mormon (for thus were they called) and now, as ye are desirous to come into the fold of God, and to be called his people, and are willing to bear one another's burdens, that they may be light; Yea, and are willing to mourn with those that mourn; yea, and comfort those that stand in need of comfort, and to stand as witnesses of God at all times and in all things, and in all places that ye may be in, even until death, that ye may be redeemed of God, and be numbered with those of the first resurrection, that ye may have eternal life—Now I say unto you, if this be the desire of your hearts, what have you against being baptized in the name of the Lord, as a witness before him that ye have entered into a covenant with him, that ye will serve him and keep his commandments, that he may pour out his Spirit more abundantly upon you?"

So, is there a "hell?"[635] Do those who go there suffer? How difficult is the suffering?[636]

How can it be flattery for the devil to tell someone "I am no devil?" Would his appearance to someone as an "angel of light" be flattery?[637] Did the devil attempt to do this with Joseph Smith?[638] How was Joseph able to determine the devil was the devil, rather than an "angel of light" when he appeared? Did Joseph learn something about detecting evil spirits from this encounter? What did Michael do to teach Joseph how to detect the devil? What did Joseph later teach about how to detect the devil?[639] What kind of a handshake would you expect to be used to detect a true messenger?

---

[635] D&C 19:15 "Therefore I command you to repent—repent, lest I smite you by the rod of my mouth, and by my wrath, and by my anger, and your sufferings be sore—how sore you know not, how exquisite you know not, yea, how hard to bear you know not."

[636] D&C 19:16–18 "For behold, I, God, have suffered these things for all, that they might not suffer if they would repent; But if they would not repent they must suffer even as I; Which suffering caused myself, even God, the greatest of all, to tremble because of pain, and to bleed at every pore, and to suffer both body and spirit—and would that I might not drink the bitter cup, and shrink—"

[637] 2 Nephi 9:9 "And our spirits must have become like unto him, and we become devils, angels to a devil, to be shut out from the presence of our God, and to remain with the father of lies, in misery, like unto himself; yea, to that being who beguiled our first parents, who transformeth himself nigh unto an angel of light, and stirreth up the children of men unto secret combinations of murder and all manner of secret works of darkness."

[638] D&C 128:20 "And again, what do we hear? Glad tidings from Cumorah! Moroni, an angel from heaven, declaring the fulfilment of the prophets—the book to be revealed. A voice of the Lord in the wilderness of Fayette, Seneca county, declaring the three witnesses to bear record of the book! The voice of Michael on the banks of the Susquehanna, detecting the devil when he appeared as an angel of light! The voice of Peter, James, and John in the wilderness between Harmony, Susquehanna county, and Colesville, Broome county, on the Susquehanna river, declaring themselves as possessing the keys of the kingdom, and of the dispensation of the fulness of times!"

[639] D&C 129:8 "If it be the devil as an angel of light, when you ask him to shake hands he will offer you his hand, and you will not feel anything; you may therefore detect him."

Have others been confronted by Satan appearing as an angel?[640] Now if one were deceived by the devil, thinking him an angel of light, would the devil teach them false doctrines?[641]

Would the false doctrines make them and those hearing from them feel secure, or would it stir them up to repentance?

What does it mean for the devil to claim "there is none?" I'm reminded of Peter asking a minister if he knew who he (the minister) worked for. The minister did not know, and so Peter informed him he worked for the devil. We don't think about that much anymore, but it is nonetheless the case that there are many people offering instruction who are really either in the employ of the devil, or using the precepts of men as the fodder (food for livestock) for their teaching.

What comes to mind with the image of the devil "whispering in their ears?" How close must the devil come to be whispering into a person's ears? How attentive must the devil become to his target?

Why "awful chains" and not just "chains?" Are there "chains" that are not "awful?" Why would these particular chains always become "awful?"[642]

---

[640] Moses 1:12 "And it came to pass that when Moses had said these words, behold, Satan came tempting him, saying: Moses, son of man, worship me."

[641] Alma 30:53 "But behold, the devil hath deceived me; for he appeared unto me in the form of an angel, and said unto me: Go and reclaim this people, for they have all gone astray after an unknown God. And he said unto me: There is no God; yea, and he taught me that which I should say. And I have taught his words; and I taught them because they were pleasing unto the carnal mind; and I taught them, even until I had much success, insomuch that I verily believed that they were true; and for this cause I withstood the truth, even until I have brought this great curse upon me."

[642] Alma 12:11 "And they that will harden their hearts, to them is given the lesser portion of the word until they know nothing concerning his mysteries; and then they are taken captive by the devil, and led by his will down to destruction. Now this is what is meant by the chains of hell."
2 Nephi 1:13 "O that ye would awake; awake from a deep sleep, yea, even from the sleep of hell, and shake off the awful chains by which ye are bound, which are the chains which bind the children of men, that they are carried away captive down to the eternal gulf of misery and woe."

What does it mean that "there is no deliverance" from these chains? Why would there be no more deliverance provided?

The verses we are considering are part of a careful message and cannot be separated from each other. They blend together. So when considering this portion of the message you must also keep in mind the other things that went before in Nephi's sermon.

I am awestruck by this great prophet's message. It inspires fear for my fellow man when I read it. The plight in which some men find themselves by the traditions handed to us seem to be such a trap as to defy escape. What can I say to liberate them? What can I do to help them escape? Who am I to even dare think I can make any difference? What petitions might I weary the Lord with to help avert this end for others?

We seem to all be asleep and incapable of noticing this terrible warning. Why cannot we all awake and arise and put on the beautiful garments, going forth to meet with the Bridegroom?[643]

Perhaps some of you may make a difference in this battle. All of our souls are at risk and we seem more interested in preserving our current circumstances than in understanding them.

This Book of Mormon is alarming when we consider it a warning for us. Not at all the docile and superficial text we can turn it into when studying 8 chapters in a single 50-minute Gospel Doctrine class—reduced by the time taken for announcement, opening and closing prayers, and witty banter exchanged among affable Saints as part of our renewal of weekly fellowship. Those things are good, of course, but the book commands deeper attention.

---

[643] Moroni 10:31 "And awake, and arise from the dust, O Jerusalem; yea, and put on thy beautiful garments, O daughter of Zion; and strengthen thy stakes and enlarge thy borders forever, that thou mayest no more be confounded, that the covenants of the Eternal Father which he hath made unto thee, O house of Israel, may be fulfilled."
D&C 133:10 "Yea, let the cry go forth among all people: Awake and arise and go forth to meet the Bridegroom; behold and lo, the Bridegroom cometh; go ye out to meet him. Prepare yourselves for the great day of the Lord."

If I had to say one thing has done more to bring me into harmony with the Lord than any other thing it would be this: I have taken the Book of Mormon seriously. I have assumed it is an authentic and ancient text written by prophetic messengers whose words ought to be studied for how they can change my life. Though all the world may treat it lightly, I have tried to not do so. For that I believe the Lord's approval has been given to an otherwise foolish, vain, error-prone and weak man.

Take the Book of Mormon seriously. Apply it to yourself. Not as a means to judge others, but as a means to test your own life. It is one thing to evaluate our circumstances, which the book compels us to do, but we needn't go further than to realize our terrible plight. From that moment the warning should work inside ourselves to help us improve within, see more clearly our day, think more correctly about what is going on, and act more consistent with the Lord's purposes.

The Book of Mormon is the most correct book available. A person can get closer to God by abiding its precepts than with any other book.

2 Nephi 28:23

> "Yea, they are grasped with death, and hell; and death, and hell, and the devil, and all that have been seized therewith must stand before the throne of God, and be judged according to their works, from whence they must go into the place prepared for them, even a lake of fire and brimstone, which is endless torment."

This is a continuation of the warning. Nephi wants us to take quite seriously his warnings.

When you read words like these it becomes apparent the only safe way to measure his warning is to apply it directly and personally to ourselves. To think this was meant only for "others" is too complacent.

When the truth has made you angry, and you have forfeited the option of repentance extended to you, the "grasp of death" is upon you. You will remain subject to "death and hell." Being "seized" by these two things, as you stand before the "throne of God" you will be certain that there will be, for you, a continuation of "the deaths."[644]

Judgment is based "according to their works."[645] Joseph ties sealing power to these "works" which must be done under this authority and then recorded to become binding. This is the practice of the

---

[644] D&C 132:25 "Broad is the gate, and wide the way that leadeth to the deaths; and many there are that go in thereat, because they receive me not, neither do they abide in my law."

[645] Revelation 20:12–13 "And I saw the dead, small and great, stand before God; and the books were opened: and another book was opened, which is *the book* of life: and the dead were judged out of those things which were written in the books, according to their works. And the sea gave up the dead which were in it; and death and hell delivered up the dead which were in them: and they were judged every man according to their works."

D&C 128:6–8 "And further, I want you to remember that John the Revelator was contemplating this very subject in relation to the dead, when he declared, as you will find recorded in Revelation 20:12—*And I saw the dead, small and great, stand before God; and the books were opened; and another book was opened, which is the book of life; and the dead were judged out of those things which were written in the books, according to their works.* You will discover in this quotation that the books were opened; and another book was opened, which was the book of life; but the dead were judged out of those things which were written in the books, according to their works; consequently, the books spoken of must be the books which contained the record of their works, and refer to the records which are kept on the earth. And the book which was the book of life is the record which is kept in heaven; the principle agreeing precisely with the doctrine which is commanded you in the revelation contained in the letter which I wrote to you previous to my leaving my place—that in all your recordings it may be recorded in heaven. Now, the nature of this ordinance consists in the power of the priesthood, by the revelation of Jesus Christ, wherein it is granted that whatsoever you bind on earth shall be bound in heaven, and whatsoever you loose on earth shall be loosed in heaven. Or, in other words, taking a different view of the translation, whatsoever you record on earth shall be recorded in heaven, and whatsoever you do not record on earth shall not be recorded in heaven; for out of the books shall your dead be judged, according to their own works, whether they themselves have attended to the ordinances in their own *propria persona*, or by the means of their own agents, according to the ordinance which God has prepared for their salvation from before the foundation of the world, according to the records which they have kept concerning their dead."

church. It is and has always been the practice of those having such authority. They not only perform the work, but upon having done so they create a record of having done so.

Upon being judged, they go "into the place prepared for them." This place is, for those who are grasped with "death and hell" called "a lake of fire and brimstone." A lake because it engulfs them so tightly they are flooded with the guilt. Fire because it is designed to purge and refine. Brimstone because of the bitterness of the experience. The torment there is "endless" meaning from God.[646]

This purging does not confer blessings, but merely balances out the claims of justice for those who would not accept mercy.[647]

Crying repentance is to warn, so the claims of justice may be avoided by obtaining mercy through Christ. Christ's mercy is offered to all, but will only be received in full by few. All will be resurrected because of His sacrifice[648], and those who died without law will not

---

[646] D&C 19:4–12 "And surely every man must repent or suffer, for I, God, am endless. Wherefore, I revoke not the judgments which I shall pass, but woes shall go forth, weeping, wailing and gnashing of teeth, yea, to those who are found on my left hand. Nevertheless, it is not written that there shall be no end to this torment, but it is written *endless torment.* Again, it is written *eternal damnation;* wherefore it is more express than other scriptures, that it might work upon the hearts of the children of men, altogether for my name's glory. Wherefore, I will explain unto you this mystery, for it is meet unto you to know even as mine apostles. I speak unto you that are chosen in this thing, even as one, that you may enter into my rest. For, behold, the mystery of godliness, how great is it! For, behold, I am endless, and the punishment which is given from my hand is end Endless punishment is God's punishment."

[647] D&C 19:15–19 "Therefore I command you to repent—repent, lest I smite you by the rod of my mouth, and by my wrath, and by my anger, and your sufferings be sore—how sore you know not, how exquisite you know not, yea, how hard to bear you know not. For behold, I, God, have suffered these things for all, that they might not suffer if they would repent; But if they would not repent they must suffer even as I; Which suffering caused myself, even God, the greatest of all, to tremble because of pain, and to bleed at every pore, and to suffer both body and spirit—and would that I might not drink the bitter cup, and shrink—Nevertheless, glory be to the Father, and I partook and finished my preparations unto the children of men."

[648] 1 Corinthians 15:22 "For as in Adam all die, even so in Christ shall all be made alive."

be punished for their ignorance[649], but to receive the full benefit of His atonement must do as He commands.[650]

Those who love others and want their eternal welfare will invite everyone to repent and come to Christ. The prospect of others suffering needlessly because they would not repent is a great horror to them. This is why Nephi's words are at times so blunt. This is why he wants to stir us all up to our terrible situation. It is merciful to speak to us in these frank terms.

I know some who have read these words of counsel from Nephi and find them objectionable. However, Isaiah spoke against those whose words were "smooth" but filled with deceit.[651] To people who are content and filled with pride, it takes a great deal of candor to bring them to their senses.[652] Nephi's warnings are intended to save as many of the gentiles who read his record from self-destruction as he can bring to repentance. It is better for us to take counsel from his hand than to dismiss his teachings. *He can only warn his readers. Since we are his readers, he must be speaking to us.*

---

[649] D&C 76:71–72 "And again, we saw the terrestrial world, and behold and lo, these are they who are of the terrestrial, whose glory differs from that of the church of the Firstborn who have received the fulness of the Father, even as that of the moon differs from the sun in the firmament. Behold, these are they who died without law;". See also D&C 45 and D&C 54.

[650] D&C 132:22–23 "For strait is the gate, and narrow the way that leadeth unto the exaltation and continuation of the lives, and few there be that find it, because ye receive me not in the world neither do ye know me. But if ye receive me in the world, then shall ye know me, and shall receive your exaltation; that where I am ye shall be also."

[651] Isaiah 30:10 "Which say to the seers, See not; and to the prophets, Prophesy not unto us right things, speak unto us smooth things, prophesy deceits:"

[652] Enos 1:23 "And there was nothing save it was exceeding harshness, preaching and prophesying of wars, and contentions, and destructions, and continually reminding them of death, and the duration of eternity, and the judgments and the power of God, and all these things—stirring them up continually to keep them in the fear of the Lord. I say there was nothing short of these things, and exceedingly great plainness of speech, would keep them from going down speedily to destruction. And after this manner do I write concerning them."

2 Nephi 28:24–25

"Therefore, wo be unto him that is at ease in Zion! Wo be unto him that crieth: All is well!"

The word "therefore" ties all that went before to this warning about "Zion." The threat of damnation, the pronouncement of "wo's", and the cautions about false teachers spreading false teachings are all designed to cause unease to Zion. That would be us. Or it would be what we claim about ourselves.

It is foolish to turn Nephi's message into a warning to some other latter-day group. The gentiles, who have received the Book of Mormon, and who claim they are better than others, puffed up with conceit about being chosen and highly favored of God, are the ones who would identify themselves as "Zion" in Nephi's prophecy. Not others. *Us.*

If you have reacted to the previous discussion with the notion that the interpretation given is really just my "opinion," and not an actual warning targeting the Latter-day Saints, you should reconsider. Although Nephi's message has been construed to apply to other faiths, (and the language certainly permits it) this part of Nephi's sermon makes the conclusion inevitable. He is not warning others. He is not primarily targeting the world of the last days. He is warning and attempting to save the souls of those who receive his writings and self-identify themselves as "Zion."

This means if we are "Zion" we can never be "at ease." We can never relent. Self-praise and assuring words that make us relax are not only false, they cheat us whenever they remove the burden of repentance we must bear.

There can be no ease. There can be no determination that "all is well" until we have repented and come to Christ. When Christ has forgiven us, we can know we are forgiven. When Christ has promised us eternal life, we can know we have eternal life. Until then, we remain at risk and in jeopardy every hour we are here.[653] When, however, you know you are sealed up to eternal life, you have the more sure word of prophecy or the testimony of Jesus.[654]

When can a person know they have a part in Zion? When the Lord Himself has made them a citizen. When the description given below is the description of their lives, then they may know it will be well with them:

> "They are they who received the testimony of Jesus, and believed on his name and were baptized after the manner of his burial, being buried in the water in his name, and this according to the commandment which he has given—That by keeping the commandments they might be washed and cleansed from all their sins, and receive the Holy Spirit by the laying on of the hands of him who is ordained and sealed unto this power; And who overcome by faith, and are sealed by the Holy Spirit of promise, which the Father sheds forth upon all those who are just and true. They are they who are the church of the Firstborn. They are they into whose hands the Father has given all things—They are they who are priests and kings, who have received of his fulness, and of his glory; And are priests of the Most High, after the order of Melchizedek, which was after the order of Enoch, which was after the order of the Only Begotten Son. Wherefore, as it is written, they are gods, even the sons of God—Wherefore, all things are theirs, whether life or death, or things present, or things to come, all are theirs and they are Christ's, and Christ is God's. And they shall overcome all things." (D&C 76:51–60)

---

[653] 1 Corinthians 15:30 "And why stand we in jeopardy every hour?"

[654] D&C 131:5 (May 17, 1843.) The more sure word of prophecy means a man's knowing that he is sealed up unto eternal life, by revelation and the spirit of prophecy, through the power of the Holy Priesthood."

These are they who have been told by the voice of God from heaven that they have eternal life. They are those who have obtained a hope in Christ.

When the Gospel of Christ is taught, it is always the purpose to bring people to this point. It is not Christ's Gospel when the teachings fall short of declaring this to the audience. Nephi was not trying to get you to improve your behavior or to become a good citizen. He was not attempting to make you a conservative, mainstream American. He was warning you to flee from this corrupt and failing society to a higher place where you can obtain communion with the Church of the Firstborn. A place where you join the household of God.

Zion is not and has never been the product of an institutional organization on this earth. It is a byproduct of there being citizens of heaven living here. Zion is the only way such persons can live with one another. First obtain a hope in Christ, and then all things will be added to you.

Why, then, should there be no ease among us? Because we have too few for the Lord to bring again Zion. Until then we do not have Zion, and our false claims to it only serve to make us at ease while there remains yet a great unfinished labor to perform.

It is Nephi's love for us, his desire to see us saved and happy, that causes him to use such harsh words of warning. He knows what we lack. He wants us to overcome it all and join him in the chorus singing anthems of praise, because our joy cannot be expressed without such songs![655]

2 Nephi 28:26

"Yea, wo be unto him that hearkeneth unto the precepts of men, and denieth the power of God, and the gift of the Holy Ghost!"

Now we return to Nephi's theme. Don't listen to the "precepts of men." This warning is not for the teachers or leaders. Nephi is not saying to them: "don't teach with your own learning." He has already consigned them to hell.[656] Now he is speaking to the "few, who are

---

[655] D&C 84:98–102 "Until all shall know me, who remain, even from the least unto the greatest, and shall be filled with the knowledge of the Lord, and shall see eye to eye, and shall lift up their voice, and with the voice together sing this new song, saying:
The Lord hath brought again Zion;
The Lord hath redeemed his people, Israel,
According to the election of grace,
Which was brought to pass by the faith
And covenant of their fathers.
The Lord hath redeemed his people;
And Satan is bound and time is no longer.
The Lord hath gathered all things in one.
The Lord hath brought down Zion from above.
The Lord hath brought up Zion from beneath.
The earth hath travailed and brought forth her strength;
And truth is established in her bowels;
And the heavens have smiled upon her;
And she is clothed with the glory of her God;
For he stands in the midst of his people.
Glory, and honor, and power, and might,
Be ascribed to our God; for he is full of mercy,
Justice, grace and truth, and peace,
Forever and ever, Amen."

[656] 2 Nephi 28:15 "O the wise, and the learned, and the rich, that are puffed up in the pride of their hearts, and all those who preach false doctrines, and all those who commit whoredoms, and pervert the right way of the Lord, wo, wo, wo be unto them, saith the Lord God Almighty, for they shall be thrust down to hell!"

the humble followers of Christ."[657] In place of three "wo's" there is only one.

Nephi pronounces a "wo" upon those who "hearken" or accept the "precepts of men." They will be condemned. Their hopes will not be realized. They will suffer setbacks in their progression and will not attain to the hopes they might have otherwise attained. But their offense is less than that of the "lead them" and "cause them to err."[658]

If you "hearken" to the "precepts of men," you are denying "the power of the God, and the gift of the Holy Ghost." It is necessary for you to both deny God's power and rebel against the gift of the Holy Ghost in order for you to "hearken to the precepts of men." God's power was designed to keep you from making these errors. The gift of the Holy Ghost was given to lead you to the knowing the truth of all things.[659] When, therefore, you hearken to men's precepts you are not confirming through the Spirit that what is being taught is merely man's precepts.

With a tool like the Holy Ghost available to you, you are accountable for what teachings you accept. It is possible for you to listen to a teacher whose precepts are dark and to know as he speaks that the Spirit does not ratify his words. It is your responsibility to weigh all things and hold onto only those things which are good.[660]

---

[657] 2 Nephi 28:14 "They wear stiff necks and high heads; yea, and because of pride, and wickedness, and abominations, and whoredoms, they have all gone astray save it be a few, who are the humble followers of Christ; nevertheless, they are led, that in many instances they do err because they are taught by the precepts of men."

[658] 2 Nephi 28:14 "They wear stiff necks and high heads; yea, and because of pride, and wickedness, and abominations, and whoredoms, they have all gone astray save it be a few, who are the humble followers of Christ; nevertheless, they are led, that in many instances they do err because they are taught by the precepts of men."

[659] Moroni 10:5 "And by the power of the Holy Ghost ye may know the truth of all things."

[660] 1 Thessalonians 5:21 "Prove all things; hold fast that which is good."

When Jesus was asked about two witnesses He said He was one, the other was His Father, who also bore witness of Him. If they did not listen to the power of the Father, nor incline their hearts to receive the witness of the Spirit, then they could not know the Father, and could not receive that second witness.[661] Nephi is saying the same thing. That is, no man teaching the precepts of men should be able to deceive you. Rather, for every teaching and every teacher, there should be a second witness coming from above which bears witness to you that you are hearing the truth.

So many Latter-day Saint teachers resort to sentimentality and emotion in their teaching, talks, books and testimonies. Some are fooled into thinking an emotional reaction is the same as a witness of the Spirit. Emotions rarely communicate light and truth or intelligence. The Spirit bears witness of the truth, conveys light and intelligence, and may not at all be emotional. Or, if emotions are involved, it may be fear[662], dread[663], or even horror at what you encounter.[664]

---

[661] John 8:17–19 "It is also written in your law, that the testimony of two men is true. I am one that bear witness of myself, and the Father that sent me beareth witness of me. Then said they unto him, Where is thy Father? Jesus answered, Ye neither know me, nor my Father: if ye had known me, ye should have known my Father also."

[662] Isaiah 6:5 "Then said I, Woe is me! for I am undone; because I am a man of unclean lips, and I dwell in the midst of a people of unclean lips: for mine eyes have seen the King, the Lord of hosts."

[663] Genesis 28:17 "And he was afraid, and said, How dreadful is this place! this is none other but the house of God, and this is the gate of heaven."

[664] Genesis 15:12–18 "And when the sun was going down, a deep sleep fell upon Abram; and, lo, an horror of great darkness fell upon him. And he said unto Abram, Know of a surety that thy seed shall be a stranger in a land that is not theirs, and shall serve them; and they shall afflict them four hundred years; And also that nation, whom they shall serve, will I judge: and afterward shall they come out with great substance. And thou shalt go to thy fathers in peace; thou shalt be buried in a good old age. But in the fourth generation they shall come hither again: for the iniquity of the Amorites is not yet full. And it came to pass, that, when the sun went down, and it was dark, behold a smoking furnace, and a burning lamp that passed between those pieces. In the same day the Lord made a covenant with Abram, saying, Unto thy seed have I given this land, from the river of Egypt unto the great river, the river Euphrates:"

Mere sentimentality is a false substitute for the witness of the Spirit. Joseph Smith explained it this way:

> "When you feel pure intelligence flowing into you, it may give you sudden strokes of ideas, so that by noticing it, you may find it fulfilled the same day or soon; (i.e.) those things that were presented unto your minds by the Spirit of God, will come to pass; and thus by learning the Spirit of God and understanding it, you may grow into the principle of revelation, until you become perfect in Christ Jesus." (*TPJS*, 151.)

The warning from Nephi about how you deny the power of God, you reject the gift of the Holy Ghost whenever you "hearken to the precepts of men" is based on this principle. You have the tools to detect when you are being taught by men using the arm of flesh to advance an idea or notion. You are accountable, hence the "wo" pronounced on you by Nephi.

Ask yourself the following questions as you hear a teacher:

- Does he teach you to come to Christ?
- Do the teachings convey intelligence upon you, or just sentiment?
- Do they awaken inside you light and truth that you hadn't considered before?
- Are the teachings based on the revelations of heaven, or some study, analysis or tool developed by academics?
- Are you encouraged to seek for a confirmation from the Spirit?
- Did you learn something new, but find yourself feeling you have known it before?
- Whether it causes dread, fear, or even horror, does the Spirit tell you, nonetheless, it is of God?
- Are you more inclined to get on your knees and call upon God because of what you have learned?

- Does the speaker merely want you to honor her, or an institution?

- Does the speaker hold him/herself out as an expert or someone with impressive credentials?

- Does he rely on status or office as the reason to trust his teaching, or instead rely on the truthfulness of his message? No power or influence can or ought to be exerted by virtue of office or position, only by persuasion and pure knowledge.[665]

- Are the words noble and great, despite your view of the person who is delivering them?

You may be surprised when you ask such questions at what you learn. Nephi is saying it is *your* own responsibility if you allow yourself to be taken in by the precepts of men. Wo unto you if you do.

2 Nephi: 28:28

"And in fine, wo unto all those who tremble, and are angry because of the truth of God! For behold, he that is built upon the rock receiveth it with gladness; and he that is built upon a sandy foundation trembleth lest he shall fall."

This is the constant problem. People do not care about religion. So when someone like Nephi delivers a message to the audience that is threatening because it contradicts their presumptions, they get upset. They are fearful. They "tremble, and are angry." When Nephi puts out the message, he knows those he addresses are going to react in a very negative way. He will become the object of their distrust and dislike.

---

[665] D&C 121:41–42 "No power or influence can or ought to be maintained by virtue of the priesthood, only by persuasion, by long-suffering, by gentleness and meekness, and by love unfeigned; By kindness, and pure knowledge, which shall greatly enlarge the soul without hypocrisy, and without guile—"

But Nephi reminds the audience that it isn't him they have a problem with. It is "the truth of God."

There are two reactions: One is anger, because it condemns them. The other is gladness. Those who are "built upon the rock"— meaning Christ—have their hope and faith in Him, for He is the "Rock of Heaven"[666] and they "receive it with gladness."

Those who are "built upon a sandy foundation" will "tremble." This would mean they are struck with fear. They are afraid of the message. They fear because they begin to realize their religious convictions may be wrong. They are afraid they "shall fall," or in other words, if the message is true then they may be doomed and their high hopes dashed.

They would rather be angry and try and suppress the message than to receive it and repent. If someone has a good heart, then any warning is appreciated. Even if it informs them they are mistaken. They want truth. So a warning is appreciated when it permits them to correct their errors. These people are built upon the Rock, because truth alone determines what they will accept. They "hearken to the truth" because they are interested in knowing truth.

This message from Nephi reminds all of us about the difference between those who are grounded in the testimony of Jesus (the Rock) and those who hope their brand of religion will aid them (the sand). False hopes are quickly threatened when exposed to the truth. Knowledge that you are built upon the testimony of Jesus, however, cannot be shaken. Critics will be ground into dust by such a stone,

---

[666] Moses 7:53 "And the Lord said: Blessed is he through whose seed Messiah shall come; for he saith—I am Messiah, the King of Zion, the Rock of Heaven, which is broad as eternity; whoso cometh in at the gate and climbeth up by me shall never fall; wherefore, blessed are they of whom I have spoken, for they shall come forth with songs of everlasting joy."

but will not damage it.[667] Those with such knowledge would suffer death, but not deny the Lord.[668] Though called upon to suffer for His name, they will not submit, but choose to die secure in the knowledge they have of Christ.[669]

This kind of faith requires sacrifice, as explained in the Lectures on Faith previously posted. The Book of Mormon calls it "knowledge" and that lecture requires you "actually know the course you are pursuing is pleasing to God." That is, whether you call it "faith" as the Lectures do, or "knowledge" as the Book of Mormon does, it is the same. You must come to know Christ has accepted your sacrifices. You should re-read that if you want to reacquaint yourself with the requirements for gaining such faith.

2 Nephi 28:29

"Wo be unto him that shall say: We have received the word of God, and we need no more of the word of God, for we have enough!"

This general principle is addressed first. Nephi will build on it in the following verses. But the first statement is the broadest.

An earlier "wo" was pronounced upon those who rely on the uninspired teachings of men who use their own precepts. Now he adds a second "wo" to those who also deny the need for continuing

---

[667] Daniel 2:45 "Forasmuch as thou sawest that the stone was cut out of the mountain without hands, and that it brake in pieces the iron, the brass, the clay, the silver, and the gold; the great God hath made known to the king what shall come to pass hereafter: and the dream *is* certain, and the interpretation thereof sure."

[668] Mosiah 17:1–0 "Yea, and I will suffer even until death, and I will not recall my words, and they shall stand as a testimony against you. And if ye slay me ye will shed innocent blood, and this shall also stand as a testimony against you at the last day."

[669] D&C 138:13–14 "And who had offered sacrifice in the similitude of the great sacrifice of the Son of God, and had suffered tribulation in their Redeemer's name. All these had departed the mortal life, firm in the hope of a glorious resurrection, through the grace of God the Father and his Only Begotten Son, Jesus Christ."

revelation. We claim we are unlike all other faiths because we believe in the concept of continuing revelation. However, that notion is greatly modified by us to the point where the continuation of revelation is so limited, so curtailed, and so distrusted that we are generally unacquainted with any new revelation.

Do we hear of visions and visitations? Not much, if at all. We think that such things are reserved for leaders. For example, if Elijah were to return with a message to someone, we would expect the person with whom he would visit would be the church President. If it were someone other than the church President, we would instantly be suspicious because Elijah wasn't following the "chain of authority" *as we expect*. [Interestingly, as soon as you know Elijah was involved you should consider that another line of authority may be created.] So even if we heard from Elijah, it would cause us trouble and likely be rejected as too irregular. This would be true of other heavenly messengers, as well.

What visitations could we tolerate? Pretty much we'd only think it appropriate for an ancestor to visit with a descendant to give a family message. A deceased great-grandfather coming to bring a message about one of his descendants would seem to fit within the whole "chain of authority" model we have created. Family business. Seems to be acceptable. However, even then, we would expect the person involved to "keep it to themselves" because it was inappropriate to share things like that. Too personal. Too sacred. Too much information of a deeply personal nature to warrant talking about it with others.

What if the great-grandfather were Abraham? Would that fit the model? What if his concerns ran to all who are living? Would that family be large enough to warrant talking about it with almost anyone? Oops, we're back to the whole "chain of authority" argument again, and would expect Abraham to limit his visit to the chief Mormon-in-charge. So a visit by Abraham would be suspect as well.

What if the message were from John the Beloved? He has a continuing ministry to visit with people and bring them to salvation. In
fact, his ministry includes visiting with those who will be "heirs of
salvation who dwell on the earth."[670] Still, if a person had him minister to him, we would not want to hear about it, would question the
propriety, and wonder why John would come when other perfectly
authoritative men are living on the earth inside the church holding
the same keys as John. So, that would be questioned and regarded as
irregular as well.

So as Latter-day Saints we believe in the continuation of revelation, visitations, visions, etc. so long as they conform to our limited
model, come to the right person, and don't disturb anything we have
going on at the present. Which is to say we don't believe in continuing revelation much at all.

What about Christ? Can He visit with anyone whom He deigns to
visit? That's a little closer call, because He seems to have promised to
come to all. He also displayed remarkably democratic tendencies
both on the day of His resurrection, and when visiting the Nephites.
(I've explained His disregard for the church hierarchy He established
on the day of His resurrection in *Come, Let Us Adore Him*.) He seems
much less interested in respecting established religious authority than
we do. So we might allow the Lord to visit with someone, but, then
we wouldn't want to hear many details because that would be wrong

---

[670] D&C 7:1–6 "And the Lord said unto me: John, my beloved, what desirest thou? For
if you shall ask what you will, it shall be granted unto you. And I said unto him: Lord,
give unto me power over death, that I may live and bring souls unto thee. And the Lord
said unto me: Verily, verily, I say unto thee, because thou desirest this thou shalt tarry
until I come in my glory, and shalt prophesy before nations, kindreds, tongues and
people. And for this cause the Lord said unto Peter: If I will that he tarry till I come,
what is that to thee? For he desired of me that he might bring souls unto me, but thou
desiredst that thou mightest speedily come unto me in my kingdom. I say unto thee,
Peter, this was a good desire; but my beloved has desired that he might do more, or a
greater work yet among men than what he has before done. Yea, he has undertaken a
greater work; therefore I will make him as flaming fire and a ministering angel; he shall
minister for those who shall be heirs of salvation who dwell on the earth."

for some reason. Probably "casting pearls before swine" or "profaning" or "disrespecting the line of authority" or something. Not sure which one, but there's got to be a prohibition against it somewhere.

So we have tendencies that are difficult to put into a hard and fast rule, but I'm going to attempt it.

Rule 1: We believe in continuing revelation; predicated upon the following:

(a) Mostly to the President of the church,

(b) but with others whenever:

- It is a grandparent who lived sometime during the restoration or had some unique reason to be coming back, but never:

    - an ancestor so long back they would be Biblical, because that puts us back into (a) above;

    - if they have a message which would be of general interest, because that puts us back into (a) above;

    - if the visit involves knowing something or clarifying something which might be sacred, because such things are wrong to discuss or acknowledge.

- It is the Lord, but that's because He pretty much gets to do what He wants to do; except if it's important we'd want Him to explain why He didn't follow (a) above—and it better be a pretty good reason or else we'll have to question the report.

Well, We believe all that God has revealed to authorized people in positions of authority, all that He does now reveal, and we believe that He will yet reveal to the proper channels many great and important things pertaining to the Kingdom of God; and that once it has been reviewed by the Correlation Department and published by Deseret Book it will become something which we can all accept as being from an authorized source and reliable.

Until that happens, we have absolutely received enough of the word of God and we don't need any more of the word of God. And, by damn, if someone comes claiming revelation or an independent apostolic witness of the Lord's resurrection we will want them to cut off an arm or some other member of the body and then restore it again, so that we may know he has come with power. I'm quite confident that ought to satisfy our need to see a sign before we will believe a proposition.

Now we know for certain Nephi's warning is to those *other faiths* that do not accept continuing revelation and not to us. However, as to those, Nephi has pronounced a prior "wo" for their acceptance of the precepts of men, and now a second "wo" upon them for their refusal to accept continuing revelation. These begin to mount up and ought to worry those to whom these concerns are addressed, *whoever* they may be. Perhaps Nephi should have written his book for those people, instead of us good folks who read the book and know for certain that we're alright.

2 Nephi 28:30

"For behold, thus saith the Lord God: I will give unto the children of men line upon line, precept upon precept, here a little and there a little; and blessed are those who hearken unto my precepts, and lend an ear unto my counsel, for they shall learn wisdom; for unto him that receiveth I will give more, and from them that shall say, We have enough, from them shall be taken away even that which they have."

Here Nephi shows he is the prophetic precedent upon which others would build. We often quote Alma for this idea, because Alma lays it out more completely. But Alma's teaching has its root in Nephi's warning here.[671]

Notice the Lord's promise that He will "give unto the children of men." He is liberal and does not upbraid us for asking.[672] Indeed, He admonishes us to seek, ask and knock.[673]

Notice that "unto him that receiveth" is the singular. It isn't "those" but "him." Meaning each of us individually may come to Him and ask and receive. However, "from them that shall say, We have enough" is plural. Meaning, there are many who could have been taught, had they not shut the doors. The collective will resist new revelation, even when it continues. They will shut their minds and not tolerate learning of truths.

When, however, groups close their minds it becomes impossible to keep what they have. It is inevitable that "from them shall be taken away even that which they have." Meaning, that we are either in

---

[671] Alma 12:9–11 "And now Alma began to expound these things unto him, saying: It is given unto many to know the mysteries of God; nevertheless they are laid under a strict command that they shall not impart only according to the portion of his word which he doth grant unto the children of men, according to the heed and diligence which they give unto him. And therefore, he that will harden his heart, the same receiveth the lesser portion of the word; and he that will not harden his heart, to him is given the greater portion of the word, until it is given unto him to know the mysteries of God until he know them in full. And they that will harden their hearts, to them is given the lesser portion of the word until they know nothing concerning his mysteries; and then they are taken captive by the devil, and led by his will down to destruction. Now this is what is meant by the chains of hell."

[672] James 1:5–6 "If any of you lack wisdom, let him ask of God, that giveth to all *men* liberally, and upbraideth not; and it shall be given him. But let him ask in faith, nothing wavering. For he that wavereth is like a wave of the sea driven with the wind and tossed."

[673] Matthew 7:7–11 "Ask, and it shall be given you; seek, and ye shall find; knock, and it shall be opened unto you: For every one that asketh receiveth; and he that seeketh findeth; and to him that knocketh it shall be opened. Or what man is there of you, whom if his son ask bread, will he give him a stone? Or if he ask a fish, will he give him a serpent? If ye then, being evil, know how to give good gifts unto your children, how much more shall your Father which is in heaven give good things to them that ask him?"
D&C 88:63 "Draw near unto me and I will draw near unto you; seek me diligently and ye shall find me; ask, and ye shall receive; knock, and it shall be opened unto you."

a process of restoration or apostasy. The instant we stop restoring truths, we begin to lose them. You cannot just keep what Joseph restored to you. That will be lost. You either continue on and receive on-going revelation and new visions, visitations and restoration, or else you begin to forfeit what you already have. So soon as you walk away from one precept, from one doctrine, from one ordinance, you have begun the process of apostasy or falling away.

This environment is not static. It is always in change. Either it is being built up, created and newly formed, or it is decaying, dying and falling apart. It never holds static. This is because the things of this world testify of Christ's Gospel.[674] The path is only upward. So soon as you stray from it, you lose the path. This is why you take the shoes from off your feet and put them on again as a symbol that you accept the path. You never remove them again, because once upon that path you are to remain so. The path is accompanied by greater light and truth, going from grace to grace until you receive a fullness.[675]

Nephi is telling us how to receive the fullness. It comes only through revelation and the opening of heaven. You may be anointed to become kings and priests, but the realization of these blessings depends upon your faithfulness. If you are true and faithful the time will come when you will be called up and anointed, whereas now it is all conditional. Only Christ can remove the conditions. To have Him do that requires Him, as the Word, to intercede on your behalf. It

---

[674] Moses 6:63 "And behold, all things have their likeness, and all things are created and made to bear record of me, both things which are temporal, and things which are spiritual; things which are in the heavens above, and things which are on the earth, and things which are in the earth, and things which are under the earth, both above and beneath: all things bear record of me."

[675] D&C 93:19, 26–28 "I give unto you these sayings that you may understand and know how to worship, and know what you worship, that you may come unto the Father in my name, and in due time receive of his fulness. . . . The Spirit of truth is of God. I am the Spirit of truth, and John bore record of me, saying: He received a fulness of truth, yea, even of all truth; And no man receiveth a fulness unless he keepeth his commandments. He that keepeth his commandments receiveth truth and light, until he is glorified in truth and knoweth all things."

requires Him to confirm by His own voice from heaven that you are His, and to establish His covenant directly with you.

Whether it is the words of an old book or the words of an older ceremony it is the same. They can't save you. Only following the exact same path as the ancients followed can result in arriving at the same end. As the 6th Lecture from the *Lectures on Faith* states:

> "When a man has offered in sacrifice all that he has for the truth's sake, not even withholding his life, and believing before God that he has been called to make this sacrifice, because he seeks to do his will, he does know most assuredly that God does and will accept his sacrifice and offering, and that he has not nor will not seek his face in vain. Under these circumstances then, he can obtain the faith necessary for him to lay hold on eternal life. It is in vain for persons to fancy to themselves that they are heirs with those, or can be heirs with them, who have offered their all in sacrifice, and by this means obtained faith in God and favor with him so as to obtain eternal life, unless they in like manner offer unto him the same sacrifice, and through that offering obtain the knowledge that they are accepted of him."

What role does revelation play? Without it no person can be saved.

Who must receive the revelation? Each person for themselves.

What happens when revelation stops? To the person for whom revelation has ended, there is no salvation[676], and they will immediately begin to lose what they were previously given. To the people who refuse to receive more, "from them shall be taken away even that which they have."

---

[676] Moroni 7:37–38 "Behold I say unto you, Nay; for it is by faith that miracles are wrought; and it is by faith that angels appear and minister unto men; wherefore, if these things have ceased wo be unto the children of men, for it is because of unbelief, and all is vain. For no man can be saved, according to the words of Christ, save they shall have faith in his name; wherefore, if these things have ceased, then has faith ceased also; and awful is the state of man, for they are as though there had been no redemption made."

Nephi has declared it, using authority from God to do so. We either accept his counsel and warnings or reject it at our peril.

2 Nephi 28:31

"Cursed is he that putteth his trust in man, or maketh flesh his arm, or shall hearken unto the precepts of men, save their precepts shall be given by the power of the Holy Ghost."

Now we move beyond the wo's to cursing. Cursing by one holding authority to seal is a terrible thing to encounter. However, we should expect that one having that authority, possessing correct knowledge, along with the ability to lead into light and truth, would do all he could to be clear about a matter so those who read what he has said will understand unmistakably the responsibilities they face. Nephi is discharging a duty, and doing so with our best interests in mind. We shouldn't take offense. We should be grateful even if it is painful to read.

So again we confront the phrase "trust in man" along with "maketh flesh his arm." Have you considered the meaning of these terms? Have you thought about them as symbols?

"Trust in man" is another way of describing reliance on man to save. Man's theories or hopes or vain formulas as the path to God is another way to describe "trust in man." Do you want a preacher who will give you the philosophies of men mingled with scripture?

Something from _Bartlett's Familiar Quotations_ to "flesh out" the meaning of a phrase in scripture? A little story of personal experience from your own life, to personalize the meaning of a verse from the Bible? Will you trade that for an inspired warning that your soul is in jeopardy and you are cursed because of what you accept in place of the power of the Holy Ghost as your guide?

"Maketh flesh his arm" is another way of saying the "strength" of man, rather than the "strength" of God. The arm is also the means by which a sign or covenant might be set forth. By putting the "flesh his arm" rather than the signs of priestly authority from a true messenger, the implication is that any surrogate for God will do if they just have a few bona-fides. Credentials will be enough. Have they been to college and received training for the ministry? A man cannot preach unless he's been trained for the ministry, you see. Are they a scholar? We like to defer to them. We quote them, study them, and believe in their techniques and methods.

But Nephi keeps thundering back: No man's precepts should be accepted when they do not originate in revelation and the Holy Ghost. Without a connection to revelation and the Holy Ghost, the teachings are all the arm of flesh. If you want to trust in that, you will be cursed.

Nephi puts it into two, opposing camPsalms There are only two. There are either inspired teachings, given by revelation and confirmed by the Holy Ghost, or they are man's understanding. The first will save you. The other will curse you. There is no happy marriage. You cannot have both. This sword cuts both ways, and forces you to make a decision. Your eternity will be affected by the decision. So either you find the right way and follow it, or you are relying upon men and will in the end be cursed.

Interesting choice. Terrible dilemma. Glad we are absolutely guaranteed that the men we trust to lead us cannot ever lead us astray. Or the majority of them won't anyway. Because if we had to rely only on something as flimsy as the Holy Ghost to choose we would be forced to fast and pray, be humble and penitent to solve this terrible dilemma for us; working out our salvation with fear and trembling before God.[677]

---

[677] Philippians 2:12 "Wherefore, my beloved, as ye have always obeyed, not as in my presence only, but now much more in my absence, work out your own salvation with fear and trembling."

I'm glad we don't have to go through that. We're the best of heaven and have come down to strut and fret our hour upon the stage, all the while enwrapped in several layers of guaranteed eternal life insurance policies paid for by the blood of martyrs and pioneers who suffered so we might be able to live comfortably. We are just GOOD people. They envied us. Everyone has, you know. The prophets all looked down from antiquity and longed to live among us, the favored few . . .

Oh, wait a minute, I got carried away. I forgot we were trying to understand Nephi's message. For a minute there I was too wrapped up in our own message. Well, to return to Nephi—someone's going to be cursed for trusting in men. Only those whose precepts and teachings originate in the Holy Ghost are going to be saved. It is a terrible burden to confront. It almost makes us want to turn away in sorrow rather than continue on following our Lord.[678] But, then again, who else has the words of eternal life other than Him?

2 Nephi 28:32

"Wo be unto the Gentiles, saith the Lord God of Hosts! For notwithstanding I shall lengthen out mine arm unto them from day to day, they will deny me; nevertheless, I will be merciful unto them, saith the Lord God, if they will repent and come unto me; for mine arm is lengthened out all the day long, saith the Lord God of Hosts."

After all these warnings, the mention of Zion, the foolishness of following the "precepts of men" Nephi turns again to identifying the most relevant group being warned. It is "the gentiles" (or us). As he considers our collective effort and how we allow the "precepts of

---

[678] John 6:65–67 "And he said, Therefore said I unto you, that no man can come unto me, except it were given unto him of my Father. From that *time* many of his disciples went back, and walked no more with him. Then said Jesus unto the twelve, Will ye also go away?"

men" to be our guide, he states his overall conclusion about our performance: "Wo be unto the Gentiles, saith the Lord God of Hosts!"

This is the third wo. And it is accompanied by a three name title. This time incorporating the "Hosts" or Family of God. This is the Father's judgment upon us. His status as the "Lord God of Hosts" is clearly intended to let us know those proud gentiles who rely upon the sparks of their own fire as their light will lay down in sorrow.[679]

When the Lord's open arm is extended all the day, they reject Him and walk away. They prefer their own false ideas to the truth found in Christ. In the end they have "denied the Lord" because all His efforts toward them have been rejected.

Still, despite all these failings, and all the wo's pronounced upon them, it is *not* the Lord's failure. It is the gentiles. Even now the Lord would welcome them "if they will repent and come to Him." His arm is yet "lengthened out all the day long." So long as life remains, He is pleading for our repentance. So long as we are here, He will welcome our repentance. And, so we do not miss the point, He also uses a three-name title when extending the plea to us for our repentance. He is speaking on behalf of, and as the chief among, all the "Hosts of heaven." The entire council would welcome us back, if we would but return.

Can you not sense the agony of this plea? Can you not feel the mercy God would grant to any penitent soul? Despite this, men prefer their arrogance, their own precepts, their own false teachings to being taught by the Holy Spirit. We refuse to repent because we prefer our false teachings. We prefer our traditions that build up our pride, and tell us we are going to be exalted because we are good and

---

[679] Isaiah 50:11 "Behold, all ye that kindle a fire, that compass *yourselves* about with sparks: walk in the light of your fire, and in the sparks *that* ye have kindled. This shall ye have of mine hand; ye shall lie down in sorrow."

2 Nephi 7:11 "Behold all ye that kindle fire, that compass yourselves about with sparks, walk in the light of your fire and in the sparks which ye have kindled. This shall ye have of mine hand—ye shall lie down in sorrow."

deserve God's favor. We've put up with tithing, and with faithful meeting attendance, and followed faithfully all kinds of leaders in every ward and stake we've ever attended. We've passed temple recommend interviews and attended faithfully our tithing settlement meetings—in short we think we've done everything God could possibly ask of us.

Except we have NOT repented and come to Christ. Had we done that, we would have been embraced in those opened arms of our Lord. In five points of contact with a loving God, we would have heard unspeakable things and know we escaped the wo's pronounced by Nephi.

Nephi's assessment of the gentile performance is consistently pessimistic. Coupled with Nephi's description of a consistently open and accepting Lord who would welcome us at any time were we willing to repent.

Nephi's message gets mangled in our distorted cultural rewriting of meanings. When someone points out what he's saying, it produces anger and resentment. The result is not particularly encouraging for the gentiles. Not merely because of Nephi's prophetic words, but also because of our reaction to them.

In the preceding verses Nephi has changed from giving his own advice and counsel to quoting the Lord. He began in verse 30 with the words: "behold, thus saith the Lord" and continues quoting Him through the end of that chapter and into the next.

The third "wo" was pronounced by Nephi as a quote from the Lord. The "cursing of the gentiles" was pronounced by Nephi as a quote from the Lord.

Now I didn't point that out as we went through the materials. It is significant enough that it requires additional attention.

Christ has divided judgment up into two separate functions. For those who will be blessed, He will delegate the honor of blessing to others, including His twelve at Jerusalem[680] and twelve Nephite disciples. Their judgment is honorary, however, because they are given no discretion in the matter. The Lord will decide the judgment. It is His alone, so as to insure it will be the right decision.[681] For those who are to be cursed, however, Christ will be the one who pronounces the judgment.[682]

It is of terrible significance that these statements come from the Lord who alone holds the right to judge. He sacrificed His life for all, and is the Savior and Redeemer, seeking to save all who will come to Him. This is the same Lord who pronounces the words through Nephi:

> "Cursed is he that putteth his trust in man, or maketh flesh his arm, or shall hearken unto the precepts of men, save their precepts shall be given by the power of the Holy Ghost. Wo be unto the Gentiles, saith the Lord God of Hosts!" (2 Nephi 28:31–32.)

The message is delivered by Nephi. The words are the Lord's. The merciful and loving Christ who suffered for all that they might

---

[680] Matthew 19:28 "And Jesus said unto them, Verily I say unto you, That ye which have followed me, in the regeneration when the Son of man shall sit in the throne of his glory, ye also shall sit upon twelve thrones, judging the twelve tribes of Israel."
1 Nephi 12:9 "And he said unto me: Thou rememberest the Twelve Apostles of the Lamb? Behold they are they who shall judge the twelve tribes of Israel; wherefore, the twelve ministers of thy seed shall be judged of them; for ye are of the house of Israel."

[681] 3 Nephi 27:27 "And know ye that ye shall be judges of this people, according to the judgment which I shall give unto you, which shall be just. Therefore, what manner of men ought ye to be? Verily I say unto you, even as I am."

[682] D&C 29:27–29 "And the righteous shall be gathered on my right hand unto eternal life; and the wicked on my left hand will I be ashamed to own before the Father; Wherefore I will say unto them—Depart from me, ye cursed, into everlasting fire, prepared for the devil and his angels. And now, behold, I say unto you, never at any time have I declared from mine own mouth that they should return, for where I am they cannot come, for they have no power."

not suffer if they would repent[683] is announcing His pessimism about the latter-day gentile effort to obtain repentance. Why do we seem destined to fail? Why is repentance so difficult for us? What terrible "precepts of men" hold us bound in chains that we cannot break free.

Several have made comments on the question of how we are to repent and come to Christ. There is a fundamental first step to be taken which the Lord has explained repeatedly in His teachings. I have written about this often, including in my first and last books.

In the chapter on the Atonement in *Come, Let Us Adore Him* there is an explanation given of what Christ suffered and what obligations are devolving on us as a result. We must do as He did, suffer in like manner, and forgive all offenses. His infinite suffering cannot be replicated in one sense, but in our own sphere and time we do suffer offenses and abuses. We are required to forgive as He forgave. It is our own forgiveness of others that qualifies us to receive forgiveness from Him. When we harbor grudges and resentments, we cut ourselves off from His Atonement. IF we are to be forgiven we must in turn FORGIVE others. In *The Second Comforter* it is shown how we must make intercession on behalf of others, even our enemies, if we are to have a hope in Christ. We must lay down the burden of sin to enter into His presence. Much of that "sin" in each of our lives has been the offenses against us, and the resentment and anger we hold from these abuses. There are people who have done you wrong. There are some who did so intentionally. When you forgive them, and plead on their behalf for the Lord to also forgive them in sincerity and love, you are not far from the Kingdom of Heaven. Your Lord did this. You must do as He did to be like Him. It is the only way to understand your Lord. In this, you must suffer as He did,

---

[683] D&C 19:16 "For behold, I, God, have suffered these things for all, that they might not suffer if they would repent;"

choosing to forgive offenses rather than to seek justice. When you show mercy, you merit mercy. The beginning of repentance is found in forgiving others.

Your just claims for retribution must be surrendered. Your worthy desire to have vindication must be abandoned. Your right to have judgment against the ones who abused you must be forfeited. And you must go on to pray for their forgiveness.

If you have read all I have written you already know this. I am disappointed to have those who have not read what I've written trying to make sense of this blog. It will make absolutely no sense if it is not seen as an extension of what I've already covered. Even this brief statement about the relationship between your own salvation and redemption through following Christ is a brief note, a cryptic signal, and altogether inadequate to explain the matter. The careful, patient and fulsome explanation has been laid out elsewhere in what I've written. You must go there to see why, along with the many places in scripture where the Lord has made the matter clear.

Nephi takes no delight in pronouncing these wo's and writing the "cursing" the latter-day gentiles face. The Lord takes even less. He suffered and died to make salvation possible for these very same latter-day gentiles. He would save them all. But to do so it is absolutely necessary to bluntly warn those whom He loves. Enos recorded his own ministry and how it was affected by the audience he addressed: "And there was nothing save it was exceeding harshness, preaching and prophesying of wars, and contentions, and destructions, and continually reminding them of death, and the duration of eternity, and the judgments and the power of God, and all these things—stirring them up continually to keep them in the fear of the Lord. I say there was nothing short of these things, and exceedingly great plainness of speech, would keep them from going down speedily to destruction. And after this manner do I write concerning them."[684]

Why would a joyful Lord, who delights in our own happiness, speak in terms of "wo's" and "cursing" to us? What is it about us as His audience that compels Him to rebuke us? Have you thought of the standard in D&C 121 ("reproving betimes with sharpness when moved upon by the Holy Ghost") as part of this rebuke?[685]

He so completely loves us that John equated Him with love.[686] Can you imagine the frustration it causes our Lord to have to speak in these terms to us?

Why do we not repent? Why do we harbor and protect our sins? Why do we worship men rather than God? Why do we cleave to the precepts of men rather than the Holy Ghost? Why do we resist the truth when it is declared to us. Why do we demand that the truth be conformed to our understanding of the precepts of men? Why do we measure the things of God against our own traditions? Why do we not abandon instantly our false notions, and stop arguing against

---

[684] Enos 1:23 "And there was nothing save it was exceeding harshness, preaching and prophesying of wars, and contentions, and destructions, and continually reminding them of death, and the duration of eternity, and the judgments and the power of God, and all these things—stirring them up continually to keep them in the fear of the Lord. I say there was nothing short of these things, and exceedingly great plainness of speech, would keep them from going down speedily to destruction. And after this manner do I write concerning them."

[685] D&C 121:41–46 "No power or influence can or ought to be maintained by virtue of the priesthood, only by persuasion, by long-suffering, by gentleness and meekness, and by love unfeigned; By kindness, and pure knowledge, which shall greatly enlarge the soul without hypocrisy, and without guile— Reproving betimes with sharpness, when moved upon by the Holy Ghost; and then showing forth afterwards an increase of love toward him whom thou hast reproved, lest he esteem thee to be his enemy; That he may know that thy faithfulness is stronger than the cords of death. Let thy bowels also be full of charity towards all men, and to the household of faith, and let virtue garnish thy thoughts unceasingly; then shall thy confidence wax strong in the presence of God; and the doctrine of the priesthood shall distil upon thy soul as the dews from heaven. The Holy Ghost shall be thy constant companion, and thy scepter an unchanging scepter of righteousness and truth; and thy dominion shall be an everlasting dominion, and without compulsory means it shall flow unto thee forever and ever."

[686] 1 John 4:8 "He that loveth not knoweth not God; for God is love."

the truth which is in Christ? Why do we think any institution, fellowship, association or man can lead us to salvation instead of Christ
alone who can save?[687]

How long will you harden your heart against your Lord, whose
pleas are aimed only at saving your soul? Why turn away and say that
you prefer membership in a great and spacious building, pointing an
accusing finger at those who would lead you to eternal life?[688] Our
awards and honors are nothing. Your recognition and praise is corro-
sion. Everything here is doomed to decay, rot and fail.[689] This is the
Telestial Kingdom. Everything here, every institution, organization
and order is Telestial. None of it will survive death.[690] Even the one

---

[687] 2 Nephi 31:19 "And now, my beloved brethren, after ye have gotten into this strait
and narrow path, I would ask if all is done? Behold, I say unto you, Nay; for ye have
not come thus far save it were by the word of Christ with unshaken faith in him, relying wholly upon the merits of him who is mighty to save."

[688] 1 Nephi 8:26–31 "And I also cast my eyes round about, and beheld, on the other
side of the river of water, a great and spacious building; and it stood as it were in the
air, high above the earth. And it was filled with people, both old and young, both male
and female; and their manner of dress was exceedingly fine; and they were in the attitude of mocking and pointing their fingers towards those who had come at and were
partaking of the fruit. And after they had tasted of the fruit they were ashamed, because of those that were scoffing at them; and they fell away into forbidden paths and
were lost. And now I, Nephi, do not speak all the words of my father. But, to be short
in writing, behold, he saw other multitudes pressing forward; and they came and caught
hold of the end of the rod of iron; and they did press their way forward, continually
holding fast to the rod of iron, until they came forth and fell down and partook of the
fruit of the tree. And he also saw other multitudes feeling their way towards that great
and spacious building."

[689] Matthew 6:19–20 "Lay not up for yourselves treasures upon earth, where moth and
rust doth corrupt, and where thieves break through and steal: But lay up for yourselves
treasures in heaven, where neither moth nor rust doth corrupt, and where thieves do
not break through nor steal:"

[690] D&C 132:7 "And verily I say unto you, that the conditions of this law are these: All
covenants, contracts, bonds, obligations, oaths, vows, performances, connections, associations, or expectations, that are not made and entered into and sealed by the Holy
Spirit of promise, of him who is anointed, both as well for time and for all eternity,
and that too most holy, by revelation and commandment through the medium of mine
anointed, whom I have appointed on the earth to hold this power (and I have appointed unto my servant Joseph to hold this power in the last days, and there is never
but one on the earth at a time on whom this power and the keys of this priesthood are
conferred), are of no efficacy, virtue, or force in and after the resurrection from the
dead; for all contracts that are not made unto this end have an end when men are dead."

association intended to endure (the family) will not endure unless it is through the Holy Spirit of Promise.

If you are going to be rescued from this Telestial Kingdom, it will be Christ who rescues you. His arm has been stretched out to you as long as you have been here, and it will remain stretched out until you depart here. If you are not saved, it will be because of your rejection of Him, not His rejection of you. He has done all He could. He has sent stern warnings, warm invitations, cheerful messengers, the dignified and the undignified, to show in all things He is willing to meet you more than half way. Those who reject these widely different invitations are accountable for their failure.[691]

---

[691] Matthew 11:7–24 "And as they departed, Jesus began to say unto the multitudes concerning John, What went ye out into the wilderness to see? A reed shaken with the wind? But what went ye out for to see? A man clothed in soft raiment? behold, they that wear soft *clothing* are in kings' houses. But what went ye out for to see? A prophet? yea, I say unto you, and more than a prophet. For this is *he,* of whom it is written, Behold, I send my messenger before thy face, which shall prepare thy way before thee. Verily I say unto you, Among them that are born of women there hath not risen a greater than John the Baptist: notwithstanding he that is least in the kingdom of heaven is greater than he. And from the days of John the Baptist until now the kingdom of heaven suffereth violence, and the violent take it by force. For all the prophets and the law prophesied until John. And if ye will receive *it,* this is Elias, which was for to come. He that hath ears to hear, let him hear. But whereunto shall I liken this generation? It is like unto children sitting in the markets, and calling unto their fellows, And saying, We have piped unto you, and ye have not danced; we have mourned unto you, and ye have not lamented. For John came neither eating nor drinking, and they say, He hath a devil. The Son of man came eating and drinking, and they say, Behold a man gluttonous, and a winebibber, a friend of publicans and sinners. But wisdom is justified of her children. Then began he to upbraid the cities wherein most of his mighty works were done, because they repented not: Woe unto thee, Chorazin! woe unto thee, Bethsaida! for if the mighty works, which were done in you, had been done in Tyre and Sidon, they would have repented long ago in sackcloth and ashes. But I say unto you, It shall be more tolerable for Tyre and Sidon at the day of judgment, than for you. And thou, Capernaum, which art exalted unto heaven, shalt be brought down to hell: for if the mighty works, which have been done in thee, had been done in Sodom, it would have remained until this day. But I say unto you, That it shall be more tolerable for the land of Sodom in the day of judgment, than for thee."

The Lord continually asks: "What more could I have done?"[692]

Apparently we will only accept the "precepts of men" and trust the "arm of flesh" and therefore merit the coming disappointments.

---

[692] Jacob 5:41, 47, 49, 75 "And it came to pass that the Lord of the vineyard wept, and said unto the servant: What could I have done more for my vineyard? . . . But what could I have done more in my vineyard? Have I slackened mine hand, that I have not nourished it? Nay, I have nourished it, and I have digged about it, and I have pruned it, and I have dunged it; and I have stretched forth mine hand almost all the day long, and the end draweth nigh. And it grieveth me that I should hew down all the trees of my vineyard, and cast them into the fire that they should be burned. Who is it that has corrupted my vineyard? . . . And it came to pass that the Lord of the vineyard said unto the servant: Let us go to and hew down the trees of the vineyard and cast them into the fire, that they shall not cumber the ground of my vineyard, for I have done all. What could I have done more for my vineyard? . . . And it came to pass that when the Lord of the vineyard saw that his fruit was good, and that his vineyard was no more corrupt, he called up his servants, and said unto them: Behold, for this last time have we nourished my vineyard; and thou beholdest that I have done according to my will; and I have preserved the natural fruit, that it is good, even like as it was in the beginning. And blessed art thou; for because ye have been diligent in laboring with me in my vineyard, and have kept my commandments, and have brought unto me again the natural fruit, that my vineyard is no more corrupted, and the bad is cast away, behold ye shall have joy with me because of the fruit of my vineyard."
2 Nephi 15:4 "What could have been done more to my vineyard that I have not done in it? Wherefore, when I looked that it should bring forth grapes it brought forth wild grapes."

2 NEPHI 29

2 Nephi 29:1–2

"But behold, there shall be many—at that day when I shall proceed to do a marvelous work among them, that I may remember my covenants which I have made unto the children of men, that I may set my hand again the second time to recover my people, which are of the house of Israel; And also, that I may remember the promises which I have made unto thee, Nephi, and also unto thy father, that I would remember your seed; and that the words of your seed should proceed forth out of my mouth unto your seed; and my words shall hiss forth unto the ends of the earth, for a standard unto my people, which are of the house of Israel;"

The thought "there shall be many" will be concluded in verse 3, and will be discussed there.

The day of the Lord's "marvelous work" will be when He "remembers [His] covenants" made previously to "the children of men." Those covenants to "the children of men" are all inclusive. This will include promises made to all mankind, without regard to their status as Israel, gentile, heathen, or even if they are living or dead as the work begins. It is the Lord's covenants made in the pre-earth councils, and is for all mankind.

As fulfillment of these complete covenants, the Lord will "set [His] hand again the second time to recover my people." Now the focus moves from "the children of men" to a sub-set of those He calls "my people." His people are, by definition, necessarily affiliated with "the house of Israel" through covenant. These would include those called the "remnant" as well as those believing "gentiles" who accept the covenant and return through repentance to Christ.

Why do we see layers of covenants or promises referred to here? Why the covenants made "unto the children of men?" Why then further "the house of Israel?" Why further "promises made unto Nephi?" Why still further "thy father" [meaning Lehi]? Why a work which will affect all these groups? And, finally, why does all of the foregoing return to "remembering Nephi's seed?" What role does Nephi's seed, or remnant fulfill in the promises made to all mankind?

Why does the Lord make a covenant with all humanity, but then reiterate the covenant with Abraham? Why do the covenants get repeated through Isaac and Jacob, the last of whom supplies the name of the covenant people "Israel?" Why, after all those covenant recipients do the covenants get renewed with Lehi? Why immediately following Nephi do the covenants get renewed yet again in Nephi? Why does the Lord engage in this covenant making process to tie together the events of history and the lives of men? Can He still do this today? Does He still expect or want to enter into covenants with men today to further His purposes? Do those covenants necessarily get confined to an institution or priestly process rather than through Him, directly? Why not?

When we get to Nephi's descendants, why are they the ones who are to provide "a standard unto my people, which are of the house of Israel?" What does this say about the significance of the Book of Mormon? Why is it the "standard unto the Lord's people?" What does that do to clarify the condemnation resting upon the church under D&C 84:57?[693] How important is "the standard" established by the Lord? Why would Joseph Smith say the "fullness of the gospel" is contained in the Book of Mormon?

Why does the title page of the Book of Mormon, which was part of the translated record, contain this description: "Which is to show unto the remnant of the House of Israel what great things the Lord hath done for their fathers; and that they may know the covenants of the Lord, that they are not cast off forever—And also to the convincing of the Jew and Gentile that Jesus is the Christ, the Eternal God, manifesting himself unto all nations."

What does it mean that these words shall "hiss forth to the ends of the earth?"

Did you notice the Lord taking personal credit for the words of the Book of Mormon? What does the phrase "the words of your seed should proceed forth *out of my mouth* unto your seed; and *my words* shall hiss forth unto the ends of the earth?" How does the Lord taking personal credit for these words affect the Book of Mormon's significance?

2 Nephi 29:3

"And because my words shall hiss forth—many of the Gentiles shall say: A Bible! A Bible! We have got a Bible, and there cannot be any more Bible."

This is one of the great missionary scriptures. It is used to show the Book of Mormon already anticipated an argument against it, and as a result shows there is no reason to reject the Book of Mormon because there is already an existing, recognized volume of scripture.

---

[693] D&C 84:57 "And they shall remain under this condemnation until they repent and remember the new covenant, even the Book of Mormon and the former commandments which I have given them, not only to say, but to do according to that which I have written—"

The gentiles are prone to prefer the Bible to the Book of Mormon. We emphasized the Book of Mormon for a few years, but found that other faiths were critical because we were not using the Bible as we should. So there has been a conscious effort to re-emphasize the Bible and de-emphasize the Book of Mormon. This has been done to broaden our appeal to members of other faiths.

The gravamen of the argument is in the words: "there cannot be any more Bible." The idea there are other words of God, requiring equal respect to the words in the Bible, is a shocking heresy for many of the gentiles. Remember that first phrase in the first verse: "Behold there shall be many" who are going to say this. The "many" are the gentiles, and their criticism will be Bible-based.

So, how are we doing with this idea? Do we prefer the Biblical teachings to those of the Book of Mormon? Do we spend more time with the Bible than the Book of Mormon in our own individual study? If we had to choose one as the "standard for our people" which one would we choose? The Book of Mormon (as verse 2 suggests) or the Bible (as verse 3 suggests)? The Lord's standard is the Book of Mormon. The gentile standard will be the Bible. Once again we are at odds with Historic Christianity.

This is not to say we disrespect the Bible. We don't. We accept it as scripture. It is an admittedly valuable standard work, to be used in study and receiving knowledge of the things of God. Indeed, among other things the Book of Mormon testifies of the truth of the Bible. Therefore the Bible is certainly accepted as a work of importance and value to us in matters of faith. But only one can assume primacy. The primary one for us is the Book of Mormon.

We may be justified in our attachment to and affection for the Bible. But the Book of Mormon must be preeminent. Our respect and affection for the Doctrine and Covenants, Temple and church organization is also well placed and should inform our understanding and behavior. But the Book of Mormon was intended to be the primary means for the Lord to impart understanding to us.

Much has has been written and said about this volume of scripture, but we are only now beginning to understand what we are looking at.

In *Eighteen Verses* I have shown how little we have done so far with this book of scripture. I have never attempted to be exhaustive in any discussion about the book. In a decade of teaching weekly about the book, where I only went from 1 Nephi 1:1 to Jarom 1:4, the discussion was not exhaustive.

This book was a gift to us. We ought not think the Bible has more to offer than what we find in "the most correct book" because a "man can get closer to God by abiding the precepts [of the Book of Mormon] than any other book," just as Joseph Smith said.

The primary text of scripture I have used in *The Second Comforter, Nephi's Isaiah,* and *Eighteen Verses* has been the Book of Mormon. The primary text used in this blog is the Book of Mormon.

Until we understand that book, I fail to see why we think we should have more. There is more in that book than we've noticed. The first step ought be to notice what we have. Then things will be added. However, until we have taken the Book of Mormon seriously, I fail to see why the most important message for us——found within that book—should not be the first thing to be understood.

2 Nephi 29:4–5

"But thus saith the Lord God: O fools, they shall have a Bible; and it shall proceed forth from the Jews, mine ancient covenant people. And what thank they the Jews for the Bible which they receive from them? Yea, what do the Gentiles mean? Do they remember the travails, and the labors, and the pains of the Jews, and their diligence unto me, in bringing forth salvation unto the Gentiles? O ye Gentiles, have ye remembered the

Jews, mine ancient covenant people? Nay; but ye have cursed them, and have hated them, and have not sought to recover them. But behold, I will return all these things upon your own heads; for I the Lord have not forgotten my people."

If you wonder at the Lord's patience and willingness to forgive, you have an answer here. The Lord's respect for and defense of the "Jews" as His "ancient covenant people" is unmitigated by any criticism of them. Instead He points to their "travails, and the labors, and the pains of the Jews" experienced in bringing forth this Biblical record.

The Jews deserve our thanks, our gratitude, and our respect for this great work of preserving the record.

Twice the Lord calls the Jews His "ancient covenant people." The Bible is a record of rebellion, persecution of the righteous, and slaying of prophets. It is a record of a fallen people who were often in apostasy, resisting true prophets calling for repentance, and suffering the judgment and condemnation of God. When the New Testament record (also a product of Jewish writers—even in the case of Luke who, though born to gentile parents, was converted to Judaism) came into existence it was the Jews who resisted and persecuted the Lord. Yet He still calls them His "ancient covenant people." He insists we have been ungrateful to the Jews for their work on the Bible.

This is the Lord speaking in the first person. Nephi is quoting Him. These are the same people Lehi taught would be the only ones "who would crucify their God."[694] Yet despite that, Christ refers to them as His "ancient covenant people" to whom we owe a debt of gratitude! How merciful is our Lord?

---

[694] 2 Nephi 10:3 "Wherefore, as I said unto you, it must needs be expedient that Christ—for in the last night the angel spake unto me that this should be his name—should come among the Jews, among those who are the more wicked part of the world; and they shall crucify him—for thus it behooveth our God, and there is none other nation on earth that would crucify their God."

Now, those who produced the Bible text are not merely the believers, true prophets, and victims of Jewish hostility and persecution. The text may have originated with the prophets, but it passed quickly into the hands of the priests and Levites, scholars and Rabbis. These others may not have had the same divine inspiration and association with angels, but they nevertheless attended with strict discipline to preserving the record of the prophets. Even those who directly challenged the Lord included the scribes who worked to preserve the records of the prophets. These "labors" and "pains" and "diligence" have produced gratitude from the Lord!

If He is willing to thank them, how generous is our Lord in His thanks to mankind! How ungrateful are we?

We tend to see those with whom we differ as enemies. But the Lord does not want us to approach religious disagreement in this way. Instead he would have us "recover" them. He says: "ye have cursed them, and have hated them, and have not sought to recover them." As Joseph Smith's History recounts, his persecutors ought "to have treated me kindly, and if they supposed me to be deluded to have endeavored in a proper and affectionate manner to have reclaimed me."695 That is the only way to obtain agreement—

---

695 JS–H 1:28 "During the space of time which intervened between the time I had the vision and the year eighteen hundred and twenty-three—having been forbidden to join any of the religious sects of the day, and being of very tender years, and persecuted by those who ought to have been my friends and to have treated me kindly, and if they supposed me to be deluded to have endeavored in a proper and affectionate manner to have reclaimed me—I was left to all kinds of temptations; and, mingling with all kinds of society, I frequently fell into many foolish errors, and displayed the weakness of youth, and the foibles of human nature; which, I am sorry to say, led me into divers temptations, offensive in the sight of God. In making this confession, no one need suppose me guilty of any great or malignant sins. A disposition to commit such was never in my nature. But I was guilty of levity, and sometimes associated with jovial company, etc., not consistent with that character which ought to be maintained by one who was called of God as I had been. But this will not seem very strange to any one who recollects my youth, and is acquainted with my native cheery temperament."

persuasion, gentleness, meekness and love unfeigned.[696] Instead of "holding a court" against someone, we ought to preach the Gospel to them and teach them the truth with love and meekness. It is clear the Lord is showing by example how our attitudes ought to be displayed with those who persecute and reject us. But, then again, He taught the same thing in the Sermon on the Mount (Matthew 5, 6, 7) and in how He lived[697] and died[698]. Oddly we would convict and excommunicate the adulterer, but our Lord would not. Nor does He who holds the greatest claim to condemn the Jews condemn them. Instead He says we ought to have gratitude for their pains, labors and diligence.

What does our ingratitude merit us? It merits us judgment. For the same judgment we apply to them will in turn be applied to us. We will see it used as the basis for His rejection of us: "I will return all these things upon your own heads; for I the Lord have not forgotten my people."

Being a religious people is fine; but being a self-righteous people has always been perilous. It is no different today. We should use the scriptures to inform our inner life. It is meant for internal use only. External application is likely to cause burning.

In the early church of this dispensation, the purpose of a church court was to obtain a confession. If someone confessed during the court, or immediately before, they would be forgiven and the court

---

[696] D&C 121:41–42 "No power or influence can or ought to be maintained by virtue of the priesthood, only by persuasion, by long-suffering, by gentleness and meekness, and by love unfeigned; By kindness, and pure knowledge, which shall greatly enlarge the soul without hypocrisy, and without guile—"

[697] John 8:10–11 "When Jesus had lifted up himself, and saw none but the woman, he said unto her, Woman, where are those thine accusers? hath no man condemned thee? She said, No man, Lord. And Jesus said unto her, Neither do I condemn thee: go, and sin no more."

[698] Luke 23:34 "Then said Jesus, Father, forgive them; for they know not what they do. And they parted his raiment, and cast lots."

would end. If someone got excommunicated because of a sin, and they confessed the next day, they would be reinstated the next day. Once the confession was made, forgiveness was more or less immediate. Take a look at that early history. It is interesting.

For those who are excommunicated, we rarely see them again. The numbers are overwhelming against their return. So essentially an excommunication means the end of that person, oftentimes also his/her immediate family, and the descendants of those.

Sin is wrong, and needs to result in repentance and change. But for the most part that is between the person and the Lord. When it involves others, it also includes them, too. But we sometimes cause a great deal of unintended consequences to even the unborn when we excommunicate.

2 Nephi 29:6–7

"Thou fool, that shall say: A Bible, we have got a Bible, and we need no more Bible. Have ye obtained a Bible save it were by the Jews? Know ye not that there are more nations than one? Know ye not that I, the Lord your God, have created all men, and that I remember those who are upon the isles of the sea; and that I rule in the heavens above and in the earth beneath; and I bring forth my word unto the children of men, yea, even upon all the nations of the earth?"

This is a continuing statement made to Nephi by the Lord. Besides the sermons delivered in the New Testament and Third Nephi, this is one of the most extensive revelations to be found given by Christ. Given its length, and the fact it is a quote from the Lord, we are compelled to take note. The Lord is doing all He can to draw our attention to the fact that the Book of Mormon *must* be valued above the Bible. It *must* take its place in latter-day study of God's acts among men.

To say you have enough information from God is foolish. God "created all men," and as a result He "remembers all men." He will "bring forth [His] word unto the children of men" in whatever place, time and circumstance as He decides. He cannot be circumscribed by our preferences or false understanding. He can and does exercise the prerogative to speak to whomever He decides.

When the Book of Mormon came forth, all people were startled at the idea God had more to say. They thought it an odd thing for anyone to claim there was yet more scripture. Joseph was persecuted and hated for announcing he had a new volume of scripture.

Now, some 180 years later we think the Lord is bound to talk to a specific person, in a specific way, and that anyone else or anywhere else is beyond the Lord's capacity to accomplish. In our own way, we are also bound to a tradition which excludes the Lord's prerogatives; we just redefine the box we confine the Lord.

He "brings forth His word" without regard to our views, and to "all the nations of the earth." Now "nations" is not the same thing as we regard it today. The "nations" at the time of the Book of Mormon were something we would call "people" or "ethnicity" like the Israelites.

The definition of an "isle of the sea" includes everything that is not part of the great Euro-Asian-African land mass. Although we regard North America as a continent, in the Book of Mormon vernacular it is an "isle of the sea."[699] Further, most of Israel was relo-

---

[699] 2 Nephi 10:20 "And now, my beloved brethren, seeing that our merciful God has given us so great knowledge concerning these things, let us remember him, and lay aside our sins, and not hang down our heads, for we are not cast off; nevertheless, we have been driven out of the land of our inheritance; but we have been led to a better land, for the Lord has made the sea our path, and we are upon an isle of the sea."

cated onto the isles of the sea.[700] So when the Lord affirms He speaks to those on the "isles of the sea" He is confirming that there are multiple locations, involving multiple parties, each one of which has received sacred communication from Him. There are, in short, still a great deal of His words which have not as yet come to our attention. They are coming. When they do, we are warned to take care in what we choose to reject.

When I was first investigating the church, this argument was presented to me by the missionaries in one of the first discussions. I have to admit the proposition made such sense to me that I found it completely persuasive. The idea that God would not be in communication with the vast majority of mankind living separate from Palestine during the Lord's life seemed to be a sort of abandonment by the Lord. If He is the God of all mankind, then ought He not speak to all mankind?

The "wise men from the east" were not locals to Palestine. Yet they remained both connected to, and watching for signs involving the birth of the Lord. If them, why not others? The Book of Mormon answers this query. This idea was too persuasive for me to find doubt.

If God does remember all mankind, and speaks to the various nations over time, then the failure to keep the information intact is also explained. The Book of Mormon shows what and how a society's faith fails and is lost. It explains how very careless mankind is with knowledge given by God.

Riddles of history are better answered both directly and indirectly in the Book of Mormon than any other text, including the Bible.

---

[700] 1 Nephi 22:4 "And behold, there are many who are already lost from the knowledge of those who are at Jerusalem. Yea, the more part of all the tribes have been led away; and they are scattered to and fro upon the isles of the sea; and whither they are none of us knoweth, save that we know that they have been led away."

2 Nephi 29:8

"Wherefore murmur ye, because that ye shall receive more of my word? Know ye not that the testimony of two nations is a witness unto you that I am God, that I remember one nation like unto another? Wherefore, I speak the same words unto one nation like unto another. And when the two nations shall run together the testimony of the two nations shall run together also."

Why would anyone complain or murmur because God has spoken? We do. Somehow we get offended at the very idea God can or has spoken further. It is disturbing. It requires us to learn more, and may require us to change. It is inconvenient. It is troubling.

But new information from God should always be welcomed. It should be exciting and delightful, even if it requires us to change.

Not only does the Lord remember all nations, but He "speaks the same words unto one nation like unto another." Meaning two things: First, the records are going to agree on doctrine, ordinances and practice. There will not be some shocking departure from what we have already learned. But, second, we may find that other records have done a better job of preserving deeper insight into the history or truths than have we.

At one time the record written by Moses contained what is now in the Pearl of Great Price. At one time the record written by Abraham also found in the Pearl of Great Price was among the Biblical record. However, they were lost until they were restored through Joseph Smith. At one time the Biblical record contained the prophecies of Zenos and Zenock, only a small portion of which are still available through the Book of Mormon.

Although the records will agree, that does not mean there will not be significant additions to our understanding as a result of these becoming available. Even the record of the Nephites is sealed, and that of the Jaredites only partially translated.[701] Joseph and Sidney were forbidden to give the full account of the vision of the afterlife.[702] So you must not presume that "the same words" will be identical to the teachings preserved in our records. They may include much more.

It is also interesting how the Book of Mormon contains so much more information upon close inspection that it appears to have in a quick read. It is a measure of how seriously we take the Lord's words as to how carefully we search the text.

As I've pointed out, most of the Book of Mormon scholarship is devoted to the question of the book's authenticity. Word studies, Jewish idioms, internal consistencies, author variances and other examinations of the book have dominated the Book of Mormon library we have produced. I have proceeded from the premise that the book is authentic, that it is what it claims to be, and worthy of respect. Then, based on that premise, I've asked what the book teaches. The result has been more than edifying, it has been at times shocking. I've found that most of the deepest doctrines taught by Joseph Smith can be found in the Book of Mormon. When his revelations reach the greatest heights, the Book of Mormon equals what is revealed.

We tend to view the Book of Mormon as a "basic" version of doctrine, because we all know there are sealed portions yet to be revealed. However, I think that attitude is wrong. Everything in the

---

[701] Ether 1:4–5 "Therefore I do not write those things which transpired from the days of Adam until that time; but they are had upon the plates; and whoso findeth them, the same will have power that he may get the full account. But behold, I give not the full account, but a part of the account I give, from the tower down until they were destroyed."

[702] D&C 76:114–115 "But great and marvelous are the works of the Lord, and the mysteries of his kingdom which he showed unto us, which surpass all understanding in glory, and in might, and in dominion; Which he commanded us we should not write while we were yet in the Spirit, and are not lawful for man to utter;"

sealed portion is already in the book we have in front of us. But to find it we must look more carefully at the text than we generally do.

I keep hoping that by showing respect to the text we can accomplish two things: First, please the Lord and remove our condemnation from neglecting this valuable ancient record. Second, increase our respect for the value of doctrine. Without the unique doctrines restored through the Book of Mormon, we may as well be Presbyterian or Methodist.

These verses promise us that the testimonies of differing nations will agree. They will all testify both of Jesus Christ as Redeemer and Savior, and provide the means by which we can come to Him and be saved.

The numerous examples of the Book of Mormon all converge on knowing Christ. Indeed, the text has more examples of Christ ministering through the veil to mortal men than any other record, including His Judean ministry. It is a veritable treasure of Second Comforter experiences. If you want to know Christ, the Book of Mormon is your best guide.

2 Nephi 29:9

"And I do this that I may prove unto many that I am the same yesterday, today, and forever; and that I speak forth my words according to mine own pleasure. And because that I have spoken one word ye need not suppose that I cannot speak another; for my work is not yet finished; neither shall it be until the end of man, neither from that time henceforth and forever."

The assurance to us by the Lord that He is the "same yesterday, today and forever" appears often in scripture. (See, e.g., four times by Nephi including 1 Nephi 10:18; 2 Nephi 2:4; 2 Nephi 27:23, and above; Alma 31:17; Mormon 9:9; Moroni 10:19; D&C 20:12; and

D&C 35:1, among other places.) Why do you suppose the Lord wants us to trust in this idea? What is it about the Lord's "sameness" that is important for us to understand?

Are the Lord's expectations different from one generation to the next? Are His teachings? Are His ordinances? Can we discard what He has given us and be justified? If His expectations are as un-changed as He is, then how important is it for us to study and retain all that He has given by revelation to mankind? How important is it to keep ordinances entirely intact?

If the Lord does not change, and the story of the Nephite people is a story of temporary success followed by ultimate failure, then how relevant is that account for us? Does temporary success in re-pentance guarantee constant favor from the Lord? When the Book of Mormon follows splinter groups in the narrative, because the splinters kept the commandments of God better, does that preserve a relevant lesson for those reading the book today? If so, how?

If the Lord "speaks forth [His] own words according to [His] own pleasure" then how can we control to whom and when He is permitted to speak? If He reserves to Himself this right, what effect does our system of recognizing an authoritative message from Him have upon His right to speak? Did the revelation given to Oliver Cowdery that told him that he could not write commandments, but only according to wisdom, and never command Joseph Smith who presided over Oliver, establish a binding precedent on the Lord?[703] If so, what limit does that place on the Lord? Does the limitation on someone being sent forth as a missionary to preach the Gospel, and the requirement they be "regularly ordained by the heads of the

---

[703] D&C 28:4–6 "And if thou art led at any time by the Comforter to speak or teach, or at all times by the way of commandment unto the church, thou mayest do it. But thou shalt not write by way of commandment, but by wisdom; And thou shalt not com-mand him who is at thy head, and at the head of the church;"

church" limit the Lord's ability to speak His own words?[704] If so, in what way?

Does the revelation to Joseph Smith informing the Church in 1831 that no one other than Joseph Smith is to receive commandments and revelations for the Church limit the Lord's ability to speak to anyone else?[705] In particular, what of the Lord's counsel that this limitation was intended as "a law unto you, that ye receive not the teachings of any that shall come before you as revelations or commandments; And this I give unto you that you may not be deceived, that you may know they are not of me." (*Ibid.* verses 5–6.) Does that prevent Him from speaking "according to His own pleasure?"

What about the 1830 revelation given to Joseph Smith that no one other than Joseph Smith is to receive revelations and commandments in the church?[706] Does that limit the Lord's ability to speak according to His own pleasure?

Do the promises given to Joseph Smith apply directly and continually as the binding precedent and complete limitation on the Lord's capacity to speak to us? If so, then can He still speak to individual members of the church but without providing a "revelation

---

[704] D&C 42:11 "Again I say unto you, that it shall not be given to any one to go forth to preach my gospel, or to build up my church, except he be ordained by some one who has authority, and it is known to the church that he has authority and has been regularly ordained by the heads of the church."

[705] D&C 43:1–6 "O hearken, ye elders of my church, and give ear to the words which I shall speak unto you. For behold, verily, verily, I say unto you, that ye have received a commandment for a law unto my church, through him whom I have appointed unto you to receive commandments and revelations from my hand. And this ye shall know assuredly—that there is none other appointed unto you to receive commandments and revelations until he be taken, if he abide in me. But verily, verily, I say unto you, that none else shall be appointed unto this gift except it be through him; for if it be taken from him he shall not have power except to appoint another in his stead. And this shall be a law unto you, that ye receive not the teachings of any that shall come before you as revelations or commandments; And this I give unto you that you may not be deceived, that you may know they are not of me."

[706] D&C 28:2 "But, behold, verily, verily, I say unto thee, no one shall be appointed to receive commandments and revelations in this church excepting my servant Joseph Smith, Jun., for he receiveth them even as Moses."

and commandment" to the entire church? For example, do we expect only President Monson to receive revelation on the individual members of your own family? How is President Monson supposed to be doing that for the families of some 13 million church members? If that isn't possible, then what about the approximate 2,000 stakes? Do we expect only President Monson to receive revelation about each of these divisions? If the stake presidents have been delegated responsibility, then can the stake president receive all revelation for each family within the stake? Can the stake president alone receive revelation for the families of his stake?

If each person is intended to receive some revelation for themselves, is that an absolute bar to receiving revelation for another? If, for example, someone were not in your ward, not in your stake, not even living in your state, but asked you to give them a blessing because of illness or injury, are you entitled to receive revelation while giving the blessing? Even if you have no connection to this person by family or church calling? Should you proceed with the blessing? If so, would you expect the Lord to assist, give revelation, and even inspire a commandment to the person if it were appropriate?

How hard and fast are the rules we impose on the Lord? Does His statement that He alone will decide when and to whom He speaks according to "His own pleasure" need to be weighed as part of the equation? If He cannot speak to anyone other than Joseph Smith, then did Joseph's death prevent Him from speaking further? If He cannot speak to anyone other than Joseph's successors in the office of President of the High Priesthood, then what if the occupant of that office is ill, infirm, or disabled?

Would the "system" govern, or the Lord's "own pleasure" govern? If it is "His own pleasure" then how can we possibly know when He speaks? What about the Lord's house being a house of order? Once He has a church established, should we trust He will confine His efforts to that church alone?

I suppose all these questions are answered by the Lord adding to "His own pleasure" that "because that I have spoken one word ye need not suppose that I cannot speak another; for my work is not yet finished; neither shall it be until the end of man, neither from that time henceforth and forever."

In the final analysis, it is left to us to fast, pray, seek the guidance of the Spirit, and to find where the Lord's own pleasure in speaking is to be found. I do not expect someone other than the presiding authorities to conduct the affairs of the church. Nor would I expect anyone would organize a ward or stake other than someone having authority over that responsibility, regularly recognized by the church. I would not expect to either pay tithing to, nor be asked to pay tithing to, someone other than a Bishop in the church. But, just as Elder F. Enzio Busche encountered gifted sisters with the gift of prophecy and visions, I do not believe revelation is or can be confined to any single office, person, or group. (See F. Enzio Busche's book, *Yearning for the Living God*.) While serving in various church leadership positions, including as a General Authority, he encountered gifted women with spiritual capacities who astonished him. But, to his credit, he did not doubt them.

God speaks according to His own pleasure. He cautions you that just because He says one thing at one time, He is never limited in what He may say at another time; even if you think it contradicts His earlier statements. He is living and He has the final decision in what He says and to whom He speaks. We must not forget that principle. Even though we may not like the uncertainty this introduces to our trusted systems. He alone will remain in control.

2 Nephi 29:10–11

"Wherefore, because that ye have a Bible ye need not suppose that it contains all my words; neither need ye suppose that I have not caused more to be written. For I command all men, both in the east and in the west, and in the north, and in the south, and in the islands of the sea, that they shall write the words which I speak unto them; for out of the books which shall be written I will judge the world, every man according to their works, according to that which is written."

Within the Book of Mormon, as a new volume of scripture, is the caution that even it is incomplete. What a marvel that is if you think about it. Here's a new revelation telling us that there are other revelations that aren't included in either the Book of Mormon or the Bible.

Everyone nation, from time to time, received sacred messages from the Lord! No matter where they are—east, west, north or south, He's been in touch. They have written it down. The records are sacred, and He watches over them. They will be revealed. And, the good/bad news is that from their content we will be judged.

We are judged "according to our works," but measured against "that which is written." Think about that for a moment.

What if they haven't come to light yet? Are they still written? Are they still going to be used to measure us? If we haven't seen these words, why would it be appropriate for them to be used as a measuring stick for our conduct? Was the Book of Mormon's standards binding upon us even before the record came forth?

Why does He assure us He is unchangeable? Why does He assure us He is the same yesterday, today and forever? Is the standard going to change from ancient record to ancient record? If it does not change, then are we accountable for the same standard of conduct no matter when or where we live? How can we be held to account for things that are yet to be revealed?

If we cannot be judged against something we do not know,[707] how can these words set a standard for judging even before they are published?

I want to propose a concept that appeals to my mind. When we are trying to "prove" a proposition, it is possible to set up an experiment where we control all variables but one, then see what that one variable does. How it acts, or reacts. Life here is like that, I think. A fallen Telestial Kingdom, "or the world in which you presently reside"—to quote an authoritative source—is the same place for Able and Cain, Enoch and Noah, Abraham and Nimrod, Moses and Pharaoh, Jesus and Ciaphus, Jacob and Sherem, Alma and Nehor, Joseph Smith and Thomas Sharp. Same place with all of these contemporaries. But with the exception of Enoch and Noah, (who took different routes, but nonetheless were both favored by God) all the other pairs had dramatically different outcomes? Why?

This world is a fallen, but controlled environment. We get introduced here with free will and the capacity to change. Inside that environment of a fallen world, there have been people who have come and lived with all the same limitations that we have, but who have grown to know God. Their lives are proof that it can happen. Their testimonies and records of success are part of the "proof" of God's fairness and of mankind's freedom to return to Him.

If the Bible and the Book of Mormon both attest to the fact that it is possible for mankind to overcome by faith and return to God's presence, then we have the proof needed to see how this life should

---

[707] Mosiah 3:11 "For behold, and also his blood atoneth for the sins of those who have fallen by the transgression of Adam, who have died not knowing the will of God concerning them, or who have ignorantly sinned."

be lived. We have the evidence of God's willingness to receive us, and of our own capacity to overcome and return to Him.

Testimony after testimony, experience after experience are recounted in the Book of Mormon. We have enough "proof" that this process is available and works. If we were to have more, in a different record, reaffirming the same thing involving other people, would it add any different proof than is already in our possession? If not, then can we be judged by the same standard without having the specific life stories before us to illustrate in another hundred ways how men have triumphed and men have failed?

Is it possible there are others, some of whom are still living, who may also have recorded unspeakable things? Do their words count? Are they binding upon us for no other reason than to prove that in this contemporary world of sin it remains still possible to return to God's presence?

What interesting things the Book of Mormon raises for our pondering and edification. It is a revolutionary book, in the sense it revolutionizes our understanding of how God deals with mankind.

2 Nephi 29:12

> "For behold, I shall speak unto the Jews and they shall write it; and I shall also speak unto the Nephites and they shall write it; and I shall also speak unto the other tribes of the house of Israel, which I have led away, and they shall write it; and I shall also speak unto all nations of the earth and they shall write it."

This is more than interesting. The Lord speaks, various people write what He speaks to them. These groups include:

1. Jews—we get that and it's the Bible, right?

2. Nephites—we get that too, the Book of Mormon, right?

3. Other tribes—how many? Who? When? Where? What?

4. All the nations of the earth—Now it's just too broad. What does "all the nations" mean, exactly?

So, let's take this a bit by bit, going through each one:

1. *Jews*: We have a Bible. But we DON'T have all the writings of the Jews, do we? We already referred to missing prophets Zenos and Zenok, and there are others. Look in your Bible Dictionary for "Missing Scripture" and you'll see a list. (I'm pulling your leg. If you look that up it'll refer you to "Lost Books" so go there.)

[That reminds me of a joke I tell: If I get a tattoo it'll say "Leviticus 19:28."[708] But you probably won't think that's funny.]

Anyway, the Jews recorded more both in the Old Testament and in the New Testament than we have currently. So don't get all certain the Bible is the final word from the ancient Jews. It isn't. Never was. There's more coming.

2. *Nephites*: Clearly more coming. Sealed material has not been revealed, and will be some day. Providing, of course, we were to actually merit the disclosure. So, I suppose that means don't hold your breath.

3. *Other Tribes*: We got nothing. Not even a number. The one chance we had to get a number was blown by both the disciples in Jerusalem and the Nephites. I've written about this in *The Second Comforter*. So the only way to triangulate is to either take the allegory of the Olive Tree in Jacob 5 and try to estimate—a risky proposition since it was intended to convey an overall meaning not a number—or we can work backwards from the crucifixion to the approximate 11 1/2 months later when Jesus appeared to the Nephites. Take the time spent with the Nephites, then estimate He's been busy doing that same ministry elsewhere. Divide the time taken to minister into the available time and you get something between 10 and 18 other

---

[708] Leviticus 19:28 "Ye shall not make any cuttings in your flesh for the dead, nor print any marks upon you: I *am* the Lord."

potential groups out there depending on your estimate of the time used. The record attempts to prevent us from being too accurate because it identifies three days specifically, then resorts to just "many times" to cover what may have been days or weeks.[709] However, when you read of the Nephite disciples "journeying and preaching" but coming together in "mighty prayer and fasting" and the Lord's appearance again there, it seems closer to the 10 number than the 18.[710] Well, you work it out. It's just an unknown plural number which might be greater than just a couple. And for these we have no record at all.

4. *All nations:* Nothing here, either. And no basis from which to compile an estimate.

So, from the foregoing we can see that we have some tiny fragment of the whole, and cannot even begin to construct an outline of what we are missing. But despite our ignorance, the Lord spoke to them, they wrote it, and it is available for some group to eventually read. Apparently not us. We do not even get the rest of the record

---

[709] 3 Nephi 26:13 "Therefore, I would that ye should behold that the Lord truly did teach the people, for the space of three days; and after that he did show himself unto them oft, and did break bread oft, and bless it, and give it unto them."

[710] 3 Nephi 27:1 "And it came to pass that as the disciples of Jesus were journeying and were preaching the things which they had both heard and seen, and were baptizing in the name of Jesus, it came to pass that the disciples were gathered together and were united in mighty prayer and fasting."

written on parchment and hidden by John, (referred to in the head-note to D&C 7). We only get a part of the information from it.[711]

So, there's a lot to be had. We don't have it . . . But what we do have we won't study. Well, maybe there is a cause and effect . . .

Seems to me, you don't want to talk about it. Seems to me, you just turn your pretty head and walk away. (Joe Walsh, from the James Gang era, before the heaviest toll was taken.)

So the Lord wants us to know there's ever so much out there. That we have a tiny fraction of what was once available. And we just don't seem to care. We'd rather reduce the volume of topics we study and eliminate the "mysteries" from our diet of Gospel study, so as to relieve ourselves of any responsibility for what we already possess. We are beyond dumbing down the Gospel. We're discarding it by the week. Tighter and tighter, until you are left alone, without God in the world. There's a brilliant phrase. It comes from the Book of Mormon.

---

[711] D&C 7:1–8 "And the Lord said unto me: John, my beloved, what desirest thou? For if you shall ask what you will, it shall be granted unto you. And I said unto him: Lord, give unto me power over death, that I may live and bring souls unto thee. And the Lord said unto me: Verily, verily, I say unto thee, because thou desirest this thou shalt tarry until I come in my glory, and shalt prophesy before nations, kindreds, tongues and people. And for this cause the Lord said unto Peter: If I will that he tarry till I come, what is that to thee? For he desired of me that he might bring souls unto me, but thou desiredst that thou mightest speedily come unto me in my kingdom. I say unto thee, Peter, this was a good desire; but my beloved has desired that he might do more, or a greater work yet among men than what he has before done. Yea, he has undertaken a greater work; therefore I will make him as flaming fire and a ministering angel; he shall minister for those who shall be heirs of salvation who dwell on the earth. And I will make thee to minister for him and for thy brother James; and unto you three I will give this power and the keys of this ministry until I come. Verily I say unto you, ye shall both have according to your desires, for ye both joy in that which ye have desired."

It is found at Mosiah 27:31; Alma 41:11 and Mormon 5:16.[712] Of all the phrases turned in the Book of Mormon this is the most solitary, profound and descriptive of the fall from grace mankind experiences. It is perfect, even if what it describes is perfectly horrid.

2 Nephi 29:13

> "And it shall come to pass that the Jews shall have the words of the Nephites, and the Nephites shall have the words of the Jews; and the Nephites and the Jews shall have the words of the lost tribes of Israel; and the lost tribes of Israel shall have the words of the Nephites and the Jews."

Well, happily the Jews "shall" get the Nephite words. Some day. Currently for the most part they don't want them. And, even if they did, the "words of the Nephites" will include the sealed portion, because they are certainly part of the "words" the Nephites recorded. So this will be future, even if there were Jews interested in taking the offer today.

The Nephites also "shall" have the words of the Jews. However, once again as we have seen, the words include a great volume of material spoken by Christ, recorded by the Jews, and not in anyone's current possession. So this, too, must be in the future. For now we aren't even sure of who these "Nephites" are.

---

[712] Mosiah 27:31 "Yea, every knee shall bow, and every tongue confess before him. Yea, even at the last day, when all men shall stand to be judged of him, then shall they confess that he is God; then shall they confess, who live without God in the world, that the judgment of an everlasting punishment is just upon them; and they shall quake, and tremble, and shrink beneath the glance of his all-searching eye."
Alma 41:11 "And now, my son, all men that are in a state of nature, or I would say, in a carnal state, are in the gall of bitterness and in the bonds of iniquity; they are without God in the world, and they have gone contrary to the nature of God; therefore, they are in a state contrary to the nature of happiness."
Mormon 5:16 "For behold, the Spirit of the Lord hath already ceased to strive with their fathers; and they are without Christ and God in the world; and they are driven about as chaff before the wind."

The Nephites and the Jews "shall" get the words of the lost tribes of Israel. This is a category, not a number. Remember that. So once again, future event. Don't know when. Don't know how many records. Don't even know how many groups will be included.

But all these records are inevitably to come forth. Just not yet. Why?

Read Mormon's explanation:

> "But behold the plates of Nephi do contain the more part of the things which he taught the people. And these things have I written, which are a lesser part of the things which he taught the people; and I have written them to the intent that they may be brought again unto this people, from the Gentiles, according to the words which Jesus hath spoken. And when they shall have received this, which is expedient that they should have first, to try their faith, and if it shall so be that they shall believe these things then shall the greater things be made manifest unto them. And if it so be that they will not believe these things, then shall the greater things be withheld from them, unto their condemnation. Behold, I was about to write them, all which were engraven upon the plates of Nephi, but the Lord forbade it, saying: I will try the faith of my people. Therefore I, Mormon, do write the things which have been commanded me of the Lord. And now I, Mormon, make an end of my sayings, and proceed to write the things which have been commanded me." (3 Nephi 26:7–12)

What if I do believe these things? What if I will accept the things which He offers? What if my faith has been tried and I am found to be deserving of more information? Can a person come out from under the condemnation referred to above, even if the rest of mankind fails to acquit themselves? Alma comes with the reply: "Yes."[713] So, as it turns out, ignorance is voluntary.

Well, shut my mouth! (That's a pun, you see.)

[Can you do puns in a religious blog? Or will the long faced and dour be offended? Well, they don't get it anyway. Hey! Why are you reading this if it offends you? Stop it!]

What do you suppose it would take for the Lord to respond to us removing the condemnation that we labor under? How should we go about trying to make that happen? I don't see it happening, do you? I'm sort of persuaded by Nephi's pessimism of the gentiles of our day. Even this mild blog discussion I am attempting has provoked ire in many readers. How we fix our collective disinterest seems a monumental enterprise beyond human ability. I fear it would take some great calamity to unfold before we would change. Then again, I think the Lord has already told us that.[714]

2 Nephi 29:14

"And it shall come to pass that my people, which are of the house of Israel, shall be gathered home unto the lands of their possessions; and my word also shall be gathered in one. And I will show unto them that fight against my word and

---

[713] Alma 12:9–11 "And now Alma began to expound these things unto him, saying: It is given unto many to know the mysteries of God; nevertheless they are laid under a strict command that they shall not impart only according to the portion of his word which he doth grant unto the children of men, according to the heed and diligence which they give unto him. And therefore, he that will harden his heart, the same receiveth the lesser portion of the word; and he that will not harden his heart, to him is given the greater portion of the word, until it is given unto him to know the mysteries of God until he know them in full. And they that will harden their hearts, to them is given the lesser portion of the word until they know nothing concerning his mysteries; and then they are taken captive by the devil, and led by his will down to destruction. Now this is what is meant by the chains of hell."

[714] D&C 1:17 "Wherefore, I the Lord, knowing the calamity which should come upon the inhabitants of the earth, called upon my servant Joseph Smith, Jun., and spake unto him from heaven, and gave him commandments;"
D&C 45:50 "And calamity shall cover the mocker, and the scorner shall be consumed; and they that have watched for iniquity shall be hewn down and cast into the fire."

against my people, who are of the house of Israel, that I am God, and that I covenanted with Abraham that I would remember his seed forever."

Now we have an estimate of the time when a general disclosure of the records of these various nations will occur. It's set in the time when the people who have survived the great distresses and wars of the last days will leave the New Jerusalem and return to their lands of possessions. That is, post-New Jerusalem, post-destruction of the wicked, and after the time when the Lord has come among them. When they are sent into their respective lands of possessions, then at last the entire record of the Lord's dealings with each nation will be "gathered in one."

So this won't be anytime soon. Well, if soon, it will be after some more dramatic events, which will take our minds off the issue of missing scripture.

What is interesting is the Lord's emphasis on those who "fight against my word." He puts this first. The fight, as He puts it, is against both "my word and my people," but it is the fight against His "word" that He lists first. This is important.

You will recall there were two different reactions to the two parts of Lehi's message. When it was repentance from their wickedness, the Jews mocked him. But when it was a message of the coming Christ, they wanted to kill him.[715] This is the war against His "word" in a nutshell. The message of hope and redemption found in Christ is what the enemies of God always seek to suppress.

---

[715] 1 Nephi 1:18–19 "Therefore, I would that ye should know, that after the Lord had shown so many marvelous things unto my father, Lehi, yea, concerning the destruction of Jerusalem, behold he went forth among the people, and began to prophesy and to declare unto them concerning the things which he had both seen and heard. And it came to pass that the Jews did mock him because of the things which he testified of them; for he truly testified of their wickedness and their abominations; and he testified that the things which he saw and heard, and also the things which he read in the book, manifested plainly of the coming of a Messiah, and also the redemption of the world."

First, distort, suppress and exclude His word. Then it follows that He has no people, because they cannot find their way back to Him.

Remember this is the great fight. It is relentlessly underway. So soon as His word becomes available, there will be forces, enemies, alliances, even good-intentions used to suppress, discard and alter His words. This is the great work of the adversary. This is the fight that gets waged first.

When the victory is won against His word, then the victory against the people is over. There cannot be any "people" belonging to Him if they do not possess His words in clarity, fullness, and with power.

What significance is there then in changing His words? Discarding His revelations? Suppressing His ordinances? Altering what He has revealed? Designating some of His word as "mysteries" that ought to be feared or avoided? Why would Joseph Smith advise us to search deeper and deeper into the mysteries of God? Why would we be told to avoid them today? What has happened in the fight against the Lord's word among us?

The purpose of His word is to establish His people. When people have His word, and obtain the light and truth that flows from it, then they are inevitably turned in their hearts to the fathers. Primarily among those fathers is the one mentioned here: Abraham. For in Abraham we see a return to the original order which preceded the flood. He inherited what "came down from the beginning" and restored the original ancient order.[716] When the "word" and "people" are again here, they are directly linked to Abraham, Isaac and Jacob and are heirs to the covenant and priesthood they held. It is a return. It is a resurrection of an ancient order, where men know God and are His friends and companions while living here in this fallen world.

The results of having the Lord's "word" is to then create a "people" who in turn are linked to "Abraham." These things all follow in turn. The fight against it is begun at the "word" to prevent the others who follow. If you can choke people off and get them to refuse His "words" then you can prevent them from ever becoming His "people" and realizing the association which brings their hearts to the fathers.

It is a consistent plan and a predictable fight. How's it going in our time? What good things have we done to preserve His word? Have we kept intact everything He handed us through Joseph? Do we possess all of the word He intended us to have, study and live? Are we thereby made into new creations, His people? Do we show the fruits of being His people? Do the visions of heaven flow over us, and angels minister to us? Do we possess knowledge of God in the sense used in the Book of Mormon? Are we in possession of all the rights and powers conferred upon Abraham?

It is an interesting interconnection the Lord refers to here. Worth reflection at a minimum. Fasting, prayer and seeking as well, perhaps.

---

[716] Abraham 1:2–3 "And, finding there was greater happiness and peace and rest for me, I sought for the blessings of the fathers, and the right whereunto I should be ordained to administer the same; having been myself a follower of righteousness, desiring also to be one who possessed great knowledge, and to be a greater follower of righteousness, and to possess a greater knowledge, and to be a father of many nations, a prince of peace, and desiring to receive instructions, and to keep the commandments of God, I became a rightful heir, a High Priest, holding the right belonging to the fathers. It was conferred upon me from the fathers; it came down from the fathers, from the beginning of time, yea, even from the beginning, or before the foundation of the earth, down to the present time, even the right of the firstborn, or the first man, who is Adam, or first father, through the fathers unto me."

2 NEPHI 30

2 Nephi 30:1

"And now behold, my beloved brethren, I would speak unto you; for I, Nephi, would not suffer that ye should suppose that ye are more righteous than the Gentiles shall be. For behold, except ye shall keep the commandments of God ye shall all likewise perish; and because of the words which have been spoken ye need not suppose that the Gentiles are utterly destroyed."

This is troubling if you understand what is said here. Let's see if we can pull it apart.

Nephi adds this direct comment to his descendants, the forebears of the remnant. Although they are the target of covenants and beneficiaries of the restoration, they too need to keep to the path. Though they are "beloved brethren" to Nephi, they are not given any unconditional promises. No one is. Everything we receive is based on what we do, think and say.[717]

---

[717] Alma 12:14 "For our words will condemn us, yea, all our works will condemn us; we shall not be found spotless; and our thoughts will also condemn us; and in this awful state we shall not dare to look up to our God; and we would fain be glad if we could command the rocks and the mountains to fall upon us to hide us from his presence."

D&C 130:20–21 "There is a law, irrevocably decreed in heaven before the foundations of this world, upon which all blessings are predicated—And when we obtain any blessing from God, it is by obedience to that law upon which it is predicated."

Note that this is not about the actual remnant, but about the Nephites who would be destroyed. These people would have access to Nephi's record until the time of Mormon, when they would be destroyed. You can see the time frame in the word usage, "Ye are" as to the Nephites, in contrast to "the Gentiles who shall be." This message is addressed to the Nephites in a time before the gentile.

What is particularly distressing is the comparison Nephi is making. He is saying that the Nephites, who possess the land of promise, needn't think themselves "more righteous than the Gentiles shall be" because if these Nephite descendants do "not keep the commandments of God" then they "shall all likewise perish." If the Nephites do not keep the commandments, they will, like the gentiles, perish.

This means that Nephi is confirming again his prophecy of the destruction of the gentiles. They are doomed. And the Nephites are similarly doomed unless they are obedient.

Despite this warning we know what happened to the Nephites. They were destroyed. The gentiles will be destroyed also.

In the case of the Nephites and the gentiles, "ye need not suppose that the Gentiles are utterly destroyed." That is, neither all the Nephites have been, nor all the gentiles will be "utterly destroyed."

Well, this is happy news indeed. Some tiny fragment of the gentiles will actually survive the destruction of the coming days! So we ought to rejoice! All is well with us after all! And coming from Nephi we know that we have a promise from one holding sealing authority who will, as I have previously pointed out, seal this prophecy.[718]

---

[718] 2 Nephi 33:13–15 "And now, my beloved brethren, all those who are of the house of Israel, and all ye ends of the earth, I speak unto you as the voice of one crying from the dust: Farewell until that great day shall come. And you that will not partake of the goodness of God, and respect the words of the Jews, and also my words, and the words which shall proceed forth out of the mouth of the Lamb of God, behold, I bid you an everlasting farewell, for these words shall condemn you at the last day. For what I seal on earth, shall be brought against you at the judgment bar; for thus hath the Lord commanded me, and I must obey. Amen."

Interestingly Nephi warns his own descendants about their pride and haughtiness. He says that these Nephite descendants, heirs of the covenant, should not think of themselves as righteous. "I, Nephi, would not suffer that ye should suppose that ye are more righteous than the Gentiles shall be." Nephi's prophecy is clear to him, and clear to his descendants. They both regarded the gentiles with pessimism. They (we) are doomed. So they saw us as something dreadful to be compared to. When Nephi confirms they ought not think themselves better than us, he is giving a strong warning indeed. The odd thing is that we read these same records, this same prophecy, and we think we're better than them! We have inverted the picture! We're good, they were bad! But Nephi is using us as the dreadful comparison, the stark warning, the terrible warning that if the Nephites do not repent they will be like us and perish.

When you pick these words apart and see the message it makes you wonder how we could have come to our inverted view. Arrogance and pride really do blind us. Almost completely. What more could Nephi have said to get us to understand?[719]

2 Nephi 30:2

> "For behold, I say unto you that as many of the Gentiles as will repent are the covenant people of the Lord; and as many of the Jews as will not repent shall be cast off; for the Lord covenanteth with none save it be with them that repent and believe in his Son, who is the Holy One of Israel."

To the extent that gentiles "will repent" they may become part of the Lord's "covenant people." They are not the remnant, but they

---

[719] 2 Nephi 32:8 "And now, my beloved brethren, I perceive that ye ponder still in your hearts; and it grieveth me that I must speak concerning this thing. For if ye would hearken unto the Spirit which teacheth a man to pray ye would know that ye must pray; for the evil spirit teacheth not a man to pray, but teacheth him that he must not pray."

may join in the covenant. If they do, then by virtue of the covenant they become "covenant people."

What is required for the gentiles to repent?

What covenant must they enter into or receive so they may be numbered among the "covenant people?" Is membership in The Church of Jesus Christ of Latter-day Saints the only thing needed to "repent" and become a "covenant people?" If not, then what else would be required?

To the extent that "the Jews will not repent" then they will be "cast off." Although history has shown how the Jews have been treated (as Nephi put it), "ye have cursed them, and have hated them, and have not sought to recover them."[720] These difficulties suffered by the Jews are preliminary. The Lord always watched over and preserved them from complete destruction. However, when the Gospel is offered to them in the last days, in the final offering to the last (who had once been first[721]), they will reject the offered renewal of the covenant at their peril. If they reject it, they "shall be cast off" because that will sever the covenant. "The Lord covenanteth with none save it be with them that repent and believe in his Son, who is the Holy One of Israel."

Although we know the Lord will extend every opportunity to the descendants for the sake of a covenant with those who have become the friends of God, there are limits. God will do all He has promised to do. He will forbear, entreat, beseech, send messengers, labor alongside with His messengers, and do all He can to reclaim the heirs

---

[720] 2 Nephi 29:5 "O ye Gentiles, have ye remembered the Jews, mine ancient covenant people? Nay; but ye have cursed them, and have hated them, and have not sought to recover them. But behold, I will return all these things upon your own heads; for I the Lord have not forgotten my people."

[721] 1 Nephi 13:42 "And the time cometh that he shall manifest himself unto all nations, both unto the Jews and also unto the Gentiles; and after he has manifested himself unto the Jews and also unto the Gentiles, then he shall manifest himself unto the Gentiles and also unto the Jews, and the last shall be first, and the first shall be last."

for the covenant's sake. In the end, however, the heirs must either accept what He offers, or be cast off.

It is extraordinary how long the Lord will extend His hand to reclaim His people. But everyone must choose to follow Him. We have our agency. We cannot be forced to follow Him. Even though He may be long-suffering and patient, He cannot compel any to be saved.[722] Unless a person is free to choose for themselves, there is no existence.[723]

If you remove the right to choose, it is not only agency that is obliterated, but it is existence itself. Though we are utterly dependent on God for our very existence, sustained from moment to moment by Him loaning us the ability to move, breathe and act[724], because we are free to make choices we exist. If you destroy the right to choose you have ended the personality of the person. [I have explained this in the beginning of *Beloved Enos*.]

Well, all of this is of no import if the gentiles do not "repent." Whenever we brush up against that subject we wind up engaged in discussions about justice, mercy, vengeance and restitution. I've written about this process in both *The Second Comforter* and *Come, Let Us*

---

[722] Moses 4:1–3 "And I, the Lord God, spake unto Moses, saying: That Satan, whom thou hast commanded in the name of mine Only Begotten, is the same which was from the beginning, and he came before me, saying—Behold, here am I, send me, I will be thy son, and I will redeem all mankind, that one soul shall not be lost, and surely I will do it; wherefore give me thine honor. But, behold, my Beloved Son, which was my Beloved and Chosen from the beginning, said unto me—Father, thy will be done, and the glory be thine forever. Wherefore, because that Satan rebelled against me, and sought to destroy the agency of man, which I, the Lord God, had given him, and also, that I should give unto him mine own power; by the power of mine Only Begotten, I caused that he should be cast down;"

[723] D&C 93:30 "All truth is independent in that sphere in which God has placed it, to act for itself, as all intelligence also; otherwise there is no existence."

[724] Mosiah 2:21 "I say unto you that if ye should serve him who has created you from the beginning, and is preserving you from day to day, by lending you breath, that ye may live and move and do according to your own will, and even supporting you from one moment to another—I say, if ye should serve him with all your whole souls yet ye would be unprofitable servants."

Adore Him . Briefly, here are some of the most important points: To be forgiven we must forgive. Not just forgive, but plead for mercy for those who have offended us. The role of accusing is left to "the accuser of the brethren" or Satan.[725] When we accuse others we interfere with their salvation. If we are the one who was offended, and we make no accusation against them, then we become their savior. Satan's right to accuse is inferior to ours as victims of the offense. We suffer in the flesh the wrongs of others. If we make no claim for justice, surrender those and seek instead for mercy on behalf of others, then Satan's accusations can have no claim upon them. We mimic Christ, follow His example, and in our own limited way also atone for the sins of others. Joseph Smith was trying to get us to understand this concept when he taught: "If you do not accuse each other, God will not accuse you. If you have no accuser you will enter heaven, and if you will follow the revelations and instructions which God gives you through me, I will take you into heaven as my back load. If you will not accuse me, I will not accuse you. If you will throw a cloak of charity over my sins, I will over yours—for charity covereth a multitude of sins." (*DHC* 4:445)

I have explained this at length in what I've written in *Come, Let Us Adore Him*. Christ said this in His ministry repeatedly. He lived it. He showed by His own example the way to obtain forgiveness for every wrong you have ever done. It is in the same way He went about atoning for sins. It is by suffering offenses and returning good. It is by forgiving those who despitefully use and abuse you. It is through loving those who are your enemies. It is by becoming sons and daughters

---

[725] Revelation 12:10 "And I heard a loud voice saying in heaven, Now is come salvation, and strength, and the kingdom of our God, and the power of his Christ: for the accuser of our brethren is cast down, which accused them before our God day and night."

of God. And it can be done in no other way.[726] If you do not forgive others, you cannot be forgiven.[727] This is why Christ, in teaching us to pray, told us we are only forgiven as we forgive others.[728] It is as we forgive that we obtain forgiveness.

The way is strait and narrow, and cannot permit you to pass through while carrying any burden of accusation, desire for revenge or even just complaint about others. When you lay down what you might justly claim against others and seek nothing for their offenses, then you are able to enter in. To be blessed, we must seek peace with those who would make war against us.[729] When we judge all others with mercy, it is with mercy alone we will be judged.[730]

For the most part, the gentiles will not repent. They will hold courts, use their time judging, exact conditions, set limits, and annotate their permanent records with notes showing what discipline a person has undergone. And happily employ control, compulsion and

---

[726] Matthew 5:38–48 "Ye have heard that it hath been said, An eye for an eye, and a tooth for a tooth: But I say unto you, That ye resist not evil: but whosoever shall smite thee on thy right cheek, turn to him the other also. And if any man will sue thee at the law, and take away thy coat, let him have *thy* cloke also. And whosoever shall compel thee to go a mile, go with him twain. Give to him that asketh thee, and from him that would borrow of thee turn not thou away. Ye have heard that it hath been said, Thou shalt love thy neighbour, and hate thine enemy. But I say unto you, Love your enemies, bless them that curse you, do good to them that hate you, and pray for them which despitefully use you, and persecute you; That ye may be the children of your Father which is in heaven: for he maketh his sun to rise on the evil and on the good, and sendeth rain on the just and on the unjust. For if ye love them which love you, what reward have ye? do not even the publicans the same? And if ye salute your brethren only, what do ye more *than others*? do not even the publicans so? Be ye therefore perfect, even as your Father which is in heaven is perfect."

[727] Matthew 6:14–15 "For if ye forgive men their trespasses, your heavenly Father will also forgive you: But if ye forgive not men their trespasses, neither will your Father forgive your trespasses."

[728] Matthew 6:12 "And forgive us our debts, as we forgive our debtors."

[729] Matthew 5:9 "Blessed *are* the peacemakers: for they shall be called the children of God."

[730] Matthew 7:2 "For with what judgment ye judge, ye shall be judged: and with what measure ye mete, it shall be measured to you again."

dominion over one another[731] right up to the time when the trumpet sounds and it is everlastingly too late. Others will justify this failure to forgive, shout praises to the abuse, and claim all compulsion and dominion is necessary to protect us from the evil. Even though our Master told us not to resist the evil, but forgive it.[732]

For the most part, the gentiles will demand they be judged by a law they cannot satisfy. Some few, however, will forgive and plead for the weaknesses and failings of others. They will forgive, and thereby be forgiven. They will obtain for themselves a judgment based only on mercy, for they have shown mercy to others. This atoning act of love and intercession will be the hallmark by which the children of God are identified in the Day of Judgment.[733] Only the peacemakers can be trusted to live in peace with one another. All others are unfit for the presence of God.

2 Nephi 30:3

"And now, I would prophesy somewhat more concerning the Jews and the Gentiles. For after the book of which I have spoken shall come forth, and be written unto the Gentiles, and sealed up again unto the Lord, there shall be many which shall believe the words which are written; and they shall carry them forth unto the remnant of our seed."

---

[731] D&C 121:37 "That they may be conferred upon us, it is true; but when we undertake to cover our sins, or to gratify our pride, our vain ambition, or to exercise control or dominion or compulsion upon the souls of the children of men, in any degree of unrighteousness, behold, the heavens withdraw themselves; the Spirit of the Lord is grieved; and when it is withdrawn, Amen to the priesthood or the authority of that man."

[732] Matthew 5:39 "But I say unto you, That ye resist not evil: but whosoever shall smite thee on thy right cheek, turn to him the other also."

[733] Matthew 5:9 "Blessed *are* the peacemakers: for they shall be called the children of God."

Nephi speaks again prophetically about our time. He makes no distinction between the Jews and "the remnant of our seed," or Nephite remnant in what he says here. The "book of which I have spoken" is the record of the Nephites. It will come forth, written as a warning to the gentiles. Here is another attempt to establish a time frame for a prophecy. It will be after the record exists, gets brought forth "unto the gentiles" and then is "sealed up again unto the Lord." We are in that era now. The record exists, even if part of it is sealed. It has come forth, at least in that part intended to be released at the point of this prophecy. And it has been "sealed up again unto the Lord." We don't have possession of it at present.

I've addressed the cover story that the Angel Moroni still has the plates in what I've written before. Briefly, the Book of Mormon tells Joseph Smith to "seal them up unto the Lord" in detail in three places. This is one of them. The other two are 2 Nephi 27:22 (giving the most detailed instruction to Joseph)[734] and Ether 5:1–4[735]. All of these instructions are to the same effect. Once the Book of Mormon has been translated, to the extent it is to come forth in our day, the plates are to be "sealed up again" by Joseph. Since he did everything else in

---

[734] 2 Nephi 27:22 "Wherefore, when thou hast read the words which I have commanded thee, and obtained the witnesses which I have promised unto thee, then shalt thou seal up the book again, and hide it up unto me, that I may preserve the words which thou hast not read, until I shall see fit in mine own wisdom to reveal all things unto the children of men."

[735] Ether 5:1–4 "And now I, Moroni, have written the words which were commanded me, according to my memory; and I have told you the things which I have sealed up; therefore touch them not in order that ye may translate; for that thing is forbidden you, except by and by it shall be wisdom in God. And behold, ye may be privileged that ye may show the plates unto those who shall assist to bring forth this work; And unto three shall they be shown by the power of God; wherefore they shall know of a surety that these things are true. And in the mouth of three witnesses shall these things be established; and the testimony of three, and this work, in the which shall be shown forth the power of God and also his word, of which the Father, and the Son, and the Holy Ghost bear record—and all this shall stand as a testimony against the world at the last day."

768 REMEMBERING THE COVENANT

the way he was instructed, there is no reason to believe he wouldn't have sealed up the record and hid it again.

Here Nephi prophesies that "there shall be many which shall believe the words which are written." Meaning that those words "written unto the gentiles" or what we have in print now, will in fact be believed by "many." They "shall believe the words." Nephi has assured us of that. Therefore, it is necessary that some group from among the gentiles distinguish itself by actually believing the words of the Book of Mormon. It will be this group which "shall carry them forth unto the remnant of" Nephi's seed. Notice that they will "believe" in the book. (That will require them to have a correct understanding of the book's content, otherwise they would have unbelief.)

Those who do not believe (or have unbelief) in the Book of Mormon will not, indeed cannot, bring the words to the remnant. They aren't qualified. They would not be able to convert any of the remnant. It will be those who actually believe in and accept the precepts of the Book of Mormon who will carry them forth unto the remnant.

Considering the otherwise direful predictions about the gentiles, this is the one way where hope may come to them. The group that believes in the Book of Mormon will necessarily have to be preserved to fulfill their responsibility to carry the words to the remnant. This is a subset of the Saints, and clearly not all of the members of the Church of Jesus Christ of Latter-day Saints. For the church itself, there remains a condemnation because of their unbelief in the book.[736] This condemnation of the church was repeated by President Benson and again by Elder Oaks.

---

[736] D&C 84:54–57 "And your minds in times past have been darkened because of unbelief, and because you have treated lightly the things you have received—Which vanity and unbelief have brought the whole church under condemnation. And this condemnation resteth upon the children of Zion, even all. And they shall remain under this condemnation until they repent and remember the new covenant, even the Book of Mormon and the former commandments which I have given them, not only to say, but to do according to that which I have written—"

If, therefore, you would like to be preserved, the manner in which that will happen, according to Nephi's prophecy, will necessarily require you to abandon the condemnation of the larger church, and become one of those who believe in the Book of Mormon. Not only to say, but to do; as Section 84 above requires.

It is surprising how much information the Book of Mormon has for us. It is even more surprising that with such detail available to us, we have done so little to understand and teach it. The words of this prophecy by Nephi ought to be proclaimed among us. However, very little attention has been given to it.

One of the effects of pride is blindness. We can't see what our pride prevents us from seeing. We have to come down to the depths of humility (to use a phrase Nephi coined in 2 Nephi 9:42). Interestingly it is only the Book of Mormon which tells us to "come down in the depths of humility."[737] Once Nephi coined the phrase, Mormon used it twice in his abridgment. It is a good phrase. It does tell us what we must do.

The great work of the Lord in this day revolves around the Book of Mormon. More instruction, prophecy and promises are contained in that book for our day than any other. You can get closer to God by abiding its precepts than any other book.

---

[737] 2 Nephi 9:42 "And whoso knocketh, to him will he open; and the wise, and the learned, and they that are rich, who are puffed up because of their learning, and their wisdom, and their riches—yea, they are they whom he despiseth; and save they shall cast these things away, and consider themselves fools before God, and come down in the depths of humility, he will not open unto them."
Helaman 6:5 "Yea, and many did preach with exceedingly great power and authority, unto the bringing down many of them into the depths of humility, to be the humble followers of God and the Lamb."
3 Nephi 12:2 "And again, more blessed are they who shall believe in your words because that ye shall testify that ye have seen me, and that ye know that I am. Yea, blessed are they who shall believe in your words, and come down into the depths of humility and be baptized, for they shall be visited with fire and with the Holy Ghost, and shall receive a remission of their sins."

Joseph Smith didn't write it. It was written by ancient prophets, sealed up to come forth in our day, and translated by the gift and power of God.

It is a perilous book. We neglect it at the risk of failure. Don't let it remain a "sealed book" for you. Anyone can come to believe in it if they are willing.

2 Nephi 30:4–5

"And then shall the remnant of our seed know concerning us, how that we came out from Jerusalem, and that they are descendants of the Jews. And the gospel of Jesus Christ shall be declared among them; wherefore, they shall be restored unto the knowledge of their fathers, and also to the knowledge of Jesus Christ, which was had among their fathers."

Once the remnant obtain a copy of the Book of Mormon, from a believing gentile hand, they will realize they are originally come out of Jerusalem. They will realize also that they are "descendants of the Jews."

It comes full circle. Those who were lost have returned again. The "prodigal" will return.[738] There will be joy at the return.

---

[738] Luke 15:11–32 "And he said, A certain man had two sons: And the younger of them said to *his* father, Father, give me the portion of goods that falleth *to me*. And he divided unto them *his* living. And not many days after the younger son gathered all together, and took his journey into a far country, and there wasted his substance with riotous living. And when he had spent all, there arose a mighty famine in that land; and he began to be in want. And he went and joined himself to a citizen of that country; and he sent him into his fields to feed swine. And he would fain have filled his belly with the husks that the swine did eat: and no man gave unto him. And when he came to himself, he said, How many hired servants of my father's have bread enough and to spare, and I perish with hunger! I will arise and go to my father, and will say unto him, Father, I have sinned against heaven, and before thee, And am no more worthy to be called thy son: make me as one of thy hired servants. And he arose, and came to his father. But when he was yet a great way off, his father saw him, and had compassion, and ran, and fell on his neck, and kissed him. And the son said unto him, Father, I have sinned against heaven, and in thy sight, and am no more worthy to be called thy son. But

This will happen as a preliminary to "the gospel of Jesus Christ [being] declared among them." The Gospel being declared requires a true message, true messengers, authority, and ordinances. That will follow the remnant receiving the Book of Mormon. To what extent the gentiles bring those things and to what extent it will require heaven's direct involvement, remains to be seen. But when the remnant reconnects, they will reconnect in every respect. The "gospel of Jesus Christ shall be declared among them!"

As a result of these events, the remnant "shall be restored unto the knowledge of their fathers." What does it mean to be restored? What knowledge? Which fathers? The Nephites, and Lehi, or to the earlier "fathers" as well? Does this include Abraham, Isaac, and Jacob?

What does it mean they will be "also [restored] to the knowledge of Jesus Christ?" What does this "knowledge" involve? What kind of relationship with Christ does this imply?

If we wonder at the "knowledge" the remnant will obtain, we have a parallel given to us: The future remnant knowledge of Christ shall be akin to that "which was had among their fathers." Meaning they will grow to know what the earlier Nephite disciples and peoples knew. What kind of knowledge does that include?

---

the father said to his servants, Bring forth the best robe, and put *it* on him; and put a ring on his hand, and shoes on *his* feet: And bring hither the fatted calf, and kill *it;* and let us eat, and be merry: For this my son was dead, and is alive again; he was lost, and is found. And they began to be merry. Now his elder son was in the field: and as he came and drew nigh to the house, he heard musick and dancing. And he called one of the servants, and asked what these things meant. And he said unto him, Thy brother is come; and thy father hath killed the fatted calf, because he hath received him safe and sound. And he was angry, and would not go in: therefore came his father out, and intreated him. And he answering said to *his* father, Lo, these many years do I serve thee, neither transgressed I at any time thy commandment: and yet thou never gavest me a kid, that I might make merry with my friends: But as soon as this thy son was come, which hath devoured thy living with harlots, thou hast killed for him the fatted calf. And he said unto him, Son, thou art ever with me, and all that I have is thine. It was meet that we should make merry, and be glad: for this thy brother was dead, and is alive again; and was lost, and is found."

When the right target receives the right Gospel, the results are dramatic. When the wrong group is entrusted with the Gospel, they tend to let it atrophy, grow dim, and become a social order without the power of godliness. The restoration was intended to cure that problem. But as with any gift from God, we must do more than to "take no thought but to ask."[739] We must pursue knowledge and act with alacrity when it is given.

If we do not do this, then the result is not a blessing, but a cursing.[740] No matter what we are offered by the Lord, we must act consistent with His will to receive the blessings offered. When we fail to fulfill the obligation He appoints to us, then we fail to obtain what was offered.[741]

Once they have been given the gospel, the remnant will not fail. Their reconnection will be as a nail in a sure place, not to be moved. Their knowledge will grow into the perfect day, just as it might with anyone who is willing to receive what Christ offers.[742] Noon at the summer solstice is a symbol of the perfect day. This year, in contrast, at midnight of the winter solstice there will be an eclipse. This would

---

[739] D&C 9:6–7 "Do not murmur, my son, for it is wisdom in me that I have dealt with you after this manner. Behold, you have not understood; you have supposed that I would give it unto you, when you took no thought save it was to ask me."

[740] D&C 124:47–48 "And it shall come to pass that if you build a house unto my name, and do not do the things that I say, I will not perform the oath which I make unto you, neither fulfil the promises which ye expect at my hands, saith the Lord. For instead of blessings, ye, by your own works, bring cursings, wrath, indignation, and judgments upon your own heads, by your follies, and by all your abominations, which you practise before me, saith the Lord."

[741] D&C 124:31–32 "But I command you, all ye my saints, to build a house unto me; and I grant unto you a sufficient time to build a house unto me; and during this time your baptisms shall be acceptable unto me. But behold, at the end of this appointment your baptisms for your dead shall not be acceptable unto me; and if you do not these things at the end of the appointment ye shall be rejected as a church, with your dead, saith the Lord your God."

[742] D&C 50:24 "That which is of God is light; and he that receiveth light, and continueth in God, receiveth more light; and that light groweth brighter and brighter until the perfect day."

be a symbol in the heavens of the opposite of the perfect day. When it arrives it undoubtedly is a sign relevant to the time. (Those things are never accidents or mere happenstance.)

The ideas begin to accumulate. Darkness and light. Free will and acceptance of what is offered by God. So many divergent roads that are offered in place of the one that remains strait and narrow, but nevertheless in a straight course before you.[743]

2 Nephi 30:6

"And then shall they rejoice; for they shall know that it is a blessing unto them from the hand of God; and their scales of darkness shall begin to fall from their eyes; and many generations shall not pass away among them, save they shall be a pure and a delightsome people."

Once the remnant is in possession of the Gospel, they will "rejoice." What does that mean? What form would "rejoicing" take as a result of receiving the Gospel?

What does it mean to "know that it is a blessing unto them from the hand of God?" How would they recognize that?

What are the "scales of darkness" which cover eyes? How would the scales have been over their eyes in the first place? What does it mean to have the scales "begin to fall from their eyes?" Does "begin to fall" mean something about a gradual process, rather than a single quick event? How do scales continue to remain in place, even as they "begin to fall?" What does that imply about the difficulty in overcoming errors because of false understanding or traditions? Even the remnant will struggle to fully remove the "scales of darkness."

---

[743] 2 Nephi 9:41 "O then, my beloved brethren, come unto the Lord, the Holy One. Remember that his paths are righteous. Behold, the way for man is narrow, but it lieth in a straight course before him, and the keeper of the gate is the Holy One of Israel; and he employeth no servant there; and there is none other way save it be by the gate; for he cannot be deceived, for the Lord God is his name."

Why are there "not many generations" involved in this process? Do you need "generations" to pass away in order to fully remove darkness?

Why is it not possible to accomplish this in a single generation?

If the Lord's purposes in redeeming the remnant will take "not many generations" then why do we think we can accomplish it in one? How gradual a process is involved?

What does it mean to become a "pure and delightsome people?" (For many editions of the Book of Mormon, this phrase used to be "white and delightsome." It was changed back to the original "pure" rather than "white" in the 1980 edition.)

Why does purity and being "delightsome" to the Lord go together?

If this process is going to involve "not many generations" then how far away are we from this unfolding?

When we read prophecy like this, we should realize we are looking at unfolding history from the Lord's perspective. We want to know what will happen in our single lifetime. We are impatient. He is interested in having us know the truth.

Nephi's prophecy gives us a perspective that helps put our own time into context. We are in a hurry. History is not. There is a great deal left to do. There is a great deal left to happen. Nephi is letting us see this lengthy agenda.

2 Nephi 30:7–8

"And it shall come to pass that the Jews which are scattered also shall begin to believe in Christ; and they shall begin to gather in upon the face of the land; and as many as shall believe in Christ shall also become a delightsome people. And it shall come to pass that the Lord God shall commence his work among all nations, kindreds, tongues, and people, to bring about the restoration of his people upon the earth."

Nephi has circled back and is reiterating his earlier prophecy, assuring us that this is the order, these are the priorities and this work is indeed universal.

The scattered Jews will begin to believe in Christ, and as they do they will be gathered again. These will also be among the people destined to become "delightsome" as a result of the Gospel.

Again, we have the reminder of the universal nature of this work. Every nation, kindred, tongue and people will be invited. The invitation is to result in a "restoration of His people upon the earth." That is, the purpose of the creation was to produce God's people. By and large that hasn't happened.

From the rebellion of Adam's children, through the almost universal rebellion at the time of Noah, mankind has been unwilling to become His people. The times when we find a "people of God" upon the earth is the exception, not the rule.

A *desire* to see Zion return is *not* the same thing as seeing its return.

I sometimes wonder if people who speak of Zion have any clue of the tremendous gulf between what that will require and who we are as a people. Having a vocabulary is not the same thing as having the heart to produce Zion.

How do people live with one another in peace? Without any poor among them? While seeking the best interest of all, and without ambition. Why would we believe we can get that great task done in a short effort in our day? There is no precedent living in anything like Zion, in this or the last seven generations.

Having the Gospel understood is the first step, of course. As a group, there is such a poor command of the scriptures that we have some considerable study before us. Passing familiarity with some scriptures is not of much use. They are the standard given to us to help reveal the basis for becoming a covenant people.

I notice how the subject of "calling and election" gets mentioned from time to time. It would be better to learn about the fundamentals of the Gospel that we are not living than to attempt to understand what lies at the end of the struggle.

Losing ourselves implies something quite distant from the self-centered worry that grows out of not knowing your standing before God. The first step is to pray in sincerity, asking God to soften your heart that you may believe. The steps Nephi followed are described in first few chapters of *The Second Comforter*. Those steps are not given to us merely to contemplate. They are given for us to follow.

As we see Nephi wrapping up his two books of scripture, he turns to the distant view of a return upon the earth of a "people of God." We could have been that people. We even fancy ourselves as being likely to be among such a people. But if we lived that kind of life, we would already associate with such beings here, in the flesh. We would know we have part with them, because we would be associating with heaven now, as they will do then.

There is no one else who you need to look to other than the Lord. There is enough revealed in the Book of Mormon to tell you what you must do to become part of His people. You don't need me, or a program, or a leader, other than Christ. He has offered the opportunity for each of us to become part of His people.

2 Nephi 30:9–10

"And with righteousness shall the Lord God judge the poor, and reprove with equity for the meek of the earth. And he shall smite the earth with the rod of his mouth; and with the breath of his lips shall he slay the wicked. For the time speedily cometh that the Lord God shall cause a great division among the people, and the wicked will he destroy; and he will spare his people, yea, even if it so be that he must destroy the wicked by fire."

Nephi quotes Isaiah to weave a second witness into this end-of-times description of the Lord's agenda.

Righteousness for the poor. Equity for the meek. Smiting for the earth. Death to the wicked. For the poor, why "righteousness?" For the meek, why "equity?" For the earth, why shall it be "smitten?" What is the "rod of His mouth" to be used to smite the earth?

For the wicked, it is the "breath of His lips" which will slay. Have you considered what this means? Why His "breath" when that is the mechanism that brings life to Adam,[744] and the Spirit to His disciples?[745] Does the word "breath" imply the converse of bringing life, and the removal of the Holy Spirit? If so, how do those ideas affect the meaning of the Lord's decision to "slay the wicked?" In what sense will they be "slain?"

What does it mean that "the time speedily cometh?" From what point is the measure taken to decide the "speed" of His coming? Is it from Nephi's prophecy, or from the time in which the prophecy is set?

What does it mean there will be "caused a great division?" How would that "division" manifest itself? Is it first spiritual, then physical? Or is it both from the start? If it is first a great spiritual division, followed at some point in a physical gathering together of these two groups into separate locations, how would it unfold?

How will the wicked be "destroyed?"[746] Will they also be able to destroy the people whom the Lord identifies as "His people?"[747]

---

744 Genesis 2:7 "And the Lord God formed man *of* the dust of the ground, and breathed into his nostrils the breath of life; and man became a living soul."

745 John 20:22 "And when he had said this, he breathed on *them,* and saith unto them, Receive ye the Holy Ghost:"

746 Mormon 4:5 "But, behold, the judgments of God will overtake the wicked; and it is by the wicked that the wicked are punished; for it is the wicked that stir up the hearts of the children of men unto bloodshed."

747 1 Nephi 22:16 "For the time soon cometh that the fulness of the wrath of God shall be poured out upon all the children of men; for he will not suffer that the wicked shall destroy the righteous."

What does it mean that the Lord "will spare His people, yea, even if it so be that He must destroy the wicked by fire?" Is that true? Would the Lord personally intervene to protect His people? Has He done anything like that before? If so, when? Why? Can He still do that today? In a time of tremendous upheaval and destruction, can He selectively preserve His people?[748]

---

[748] 3 Nephi 9:1–13 "And it came to pass that there was a voice heard among all the inhabitants of the earth, upon all the face of this land, crying: Wo, wo, wo unto this people; wo unto the inhabitants of the whole earth except they shall repent; for the devil laugheth, and his angels rejoice, because of the slain of the fair sons and daughters of my people; and it is because of their iniquity and abominations that they are fallen! Behold, that great city Zarahemla have I burned with fire, and the inhabitants thereof. And behold, that great city Moroni have I caused to be sunk in the depths of the sea, and the inhabitants thereof to be drowned. And behold, that great city Moronihah have I covered with earth, and the inhabitants thereof, to hide their iniquities and their abominations from before my face, that the blood of the prophets and the saints shall not come any more unto me against them. And behold, the city of Gilgal have I caused to be sunk, and the inhabitants thereof to be buried up in the depths of the earth; Yea, and the city of Onihah and the inhabitants thereof, and the city of Mocum and the inhabitants thereof, and the city of Jerusalem and the inhabitants thereof; and waters have I caused to come up in the stead thereof, to hide their wickedness and abominations from before my face, that the blood of the prophets and the saints shall not come up any more unto me against them. And behold, the city of Gadiandi, and the city of Gadiomnah, and the city of Jacob, and the city of Gimgimno, all these have I caused to be sunk, and made hills and valleys in the places thereof; and the inhabitants thereof have I buried up in the depths of the earth, to hide their wickedness and abominations from before my face, that the blood of the prophets and the saints should not come up any more unto me against them. And behold, that great city Jacobugath, which was inhabited by the people of king Jacob, have I caused to be burned with fire because of their sins and their wickedness, which was above all the wickedness of the whole earth, because of their secret murders and combinations; for it was they that did destroy the peace of my people and the government of the land; therefore I did cause them to be burned, to destroy them from before my face, that the blood of the prophets and the saints should not come up unto me any more against them. And behold, the city of Laman, and the city of Josh, and the city of Gad, and the city of Kishkumen, have I caused to be burned with fire, and the inhabitants thereof, because of their wickedness in casting out the prophets, and stoning those whom I did send to declare unto them concerning their wickedness and their abominations. And because they did cast them all out, that there were none righteous among them, I did send down fire and destroy them, that their wickedness and abominations might be hid from before my face, that the blood of the prophets and the saints whom I sent among them might not cry unto me from the ground against them. And many great destructions have I caused to come upon this land, and upon this people, because of their wickedness and their abominations. O all ye that are spared because ye were more righteous than they, will ye not now return unto me, and repent of your sins, and be converted, that I may heal you?"

What protection is there from such forces of destruction?

Have you noticed how things seem to be speeding up? Business cycles that used to take generations now play themselves out in a few years. Political dynasties are crumbling and institutions which were once impervious to change are being forced to change. Cultural norms are changing so quickly that change is itself the new culture. The days seem to be shortening, don't they.[749]

2 Nephi 30:11–15

"And righteousness shall be the girdle of his loins, and faithfulness the girdle of his reins. And then shall the wolf dwell with the lamb; and the leopard shall lie down with the kid, and the calf, and the young lion, and the fatling, together; and a little child shall lead them. And the cow and the bear shall feed; their young ones shall lie down together; and the lion shall eat straw like the ox. And the sucking child shall play on the hole of the asp, and the weaned child shall put his hand on the cockatrice's den. They shall not hurt nor destroy in all my holy mountain; for the earth shall be full of the knowledge of the Lord as the waters cover the sea."

These words, again borrowed from Isaiah, are familiar to all of us. The time frame puts it inside the larger Nephi prophecy regarding the fulfillment of covenants made to the "fathers."

What is interesting for us is the narrative of end-of-times peace and return of righteousness. This includes a "people of God" returning to inhabit the earth set inside the Book of Mormon narrative prophecy. The Book of Mormon remnant figure centrally into the progression. It (the book) comes forth, and from that time until the

---

[749] Matthew 24:22 "And except those days should be shortened, there should no flesh be saved: but for the elect's sake those days shall be shortened."

JS–Matthew 1:20 "And except those days should be shortened, there should none of their flesh be saved; but for the elect's sake, according to the covenant, those days shall be shortened."

fulfillment of the return of righteousness and peace, the book's involvement is central. The gentiles receive custody of it. Don't do much with it. Some few actually believe it. They will eventually take it to the remnant. The remnant begin to come onboard with their conversion. They increase, the gentiles decrease, the momentum builds. The gentiles ultimately get swept away, while the remnant begin to grow into the fullness of the Gospel in all its rights, ordinances, and return to the knowledge of Christ.

As the culmination of these trends, which begin small, but gain momentum as they roll forth, we see the final product for what it was always intended to become: Zion. Once the stone cut out of the mountain without hands begins to roll forth, it will not stop until it has filled the whole earth.

Among those who are destined to fulfill these events, they will "not hurt nor destroy in all" the Lord's "holy mountain." What does it mean to "not hurt?" What does it mean to "not destroy?" Why a "holy mountain?"

The earth itself will be "full of the knowledge of the Lord as the waters cover the sea." What "knowledge of the Lord" is referred to here? How completely does the water cover the sea? Will there be any need for one man to say to another "know ye the Lord" in that day, or will all who remain know Him?[750]

We imagine that day, but do not live for it. We think ourselves qualified to be part of that group. But ask yourself, do you make others hurt? Do others who hurt find relief from their pain by what you are willing to suffer, without returning evil for evil, but good for evil? Or do you believe such ideas to be "weird?" Because they are,

---

[750] Jeremiah 31:34 "And they shall teach no more every man his neighbour, and every man his brother, saying, Know the Lord: for they shall all know me, from the least of them unto the greatest of them, saith the Lord: for I will forgive their iniquity, and I will remember their sin no more."

indeed, for all we do, all we say, all we live and all we are, so alien to us that they are weird indeed.

From inside that culture, looking back at us and our time, reading our foolishness, observing our entertainment, they will think us more than "weird." They will think us utterly insane. And they will be right. We are the madmen, claiming ourselves to be righteous, while dwelling in raw sewage and celebrating revenge, discord, hatred and anger. We speak of Zion while marketing Babylon. We ask "what will sell" before we undertake any project. We study the trends of the fallen, wicked and perverse in order to adapt our faith, our words, and our conversations to appeal to Babylon. The social statistics of Latter-day Saints run about 7 years behind the larger population.

We're all headed to hell, but console ourselves that we remain "peculiar" because we are slower in our descent than the larger population. It never occurs to us that a complete break will be needed.

The Lord plans to provide that break. The question then will be whether we join with those who lament the fall of Babylon[751], or

---

[751] Revelation 18:9–11 "And the kings of the earth, who have committed fornication and lived deliciously with her, shall bewail her, and lament for her, when they shall see the smoke of her burning, Standing afar off for the fear of her torment, saying, Alas, alas, that great city Babylon, that mighty city! for in one hour is thy judgment come. And the merchants of the earth shall weep and mourn over her; for no man buyeth their merchandise any more:"

among those who will rejoice at the coming of Zion[752] Perspective is affected by what our hearts value. Unfortunately, the choice is "either-or," and not both.[753]

Well this is indeed "getting weird" . . .

2 Nephi 30:16–17

"Wherefore, the things of all nations shall be made known; yea, all things shall be made known unto the children of men. There is nothing which is secret save it shall be revealed; there is no work of darkness save it shall be made manifest in the light; and there is nothing which is sealed upon the earth save it shall be loosed."

---

[752] D&C 84:96–102 "For I, the Almighty, have laid my hands upon the nations, to scourge them for their wickedness. And plagues shall go forth, and they shall not be taken from the earth until I have completed my work, which shall be cut short in righteousness—Until all shall know me, who remain, even from the least unto the greatest, and shall be filled with the knowledge of the Lord, and shall see eye to eye, and shall lift up their voice, and with the voice together sing this new song, saying:
The Lord hath brought again Zion;
The Lord hath redeemed his people, Israel,
According to the election of grace,
Which was brought to pass by the faith
And covenant of their fathers.
The Lord hath redeemed his people;
And Satan is bound and time is no longer.
The Lord hath gathered all things in one.
The Lord hath brought down Zion from above.
The Lord hath brought up Zion from beneath.
The earth hath travailed and brought forth her strength;
And truth is established in her bowels;
And the heavens have smiled upon her;
And she is clothed with the glory of her God;
For he stands in the midst of his people.
Glory, and honor, and power, and might,
Be ascribed to our God; for he is full of mercy,
Justice, grace and truth, and peace,
Forever and ever, Amen."

[753] Luke 16:13 "No servant can serve two masters: for either he will hate the one, and love the other; or else he will hold to the one, and despise the other. Ye cannot serve God and mammon."

This is another confirmation by Nephi of what was written before. The Nephites will have the records of the Jews and lost tribes of Israel, and the Jews and the lost tribes will have the records of the Nephites. "The things of all nations" will include these various Divine messages and teachings given to the various nations/people of the earth. The "children of men" in that day will have available to them the records that allow them to see how the knowledge of the Lord will cover the earth as the waters cover the sea. They will realize that these distant echoes of the Gospel which appear in other faiths, traditions and sacred texts were, at one time, an authentic communication from the Lord or His servants.

So much of what appears to contradict will be found to have a common root. The things that have been sealed and kept from public discourse will become part of the public dialogue. We will not have the same requirement for "secrets" to be kept. But "nothing which is secret" will remain so. It will all "be revealed."

When the truth is unsealed, so are the conspiracies, the foolishness and the ambitions that have worked to keep the truth from becoming known. None of the "work of darkness" which has been afoot will be kept from public view, but "it shall be manifest in the light." Whatever excuses men have had to suppress the truth, deny the Spirit, and employ the "arm of flesh" as their guide will be exposed for what they are. They will put on display. The wisdom of the wise will be seen for the foolishness it was. The strength of man's arm, the studied foolishness gained from social sciences, opinion polling, focus groups and other attempts to figure out where the ignorant are going and jump in front of the trend to feign leadership, will be seen for what it was. The endless praise and adoration given to these foolish and weak political, governmental, business, educational and "moral" leaders will be seen for what it was.

Oh the wisdom of God and the foolishness of men! When men are educated they think they are wise.[754] All the studied ignorance of men will be recognized as foolishness, rather than as wisdom as it is now.[755] Then the fools will at last shut their mouths and cease to thunder out their errors.[756]

You can almost feel Nephi's relief as he contemplates this outcome. The final vindication of the truth. The final conquest of the foolishness of men. It is consoling to consider that this odd and corrupt world we find ourselves in will at some point finally end. The truth will be vindicated. The errors and evil we enshrine in our institutions and art will collapse. We will emerge from behind the scales of darkness covering our eyes and at last see things as they are in the light of heaven.

I'm thinking the most common reaction will be "oops" or some four letter equivalent . . .

You realize you can fix that today, right? You know the Gospel intends to take you out of this fallen world and into that kind of light even now, right? That was what Christ was trying to do all along. That is why He's provided the scriptures (primarily the Book of Mormon for us) to help us catch on before the terrible end is upon us. So you can do something about all this.

Or you can think it just "weird," remain as you are, and enjoy the decline. 'Cuz lotsa folks is do'in just that, ya know . . .

---

[754] 2 Nephi 9:28 "O that cunning plan of the evil one! O the vainness, and the frailties, and the foolishness of men! When they are learned they think they are wise, and they hearken not unto the counsel of God, for they set it aside, supposing they know of themselves, wherefore, their wisdom is foolishness and it profiteth them not. And they shall perish."

[755] 1 Corinthians 3:19 "For the wisdom of this world is foolishness with God. For it is written, He taketh the wise in their own craftiness."

[756] Isaiah 52:15 "So shall he sprinkle many nations; the kings shall shut their mouths at him: for *that* which had not been told them shall they see; and *that* which they had not heard shall they consider."

2 Nephi 30:18

"Wherefore, all things which have been revealed unto the children of men shall at that day be revealed; and Satan shall have power over the hearts of the children of men no more, for a long time. And now, my beloved brethren, I make an end of my sayings."

The truth will be revealed. But truth of this nature will involve something else. Satan will have no power. When we gather enough light and truth, Satan's influence and power ends. We find that Satan is "cast out" because he can no longer deceive.

His primary tool is the lie. When there is enough truth, there is no longer any reason to believe or teach a lie. Therefore, he has lost power.

His secondary tool is the lusts and appetites of the flesh. When these are controlled, he is rendered completely ineffective. He is bound.

Once the lies are exposed and the appetites of the flesh are subdued, the hearts of men are freed from captivity. Nephi is describing a future day when this will be the the common situation for mankind.

Of course, this doesn't have to be a future day. It is possible to gain enough light and truth today so the lies are exposed to your view. It is also possible to subdue the appetites of the flesh. In any event, the desires, appetites and passions ought to be kept within the bounds which the Lord prescribes. We say that, but we don't often do that. Most people are not willing to actually subdue their desires, passions and appetites. It seems weird to suppress the desire for revenge, to actually turn the other cheek, and to return good for evil. In short, it would appear the Savior's conduct in willingly going to His death without accepting Peter's offer to use the sword in His defense was a bit nutty. At least from the perspective of the damned. (They can't even stop watching pornography. Latter-day "*Saint*" indeed. What's saintly about the vengeful, lustful, and gluttonous? But that's an aside . . .)

Binding Satan so he has no "power over the hearts of the children of men" is an interesting phrase. Why "power?" Why "power over the hearts?" Why "children of men" rather than sons of God? (See the dialogue between Moses and Satan where Moses refers to himself as a "son of God" but Satan calls him a "son of man" in Moses 1:12–13.)[757] Isn't that interesting?

Why is it that such power over the hearts of the children of men will be lost? It is as if entry into a Terrestrial World will bring about the binding of Satan, even before becoming a "son of God," and beginning the final journey into the Lord's presence. This is interesting—as if Nephi understood the Temple itself.[758]

Satan's power is lost for a "long time" but not forever. Why? How will Satan be loosed again?[759] I've described this event and the reasons in "The Great Competition" in *Ten Parables*.

The final phrase is because Nephi was through with his message for a while. He may have intended to take his writing up again, but

---

[757] Moses 1:12–13 "And it came to pass that when Moses had said these words, behold, Satan came tempting him, saying: Moses, son of man, worship me. And it came to pass that Moses looked upon Satan and said: Who art thou? For behold, I am a son of God, in the similitude of his Only Begotten; and where is thy glory, that I should worship thee?"

[758] 2 Nephi 5:16 "And I, Nephi, did build a temple; and I did construct it after the manner of the temple of Solomon save it were not built of so many precious things; for they were not to be found upon the land, wherefore, it could not be built like unto Solomon's temple. But the manner of the construction was like unto the temple of Solomon; and the workmanship thereof was exceedingly fine."

[759] Revelation 20:7 "And when the thousand years are expired, Satan shall be loosed out of his prison,"
D&C 43:31 "For Satan shall be bound, and when he is loosed again he shall only reign for a little season, and then cometh the end of the earth."
D&C 88:110 "And so on, until the seventh angel shall sound his trump; and he shall stand forth upon the land and upon the sea, and swear in the name of him who sitteth upon the throne, that there shall be time no longer; and Satan shall be bound, that old serpent, who is called the devil, and shall not be loosed for the space of a thousand years."

the final phrase indicates he was done for the time. We cannot tell how long it was between the last verse of chapter 30 and the first verse of chapter 31. When he takes up his writing again, he is clearly ending his ministry. How long he took to compose his final thoughts is undisclosed. But this will be an old man, finishing his mortal warning to us.

2 NEPHI 31

2 Nephi 31:1

"And now I, Nephi, make an end of my prophesying unto you, my beloved brethren. And I cannot write but a few things, which I know must surely come to pass; neither can I write but a few of the words of my brother Jacob."

Don't make any mistakes, Nephi was a prophet. He knew he was a prophet. He also knew his testimony and explanations were indeed prophesy. So, in case you were wondering, here he removes any doubt. He is "making an end of my prophesying unto you." And he identifies "you" to mean his "beloved brethren." Who would that be? Could gentiles be included as his "beloved brethren?" What would a gentile have to do or be in order to qualify for that description? Then why aren't you doing that?

Why "cannot" he "write but a few things" further? Is there a limit put upon his prophecy for us?[760] Would he have liked to have said

---

[760] 1 Nephi 14:28 "And behold, I, Nephi, am forbidden that I should write the remainder of the things which I saw and heard; wherefore the things which I have written sufficeth me; and I have written but a small part of the things which I saw."

more? Does he assure us what he did write is true and complete as far as permitted to be written?[761]

What does it mean that he knows it "must surely come to pass?" How can he know that? What does it mean about the information we have in his record? How closely was the information given in conformity with what the Lord wanted him to reveal? How seriously should we take the record or prophecy of Nephi?

Why does Nephi refer again to his brother Jacob? What did Nephi and Jacob have in common in their faith and knowledge?[762] What does this imply about the validity of their testimony, their prophecy, their commission to deliver words of warning? What level of attention should their words attract from us? If we give them strict heed, will they lead us in the way of life and salvation?

As he ends his record, an aging and dying prophet whose journey began on another continent, is pleading to us to save ourselves. He has been such a significant source of faith in moments of despair, that when the Lord was reminding Joseph Smith of faith in troubled times, He drew directly from Nephi's life. Joseph was in Liberty Jail, abandoned by force of arms by his people, who had been evicted from Missouri. The governor had ordered the extermination of Mormons if they remained. Joseph's people had been killed, mobbed, evicted, driven in the snow from Missouri, their property pillaged, their women abused, and their houses burned. In a dungeon cell, Joseph was lamenting his plight. He felt abandoned by the

---

[761] 1 Nephi 14:30 "And now I make an end of speaking concerning the things which I saw while I was carried away in the spirit; and if all the things which I saw are not written, the things which I have written are true. And thus it is. Amen."

[762] 2 Nephi 11:2–3 "And now I, Nephi, write more of the words of Isaiah, for my soul delighteth in his words. For I will liken his words unto my people, and I will send them forth unto all my children, for he verily saw my Redeemer, even as I have seen him. And my brother, Jacob, also has seen him as I have seen him; wherefore, I will send their words forth unto my children to prove unto them that my words are true. Wherefore, by the words of three, God hath said, I will establish my word. Nevertheless, God sendeth more witnesses, and he proveth all his words."

Saints, and by God. As he pled for relief, the Lord told him to face adversity without complaint, because it would ultimately be for his good. When the Lord spoke and reminded Joseph of moments of despair over which faith and hope triumphed, he told Joseph:

". . . if the billowing surge conspire against thee; if fierce winds become thine enemy; if the heavens gather blackness, and all the elements combine to hedge up the way; and above all, if the very jaws of hell shall gape open the mouth wide after thee, know thou, my son, that all these things shall give thee experience, and shall be for thy good." (D&C 122:7)

One of the moments used was taken from Nephi's life.

"Wherefore, they knew not whither they should steer the ship, insomuch that there arose a great storm, yea, a great and terrible tempest, and we were driven back upon the waters for the space of three days; and they began to be frightened exceedingly lest they should be drowned in the sea; nevertheless they did not loose me. And on the fourth day, which we had been driven back, the tempest began to be exceedingly sore. And it came to pass that we were about to be swallowed up in the depths of the sea. And after we had been driven back upon the waters for the space of four days, my brethren began to see that the judgments of God were upon them, and that they must perish save that they should repent of their iniquities; wherefore, they came unto me, and loosed the bands which were upon my wrists, and behold they had swollen exceedingly; and also mine ankles were much swollen, and great was the soreness thereof. Nevertheless, I did look unto my God, and I did praise him all the day long; and I did not murmur against the Lord because of mine afflictions." (1 Nephi 18:13–16)

It was no accident that the 116 pages were lost, compelling the use of Nephi's full record to begin the Book of Mormon. It was a "wise purpose" indeed.[763] These words were always destined to come to us unabridged, from the hand of Nephi unaltered, translated by the gift and power of God into our language by Joseph Smith. Now they confront us, inform us, elevate us, warn us and deliver to us the means of obtaining the fullness of the Gospel of Jesus Christ.

2 Nephi 31:2

> "Wherefore, the things which I have written sufficeth me, save it be a few words which I must speak concerning the doctrine of Christ; wherefore, I shall speak unto you plainly, according to the plainness of my prophesying."

Nephi has been pondering for over four decades about the great revelations given to him in the Arabian Peninsula.[764] His creation of, and inscription on the plates were after these long deliberations and reflections.

When he says "the things which I have written sufficeth me," he is putting a punctuation mark on his plates. He is saying he has finished his ministry, finished his prophecy. He has refined and set out his message in a deliberate, careful way. These books of Nephi are not internet blogs undertaken daily. They are not rapid-fire responses, nor stream-of-consciousness statements. They were planned for the ages. Born from pondering, inspired by revelation, described as prophecy by the author, and filled with light and truth if considered with care by any reader. Nephi's pronouncement that they "sufficeth me" is a powerful statement by an aging prophet.

---

[763] Words of Mormon 1:6–7 "And it came to pass that I, being *eleven years old, was carried by my father into the land southward, even to the land of Zarahemla. The whole face of the land had become covered with buildings, and the people were as numerous almost, as it were the sand of the sea."

[764] 2 Nephi 4:16 "Behold, my soul delighteth in the things of the Lord; and my heart pondereth continually upon the things which I have seen and heard."
2 Nephi 5:34 "And it sufficeth me to say that *forty years had passed away, and we had already had wars and contentions with our brethren."

Years of preparation and reflection allow him to "speak plainly" to us. There's no need to be vague. No reason to hide our plight from us. He wants us to understand. When he attempts to "speak unto you plainly, according to the plainness of my prophesying," we read into it the wrong definitions, associate his words with others who will never read the book, and consider ourselves blessed and vindicated instead of condemned, and called to repentance. We do that a lot. What good is it to read things which tell you to be proud? Why follow a religion that tells you you've no reason to repent? Everyone but you is going to hell, right?[765] Because so long as you remain affiliated with the broad mainstream of your church, God will save you. And if there's any hint of error, He will beat you with a few stripes and all will be well. Nephi has already condemned that as an error, hasn't he?[766]

If his words were plain and intended to be taken at face value, why read into them justification for yourself and your sins? Why think they condemn everyone but you? Why are they speaking in disparaging terms about *those who will never have the book*? Why did Nephi write a book *condemning only those who will never read it*? Surely, if he was in fact "plain" in his meaning, then we ought not read anything into it other than what it says and how it says it. *It must be a message to us.*

---

[765] Alma 31:17–18 "But thou art the same yesterday, today, and forever; and thou hast elected us that we shall be saved, whilst all around us are elected to be cast by thy wrath down to hell; for the which holiness, O God, we thank thee; and we also thank thee that thou hast elected us, that we may not be led away after the foolish traditions of our brethren, which doth bind them down to a belief of Christ, which doth lead their hearts to wander far from thee, our God. And again we thank thee, O God, that we are a chosen and a holy people. Amen."

[766] 2 Nephi 28:8 "And there shall also be many which shall say: Eat, drink, and be merry; nevertheless, fear God—he will justify in committing a little sin; yea, lie a little, take the advantage of one because of his words, dig a pit for thy neighbor; there is no harm in this; and do all these things, for tomorrow we die; and if it so be that we are guilty, God will beat us with a few stripes, and at last we shall be saved in the kingdom of God."

If it is addressed to us, then we have more than one "wo" pronounced upon us by Nephi. We have been warned. We need to change what we are doing. The gentiles with whom we are identified[767] are collectively condemned. We need to separate ourselves by our behavior from theirs. We need to repent.

Now, just in case you think, as a recent comment has asserted, that the Lord has sent another message vindicating us as a collective gentile body/church in D&C 1:30,[768] I would remind you that revelation came from the Lord in 1831. In the following year the Lord gave another revelation that put the church under condemnation.[769] We know that condemnation was not lifted, because of comments by President Benson and Elder Oaks.

More troubling still is the Lord's threat to reject the gentile church altogether in January of 1841 if the church did not follow His strict appointment and complete building a temple in the time He

---

[767] D&C 109:60 "Now these words, O Lord, we have spoken before thee, concerning the revelations and commandments which thou hast given unto us, who are identified with the Gentiles."

[768] D&C 1:30 "And also those to whom these commandments were given, might have power to lay the foundation of this church, and to bring it forth out of obscurity and out of darkness, the only true and living church upon the face of the whole earth, with which I, the Lord, am well pleased, speaking unto the church collectively and not individually—"

[769] D&C 84:54–58 "And your minds in times past have been darkened because of unbelief, and because you have treated lightly the things you have received—Which vanity and unbelief have brought the whole church under condemnation. And this condemnation resteth upon the children of Zion, even all. And they shall remain under this condemnation until they repent and remember the new covenant, even the Book of Mormon and the former commandments which I have given them, not only to say, but to do according to that which I have written—That they may bring forth fruit meet for their Father's kingdom; otherwise there remaineth a scourge and judgment to be poured out upon the children of Zion."

provided.[770] The warning was given that even if the temple were built, we would still be condemned if we failed to do what He said.[771]

Did we keep the appointment given us? The Nauvoo Temple was not completed before Joseph Smith died. The endowment was not completed by Joseph, but Brigham Young was told he had to finish it.[772] Did we keep the appointment? Have we been able to avoid being rejected as a church? Have our covenants been fulfilled?

Why do we repeat endlessly the praise from 1831 but ignore the threatened rejection that came in 1841? From January of 1841, until Joseph's death in June of 1844, we had three and a half years to complete the Nauvoo Temple. Was that "sufficient time" to do what was required of us? If so, we did not complete it. Why was Joseph taken? Was that any indication about when the "sufficient time" expired? If so, what then? Where would that leave us?

Is our best hope to be found in the messages and warnings of the Book of Mormon? Can there be gentiles found who will believe its message? How carefully ought we study it?

Did you know the church had almost no use for the Book of Mormon until Hugh Nibley's efforts? (You know that if you've read *Eighteen Verses*.) Hugh Nibley, by his efforts beginning in the 1950's, practically discovered the Book of Mormon for the church. He's gone now.

---

[770] D&C 124:31–32 "But I command you, all ye my saints, to build a house unto me; and I grant unto you a sufficient time to build a house unto me; and during this time your baptisms shall be acceptable unto me. But behold, at the end of this appointment your baptisms for your dead shall not be acceptable unto me; and if you do not these things at the end of the appointment ye shall be rejected as a church, with your dead, saith the Lord your God."

[771] D&C 124:47–48 "And it shall come to pass that if you build a house unto my name, and do not do the things that I say, I will not perform the oath which I make unto you, neither fulfil the promises which ye expect at my hands, saith the Lord. For instead of blessings, ye, by your own works, bring cursings, wrath, indignation, and judgments upon your own heads, by your follies, and by all your abominations, which you practise before me, saith the Lord."

[772] See previous commentary on 1 Nephi 13:33–34.

Even though Moses was taken from ancient Israel, and with him the authority of the priesthood,[773] the ancient Israelites remained the Lord's people. He still worked through them and sent them messengers from time to time. These messengers were rarely the High Priest. Although in Samuel's case he displaced the High Priest.[774] They were sent from time to time. Their qualifications were private,

---

[773] D&C 84:25–26 "Therefore, he took Moses out of their midst, and the Holy Priesthood also; And the lesser priesthood continued, which priesthood holdeth the key of the ministering of angels and the preparatory gospel;"

[774] 1 Samuel 3:1–21 "And the child Samuel ministered unto the Lord before Eli. And the word of the Lord was precious in those days; *there was* no open vision. And it came to pass at that time, when Eli *was* laid down in his place, and his eyes began to wax dim, *that* he could not see; And ere the lamp of God went out in the temple of the Lord, where the ark of God *was,* and Samuel was laid down *to sleep;* That the Lord called Samuel: and he answered, Here *am* I. And he ran unto Eli, and said, Here *am* I; for thou calledst me. And he said, I called not; lie down again. And he went and lay down. And the Lord called yet again, Samuel. And Samuel arose and went to Eli, and said, Here *am* I; for thou didst call me. And he answered, I called not, my son; lie down again. Now Samuel did not yet know the Lord, neither was the word of the Lord yet revealed unto him. And the Lord called Samuel again the third time. And he arose and went to Eli, and said, Here *am* I; for thou didst call me. And Eli perceived that the Lord had called the child. Therefore Eli said unto Samuel, Go, lie down: and it shall be, if he call thee, that thou shalt say, Speak, Lord; for thy servant heareth. So Samuel went and lay down in his place. And the Lord came, and stood, and called as at other times, Samuel, Samuel. Then Samuel answered, Speak; for thy servant heareth. And the Lord said to Samuel, Behold, I will do a thing in Israel, at which both the ears of every one that heareth it shall tingle. In that day I will perform against Eli all *things* which I have spoken concerning his house: when I begin, I will also make an end. For I have told him that I will judge his house for ever for the iniquity which he knoweth; because his sons made themselves vile, and he restrained them not. And therefore I have sworn unto the house of Eli, that the iniquity of Eli's house shall not be purged with sacrifice nor offering for ever. And Samuel lay until the morning, and opened the doors of the house of the Lord. And Samuel feared to shew Eli the vision. Then Eli called Samuel, and said, Samuel, my son. And he answered, Here *am* I. And he said, What *is* the thing that *the Lord* hath said unto thee? I pray thee hide *it* not from me: God do so to thee, and more also, if thou hide *any* thing from me of all the things that he said unto thee. And Samuel told him every whit, and hid nothing from him. And he said, It *is* the Lord: let him do what seemeth him good. And Samuel grew, and the Lord was with him, and did let none of his words fall to the ground. And all Israel from Dan even to Beer-sheba knew that Samuel *was* established *to be* a prophet of the Lord. And the Lord appeared again in Shiloh: for the Lord revealed himself to Samuel in Shiloh by the word of the Lord."

as the Lord told Moses they would be.[775] I have no doubt Hugh Nibley was sent to us. If you've paid close attention, his departure has created an intellectual collapse at the center of the faith, with various egos contending to be noticed. They aspire to put upon them Hugh Nibley's mantle. They are not made of the same stuff, called with the same calling, nor endowed with the same capacities.

I doubt we'll see someone like him again. Perhaps we may someday see someone with an equally important message, but among those born in this dispensation, there is none to compare to Brother Nibley.

2 Nephi 31:3

"For my soul delighteth in plainness; for after this manner doth the Lord God work among the children of men. For the Lord God giveth light unto the understanding; for he speaketh unto men according to their language, unto their understanding."

This raises an interesting side issue. Nephi's explanation of how God speaks to different people "according to their language" is something worth explaining. We have a great example in the visit of John the Baptist to Joseph and Oliver found in JS–H 1:68–70 and

---

[775] Numbers 12:6 "And he said, Hear now my words: If there be a prophet among you, I the Lord will make myself known unto him in a vision, *and* will speak unto him in a dream."

Oliver's account in the footnote there[776]. The language they quote from John the Baptist is phrased differently by each of them, although both are quoting the angel. Angel's leave an impression. Notwithstanding Joseph Fielding Smith's teaching that memory from such things fade with time, my experience tells me quite the contrary. Such things are distinct and memorable. Often, if you need to hear a quote, the person who received it can quote word-for-word what they were told many years later; particularly when the quote is a declarative statement of what is to be or what is conferred. When, therefore, Joseph and Oliver give two different accounts of the quote, I understand this not to be a contradiction, but an example of the thing Nephi is referring to in this verse.

The communication of angels is not usually verbal in the traditional sense of verbal communication. That is, no air is being vibrated. Rather, the form the communication takes is for the angel to "speak" by delivering to the mind of the person spoken to the concept or declaration to be understood. Then the person, receiving the concept or declaration into their mind, is obliged to convert into words the message received. If the vocabulary of the recipient is German, they will use German to reduce the message to words. If English, they will use English. If their vocabulary is rich and complex, the words may be more exact. If their vocabulary is simple, the words may be simple.

---

[776] JS–H 1:68–70 "We still continued the work of translation, when, in the ensuing month (May, 1829), we on a certain day went into the woods to pray and inquire of the Lord respecting baptism for the remission of sins, that we found mentioned in the translation of the plates. While we were thus employed, praying and calling upon the Lord, a messenger from heaven descended in a cloud of light, and having laid his hands upon us, he ordained us, saying: *Upon you my fellow servants, in the name of Messiah, I confer the Priesthood of Aaron, which holds the keys of the ministering of angels, and of the gospel of repentance, and of baptism by immersion for the remission of sins; and this shall never be taken again from the earth until the sons of Levi do offer again an offering unto the Lord in righteousness.* He said this Aaronic Priesthood had not the power of laying on hands for the gift of the Holy Ghost, but that this should be conferred on us hereafter; and he commanded us to go and be baptized, and gave us directions that I should baptize Oliver Cowdery, and that afterwards he should baptize me."

However one comes into the presence of God or His angelic ministers, once there, the thoughts that come to the person will conform to their understanding, their vocabulary, their manner of phrasing. The underlying purpose is always the same: to make the communication plain to the understanding of the person visited.

It is also true that the Lord "giveth light unto the understanding" and does so according to the heed and diligence we give to what we have already received.[777] We cannot understand some things even if they are explained to us if we do not have the necessary light to permit that understanding. Light and truth attract one another.

When we approach God, we do so by degrees not merely by study. We find ourselves gaining light that quickens our understanding. What we cannot understand at first, gains clarity only after a period of living true to the things we already have.

The commandments are not something we follow to please God, but something we do to understand God. Living true to what we believe He expects of us, allows us to gain an appreciation for what kind of Being He truly is. In that sense, the commandments are not so much burdens to bear, but revelations to understand.

The greatest understanding, of course, does not lie in strict conformity to the letter of any law or commandment, but the insight obtained from the underlying principle you discover as you follow it. Commandments should soften or break your heart, not harden it. When a commandment hardens the heart of the follower, they have misunderstood the commandment altogether. This was the case with

---

[777] Alma 12:9 "And now Alma began to expound these things unto him, saying: It is given unto many to know the mysteries of God; nevertheless they are laid under a strict command that they shall not impart only according to the portion of his word which he doth grant unto the children of men, according to the heed and diligence which they give unto him.

D&C 50:24 "That which is of God is light; and he that receiveth light, and continueth in God, receiveth more light; and that light groweth brighter and brighter until the perfect day."

the accusers of Christ, who followed the underlying intent with perfection, while breaking the superficial requirements regularly.

None of it will become "plain" to the follower until they have done and understood what the commandments were attempting to reveal to them. When, however, you encounter a Nephi, you have someone who now sees the issues plainly. It was meant for us all to see them plainly.

2 Nephi 31:4

> "Wherefore, I would that ye should remember that I have spoken unto you concerning that prophet which the Lord showed unto me, that should baptize the Lamb of God, which should take away the sins of the world."

This puts us back into the narrative Nephi wrote much earlier in his first book. He described this in 1 Nephi.[778] Although the Lord's mortal ministry was future, and separated by more than half-a-millennium, Nephi witnessed it. The Lord is able to make witnesses of His mortal ministry even of someone who lived at another time and place, as He has done with Nephi.

During that vision, Nephi saw more than the Lord's mortal ministry. He was shown the entire history of the world through the end of time. However, Nephi was only permitted to bear selective testimony of what he saw. Others were given responsibility for testifying to portions of what Nephi saw, but was not permitted to record. He saw it all. He was to record only some of what he saw. He was told at a certain point that the responsibility for recording it became John

---

[778] 1 Nephi 11:27 "And I looked and beheld the Redeemer of the world, of whom my father had spoken; and I also beheld the prophet who should prepare the way before him. And the Lamb of God went forth and was baptized of him; and after he was baptized, I beheld the heavens open, and the Holy Ghost come down out of heaven and abide upon him in the form of a dove."

the Beloved's and not Nephi's.[779] Nephi saw it, John the Beloved saw it, and others, including Isaiah, also saw it.[780] I've explained this in *Nephi's Isaiah*.

Here Nephi returns to the Lord's baptism to begin an explanation of "the doctrine of Christ"[781] so that Nephi's testimony refocuses the reader on the path required for salvation. Since Nephi's primary reason for writing is to save others, he cannot finish without a final direct appeal for all to understand the "doctrine of Christ."

What is the difference between "the doctrine of Christ" and the "Gospel of Jesus Christ?" How do they relate to one another?

Here Nephi has linked together four distinct thoughts: First he has 1) already described the prophet which 2) the Lord had shown to Nephi. This was the earlier vision described above. That prophet 3)

---

[779] 1 Nephi 14:19–28 "And I looked and beheld a man, and he was dressed in a white robe. And the angel said unto me: Behold one of the twelve apostles of the Lamb. Behold, he shall see and write the remainder of these things; yea, and also many things which have been. And he shall also write concerning the end of the world. Wherefore, the things which he shall write are just and true; and behold they are written in the book which thou beheld proceeding out of the mouth of the Jew; and at the time they proceeded out of the mouth of the Jew, or, at the time the book proceeded out of the mouth of the Jew, the things which were written were plain and pure, and most precious and easy to the understanding of all men. And behold, the things which this apostle of the Lamb shall write are many things which thou hast seen; and behold, the remainder shalt thou see. But the things which thou shalt see hereafter thou shalt not write; for the Lord God hath ordained the apostle of the Lamb of God that he should write them. And also others who have been, to them hath he shown all things, and they have written them; and they are sealed up to come forth in their purity, according to the truth which is in the Lamb, in the own due time of the Lord, unto the house of Israel. And I, Nephi, heard and bear record, that the name of the apostle of the Lamb was John, according to the word of the angel. And behold, I, Nephi, am forbidden that I should write the remainder of the things which I saw and heard; wherefore the things which I have written sufficeth me; and I have written but a small part of the things which I saw."

[780] 1 Nephi 14:26 "And also others who have been, to them hath he shown all things, and they have written them; and they are sealed up to come forth in their purity, according to the truth which is in the Lamb, in the own due time of the Lord, unto the house of Israel."

[781] 2 Nephi 31:2 "Wherefore, the things which I have written sufficeth me, save it be a few words which I must speak concerning the doctrine of Christ; wherefore, I shall speak unto you plainly, according to the plainness of my prophesying."

should baptize the Lamb of God during the Lord's mortal ministry. The Lord, who is the Lamb of God 4) should take away the sins of the world.

This is a specific time and setting. It involves a specific event and two persons: John the Baptist and Jesus Christ. Nephi has seen the event, and reminds us of it as a baseline from which to reconstruct the "doctrine of Christ."

Remember that the Jews who confronted John the Baptist did not ask him what ordinance he was performing. They did not ask why he was performing the ordinance. They only asked what authority permitted him to be performing an ordinance which they already understood and undoubtedly already practiced. Why would John baptize if he were not Christ, or Elias (in that context meaning Elijah), or another returning prophet who already had the authority.[782] The inquisitors already understood the ordinance.

Baptism was a pre-Christian ordinance. Because of historic interests which conflict with one another, both the Jews and the Christians downplay or ignore that truth.

Look at the wording above and ask yourself: Why, when the vision is shown to Nephi, is Christ identified as "the Lord?" Then, when Nephi beholds His baptism, why does he refer to Christ as "the Lamb of God?" The same person, at first identified as "the Lord," and then identified as "the Lamb of God." Why these two

---

[782] John 1:19–28 "And this is the record of John, when the Jews sent priests and Levites from Jerusalem to ask him, Who art thou? And he confessed, and denied not; but confessed, I am not the Christ. And they asked him, What then? Art thou Elias? And he saith, I am not. Art thou that prophet? And he answered, No. Then said they unto him, Who art thou? that we may give an answer to them that sent us. What sayest thou of thyself? He said, I *am* the voice of one crying in the wilderness, Make straight the way of the Lord, as said the prophet Esaias. And they which were sent were of the Pharisees. And they asked him, and said unto him, Why baptizest thou then, if thou be not that Christ, nor Elias, neither that prophet? John answered them, saying, I baptize with water: but there standeth one among you, whom ye know not; He it is, who coming after me is preferred before me, whose shoe's latchet I am not worthy to unloose. These things were done in Bethabara beyond Jordan, where John was baptizing."

identities? Why would it be so clear to Nephi that the Lord holds these two identities that he would use them in this single verse to make Christ's identity and deeds clear to the reader? How do the different names/titles help us to better understand Christ?

Why is a pre-Christian prophet commissioned to know and write about these things? Why would the Nephite descendants from the time of this writing through the time of Moroni all be entitled to know about this event? What importance is it for us to understand this about Christ?

Well, let's push further into the "doctrine of Christ" to see what it may persuade us to do or believe.

2 Nephi 31:5

> "And now, if the Lamb of God, he being holy, should have need to be baptized by water, to fulfill all righteousness, O then, how much more need have we, being unholy, to be baptized, yea, even by water!"

This is a missionary proof text, used to persuade everyone to get baptized. They used it on me. It worked. I got baptized.

How undeniably essential is baptism as a result of this argument? Does it seem to you that if Christ Himself needed to be baptized that without it it would not be possible for anyone to please God? If Christ needed it, then undoubtedly all of Christ's inferiors need it as well. The only exception seems to be those children who are not accountable, and for whom Christ's atonement will be applied because of the justice and mercy applied to such unaccountable young souls.[783] They need no baptism. But all of us do. Without it we have no hope for redemption.

It is indisputable from this verse that baptism is essential. But the question remains "why?" Why would this ordinance be required for residing in God's presence in the eternal worlds? We know, of course, that all such matters were ordained before the foundation of the world, and cannot be changed now.[784] But that does not answer the question of "why?"

Have you ever inquired to know why? It is not answered in scripture. It is only implied. Sometimes the best place to look for an answer is to go back to the beginning. Reading the account of Adam's baptism (who was the first to receive the ordinance in mortality) we find a few things. By the water we keep the commandment.[785] The first man was taken by the Spirit and baptized, put under the water and brought forth out of the water again.[786] After he had been buried in the water and brought forth again, he was told he had been

---

[783] Moroni 8:20–22 "And he that saith that little children need baptism denieth the mercies of Christ, and setteth at naught the atonement of him and the power of his redemption. Wo unto such, for they are in danger of death, hell, and an endless torment. I speak it boldly; God hath commanded me. Listen unto them and give heed, or they stand against you at the judgment-seat of Christ. For behold that all little children are alive in Christ, and also all they that are without the law. For the power of redemption cometh on all them that have no law; wherefore, he that is not condemned, or he that is under no condemnation, cannot repent; and unto such baptism availeth nothing—"

[784] D&C 130:20–21 "There is a law, irrevocably decreed in heaven before the foundations of this world, upon which all blessings are predicated—And when we obtain any blessing from God, it is by obedience to that law upon which it is predicated."

[785] Moses 6:60 "For by the water ye keep the commandment; by the Spirit ye are justified, and by the blood ye are sanctified;"

[786] Moses 6:64 "And it came to pass, when the Lord had spoken with Adam, our father, that Adam cried unto the Lord, and he was caught away by the Spirit of the Lord, and was carried down into the water, and was laid under the water, and was brought forth out of the water."

born again of the Spirit.[787] Before any of the ordinance happened, however, Adam was told this:

> "behold, all things have their likeness, and all things are created and made to bear record of me, both things which are temporal, and things which are spiritual; things which are in the heavens above, and things which are on the earth, and things which are in the earth, and things which are under the earth, both above and beneath: all things bear record of me." (Moses 6:63)

Did you catch that?

Just before Adam's baptism the Lord explains to Adam that the reason for "all things" being as they are is "to bear record of me [meaning Christ]." Baptism is designed to bear testimony of Christ. How so? In what way does baptism tell us about Christ?

Christ died, was buried, and on the third day arose from the dead.[788] He said He would do that before His crucifixion.[789] His disciples did not understand this prophecy.[790]

Baptism is a reenactment of Christ's death and resurrection. Once you have been placed under the water you are cut off from the breath of life. If you remain under the water for too long, you will die. While there, you are only able to survive by holding your breath. You retain the power to live, if you return to the surface soon enough, but your life is dependent upon the one performing the ordinance.

---

[787] Moses 6:65 "And thus he was baptized, and the Spirit of God descended upon him, and thus he was born of the Spirit, and became quickened in the inner man."

[788] D&C 20:23 "He was crucified, died, and rose again the third day;"

[789] Mark 8:31 "And he began to teach them, that the Son of man must suffer many things, and be rejected of the elders, and of the chief priests, and scribes, and be killed, and after three days rise again."
Luke 18:33 "And they shall scourge *him,* and put him to death: and the third day he shall rise again."

[790] Luke 18:34 "And they understood none of these things: and this saying was hid from them, neither knew they the things which were spoken."

They must lift you back to return you to life. Just as Christ needed the power of His Father, we also need the power of the officiator to raise us back to life. It is as if the life of Christ has been beautifully choreographed. Christ was sent to lay down His life and take it up again. That is what He did. As Joseph Smith explained in the King Follett Discourse: "The scriptures inform us that Jesus said, as the Father hath power in himself, even so hath the Son power—to do what? Why, what the Father did. The answer is obvious—in a manner to lay down his body and take it up again. Jesus, what are you going to do? To lay down my life as my Father did, and take it up again. Do you believe it? If you do not believe it you do not believe the Bible. The scriptures say it, and I defy all the learning and wisdom and all the combined powers of earth and hell together to refute it. Here, then, is eternal life—to know the only wise and true God; and you have got to learn how to be gods yourselves, and to be kings and priests to God, the same as all gods have done before you, namely, by going from one small degree to another, and from a small capacity to a great one; from grace to grace, from exaltation to exaltation, until you attain to the resurrection of the dead, and are able to dwell in everlasting burnings, and to sit in glory, as do those who sit enthroned in everlasting power."

First we receive an ordinance which shows us the way by symbols. We are shown the way back to redemption and resurrection, but must see it with the eyes of faith, before we behold it as it truly is.[791] If we are to rise from the dead and have eternal life in Christ, we must first enact that event through the ordinance which points to the reality of our future rise from the dead.

---

[791] Ether 12:19 "And there were many whose faith was so exceedingly strong, even before Christ came, who could not be kept from within the veil, but truly saw with their eyes the things which they had beheld with an eye of faith, and they were glad."

Ordinances are the preliminary act, designed to bear testimony of the real event. They are not the real thing, but a "type" of the real thing. They must be seen through the eyes of faith[792] to allow us to gain the faith necessary to obtain the real thing. Before you are resurrected in a whole, complete, and glorified fashion you must first voluntarily agree to enact that future event, looking forward in faith to that future day. Before you enter into the Lord's presence, you must first enact that in the Temple, looking forward in faith to that future day.

All things point to Christ. However, only those who have the faith to see within them the underlying reality with the "eyes of faith" will obtain to the final promises and covenants intended for all of us to obtain.

2 Nephi 31:6–7

"And now, I would ask of you, my beloved brethren, wherein the Lamb of God did fulfill all righteousness in being baptized by water? Know ye not that he was holy? But notwithstanding he being holy, he showeth unto the children of men that, according to the flesh he humbleth himself before the Father, and witnesseth unto the Father that he would be obedient unto him in keeping his commandments."

Although Christ was the one mortal upon whom death could make no claim (He being holy), He nonetheless obeyed the same conditions as everyone else. Notwithstanding His holiness, His right to face judgment and not be condemned, He set the example. No one else could face the judgment and pass. Therefore, everyone other than Him would require baptism for repentance and remission of their sins. He did not. He determined to obey anyway so everyone could see the strait path by which they can obtain hope.

---

[792] Ibid.

He was flesh. He was mortal. He could (and did) die. Though death could not claim Him, He was to die. Baptism is the great symbol of death and resurrection, and He is the resurrection. He lived the symbol as well as the reality, so all others could have part in that victory. The symbol to point the way. The reality to open the way. We are in turn "shown the way" by what He did.

He also "witnesses" before "the Father that he would be obedient unto Him."

Think about the command of understanding Nephi is exhibiting here. He is telling us that Christ's mortal ministry would include these very specific events for these very specific reasons. This was what he was permitted to tell us. What other information was within his knowledge which he was forbidden from sharing? Does this level of understanding by Nephi tell you something about what can be learned from the Lord if you are diligent in following His path? Why, if you can see what may be available, would you not be willing to do whatever is asked of you in order to receive something similar in your own life?

Well, the foundation of the "doctrine of Christ" begins by seeing Christ's example, learning of the necessity of baptism and obedience to the will of God. That is where everyone must begin. If you start right, you are likely to continue in the right way. But if you do not begin aright, then you are not likely to have any ability to return and find the right way. You cannot enter in by some other way. If you enter in the right way, you will begin to recognize the True Shepherd's voice.[793] This is the beginning. It is as important to the doctrine of Christ as all that will follow.

2 Nephi 31:8–9

> "Wherefore, after he was baptized with water the Holy Ghost descended upon him in the form of a dove. And again, it showeth unto the children of men the straitness of the path, and the narrowness of the gate, by which they should enter, he having set the example before them."

This is an interesting cause-and-effect. Once Christ was baptized, "the Holy Ghost descended upon Him" as a result of the baptism. Now, true enough an ordinance was instituted by which hands are laid upon a person, post-baptism, where the "gift of the Holy Ghost" is bestowed. This practice was instituted by Christ.[794] However, in the case of Christ's own baptism, no hands were put upon Him. He was baptized. The Holy Ghost descended upon Him.

It is clear that baptism is a gate through which all must pass. Immediately after the ordinance, the Holy Ghost must become the companion of those who are redeemed.

Christ set the example. We are obligated to follow the example.

Receiving baptism without also receiving the Spirit renders the event incomplete. Nephi will explain the essential nature of the Holy

---

[793] John 10:1–5 "Verily, verily, I say unto you, He that entereth not by the door into the sheepfold, but climbeth up some other way, the same is a thief and a robber. But he that entereth in by the door is the shepherd of the sheep. To him the porter openeth; and the sheep hear his voice: and he calleth his own sheep by name, and leadeth them out. And when he putteth forth his own sheep, he goeth before them, and the sheep follow him: for they know his voice. And a stranger will they not follow, but will flee from him: for they know not the voice of strangers."

[794] Acts 8:14–17 "Now when the apostles which were at Jerusalem heard that Samaria had received the word of God, they sent unto them Peter and John: Who, when they were come down, prayed for them, that they might receive the Holy Ghost: (For as yet he was fallen upon none of them: only they were baptized in the name of the Lord Jesus.) Then laid they *their* hands on them, and they received the Holy Ghost."

Ghost in the redemption process in a few more verses. It is clear that the Holy Ghost is the instrumentality by which redemption itself comes. The Spirit is the guide which will lead back to the Lord's presence. Without the guide, the doctrine of Christ is incomplete.

The water is something that we must pass through to keep the law. It is the companionship of the Spirit which makes you justified, by leading you to do what is right. It is the resulting application of Christ's blood on your behalf that will sanctify you.[795] You cannot receive sanctification without first receiving baptism and then also the Holy Ghost.

If there is no other way, and all must comply, then the way is both "strait" and "narrow."

Christ's example is the only one for us to follow to obtain hope for our own salvation. He is the "prototype of the saved man" (Lecture 7, *Lectures on Faith*, paragraph 9). If it was necessary for Him, it is the more necessary for us.

Baptism is one thing, accepting the Holy Ghost is another. The one is objective, and openly visible when the act happens. The other is internal, involving welcoming a member of the Godhead into your life.

I remember kneeling on an Atlantic beach in the cool sand at the setting of the sun on the day of my baptism. The Atlantic is cold in September, and I was chilled from the ordinance, still wet while kneeling, and shivering as the elders began the ordinance. When, however, they said: "receive the Holy Ghost" I remember becoming warm, beginning at my scalp and flowing downward until my entire body was warm and calm. It was palpable. It was physical. To me the experience was no less dramatic than the descent of the Holy Ghost "in the form of a dove" on the day of Christ's baptism. It was every

---

[795] Moses 6:60 "For by the water ye keep the commandment; by the Spirit ye are justified, and by the blood ye are sanctified;"

bit as objective, as physical and as memorable as any other distinct event in my life.

More importantly, I began to experience the fruits of that event immediately. What followed for me, within the hour of my baptism, was akin to what Joseph and Oliver experienced.[796] Within days I found also that the scriptures began to have far more distinct and clear meaning than ever before, again just as Joseph and Oliver found.[797]

It was clear to me that the Holy Ghost imparts something altogether more significant than what I alone could do, understand, or accomplish. It expanded capacity, enlightened and informed the mind, and led to understanding things which were unknown and unknowable before.

This process is not just mandatory. It is a far superior way to experience life than to live alone, without God in the world.[798] It is a blessing, a gift. The "gift of the Holy Ghost" is, without question, the great "gift" coming from God to aid us in our return to Him.

---

[796] JS–H 1:73 "Immediately on our coming up out of the water after we had been baptized, we experienced great and glorious blessings from our Heavenly Father. No sooner had I baptized Oliver Cowdery, than the Holy Ghost fell upon him, and he stood up and prophesied many things which should shortly come to pass. And again, so soon as I had been baptized by him, I also had the spirit of prophecy, when, standing up, I prophesied concerning the rise of this Church, and many other things connected with the Church, and this generation of the children of men. We were filled with the Holy Ghost, and rejoiced in the God of our salvation."

[797] JS–H 1:74 "Our minds being now enlightened, we began to have the scriptures laid open to our understandings, and the true meaning and intention of their more mysterious passages revealed unto us in a manner which we never could attain to previously, nor ever before had thought of. In the meantime we were forced to keep secret the circumstances of having received the Priesthood and our having been baptized, owing to a spirit of persecution which had already manifested itself in the neighborhood."

[798] Alma 41:11 "And now, my son, all men that are in a state of nature, or I would say, in a carnal state, are in the gall of bitterness and in the bonds of iniquity; they are without God in the world, and they have gone contrary to the nature of God; therefore, they are in a state contrary to the nature of happiness."

2 Nephi 31:10–11

"And he said unto the children of men: Follow thou me. Wherefore, my beloved brethren, can we follow Jesus save we shall be willing to keep the commandments of the Father? And the Father said: Repent ye, repent ye, and be baptized in the name of my Beloved Son."

Notice the "prophetic-perfect" tense, where Nephi speaks of the Lord's future conduct as if it were in the past. This is what happens when a prophet speaks in prophecy. To the prophet, the events are in the past because he was shown it *before* writing it. Although the event has not occurred yet, the prophet remembers it in his mind and to him it is a past event.

This "remembering" the future makes the mind of the prophet akin to the mind of God.

Nephi again addresses his "beloved brethren" in this plea. Can we "follow Jesus" and not keep commandments? Is "be willing to keep the commandments" the same as "keeping the commandments?" Are all commandments to be kept? What about those that create conflict? How did Christ resolve the conflict between the commandment to do good and honor God on the Sabbath, with the commandment to do no work on the Sabbath? Are some commandments objective and without conflict (like baptism) while others may conflict with each other? Can you keep them all? Do you think you even know them all? How do you resolve conflicts? How do you make up for the wrongs you do in ignorance?[799]

Notice the quote Nephi reports from "the Father." Again, Nephi is telling us something about his associations. He says the Father has stated: "Repent ye, repent ye, and be baptized in the name of my

---

[799] Mosiah 3:11 "For behold, and also his blood atoneth for the sins of those who have fallen by the transgression of Adam, who have died not knowing the will of God concerning them, or who have ignorantly sinned."

Beloved Son." You can search all the scriptures and you will find this quote appears in this one place. Nephi is quoting the Father. Where did Nephi get the quote from if it does not otherwise appear in scripture?

What does that tell you about Nephi? What does it tell you about the Father's view of baptism? What does it tell you about the actions of Christ and the will of the Father? Why does the Father refer to Christ as "my Beloved Son" while speaking of baptism?

With what emotion does the Father express Himself about Christ? Does that emotion attach to any of those who do as Christ did? Does it please the Father when we are baptized? Why?

What is God's work?[800] How does baptism relate to this work? How do we "follow Christ" without seeking to do everything He did? Can we do all He did? Why did Joseph say we must go from one exaltation to another? What does Joseph refer to when he explained: "you have got to learn how to be gods yourselves, and to be kings and priests to God, the same as all gods have done before you, namely, by going from one small degree to another, and from a small capacity to a great one; from grace to grace, from exaltation to exaltation, until you attain to the resurrection of the dead, and are able to dwell in everlasting burnings, and to sit in glory, as do those who sit enthroned in everlasting power." (King Follett Discourse.) This was long after Joseph received the Vision of the Three Degrees of Glory found in Section 76. Section 76 was received February 16, 1832 while the King Follett Discourse was given April 7, 1844. Remember that all of what was seen in the vision was not recorded by Joseph: "But great and marvelous are the works of the Lord, and the mysteries of his kingdom which he showed unto us, which surpass all understanding in glory, and in might, and in dominion; Which he commanded

---

800 Moses 1:39 "For behold, this is my work and my glory—to bring to pass the immortality and eternal life of man."

us we should not write while we were yet in the Spirit, and are not lawful for man to utter."[801] Why would some things be known to a prophet but "not lawful" for him to reveal to others?

What does the idea of "following Christ" imply, if it were taken to its fullest extent? Why would that require someone to go "from one small degree to another?" What would be involved for someone to pass "from exaltation to exaltation," as Joseph mentions in this discourse in April 1844? How fully must we follow Christ?

If it is God's work to bring to pass immortality and eternal life for His children, then must God work out salvation for His children to confer upon them immortality and eternal life? If another becomes "like God" will they undertake the same work? Will it require the same price to be paid? Is there another way?

2 Nephi 31:12

"And also, the voice of the Son came unto me, saying: He that is baptized in my name, to him will the Father give the Holy Ghost, like unto me; wherefore, follow me, and do the things which ye have seen me do."

Notice that immediately following the quote from the Father, Nephi adds a quote from the Son. Here Nephi makes it clear that the Father said to Nephi what is quoted in verse 11, because he adds, "And also, the voice of the Son came unto me, saying . . . " As soon as the Father stopped speaking, the Son added the comment he now quotes.

This contradicts what is an often referred to Mormon legend. Our legend is that the Father does nothing other than introduce the Son.

---

[801] D&C 76:114–115 "But great and marvelous are the works of the Lord, and the mysteries of his kingdom which he showed unto us, which surpass all understanding in glory, and in might, and in dominion; Which he commanded us we should not write while we were yet in the Spirit, and are not lawful for man to utter;"

This comes from a misreading of the Joseph Smith Translation of John 1:18. This verse is rendered in the JKV as follows:

> "No man hath seen God at any time; the only begotten Son, which is in the bosom of the Father, he hath declared him."

In the JST it is changed to read:

> "No man hath seen God at any time except he hath borne record of the Son; the only begotten Son, which is in the bosom of the Father, he hath declared him."

This is the basis for asserting the Father doesn't ever speak, apart from introducing and bearing testimony of the Son. It is clearly a false notion, however, as the Father has many quoted words in the Book of Mormon. The fact the myth exists is, once again, evidence of how little we have as a people studied the Book of Mormon.

Well, returning to this verse, we find that the promise of the Holy Ghost is made by the Father! That is, Christ is saying when the Holy Ghost is sent, it is a gift from "the Father." Indeed it is! The Father of our spirits[802] has given us all that spirit which dwells within us.[803]

First the Father tells us to be baptized and follow Christ. Then Christ adds to it the plea: If you do that you will receive the Holy Ghost as a gift from the Father. So "follow me, and do the things which ye have seen me do."

How seamless the will of the Father is with the desire of His Son!

How eager are both the Father and the Son for us to come to them!

---

[802] Hebrews 12:9 "Furthermore we have had fathers of our flesh which corrected *us*, and we gave *them* reverence: shall we not much rather be in subjection unto the Father of spirits, and live?"

[803] D&C 130:22 "The Father has a body of flesh and bones as tangible as man's; the Son also; but the Holy Ghost has not a body of flesh and bones, but is a personage of Spirit. Were it not so, the Holy Ghost could not dwell in us."

How consistent is the message we receive from both the Father and the Son!

There is no other record in all scripture that puts together the promises of the Father and the plea of the Son like Nephi has done here!

How great a prophet was Nephi! How trusted and familiar must he have been with both the Father and the Son to be able to deliver this message to us!

Let it sink in. Let it be understood. Then, realize Nephi was a man just like you and I. He suffered, toiled, was rejected, fled and worked in obscurity to follow God against the active opposition of his own brothers. His knowledge and experiences are open to all. If you have not realized before, now you should realize why Nephi forms the bedrock example in *The Second Comforter* to lay out the process of returning to God's presence. Among prophets, Nephi was a pillar of light, whose understanding reached into heaven itself.

Perhaps we should have been giving him more attention for the last 180 years. Well, it's not too late for you to begin to do so now.

2 Nephi 31:13

"Wherefore, my beloved brethren, I know that if ye shall follow the Son, with full purpose of heart, acting no hypocrisy and no deception before God, but with real intent, repenting of your sins, witnessing unto the Father that ye are willing to take upon you the name of Christ, by baptism—yea, by following your Lord and your Savior down into the water, according to his word, behold, then shall ye receive the Holy Ghost; yea, then cometh the baptism of fire and of the Holy Ghost; and then can ye speak with the tongue of angels, and shout praises unto the Holy One of Israel."

Now we get the explanation of what it means to "follow Christ." It is not merely the act itself, but the underlying intent of the act. To follow Him requires:

- Full purpose of heart. What does that imply or require?
- Acting no hypocrisy. How so?
- No deception before God. Can a man deceive God?
- Real intent. What does "real intent" include?
- Repenting of your sins. How does one repent of their sins?
- Witnessing unto the Father: How do you witness to Him?
- Willing to take upon you the name of Christ. How?

The only way I can think to touch upon Nephi's meaning is to get personal about this process. It is by how I have lived that I have come to understand Nephi's meaning.

I remember as the missionaries were teaching me that I came to the conviction that the restoration of the Gospel had indeed happened. It was not a happy thought. I did *not* want to become a Mormon. It seemed like a terrible change to attempt to make, in what was an otherwise content life at the time. As a lifestyle some of it seemed to have merit. Not drinking, smoking and living a higher moral standard certainly made some sense to me. But the association with Mormons had no appeal to me at the time. I thought them shallow and artificial in many ways, and did not want to become immersed in a society that seemed to be either a pretense, or if not, then living a standard I could never attain.

I reluctantly accepted baptism, not because I wanted to become Mormon, but because I truly believed it was the restored Gospel of Jesus Christ. However humiliating it may be to associate with a social group I had practically nothing in common, it was the right thing to do before God. I told God that I was doing this because of Him, and that I doubted I could live these standards, doubted I could be happy among these odd people, that I did not know if they were really sincere, but that I was. I intended to try to leave such sins behind as I understood I was committing, and to attempt to become part of the artificial life-form known as "Mormon." But I doubted my capacity to continue on to the end. In all this I was absolutely sincere, but completely hopeless about what it would result in over the long run.

I was, in fact, willing to take upon me these obligations as a matter between me and God. However badly it may turn out between me and other Mormons, I expected that as between me and God it would be better than alright. I thought it would please Him.

So I was baptized.

Oddly, upon baptism things changed. A great deal, in fact. What seemed unlikely for me to be able to do under my own capacity, became almost second-nature. These people who I feared I could never fit in with became my brothers and sisters. It took a surprisingly short time and I found that what I feared most was the lightest of burdens to carry. Associating with other Mormons was delightful. I found that I loved the Mormons and I loved being one of them. It ceased to be "them" and "me" but turned into "us" and "we."

And, by damn, we are a peculiar lot. We're the oddest people on the planet. Peculiar doesn't even begin to capture our quirkiness, phobias, longings, hopes, aspirations, misunderstandings, convictions, genius mixed with stupidity, juxtapositions of truth and error, traditions and deep doctrines. We're a cacophony, really. But underlying it all is a hope that we are on the right track and a conviction that we're going to please God even if it requires us to offend Him.

I appreciate the faith restored through Joseph at a whole different level than the one which brought me into the fold. It IS true. Abidingly and without any failing, the faith restored through Joseph is the Gospel of Jesus Christ.

The sad truth is, however, that faith has not been preserved as Joseph brought it back. Even from the time I was baptized in the waning four months of President Lee's administration until today, the faith has undergone a radical revisionism. Today it isn't even what President Kimball presided over. It is becoming increasingly altered, bureaucratized, regimented and turning into a religious product managed by an increasingly menacing middle-management which prefers rules and regulations to the Spirit and truth. They manage it as if it is another Fortune 500 company whose product line is religion and religious paraphernalia. The Spirit increasingly withdraws from our councils, our conferences, our private as well as public conversations, because it is grieved, and not many people seem to notice as it does so.

The faith I joined still exists. But it is covered by layers of sediment making it progressively more difficult to breathe life into it. That original faith, the one that attracted me, was always meant to connect the believer to Christ. Directly, and without intermediaries. Each Saint was to be a prophet, because the testimony of Jesus is the spirit of prophecy, according to John the Beloved.

But I began this process "acting no hypocrisy" and I will finish it remaining so. My "real intent" is before God, and the resistance, opposition and criticism of men will not alter that. Indeed, it cannot. As soon as I respect the opinions of men more than the "full purpose of heart" required of me, I cease to be "willing to take upon me the name of Christ."

I understand Nephi's words. I live them. I cannot do otherwise at this point. It is for that reason, therefore, that I have been privileged to receive "the baptism of fire and of the Holy Ghost;" which has permitted me from time to time to "speak with the tongue of angels, and shout praises unto the Holy One of Israel." It has not been easy. It is certainly not what I wanted when missionaries interrupted a content life, and introduced this inconvenient faith to a reluctant 19-

year-old. It was not what I expected when the journey began before baptism, nor what I thought would then follow immediately after I was baptized. I find now, as I survey the altered and altering faith practiced by the Church I belong to, there are increasingly more troubles in living and acting with:

- Full purpose of heart
- Acting no hypocrisy
- No deception before God
- Real intent
- Repenting of my sins
- Witnessing unto the Father
- Willing to take upon me the name of Christ

But that will always remain a matter between the Father, the Lord and myself. Nephi lived these things, too. It was for that reason he understood them and was able to set them out with clarity in writing. Light and truth, which is intelligence, only come as a consequence of living it.

I will never stop being Mormon, nor forsake the faith I have accepted. I love associating with the Saints. I'm also glad to not be a part of leadership. I wouldn't want the condemnation that accompanies leading these people in the course that we are currently set. It is better to practice the faith as I understand it, explain it to those who care to listen, support those who try to keep my ward family at peace with one another, and raise my children to respect the light and truth.

I am content. More than content, I am filled with joy and hope for what lies ahead for myself and all those who have the testimony of Jesus.

2 Nephi 31:14

"But, behold, my beloved brethren, thus came the voice of
the Son unto me, saying: After ye have repented of your sins,
and witnessed unto the Father that ye are willing to keep my
commandments, by the baptism of water, and have received
the baptism of fire and of the Holy Ghost, and can speak
with a new tongue, yea, even with the tongue of angels, and
after this should deny me, it would have been better for you
that ye had not known me."

Nephi first gave us his personal testimony and witness of the
principles. Having done so, now he adds the testimony and promise
of Christ. Christ's promise and covenant are slightly different than
Nephi's formula. But the two are nevertheless in complete harmony.

The "voice of the Son" declares to Nephi, and Nephi testifies to
us, that "after ye have repented of you sins" and you have "witnessed
unto the Father that ye are willing to keep [Christ's] commandments" by receiving "baptism of water" and then have received "baptism of fire and the Holy Ghost" you will speak with "a new tongue."

How can a man speak with a "new tongue?" What does "a new
tongue" mean?

Think of Isaiah's meeting with the Lord in the Temple. He confessed how unworthy his speech had been, and how much regret he
felt at having been a man of "unclean lips".[804] His lips were unclean
because of the low, mean, vulgar and unworthy things that occupied
daily conversation. Or, as Joseph put it:

"How vain and trifling have been our spirits, our conferences,
our councils, our meetings, our private as well as public conversations—too low, too mean, too vulgar, too condescending
for the dignified characters of the called and chosen of God,

---

[804] Isaiah 6:5 "Then said I, Woe *is* me! for I am undone; because I *am* a man of unclean
lips, and I dwell in the midst of a people of unclean lips: for mine eyes have seen the
King, the Lord of hosts."

according to the purposes of His will, from before the foundation of the world!" (Letter from Liberty Jail.)

To speak with a new tongue is to speak worthily of sacred things. It is to correctly weigh the truth of a matter, know by the power of the Spirit that what is said is true and in conformity with God's will and then to speak it. It is to render sacred the vessel by the things it holds.

To speak with a new tongue is to be able to speak with the tongue of an angel because you have become an angel; or a companion of angels anyway. It is to elevate your thoughts, and then what proceeds forth from your mouth, because of what is in your thoughts. It is to reveal truth by the things you are authorized or commissioned to speak. It is to have a right to speak in the name of the Lord by His consent, His authority, His will. It is to "know, nothing doubting" that He is your Lord.[805] It is to say, without hypocrisy, without guile, without hesitation and in truth, that the power of salvation is found in Christ and that you are His. That He has entrusted to you words of life, and that salvation can be found only in Him and His words. It is to have the Word of God within you.

Can an angel fall from grace? Only by being cast out of heaven.[806] When an angel falls he becomes a devil. For these it would be better if they had never known Christ, for they have decided to crucify Him anew. Because after having had the Holy Spirit make great things known unto them they have turned against the Lord by their

---

[805] Ether 3:19 "And because of the knowledge of this man he could not be kept from beholding within the veil; and he saw the finger of Jesus, which, when he saw, he fell with fear; for he knew that it was the finger of the Lord; and he had faith no longer, for he knew, nothing doubting."

[806] 2 Nephi 2:17 "And I, Lehi, according to the things which I have read, must needs suppose that an angel of God, according to that which is written, had fallen from heaven; wherefore, he became a devil, having sought that which was evil before God."

knowing rebellion against Him.[807] They are sons of perdition, and the heavens weep over them.[808] These are they who know the battle is and always has been the Lord's, and they either align themselves with Him or against Him.

You cannot speak with the tongue of angels without having knowledge of certain things given you. The clarity with which you can declare truth is distinct from what others say or claim to know. Light and truth, which is intelligence or the glory of God[809], is not a mystery but an understood and appreciated experience where darkness has fled and God's own glory has been upon you.[810]

This is what the Gospel of Christ was intended to confer. Not just belief, or faith, but knowledge and understanding. The journey back to God's presence was always the outcome intended by the Gospel. The Gospel message is and always has been that you should receive further light and knowledge by conversing with the Lord through the veil. Not through an intermediary, but in your own behalf, face to face.

The entirety of the process may be reduced to just a few words: You are intended to receive baptism of fire and the Holy Ghost, which purges you from all sin. After being made clean, every whit, which is suggested by "fire" then through the instrumentality of the "Holy Ghost" which dwells within you you may be brought into remembrance of all things.

---

[807] D&C 76:35 "Having denied the Holy Spirit after having received it, and having denied the Only Begotten Son of the Father, having crucified him unto themselves and put him to an open shame."

[808] D&C 76:26, 31–32 "And was called Perdition, for the heavens wept over him—he was Lucifer, a son of the morning."

[809] D&C 93:36 "The glory of God is intelligence, or, in other words, light and truth."

[810] Moses 1:11 "But now mine own eyes have beheld God; but not my natural, but my spiritual eyes, for my natural eyes could not have beheld; for I should have withered and died in his presence; but his glory was upon me; and I beheld his face, for I was transfigured before him."

These are the words of both Nephi and Christ. They agree. They are the two witnesses of this doctrine and truth. Therefore, it is so.

2 Nephi 31:15

"And I heard a voice from the Father, saying: Yea, the words of my Beloved are true and faithful. He that endureth to the end, the same shall be saved."

The dialogue continues. It is clear the conversation being reported by Nephi is one where both the Son and the Father spoke to Nephi, and contributed to the dialogue. A question was posed about whether Nephi heard this in connection with his vision of Christ's mortal baptism by John the Baptist. He certainly beheld that event.[811] However, the testimony and teaching of both the Father and Son regarding baptism, as reported by Nephi in this final sermon, are separate from that event. They are an independent revelation and explanation to Nephi, where both the Father and Son taught the importance of baptism.

We also have the important condition set out of "enduring to the end" as a requisite for salvation. A while ago there was a question about the concept of "enduring to the end" and the Second Comforter. They are directly linked. You cannot have a great season of concentrated effort, followed by abandonment of purpose. If it is in you to abandon the journey, then you will never qualify to receive these blessings. The Lord knows the intent of the heart. The preceding verses describe how the Lord measures the heart. You cannot deceive Him.

---

[811] 1 Nephi 11:27 "And I looked and beheld the Redeemer of the world, of whom my father had spoken; and I also beheld the prophet who should prepare the way before him. And the Lamb of God went forth and was baptized of him; and after he was baptized, I beheld the heavens open, and the Holy Ghost come down out of heaven and abide upon him in the form of a dove."

The Lord also knows whether it is in you to "endure to the end." Whether the end has come is irrelevant to Him. He beholds all things, past, present and future.[812] Therefore, He knows if you are willing to "endure to the end" before your life has been lived.

Enduring to the end, or the fixed purpose to always serve God so that you may always have His spirit to be with you, is essential to salvation. You claim this is your determination every time you take the sacrament.[813] Whether you take this commitment seriously or not determines whether you are destined for salvation or not. It also determines if you are qualified to receive His personal ministry and comfort.

The Father declares: "Yea, the words of my Beloved are true and faithful." The reason Christ is the Father's "Beloved" is directly related to His words being "true and faithful." That is, Christ only does and says what He knows represents the Father's will. He has done this "from the beginning."[814] He represents the "Word" of the Fa-

---

[812] D&C 130:7 "But they reside in the presence of God, on a globe like a sea of glass and fire, where all things for their glory are manifest, past, present, and future, and are continually before the Lord."

[813] D&C 20:76–79 "And the elder or priest shall administer it; and after this manner shall he administer it—he shall kneel with the church and call upon the Father in solemn prayer, saying: O God, the Eternal Father, we ask thee in the name of thy Son, Jesus Christ, to bless and sanctify this bread to the souls of all those who partake of it, that they may eat in remembrance of the body of thy Son, and witness unto thee, O God, the Eternal Father, that they are willing to take upon them the name of thy Son, and always remember him and keep his commandments which he has given them; that they may always have his Spirit to be with them. Amen. The manner of administering the wine—he shall take the cup also, and say: O God, the Eternal Father, we ask thee in the name of thy Son, Jesus Christ, to bless and sanctify this wine to the souls of all those who drink of it, that they may do it in remembrance of the blood of thy Son, which was shed for them; that they may witness unto thee, O God, the Eternal Father, that they do always remember him, that they may have his Spirit to be with them. Amen."

[814] 3 Nephi 11:11 "And behold, I am the light and the life of the world; and I have drunk out of that bitter cup which the Father hath given me, and have glorified the Father in taking upon me the sins of the world, in the which I have suffered the will of the Father in all things from the beginning."

ther because you can find in Christ's words and deeds the very word of the Father.[815]

It is this that qualified Christ to be the Redeemer. His words are faithful and true. So are Nephi's. The words are the Lord's though they were delivered by a man.

Nephi, having been true and faithful in all things, was able to converse with the Father and the Son through the veil and receive from them further instruction, counsel, warning, and comfort because of the things he learned. This is the pattern for all of us. This is the culminating message of the Gospel of Christ.

2 Nephi 31:16

"And now, my beloved brethren, I know by this that unless a man shall endure to the end, in following the example of the Son of the living God, he cannot be saved."

What does it mean to "endure to the end?" It is to put up with all the difficulties of mortality? Are we simply supposed to overcome boredom, irritation, trials of our patience, and the offenses caused by others? Is that what it means to "endure?"

What about "endure to the end in following the example of the Son of the living God?" Is that something different?

What if you see errors and mistakes all around you? Is it "enduring" to keep your mouth shut? Do you need to speak up?

What about the changes that have been made or are being made which alarm you? Is it "enduring" to stay silent in the face of things that suggest this is harmful?

When I first went through the Temple, it was the understood and longstanding practice of the Saints to hold prayer circles in their homes, invoking the "True Order of Prayer" as taught in the Tem-

---

[815] D&C 93:8 "Therefore, in the beginning the Word was, for he was the Word, even the messenger of salvation—"

ple. President Kimball sent a letter to the Stake Presidents terminating that practice. I have a copy of that letter. It said that prayer circles were no longer to be practiced outside the Temple—by anyone in the church.

Then in 1990 the True Order of Prayer was altered again, with the elimination of penalties. Thereafter the name changed to the "Order of Prayer" rather than the "True Order of Prayer."

Those who went through the Temple before 1990 would know about how to conduct a prayer circle involving the True Order of Prayer. But they were instructed not to do so outside the Temple. Those who went through after 1990 would not know how to conduct a True Order of Prayer circle, because they were not instructed in the Temple in anything other than the Order of Prayer.

It was still possible for those who knew the pre-1990 form to communicate the process in the Temple to others. However, recently there has begun a practice of hushing any discussions seen taking place inside the Celestial Rooms of the Temples.

It is as if those who are in control are opposed to keeping the earlier information, and working to keep it from being preserved by others. Is it "enduring to the end" to watch these changes and say nothing? Or is it "enduring" to actually endure, to preserve, to persevere against opposition and to keep as an enduring feature of the faith, information you received if you went through the Temple before 1990? Does a person who, in all sincerity before God, believes that Isaiah's prophecy warned against this[816] "endure" if he remains silent? Or must he speak up? If so, how and to who? Which is enduring? Which is enduring to the end in following the example of the Son of the Living God? What example did Christ set in relation to this kind of a conflict? Did Christ submit, or resist authority? If

---

[816] Isaiah 24:5 "The earth also is defiled under the inhabitants thereof; because they have transgressed the laws, changed the ordinance, broken the everlasting covenant."

He did both, how does one endure while appropriately weighing those things they will submit to, and those things they will resist?

What about Nephi's warning that you "cannot be saved" if you fail to do the right kind of "enduring" to the end? If salvation itself hinges upon solving this riddle, then how carefully must you weigh what you resist and what you submit to?

It is for this reason we work out our salvation before God as Nephi has explained, acting no hypocrisy, with real intent, having faith in God, but also with fear and trembling.[817]

Indeed, God has given us a test worthy of a God. And only those worthy of becoming among the gods will be able to solve the riddle. Because only they will humble themselves, come with a contrite spirit and broken heart to offer upon the altar a sacrifice worthy of being accepted. Others will proceed in ignorance and arrogance to proudly proclaim: "I know my culture is true!" "I know all is well in Zion!" "I follow a broad and safe mainstream into a great and spacious building where there is peace, pride, success, prosperity and assurance that I am saved while all around me there are those who will be cast down to hell!" Or similar such nonsense . . . Warmed over Evangelical gibberish, with a vague Mormonesque vocabulary applied to it. Having a form of godliness, but without power. This new form of ungodliness will not be lacking in body, parts and passions, for the image of the idol raised will be the very image of the person looking in the mirror. They will think themselves destined to rule and reign over principalities, dominions, heights, depths and others. They are their own idols! What irony it all invokes! It must make the devil look up

---

[817] Mormon 9:27 "O then despise not, and wonder not, but hearken unto the words of the Lord, and ask the Father in the name of Jesus for what things soever ye shall stand in need. Doubt not, but be believing, and begin as in times of old, and come unto the Lord with all your heart, and work out your own salvation with fear and trembling before him."
Philippians 2:12 "Wherefore, my beloved, as ye have always obeyed, not as in my presence only, but now much more in my absence, work out your own salvation with fear and trembling."

to heaven and laugh still (Moses 7:26.) Perhaps we ought to see some humor in it as well . . . Or, since we're speaking of the loss of men's souls, maybe it can never be humorous. Only tragedy. Only disappointment. Only foolishness.

Where is the hope? Is there none? Yes, in repentance! Changing our course! Remembering God again! Restoring what has been lost! Returning and repenting! That's right! And Nephi has invited us to do just that.

So "enduring to the end in following the example of the Son of the living God" is not easy. Even understanding the meaning of these words is challenging. Thank you Nephi. You have proven yet again how prayerful we all must be. Let us, therefore, repent!

2 Nephi 31:17

"Wherefore, do the things which I have told you I have seen that your Lord and your Redeemer should do; for, for this cause have they been shown unto me, that ye might know the gate by which ye should enter. For the gate by which ye should enter is repentance and baptism by water; and then cometh a remission of your sins by fire and by the Holy Ghost."

You must "do the things which I have told you I have seen that your Lord and your Redeemer should do." You must "follow Him." There is no other way nor name given under heaven to obtain salvation.[818]

It was for this reason Nephi was "shown" these things. The Lord and His Father taught Nephi so he could in turn teach others, includ-

---

[818] Mosiah 5:8 "And under this head ye are made free, and there is no other head whereby ye can be made free. There is no other name given whereby salvation cometh; therefore, I would that ye should take upon you the name of Christ, all you that have entered into the covenant with God that ye should be obedient unto the end of your lives."

ing us. The message was intended to save many, not just Nephi. But we must give heed to the message when we hear it.

The "gate by which ye should enter is repentance and baptism by water." You must repent first. Then, having repented, receive baptism by water. When this is done, "then cometh a remission of your sins by fire and by the Holy Ghost."

Without the "fire" to purge the sacrifice upon the altar, it is not cleansed. It cannot become holy unless exposed to that fire.

But note—this is automatic. It is not by the laying on of hands. The laying on of hands for the gift of the Holy Ghost is not required in this teaching. Nephi, with elaboration from the Father and the Son, is teaching that this is an event that follows the process of "repentance and baptism by water." That is, the ordinance of baptism, when accompanied by repentance and done right, is the reason for this event.

Laying on of hands is for "the gift of the Holy Ghost" so there may be a companion and guide for a person. This is an ordinance. It is also the moment one is confirmed a member of the church. But it is not necessarily co-equal with receiving "fire and the Holy Ghost" as described here. There is nothing that excludes it from being coincidental in time, however. They may happen at the same moment. That is, after baptism, and while receiving the laying on of hands, one may receive both the gift of the Holy Ghost, and also fire and the Holy Ghost. As a result one is renewed in the manner described in this chapter. They are not co-equal.

Laying on of hands does not appear to be an ordinance in the Book of Mormon until the coming of Christ in 3 Nephi. The only potential exception is found in Alma 31:36, where Alma "clapped his hands upon them who were with him" and they received the Holy Ghost. This is similar to the Lord "breathing" the Holy Ghost upon

His disciples.[819] They were instructed to lay on hands, and would perform that act rather than breathing upon those who were to receive the Holy Ghost. The ordinance is different from "clapping" or from "breathing" and involves the process we follow in the church today.[820]

The baptism of fire and the Holy Ghost promised here is given without man's involvement, comes from heaven, is promised by both the Father and the Son. It is a signal of redemption, purification and holiness. It is included in the "gate" for entering into God's presence. For God is a "consuming fire" and those who enter into that presence must be able to endure that fire.[821] Without the capacity to do so, a person would be consumed by the flames.[822] The fire and the Holy Ghost are also given as a sign to the recipient that they may know it is safe for them to enter into God's presence and not be consumed. In earlier versions of the First Vision, Joseph described the "pillar of light" as a "pillar of fire" which gradually descended. He wondered if the trees would be consumed as it descended, but seeing they were not he thought it safe for him to be exposed to it as well. When it fell upon him, the vision opened up and he saw the Father and the Son.

---

[819] John 20:22 "And when he had said this, he breathed on *them,* and saith unto them, Receive ye the Holy Ghost:"

[820] D&C 33:15 "And whoso having faith you shall confirm in my church, by the laying on of the hands, and I will bestow the gift of the Holy Ghost upon them."

[821] Hebrews 12:29 "For our God *is* a consuming fire."
Deuteronomy 4:24 "For the Lord thy God *is* a consuming fire, *even* a jealous God."

[822] Leviticus 10:1–2 "And Nadab and Abihu, the sons of Aaron, took either of them his censer, and put fire therein, and put incense thereon, and offered strange fire before the Lord, which he commanded them not. And there went out fire from the Lord, and devoured them, and they died before the Lord."

Christ also entered into this glorious light on the Mount of Transfiguration.[823]

We are to do as Nephi instructs, "do the things which I have told you I have seen that your Lord and your Redeemer should do; for, for this cause have they been shown unto me, that ye might know the gate by which ye should enter."

We live below the standard Christ set for us. We needn't. Have faith. Press forward feasting on His words. You can and will find Him there.

2 Nephi 31:18

> "And then are ye in this strait and narrow path which leads to eternal life; yea, ye have entered in by the gate; ye have done according to the commandments of the Father and the Son; and ye have received the Holy Ghost, which witnesses of the Father and the Son, unto the fulfilling of the promise which he hath made, that if ye entered in by the way ye should receive."

This is the path to "eternal life." It is "strait and narrow," but it is the way to eternal life. What is eternal life?

Why is the path "strait and narrow?" Is it to deprive you of something, or is it to direct you toward the only path where abundance can be obtained? If you become connected to the "true vine," are you then able to "bear fruit?"[824] If you bear fruit, what can you

---

[823] Matthew 17:1–2 "And after six days Jesus taketh Peter, James, and John his brother, and bringeth them up into an high mountain apart, And was transfigured before them: and his face did shine as the sun, and his raiment was white as the light"

[824] John 15:4–7 "Abide in me, and I in you. As the branch cannot bear fruit of itself, except it abide in the vine; no more can ye, except ye abide in me. I am the vine, ye *are* the branches: He that abideth in me, and I in him, the same bringeth forth much fruit: for without me ye can do nothing. If a man abide not in me, he is cast forth as a branch, and is withered; and men gather them, and cast *them* into the fire, and they are burned. If ye abide in me, and my words abide in you, ye shall ask what ye will, and it shall be done unto you."

ask of Him that He will not give to you?[825] What does that mean? Have you read *Beloved Enos*? If so you will understand what is being discussed.

By doing as the Father and Son have asked, you "receive the Holy Ghost." What does it mean to have the Holy Ghost dwell within you?[826] How does a spirit dwell inside a person? How does that spirit become "Holy" and the third member of the Godhead? If the scriptures say, and Christ taught that those who receive God's word are gods, what does it mean?[827]

Did you notice the Father and Son promise the Holy Ghost, and when you receive it the Holy Ghost bears witness of the Father and Son? The first promise to you provides the last, and the last bears witness of the first. In one eternal round, the doctrine of Christ includes all members of the Godhead combined into a witness that will come to you, take up residence within you, and make you a vessel of the promises fulfilled. You are to return home, and take your abode again. Or, more correctly, permit Them to take up Their abode with you.[828]

You become the record of God's dealings with mankind. You become the promise of God's presence, for you fulfill "the promise which He hath made."

---

[825] John 15:7 "If ye abide in me, and my words abide in you, ye shall ask what ye will, and it shall be done unto you."

[826] D&C 130:22 "The Father has a body of flesh and bones as tangible as man's; the Son also; but the Holy Ghost has not a body of flesh and bones, but is a personage of Spirit. Were it not so, the Holy Ghost could not dwell in us."

[827] John 10:34–36 "Jesus answered them, Is it not written in your law, I said, Ye are gods? If he called them gods, unto whom the word of God came, and the scripture cannot be broken; Say ye of him, whom the Father hath sanctified, and sent into the world, Thou blasphemest; because I said, I am the Son of God?"

[828] John 14:23 "Jesus answered and said unto him, If a man love me, he will keep my words: and my Father will love him, and we will come unto him, and make our abode with him."

You receive the "record of heaven" or, more correctly, the Record of Heaven, for it is a proper name and title.[829] When it has come to you, then this Record of Heaven will abide with you. You will be the one who possess the "peaceable things of immortal glory." You will know "the truth of all things" for it will reside within you.[830] You will understand wisdom, for she will be with you. You will know mercy, possess truth, and be capable of performing judgment, for the judgment you judge will not be yours but will be given to you.[831] God will dwell within you.

When He appears to you, you will see Him as He is, for you will be at last like Him.[832] If you can understand this, then you will purify yourself to receive it.[833] For the baptism of fire and the Holy Ghost will purge and purify, refining you with that holy fire.[834]

This doctrine of Christ will bring you in contact with God. You were meant to return to the Family you came from. It is the homecoming you have always felt was needed. You do not belong here.

---

[829] Moses 6:61 "Therefore it is given to abide in you; the record of heaven; the Comforter; the peaceable things of immortal glory; the truth of all things; that which quickeneth all things, which maketh alive all things; that which knoweth all things, and hath all power according to wisdom, mercy, truth, justice, and judgment."

[830] Moses 6:61 "Therefore it is given to abide in you; the record of heaven; the Comforter; the peaceable things of immortal glory; the truth of all things; that which quickeneth all things, which maketh alive all things; that which knoweth all things, and hath all power according to wisdom, mercy, truth, justice, and judgment."

[831] 3 Nephi 27:27 "And know ye that ye shall be judges of this people, according to the judgment which I shall give unto you, which shall be just. Therefore, what manner of men ought ye to be? Verily I say unto you, even as I am."

[832] 1 John 3:1–2 "Behold, what manner of love the Father hath bestowed upon us, that we should be called the sons of God: therefore the world knoweth us not, because it knew him not. Beloved, now are we the sons of God, and it doth not yet appear what we shall be: but we know that, when he shall appear, we shall be like him; for we shall see him as he is."

[833] 1 John 3:3 "And every man that hath this hope in him purifieth himself, even as he is pure."

[834] Malachi 3:2 "But who may abide the day of his coming? and who shall stand when he appeareth? for he *is* like a refiner's fire, and like fullers' soap:"

There is something higher, something more holy calling to you. It is not found in an institution, or program, or award, or office. It is only found in God, who is your home.

The doctrine of Christ is the doctrine of God's return to be with you and abide with you. It is Him coming to sup with you. He has been knocking at the door all these years seeking entry into your life.[835] If you let Him come in, He will prepare a throne for you.[836] Only those who have descended will be permitted to rise. Only those who humble themselves can be exalted.[837] While all those who rule rather than serve, will be disappointed. These are they who declare themselves worthy to be followed and insist they can use compulsion. They pretend to be on the Lord's errand while they are on their own. They crave dominion over others but will be cast down. They will be denied priesthood, and be left begging for water to cool their tongues for the torment of it all.[838]

How much better is it, then, for us to repent? It seems foolish to do otherwise. I find I'm persuaded by Nephi.

---

[835] Revelation 3:20 "Behold, I stand at the door, and knock: if any man hear my voice, and open the door, I will come in to him, and will sup with him, and he with me."

[836] Revelation 3:21–22 "To him that overcometh will I grant to sit with me in my throne, even as I also overcame, and am set down with my Father in his throne. He that hath an ear, let him hear what the Spirit saith unto the churches."

[837] Matthew 23:12 "And whosoever shall exalt himself shall be abased; and he that shall humble himself shall be exalted."

[838] D&C 121:37 "That they may be conferred upon us, it is true; but when we undertake to cover our sins, or to gratify our pride, our vain ambition, or to exercise control or dominion or compulsion upon the souls of the children of men, in any degree of unrighteousness, behold, the heavens withdraw themselves; the Spirit of the Lord is grieved; and when it is withdrawn, Amen to the priesthood or the authority of that man."
Luke 16:23–24 "And in hell he lift up his eyes, being in torments, and seeth Abraham afar off, and Lazarus in his bosom. And he cried and said, Father Abraham, have mercy on me, and send Lazarus, that he may dip the tip of his finger in water, and cool my tongue; for I am tormented in this flame."

2 Nephi 31:19–20

"And now, my beloved brethren, after ye have gotten into this strait and narrow path, I would ask if all is done? Behold, I say unto you, Nay; for ye have not come thus far save it were by the word of Christ with unshaken faith relying wholly upon the merits of him who is mighty to save. Wherefore, ye must press forward with a steadfastness in Christ, having a perfect brightness of hope, and a love of God and of all men. Wherefore, if ye shall press forward, feasting upon the word of Christ, and endure to the end, behold, thus saith the Father: Ye shall have eternal life. in him,

"Once on the narrow path, are you done? Have you "arrived?" Is there "rest?"

No, you are on the path, but you cannot turn back. If you even look back, you risk moving on an uneven path.[839] You could not get this far if you hadn't followed "the word of Christ" and therefore you can only continue by following the word of Christ along the journey.

Your path is not just based on Christ's words, but also "with unshaken faith in Him." What is "unshaken faith?"

What does it mean to rely "wholly upon the merits of Him who is mighty to save?" Can you take any pride in what you have done? Can you boast of something about yourself?[840]

---

[839] Luke 9:62 "And Jesus said unto him, No man, having put his hand to the plough, and looking back, is fit for the kingdom of God."

[840] Mosiah 2:22–25 "And behold, all that he requires of you is to keep his commandments; and he has promised you that if ye would keep his commandments ye should prosper in the land; and he never doth vary from that which he hath said; therefore, if ye do keep his commandments he doth bless you and prosper you. And now, in the first place, he hath created you, and granted unto you your lives, for which ye are indebted unto him. And secondly, he doth require that ye should do as he hath commanded you; for which if ye do, he doth immediately bless you; and therefore he hath paid you. And ye are still indebted unto him, and are, and will be, forever and ever; therefore, of what have ye to boast? And now I ask, can ye say aught of yourselves? I answer you, Nay. Ye cannot say that ye are even as much as the dust of the earth; yet ye were created of the dust of the earth; but behold, it belongeth to him who created you."

What does it mean to "press forward with a steadfastness in Christ?" How would "steadfastness" be lived?

What is a "perfect brightness of hope?" I've defined that kind of "hope" in *Eighteen Verses*.

How does any person come into possession of "a love of God and of all men?" Would that come from within, or as a gift from God? Moroni prayed for the gentiles to receive grace that they might obtain charity.[841] The Lord replied that if the gentiles lack charity it would not cause any loss to Moroni, for he was saved.[842] [Once again reflecting the pessimism which the latter-day gentiles are consistently viewed by the Book of Mormon.]

Why "press forward?"

What does it mean for us to be "feasting upon the word of Christ?" Is "feasting" something more than participating in a gospel doctrine class discussion once a week? What would it require for you to "feast" upon the "word of Christ?" Is scripture study alone enough? Would you need to receive anything directly from Him to be included in the "feast?" How would that be obtained?

Did you notice once again we are reminded we must "endure to the end?" Once again, you must determine how "enduring" is to be accomplished, and what "enduring" will require.

If, however, you do these things then "behold, thus saith the Father: Ye shall have eternal life." Notice the promise of eternal life comes from the office of "the Father." It is because this final step

---

[841] Ether 12:36 "And it came to pass that I prayed unto the Lord that he would give unto the Gentiles grace, that they might have charity."

[842] Ether 12:37 "And it came to pass that the Lord said unto me: If they have not charity it mattereth not unto thee, thou hast been faithful; wherefore, thy garments shall be made clean. And because thou hast seen thy weakness thou shalt be made strong, even unto the sitting down in the place which I have prepared in the mansions of my Father."

comes from the authority to make you a son. His office is the only one which can declare "this day have I begotten thee."[843]

2 Nephi 31:21

> "And now, behold, my beloved brethren, this is the way; and there is none other way nor name given under heaven whereby man can be saved in the kingdom of God. And now, behold, this is the doctrine of Christ, and the only and true doctrine of the Father, and of the Son, and of the Holy Ghost, which is one God, without end. Amen."

This is "the way" to salvation. Nephi adds: "and there is none other way." What does it mean there "is none other way?" Does that mean any religious system, institution, process, explanation or additional doctrine cannot save you? Is it true that you either enter in through this method or you cannot be saved? Is the purpose of the other rites, rituals, ordinances and teachings merely to bring you into this one true "way and there is none other way?" Or do you need to look for additional things, helps, ordinances, confirmations, and blessings to be conferred?

What of the other Gospel rites? They did come from God, didn't they? How are we to understand the relationship between other ordinances, even "higher ordinances" and this "doctrine of Christ" being explained by Nephi?

Clearly the "doctrine of Christ" is intended to give you the underlying basis for all salvation. There is no other "name given under heaven whereby man can be saved in the kingdom of God" apart from Jesus Christ. He is the one who, by His obedience and sacrifice, put power into the plan of salvation. We know this to be true from everything declared by the prophets of God. But what about "this is

---

[843] Psalms 2:7 "I will declare the decree: the Lord hath said unto me, Thou *art* my Son; this day have I begotten thee."

the way; and there is none other way." What does that mean? Does it exclude other ordinances or processes? Does it make the Law of Moses no longer binding upon Nephi and his posterity?

Clearly following Nephi's ministry, his descendants did not abandon the Law of Moses.[844] And so, if there is "none other way," it did not mean that the Nephites were to abandon practice of the ordinances then in effect. Nor does it mean that we abandon the ordinances now in effect in our day.

It is not that the ordinances are essential, but that the **purpose** of the ordinances are essential. The underlying meaning is essential. The "doctrine of Christ" becomes possible to understand, live and receive as you follow the ordinances. They are "helps" to bring you into this correct path. You will honor them, conform to them, seek for them, in order that you may inherit the blessings of the "doctrine of Christ."

Why are ordinances instituted? They are to bring you to the point where you inherit in your body and spirit these great blessings of the "doctrine of Christ." They prepare you. Their effect is to qualify you, instruct you, advance you toward this goal of receiving the blessings found in the doctrine of Christ as expounded by Nephi in this chapter. Once ordinances have been adopted, it is then unlikely you can ignore them and receive what is promised by the "doctrine of Christ." How can you refuse what is offered and still accept the underlying gift? How can you mix ingratitude and gratitude?

---

[844] Jarom 1:5 "And now, behold, *two hundred years had passed away, and the people of Nephi had waxed strong in the land. They observed to keep the law of Moses and the sabbath day holy unto the Lord. And they profaned not; neither did they blaspheme. And the laws of the land were exceedingly strict."

Alma 25:15 "Yea, and they did keep the law of Moses; for it was expedient that they should keep the law of Moses as yet, for it was not all fulfilled. But notwithstanding the law of Moses, they did look forward to the coming of Christ, considering that the law of Moses was a type of his coming, and believing that they must keep those outward performances until the time that he should be revealed unto them."

Is it important, therefore, to keep the ordinances intact? If changed does some of the communication involved in preparing you to receive the "doctrine of Christ" lose something?

For example, without the shedding of blood there can be no covenant. Christ's blood is the culminating event which shed blood to activate a covenant between God and man. However, even after Christ's sacrifice, we are still required to offer sacrifice, and even the return of animal sacrifice will happen at some point in this final dispensation. The Law of Moses was fulfilled and will not return. However, the sacrifice of blood by animals which was before the Law of Moses will return. As Joseph Smith taught:

> "These [animal] sacrifices, as well as every ordinance belonging to the Priesthood, will, when the Temple of the Lord shall be built, and the sons of Levi be purified, be fully restored and attended to in all their powers, ramifications, and blessings. This ever did and ever will exist when the powers of the Melchizedek Priesthood are sufficiently manifest; else how can the restitution of all things spoken of by the Holy Prophets be brought to pass. It is not to be understood that the law of Moses will be established again with all its rites and variety of ceremonies; this has never been spoken of by the prophets; but those things which existed prior to Moses' day, namely, sacrifice, will be continued." (*TPJS*, 173, *DHC* 4:212)

When the penalties existed in the Temple ceremonies of our dispensation, we were reminded of the shedding of blood required for a covenant. When removed, we lose some of that memory. How would penalties involving the shedding of blood prepare people for the return of animal sacrifice? Would it help remind them that shedding blood is required to establish a covenant? Even this final Dispensation of the Fullness of Time could not be an effective covenant without the shedding of blood to seal the testament or covenant.[845]

Does the Gospel of Jesus Christ require the sacrifice of all things? (We've explained this before in relation to the Lectures on Faith.) If so, then how do we obtain the blessings we desire from the hand of God without being willing to make a similar sacrifice? If it is required, then how do we qualify to receive this baptism of fire spoken of by Nephi that will purge us from all sin and permit us to speak with a new tongue? How is this sacrifice made apart from the irrevocable commitment made within yourself to "endure to the end" by laying upon the altar everything you have, even your own life if necessary, to build up His kingdom? How, in a fallen world filled with sin, in a day where there is no sacrifice or consecration being made by others; how do you do that? What does the "doctrine of Christ" allow you to do without regard to the sins and errors you find all around you? Even if all the world is content to remain Telestial, or some few encourage only a Terrestrial law be followed, can you still find and live the "doctrine of Christ?" Does Nephi's teachings require you to be anything or anyone special or noteworthy in this life? Can you do this in private, between you and God? Can you follow the "doctrine of Christ" by what you think, ponder, pray, say, do and believe?

---

[845] D&C 135:3 "Joseph Smith, the Prophet and Seer of the Lord, has done more, save Jesus only, for the salvation of men in this world, than any other man that ever lived in it. In the short space of twenty years, he has brought forth the Book of Mormon, which he translated by the gift and power of God, and has been the means of publishing it on two continents; has sent the fulness of the everlasting gospel, which it contained, to the four quarters of the earth; has brought forth the revelations and commandments which compose this book of Doctrine and Covenants, and many other wise documents and instructions for the benefit of the children of men; gathered many thousands of the Latter-day Saints, founded a great city, and left a fame and name that cannot be slain. He lived great, and he died great in the eyes of God and his people; and like most of the Lord's anointed in ancient times, has sealed his mission and his works with his own blood; and so has his brother Hyrum. In life they were not divided, and in death they were not separated!"

This statement, which concludes the exposition on "the doctrine of Christ" is concluded using the names of "the only and true doctrine of the Father, and of the Son, and of the Holy Ghost, which is one God, without end. Amen." Although only a few will recognize this, it is a formula used when using the sealing authority. If you are aware of this, then you would realize what Nephi has done is declared that he possesses the Patriarchal Priesthood authority, which invariably includes the power to seal. He will mention "sealing" his testimony again before he concludes. But if you know this is a formula employed in connection with this authority, you will recognize it. Within the ordinances of the church, we use this formula when baptizing and again when sealing a marriage in the Temple. All other intermediate ordinances are done "in the name of Jesus Christ."

Baptism has been specifically authorized to be performed "in the name of the Father, and of the Son, and of the Holy Ghost." That authorization came from the Lord, by revelation.[846] That authorization is important and allows the formula to be used. Then, in the Temple, it is once again prescribed for use. I point it out deliberately, and knowing that the authorization of the formula is deliberate, noteworthy and important to consider as a matter of meaning.

---

[846] D&C 20:73 "The person who is called of God and has authority from Jesus Christ to baptize, shall go down into the water with the person who has presented himself or herself for baptism, and shall say, calling him or her by name: Having been commissioned of Jesus Christ, I baptize you in the name of the Father, and of the Son, and of the Holy Ghost. Amen."

42957024R00231

Made in the USA
San Bernardino, CA
11 December 2016